Selected Prose 1909–1965

Selected Prose
1909–1965

EZRA POUND

Edited, with an Introduction by William Cookson

FABER AND FABER
LONDON

First published in 1973 by
Faber and Faber Limited
3 Queen Square London W.C.1.
Printed in Great Britain by
Western Printing Services Ltd, Bristol

ISBN 0 571 09824 X

CONTENTS

3

CONTENTS

CONTENTS

THE TREATISE ON HARMONY, is included by courtesy of Peter Owen from PATRIA MIA AND THE TREATISE ON HARMONY by Ezra Pound.

5

FOREWORD

To tread delicately amid the scrapings from the cracker-barrel is no easy job and Mr. Cookson has made the best of it.

The volume would be more presentable had it been possible to remove 80% of the sentences beginning with the pronoun 'I' and more especially those with 'we'.

The substitution of 'I' by a comprehensive claim in which 'we' or 'one' is used to indicate a general law may be a pretentious attempt to expand a merely personal view into a universal law.

In sentences referring to groups or races 'they' should be used with great care.

re USURY:

I was out of focus, taking a symptom for a cause.

The cause is AVARICE.

Venice, 4th July, 1972

EZRA POUND

INTRODUCTION

In making this selection my aim has been to show the unity of Ezra Pound's vision and the integrity of his concerns. I have tried to collect the clearest statements of the beliefs from which he has made his poetry.

Yeats said, 'Poetry is truth seen with passion.' Probably too much attention has been paid to the technique of the *Cantos* at the expense of its content. It is because Pound's ideas and subject matter are important in themselves that the poetry is living. As Eliot wrote, 'I cannot see that poetry can ever be separated from something which I should call belief, and to which I cannot see any reason for refusing the name belief, unless we are to reshuffle names altogether.'[1]

The intention is to shake the idea that there is a fundamental split in Pound's work. I believe that it 'is one, indivisible, a nature extending to every detail as the nature of being oak or maple extends to every part of the oak tree or maple.'[2] This book should be read in conjunction with the *Cantos*, *The Collected Shorter Poems*, the translations, particularly those from Confucius, the *Literary Essays*, and the two full length prose books, *The Spirit of Romance* and *The Guide to Kulchur*.

I have tried to gather the core of Pound's writing on religious, musical, Confucian, historical, economic and monetary subjects together with some previously uncollected literary essays. The way in which the material has been arranged is intended to illuminate the main themes of the *Cantos*—as far as possible those articles which bear directly on the poem have been chosen. But it is the continuing vitality of the ideas, their 'now-ness' to use a word of David Jones, which I wish to stress. The book is not meant to be merely an addition to Pound scholarship or a useful guide to the *Cantos*.

The order within the eight parts is chronological. None of these sections is self-sufficient as there are cross-currents of thought between them. All essays have been printed in full, apart from two exceptions: *Ecclesiastical History* (1934) and *History and Ignorance* (1935), which were slightly cut by Mr. Pound when he went through all the material in 1971. I have included a small number of short extracts from articles

---

[1] T. S. Eliot: A Note on Poetry and Belief (*The Enemy* 1, January 1927.)

[2] *Mang Tsze: The Ethics of Mencius.* (1938). See page 96.

7

that it was not possible, for reasons of space, to include entire. I am entirely responsible for the choice and arrangement of the material.

In the notes which follow I shall discuss some of the themes of Pound's prose in relationship to his poetry.

*   *   *

'The essential thing in a poet is that he builds us his world', Pound wrote in 1915. I have opened the book with the early sequence of essays, *I Gather the Limbs of Osiris*, because it prefigures to a large extent the concerns of Pound's maturity; as its title suggests, in a sense it defines what he has been doing from the beginning. It shows that Pound had already begun to practice a form of 'ideogrammic method', though of course not under that name, some time before he had read Fenollosa's *Essay on the Chinese Written Character*. The 'New Method of Scholarship' described here as the 'method of Luminous Detail . . . certain facts give one a sudden insight into circumjacent conditions, into their causes, their effects, into sequence and law' informs the *Cantos* throughout; and Pound's perennial conception of the function of literature is clearly stated, 'If a book reveals to us something of which we are unconscious, it feeds us with its energy . . . ' *I Gather the Limbs of Osiris* also contains the germ of the idea which Eliot later developed in *Tradition and the Individual Talent*. It shows that Pound was rooted from the first in the poetry with which the *Cantos* now forms part of a living tradition–the work of Homer, Dante, Chaucer, Villon and Shakspere.

*   *   *

'Implicit in all serious works of art', wrote Wyndham Lewis, 'will be found politics, theology, philosophy–in brief, all the great intellectual departments of the human consciousness.' Or, as Pound has said, 'A work of art, any serious work vivifies a man's total perception of relations' (*History and Ignorance*, 1935).

Much twentieth century poetry has been exclusively parochial and incapable of embodying subjects other than the personal or the incidentals of everyday life. Probably the main reason that the greatness of the *Cantos* has not yet been fully comprehended is due to the peripheral role of poetry in contemporary England and America. This problem has been most clearly expressed by David Jones in his Preface to *The Anathemata*:

> We are, in our society of today, very far removed from those culture phases where the poet was explicitly and by profession the custodian, rememberer, embodier and voice of the mythus, etc. of some contained group of families, or of a tribe, nation, people, cult.

The *Cantos*, *The Anathemata* and parts of the later work of Hugh MacDiarmid belong to this most ancient poetic tradition and represent heroic attempts to reaffirm its validity to the twentieth century. In this sense Pound's epic is as American as Homer's was Greek, with at its centre the 10 Adams cantos evoking the founding of the American nation. I have included a number of Pound's essays on American history in the present selection.

*　　*　　*

The main elements in Pound's poetry and prose are neither obscure nor literary, just as they are free from the aestheticism that he buried with *Mauberley*. His writing has layers of meaning, but it is not ambiguous. Its scale of values would have been understood by Dante, Chaucer and Langland. On its simplest level, Pound's work records the fight to preserve the individual human spirit, and 'to keep the value of a local and particular character' against all forms of oppression and blurring of distinctions, throughout history. It deals with the perennial struggle of man's creative intelligence against the exploiters of 'the abundance of nature'. Confucius, St. Ambrose, Coke, Pietro Leopoldo, Jefferson, Adams, Orage, Douglas, Lenin, to name a few of the individuals he points to, affirms these values directly by documents and quotations.

The themes in Pound's prose are the same as those of his poetry and, in consequence, the prose provides the best commentary on it. Some words he wrote about Henry James in *Provincialism the Enemy* (1917) could be used with equal validity about his own writing: 'Human liberty, personal liberty, underlay all his work . . . '. This passion for liberty lies at the root of all the articles in this book, and of Pound's lifelong struggle for monetary reform and against a system that treats money as a commodity which can be bought and sold rather than as 'a ticket for the orderly distribution of what is available.' (*What is Money For?*, 1939). His dislike of monotheistic religion is part of the same struggle against intolerance, monopoly and uniformity. 'The glory of the polytheistic anschauung is that it never asserted a single and obligatory path for everyone' (*Terra Italica*, 1932).

When there seems danger that the world is losing its memory, another passage in David Jones's Preface is particularly pertinent to the *Cantos* and to the essays in *Selected Prose*, as it defines what is most 'dangerous' in them to the forces which now threaten the individual:

> Poetry is to be diagnosed as 'dangerous' because it evokes and recalls, is a kind of *anamnesis* of, i.e. is an effective recalling of, something loved. In that sense it is inevitably 'propaganda' in that any real formal expression propagands the reality which caused those forms and their content to be.

*　　*　　*

RELIGIO . . . 'The root and the spring' of Pound, beyond the rage and fragmentation of much of his writing, is his belief in a permanent world: 'Tradition inheres in the images of the gods, and gets lost in dogmatic definitions.' (*A Visiting Card*, 1942).

> 'We have', said Mencius, 'but phenomena.'
> monumenta. In nature are signatures
> needing no verbal tradition,
> oak leaf never plane leaf. John Heydon.
>
> (Canto LXXXVII)

Pound has embodied the work of the great naturalists Linnaeus and Agassiz, and he believes in what he has described as 'the intelligence working in nature and requiring no particular theories to keep it alive: a respect that is reborn in a series of sages, from Confucius, through Dante, to Agassiz.'[1] 'Respect for the kind of intelligence that enables grass seed to grow grass; the cherry-stone to make cherries.'[2] I have included in this collection his essay on W. H. Hudson which attacks the pollution and destruction of nature by usury and commercialism.

'And that the universe is alive', Pound wrote in Canto XCIV. This sense of numinous nature, 'of wood alive, of stone alive', is everywhere present in his greatest poetry and particularly in the later cantos—it is a similar quality which makes the world of *The Tempest* so profoundly poetic. As Pound wrote in *Psychology and Troubadours* (1916):[3] 'this . . . sort of mind is close on the vital universe; and the strength of the Greek beauty rests in this, that it is ever at the interpretation of this vital universe, by its signs of gods and godly attendants and oreads.'

Pound's belief in Greek deities is as strong as was Hölderlin's.

> The Gods have not returned. 'They have never left us.'
>   They have not returned.
> Cloud's processional and the air moves with their living.
>
> (Canto CXIII)

He makes us see again a beauty that has always been there; that the world has forgotten it does not make it any less real.

'Observe the phenomena of nature as one in whom the ancestral voices speak' (*Analects* VI, 11).

The serenity and stillness of Pound's Confucian writings is another aspect of this reality. 'That his ray come to point in this quiet.' (*The Classic Anthology*, Ode 305).

*   *   *

Pound's verse is characterised by rhythmic energy and melodic invention. Louis Zukofsky has said that the movement of the *Cantos*

---

[1] *Edge* 6, Melbourne, June 1957.   page 193.
[2] See *Confucius*, New Directions, 1969,   [3] *The Spirit of Romance*, Chapter V.

is that of fire and wind. 'A fanned flame in their moving' (Canto XCVIII). I have given *The Treatise on Harmony* a part to itself as it is as pertinent to Pound's poetry as it is to music. 'Rhythm is a form cut into TIME, as a design is determined SPACE.' (*A.B.C. of Reading*).

*   *   *

'Dante wrote his poems to MAKE PEOPLE THINK'[1] and this is Pound's aim in these essays. It is not to persuade the reader to accept some private system of ideas or history. Their *hilaritas* and lack of solemnity would, anyway, preclude such an intention–some of these articles are as funny as parts of the *Cantos*.

Pound has had the courage not to close his mind by accepting any system of belief based upon dogma and anyone who seeks to erect a system of this kind on his work would do well to remember what he said in *The Individual and his Milieu* (1935): 'Disciples are more trouble than they are worth when they start anchoring and petrifying their mahatmas. No man's *thought* petrifies.'

*   *   *

In the CIVILIZATION, MONEY AND HISTORY part of this book I have included some of Pound's earliest political and economic writings so that the reader will be able to trace the development of his thought on these subjects. Hugh Kenner has pointed out the significance, in this connection, of C. H. Douglas's *Economic Democracy* (1919) and two of the reviews which Pound wrote of this book in 1920 will be found here. I quote Kenner:

> We tend to suppose that money, Pound's famous obsession, entered the *Cantos* later, to their detriment. Money, on the contrary, was there all along. The poet who scrapped the early versions of the first three cantos, after publishing them three times, did so after rethinking the enterprise in the light of *Economic Democracy* . . .
>
> Douglas's vision is of communal knowledge, communal intellection, as wealth. Thus Malatesta's judgement, his factive vigour, and the traditions on which his Tempio drew, were part of the wealth of Rimini, whatever bankers might say. Currency is simply a means of bringing wealth into active existence, and distributing access to it. A mistaken accounting system, however, supposes that the currency is the wealth. It also supposes that the only way to distribute currency is to tie men down to 'work', and then pay them for the time they spend working. Douglas devoted much arithmetic to showing that this method never distributes *enough* currency to buy what is produced (hence competition for foreign markets; hence

[1] *Literary Essays*, page 204.

wars). He also proposed that as industrialisation reduces necessary work more and more, the work to which men are tied in order to circulate currency grows increasingly futile, and actually impoverishes them (and us) by taking up their time . . . And the system diversifies into useless artifacts to distribute the currency to buy the useful ones: hence clutter and debasement. And finally, mistaking currency for wealth, the accounting system allows itself to be confused by the intrinsic value of metals . . .

This book seemed to Pound an intellectual event comparable to the century's achievements in genetics and electromagnetics. It allowed one to rewrite history as a long process culminating in the discovery of the real basis of wealth. In particular, it explained the 19th century, struggling toward enlightenment while sinking into the morass of false values Ruskin had diagnosed (but Ruskin's remedy, a return to handicraft was wrong). And the war just ended had been the ultimate demonstration. If it were once understood, no more wars would be necessary. In *Mauberley* Pound shed like a skin the aesthete who does not know what is going on, the author, as it were, of the first drafts of the first cantos, and replaced him with a persona who can scrutinize the times, including wars and wasted lives, and can understand the social value of perceptivity, its function as a generator of wealth.[1]

Another major poet to be profoundly influenced by Douglas is Hugh MacDiarmid. In a fine essay on Pound, *The Return of the Long Poem* (*Perspectives*, Regnery, U.S.A., 1965), he wrote:

The values to be safeguarded in the Douglas Commonwealth are Liberty, Leisure and Culture. The will-to-plenty of the individual is to be given satisfaction, and the whole business and industrial life of society relegated to a subordinate place, somehow as in the economy of the human body many biological processes proceed automatically or semi-automatically, leaving the psychology of the human being free to develop its interests.

Systems were made for men, not men for systems (declared Major Douglas in the first chapter of his first book), and the interest of man, which is self-development, takes precedence over all systems, economic, political or theological. A ringing statement to come from an economist!

*   *   *

Pound's guiding beliefs in politics and economics can be summarised by four quotations: (1) 'The republic, the *res publica* means, or ought

[1] Hugh Kenner: *Drafts and Fragments and the Structure of the Cantos* (*Agenda*, Volume 8, Nos. 3–4, Autumn–Winter 1970). A more detailed treatment of these subjects will be found in Hugh Kenner's *The Pound Era* (Faber, 1972), pages 301–317 and 407–413.

to mean "the public convenience".' (2) 'The right aim of law is to prevent coercion, either by force or by fraud,' (3) 'Sovereignty inheres in the power to issue money, or to distribute the power to buy (credit or money) whether you have the right to do so or not.' (4) 'Civilisation depends on local control of purchasing power needed for local purposes.'

Pound has shown a more practical concern for the just distribution of wealth, and for the freedom of the individual, than vaguely 'socialist' English poets of the thirties and since. He attacked the problem of inequality and social injustice at its root—that is, in the means of distribution itself—the control and issue of money:

> Infantilism increasing to our time,
>   attention to outlet, no attention to source,
>   That is: the problem of issue.
> Who issues it? How?   (Canto LXXXVII)

As Hugh MacDiarmid has written in the article which I have already quoted, 'those of us who, like Pound, have long been interested in the Money Question are familiar with the psychological barrier most people have in this respect. They are unable to contemplate the fact that we are potbound in an arbitrary and artificial money system which has no correspondence to reality at all.'

A disinterested assessment of Pound's writings on 'coin, credit and circulation' is long overdue and it is my hope that the publication of *Selected Prose* will make this possible. Apart from *Impact*, which was published in the U.S.A. by Regnery in 1960 and included considerably cut versions of some of the articles in this book, most of this material has been unobtainable for years, although Peter Russell's publication of *Six Money Pamphlets* and *The ABC of Economics* in the early 1950s was valuable.

'. . . a nation whose measure of exchange is at the mercy of forces OUTSIDE the nation, is a nation in peril, . . . ' (*What is Money For?*, 1939). It is gradually becoming evident that Pound's ideas on monetary subjects were nearer the truth than those of 'orthodox' economists. More evidence on the way in which the MacDonald government was forced to betray its principles by non-elected international bankers has recently been released and the last Labour government was at least partially paralysed by similar external pressure. It is worth remembering that throughout the time Pound was writing his economic essays and pamphlets the Bank of England was a private institution.

Even Churchill himself realised the disastrous policies that the then governor of the Bank, Montagu Norman, had forced upon him when he was Chancellor of the Exchequer. In an interesting letter published in *The Times Business News* (20 May 1968) Lord Boothby quotes Churchill as having written to him in February 1932: 'I have gone the whole hog against gold. To hell with it! It has been used as a vile trap to destroy us . . . Surely it will become a public necessity to get rid of Montagu Norman. No man has ever been as stultified as he has been in his 14 years' policy.'

Lord Boothby ended his letter by saying 'when all is said and done' the Central Bankers 'were primarily responsible for the Second World War.' This is what Pound had maintained throughout his broadcasts and in his wartime economic writings. He had seen Europe destroy itself once, as *Mauberley* movingly records, and he fought during the thirties for a radical monetary reform which would prevent this from happening again–his broadcasts were not treason, but the logical outcome of this struggle. As he said in *For a New Paideuma* (1938), 'from now on all war in Europe is civil war, it is a man tearing at his own viscera.'

* * *

When reading some of Pound's statements in the thirties and during the Second World War we should remember his isolation throughout this period. He believed in 'a STRONG ITALY as the only possible foundation or anchor or whatever you want to call it for the good life in Europe.'[1] Sometimes, perhaps, he saw the possibility of an order and beauty which did not correspond to external, ephemeral reality. The same could be said of Virgil and Rome, or Dante and the Holy Roman Empire, but this does not invalidate their poetic vision.

Pound has been described as 'the last American living the tragedy of Europe.' In his writings and broadcasts during the war he felt he was fighting to save the principles of the American Constitution–he never advocated a fascist system of government for either England or America.

The clearest statement of Pound's position at this period is contained in a letter, dated 4 August 1943, which he wrote to Francis Biddle, United States Attorney General:

> I understand that I am under indictment for treason. I have done my best to get an authentic report of your statement to this effect. And I wish to place the following facts before you.
>
> I do not believe that the simple fact of speaking over the radio, wherever placed, can in itself constitute treason. I think that must depend on what is said, and on the motives for speaking.

---

[1] Ezra Pound: *Jefferson and/or Musso-lini* (1935). It is important to distinguish German Nazism from Italian Fascism. This Pound himself had done in one of his *New English Weekly* articles: 'Hitler sets up a parody, a sickly and unpleasant parody of fascism. He gets results of a sort, because there is a Teutonic tradition of hysteria. The Children's Crusade, mediaeval headlessness.' (*Orientation and News Sense*, January 5, 1933)

INTRODUCTION

I obtained the concession to speak over Rome radio with the following proviso. Namely that nothing should be asked of me contrary to my conscience or contrary to my duties as an American citizen. I obtained a declaration on their part of a belief in 'the free expression of opinion by those qualified to have an opinion.' . . .

This declaration was made several times in the announcement of my speeches; with the declaration 'He will not be asked to say anything contrary to his conscience, or contrary to his duties as an American citizen' (Citizen of U.S.). . . .

I have not spoken with regard to *this* war, but in protest against a system which creates one war after another, in series and in system. I have not spoken to the troops, and have not suggested that the troops should mutiny or revolt.

The whole basis of democratic or majority government assumes that the citizen shall be informed of the facts. I have not claimed to know all the facts, but I have claimed to know some of the facts which are an essential part of the total that should be known to the people.

I have for years believed that the American people should be better informed as to Europe, and informed by men who are not tied to a special interest or under definite control.

The freedom of the press has become a farce, as everyone knows that the press is controlled, if not by its titular owners, at least by the advertisers.

Free speech under modern conditions becomes a mockery if it does not include right to free speech over the radio.

And this point is worth establishing. The assumption of the right to punish and take vengeance regardless of the area of jurisdiction is dangerous. I do not mean in a small way; but for the nation.

I returned to America before the war to protest against particular forces then engaged in trying to create war and to make sure that the U.S.A. should be dragged into it.

Arthur Kitson's testimony before the Cunliffe and Macmillan commissions was insufficiently known. Brooks Adams brought to light several currents in history that should be better known. The course of events following the foundation of the Bank of England should be known, and considered in sequence: the suppression of colonial paper money, especially in Pennsylvania! [Biddle was a Philadelphian]. The similar curves following the Napoleonic wars, and our Civil War and Versailles need more attention.

We have not the right to drift into another error similar to that of the Versailles Treaty.

We have, I think, the right to a moderate expansion including defense of the Caribbean, the elimination of foreign powers from the American continent, but such expansion should not take place at the cost of deteriorating or ruining the internal structure of the U.S.A. The ruin of markets, the perversions of trade routes, in fact all the matters on which my talks have been based is of importance to the American citizen; [whom] neither you nor I should betray either in time of war *or* peace....

At any rate a man's duties increase with his knowledge. A war between the U.S. and Italy is monstrous and should not have occurred. And a peace without justice is no peace but merely a prelude to future wars. Someone must take count of these things. And having taken count must act on his knowledge; admitting that his knowledge is partial and his judgment subject to error.

It cannot be denied, whether one agrees with Pound's views at this time or not, that his stand was in accord with the principles of the founders of the American nation and it's a strange irony that it should have led to a charge of treason. This can best be shown by Jefferson's letter to William Wirt, 30 May 1811:

But for us to attempt, by war, to reform all Europe, and bring them back to principles of morality and a respect for the equal rights of nations, would show us to be only maniacs of another character.

* * *

I have devoted a part of this book to China. Pound's concern with Confucius dates from 1914–15 and he probably read him earlier. Both before, during, and after the Second World War, his work, and that of Mencius, remained a constant stronghold of order and repose in his mind amidst threatening chaos. He wrote from Pisa, after finishing his translations, *The Great Digest* and *The Unwobbling Pivot*: 'I do not know that I would have arrived at the centre of his meaning if I had not been down under the collapse of a regime.'

Pound was convinced that a just world order could only be built on the principles of the *Ta Hsio*. I quote what is perhaps the most salient passage from his translation of this text as it defines Pound's deepest beliefs and what is finest in his poetry and prose has its roots in these few sentences:

The men of old wanting to clarify and diffuse throughout the empire that light which comes from looking straight into the heart and then acting, first set up good government in their own states; wanting good government in their states, they first established order in their own families; wanting order in the home, they first disciplined themselves; desiring self-discipline, they rectified their hearts; and wanting to rectify their hearts, they sought precise verbal definitions of their inarticulate thoughts [the tones given off by the heart]; wishing to attain precise verbal definitions, they set to extend their knowledge to the utmost. This completion of knowledge is rooted in sorting things into organic categories.

As Tom Scott has written, 'I predict that the next century will see, even be dominated by, a dialogue between the U.S. and China in which Pound's poetry will take on an importance and weight not obvious at the moment: that not only has he woven a new wholeness, or at any rate potential wholeness, out of European and American, but also of Chinese, elements.'[1]

      *   *   *

Though Pound's interests extend far beyond Europe, the *Cantos* in one of its aspects, is a tragic visionary poem of European civilization written at a time when that civilization is in danger of falling apart.

> The scientists are in terror
>   and the European mind stops   (Canto CXV)

A Visiting Card (1942) and *Gold and Work* (1944), both written in Italian and included here in translation, date from not long before *The Pisan Cantos* and help us to understand them. At Pisa, Pound suffered the wreck of the Europe he loved, in actuality, which gives his vision a new depth. I think of King Lear, or the 'compound ghost' in *Little Gidding* who says, 'So I find words I never thought to speak'. The vision, 'To build the city of Dioce whose terraces are the colour of stars', remained, strengthened by suffering, 'now in the mind indestructible'.

The most recent volume of Cantos, *Drafts & Fragments of Cantos CX–CXVII*, which speak 'of men seeking good/doing evil', make us realise that Pound had probably oversimplified the world in some of his earlier writings. And he himself clearly analysed what he now considers was wrong with his 'method of opposing tyranny' in an interview published in *The Paris Review* (Summer-Fall, 1962):

What I was right about was the conservation of individual rights. If when the executive, or any other branch, exceeds its legitimate powers and no one protests, you will lose all your liberties. My method of opposing tyranny was wrong over a thirty year period; it had nothing to do with the second world war in particular. If the individual, or heretic, gets hold of some essential truth, or sees some error in the system being practiced, he commits so many marginal errors himself that he is worn out before he can establish his point.

      *   *   *

[1] Tom Scott: *The Poet as Scapegoat* (*Agenda*, Volume 7 No. 2, Spring 1959).

INTRODUCTION

Pound has both written, and acted, on a principle which he enunciated as early as 1913 in *Patria Mia* (Peter Owen): that the strength of the American genius is that 'it will undertake nothing in its art for which it will not be in person responsible.' A commitment of this kind informs all the essays in this book. It was echoed by Pound's words when he gave himself up to the American army in Genoa in 1945: 'If a man isn't willing to take some risk for his opinions, either his opinions are no good or he's no good.' The *Cantos*, whose history and economics are organically part of its vision, has poetic meaning because Ezra Pound has lived and suffered its subject matter directly.

I believe that his ideas about money and history are more often right than wrong, but even if they were proved to be mistaken, what counts for the poetry is his concern for justice in these matters; it is the economics and the history which give the *Cantos* order and profundity –without them the unsurpassed lyric beauty would lack meaning beyond aestheticism–it would have no roots in reality. Not the least of Pound's achievements has been to widen the scope of contemporary poetry to embody these subjects. When Pound's errors have been forgotten, the humanity and inclusiveness of his concerns will be remembered.

*   *   *

Pound has not written much prose since the war though he has made some important definitions which I have included in this selection. He never lost interest in monetary subjects while working on the later cantos at St. Elizabeth's Hospital. One author, scarcely mentioned in his prose, but important to this latter part of the poem, is the American historian Alexander Del Mar, whose *History of Monetary Systems* (1895) and *Barbara Villiers, a History of Monetary Crimes* (1899) confirmed much of what Pound had been writing in the thirties and forties.

The cantos written during these years incorporate many other tracts of material which are not touched on in the prose, including the work of Philostratus, John Heydon, Sir Edward Coke, Lord Herbert of Cherbury, Blackstone, Thomas Hart Benton, Joseph Rock and Linnaeus.

It is, perhaps, one of the tasks of poetry to affirm the existence of paradise even though today it can probably only exist in 'the wilds of a man's mind'. Much of *Selected Prose 1909–65* is concerned with civic order. *Rock-Drill*, *Thrones* and *Drafts & Fragments*, being written under 'the domination of benevolence' add another, essential dimension:

> Beyond civic order
> l'AMOR.   (Canto XCIV)

PART ONE
I gather the Limbs of Osiris

---

*The essential thing in a poet is that he
builds us his world.*

E.P., 1915

PART ONE

I gather the Limbs of Osiris[1]

A RATHER DULL INTRODUCTION

When I bring into play what my late pastors and masters would term, in classic sweetness, my 'unmitigated gall', and by virtue of it venture to speak of a 'New Method in Scholarship', I do not imagine that I am speaking of a method by me discovered. I mean, merely, a method not of common practice, a method not yet clearly or consciously formulated, a method which has been intermittently used by all good scholars since the beginning of scholarship, the method of Luminous Detail, a method most vigorously hostile to the prevailing mode of today–that is, the method of multitudinous detail, and to the method of yesterday, the method of sentiment and generalisation. The latter is too inexact and the former too cumbersome to be of much use to the normal man wishing to live mentally active.

Axioms are the necessary platitudes of any science, and, as all sciences must start from axioms, most serious beginnings are affairs sententious, and pedagogical, bear with me a little; let me write a few pages of commonplace, of things which we all know and upon which we for the most part agree, and if you endure to the end of them you will know upon what section of our common knowledge I am to build the airy fabric of my heresies. The former may not amuse you, but, in tolerance await, I ask you, for the irritation of the latter. These things pertain not only to education–always a painful and unpleasant process, but to an art not always the reverse.

The aim of right education is to lead a man out into more varied, more intimate contact with his fellows. The result of education, in the present and usual sense, is usually to rear between the 'product of education' and the unproduced, a barrier, a *chevaux de frise* of books and of mutual misunderstanding. This refers chiefly to education in what are still called the 'humanities', to processes by which, upon

---

[1] *The New Age,* 7 December 1911–15 February 1912. This series of articles was originally published in eleven parts and included a number of translations most of which Mr. Pound subsequently revised–these revised versions are printed in *The Translations of Ezra Pound* (Faber, 1970). I have cut those parts which are available there. Ed.

21

being examined, one becomes 'bachelor' or 'master' of the 'liberal arts', or even 'one learned in philosophy'. In matters of technical and practical education, where the object is to make a man more efficiently useful to the community, things are better managed: there is here some obvious gauge of the result.

If a man owned mines in South Africa he would know that his labourers dug up a good deal of mud and an occasional jewel, looking rather like the mud about it. If he shipped all the mud and uncut stones northward and dumped them in one heap on the shore of Iceland, in some inaccessible spot, we should not consider him commercially sound. In my own department of scholarship I should say the operations are rather of this complexion. There are many fine things discovered, edited, and buried. Much very dull 'literature' is treated in like manner. They are dumped in one museum and certain learned men rejoice in the treasure. They also complain of a lack of public interest in their operations. But let us finish our objecting. Obviously we must know accurately a great number of minute facts about any subject if we are really to know it. The drudgery and minutiae of method concern only the scholar. But when it comes to presenting matter to the public, to the intelligent, over-busy public, *bonae voluntatis*, there are certain forms of civility, consideration, and efficiency to be considered.

Any fact is, in a sense, 'significant'. Any fact may be 'symptomatic', but certain facts give one a sudden insight into circumjacent conditions, into their causes, their effects, into sequence, and law.

So-and-so was, in such-and-such a year, elected Doge. So-and-so killed the tyrant. So-and-so was banished for embezzling State funds. So-and-so embezzled but was not banished. These statements may contain germs of drama, certain suggestions of human passion or habit, but they are reticent, they tell us nothing we did not know, nothing which enlightens us. They are of any time and any country. By reading them with the blanks filled in, with the names written, we get no more intimate acquaintance with the temper of any period; but when in Burckhardt we come upon a passage: 'In this year the Venetians refused to make war upon the Milanese because they held that any war between buyer and seller must prove profitable to neither,' we come upon a portent, the old order changes, one conception of war and of the State begins to decline. The Middle Ages imperceptibly give ground to the Renaissance. A ruler owning a State and wishing to enlarge his possessions, could under one régime, in a manner opposed to sound economy, make war; but commercial sense is sapping this régime. In the history of the development of civilisation or of literature, we come upon such interpreting detail. A few dozen facts of this nature give us intelligence of a period – a kind of intelligence not to be gathered from a great array of facts of the other sort. These facts are hard to find. They are swift and easy of transmission. They govern knowledge as the switchboard governs an electric circuit.

If on no other grounds than this, namely, that the eye-sight is valuable, we should read less, far less than we do. Moreover, the best of knowledge is 'in the air', or if not the best, at least the leaven.

Being what we are, we have in certain matters an Accuracy of Sentiment. 'Wireless', 'Automobile', 'Chippendale', 'Figures out of Æschylus', are terms which convey to us definite meanings, which they would not convey to creatures of our own faculty but of an earlier time, or different in customs and in culture. 'Derby', 'Boxing Day', 'Bank-holiday', are arcana to a citizen of Oshkosh, as are 'Greece before Pericles', 'The Eighth Century', 'Trobar clus', 'sublimation' to the general reader.

Certain knowledge comes to us very easily, and we no longer think of an automobile as having a door at the back. We are, that is, modern; if we desire accuracy of sentiment about a certain picture we go to see it, if it is inaccessible we buy a photograph and make allowance for the lack of colour, we read the date of painting, the artist's name, and begin our concept of the art of a certain place and time, a concept to be enlarged and modified by whatever other masterpieces we see of like place and time, of like place, before and after, of like time and different place. A few days in a good gallery are more illuminating than years would be if spent in reading a description of these pictures. Knowledge which cannot be acquired in some such manner as that of visiting galleries is relegated to the specialist or to his shadow, the dilettante.

As for myself, I have tried to clear up a certain messy place in the history of literature; I have tried to make our sentiment of it more accurate. Accuracy of sentiment here will make more accurate the sentiment of the growth of literature as a whole, and of the Art of poetry. I am more interested in the Arts than in the histories of developments of this and that, for the Arts work on life as history works on the development of civilisation and literature. The artist seeks out the luminous detail and presents it. He does not comment. His work remains the permanent basis of psychology and metaphysics. Each historian will 'have ideas'–presumably different from other historians–imperfect inductions, varying as the fashions, but the luminous details remain unaltered. As scholarship has erred in presenting all detail as if of equal import, so also in literature, in a present school of writing we see a similar tendency. But this is aside the mark.

I am more interested in life than in any part of it. As an artist I dislike writing prose. Writing prose is an art, but it is not my art. One word more of the plan I have followed in it. I have, if you will, hung my gallery, a gallery of photographs, of perhaps not very good photographs, but of the best I can lay hold of.

In 'The Spirit of Romance' I attempted to present certain significant data on mediaeval poetry in Southern Europe, of the troubadours, of the Tuscans, of Villon, and, coming on to the Renaissance, of Lope de Vega, of Camoens, of certain poets who wrote in Latin–to make a sort of chemical spectrum of their art. I have since augmented this study with translations from Guido Cavalcanti and Arnaut Daniel. I have allowed it to impinge on my own poetry in 'Canzoni', which is a great fault in the eyes of those critics who think I should be more interested in the poetry which I write myself than in 'fine poetry as a whole'.

Personally, I think the *corpus poetarum* of more importance than any cell or phalange, and shall continue in sin.

I have, moreover, sought in Anglo-Saxon a certain element which has transmuted the various qualities of poetry which have drifted up from the south, which has sometimes enriched and made them English, sometimes rejected them, and refused combination.

This further work of mine will appear in part in book form, in part in these columns. I shall also set forth some defence of a hope which I have that this sort of work may not fail utterly to be of service to the living art. For it is certain that we have had no 'greatest poet' and no 'great period' save at, or after, a time when many people were busy examining the media and the traditions of the art.

A BEGINNING

In my opening chapter I said that there were certain facts or points, or 'luminous details', which governed knowledge as the switchboard the electric circuit. In the study of the art of letters these points are particular works or the works of particular authors.

Let us suppose a man, ignorant of painting, taken into a room containing a picture by Fra Angelico, a picture by Rembrandt, one by Velasquez, Memling, Rafael, Monet, Beardsley, Hokusai, Whistler, and a fine example of the art of some forgotten Egyptian. He is told that this is painting and that every one of these is master-work. He is, if a thoughtful man, filled with confusion. These things obey no common apparent law. He confesses, if intelligent, to an ignorance of the art of painting. If he is a natural average human he hates part of the work, perhaps violently; he is attracted, perhaps, by the subjects of some of the pictures. Apart from the subject matter he accepts the Rafael, then, perhaps, the Rembrandt or the Velasquez or the Monet or the Memling, and then the Whistler or the Angelico or the Egyptian, and last the Beardsley. Or he does it in different order. He calls some ugly and some pretty. If, however, he is a specialist, a man thoroughly trained in some other branch of knowledge, his feelings are not unlike mine when I am taken into the engineering laboratory and shown successively an electric engine, a steam-engine, a gas-engine, etc. I realise that there are a number of devices, all designed for more or less the same end, none 'better', none 'worse', all different. Each, perhaps, slightly more fit for use under certain conditions for certain objects minutely differentiated. They all 'produce power'– that is, they gather the latent energy of Nature and focus it on a certain resistance. The latent energy is made dynamic or 'revealed' to the engineer in control, and placed at his disposal.

As for me–the visitor in the engine-room–I perceive 'sources'–not ultimate sources, but sources–of light, heat, motion, etc. I realise the purpose and effect; I know it would take me some time really to understand the rules in accordance with which any engine works, and that these rules are similar and different with different engines.

To read a number of books written at different ages and in different tongues may arouse our curiosity and may fill us with a sense of our ignorance of the laws of the art in accordance with which they are written. The fact that every masterpiece contains its law within itself, self-sufficing to itself, does not simplify the solution. Before we can discuss any possible 'laws of art' we must know, at least, a little of the various stages by which that art has grown from what it was to what it is. This is simply restatement of what ought to be in every text-book, and has nothing to do with any 'new method'. The handiest way to some knowledge of these 'various stages' is, however, by 'the new method'–that of luminous detail.

Interesting works are of two sorts, the 'symptomatic' and the 'donative'; thus a sestina of Pico della Mirandola, concerned for the most part with Jove and Phoebus, shows us a Provençal form stuffed with revived classicism. Camoens' 'Os Lusiadas' has a similar value. In them we find a reflection of tendencies and modes of a time. They mirror obvious and apparent thought movements. They are what one might have expected in such and such a year and place. They register.

But the 'donative' author seems to draw down into the art something which was not in the art of his predecessors. If he also draw from the air about him, he draws latent forces, or things present but unnoticed, or things perhaps taken for granted but never examined. *Non e mai tarde per tentar l'ignoto.*[1] His forbears may have led up to him; he is never a disconnected phenomenon, but he does take some step further. He discovers, or, better, 'he discriminates'. We advance by discriminations, by discerning that things hitherto deemed identical or similar are dissimilar; that things hitherto deemed dissimilar, mutually foreign, antagonistic, are similar and harmonic.

[1] Gabriele d'Annunzio from the third episode of *La Nave* (1908); quoted   Canto XCIII, Ed.

Assume that, by the translations of 'The Seafarer' and of Guido's lyrics, I have given evidence that fine poetry may consist of elements that are or seem to be almost mutually exclusive. In the canzoni of Arnaut Daniel we find a beauty, a beauty of elements almost unused in these two other very different sorts of poetry. That beauty is, or would be if you read Provençal, a thing apparent, at least, a thing not to be helped or thrust upon you by any prose of mine. In the translations (to follow next week) I give that beauty–reproduced, that is, as nearly as I can reproduce it in English–for what it is worth. What I must now do—as the scholar–in pursuance of my announced 'method' is to justify my use of Arnaut's work as a strategic position, as 'luminous detail'.

We advance by discriminations, and to Arnaut Daniel we may ascribe discriminations. The poems of Arnaut were written in Provençe about A.D. 1180–1200, about a century, that is, before the love poems of Dante and of Guido. And if he, Arnaut, frequented one court more than another it was the court of King Richard Coeur de Lion, 'Plantagenet', in compliment to whose sister (presumably) he rimes to 'genebres' in Canzon XVI.

'*Ans per s'amor sia laurs o genebres*'–'Her love is as the laurel or the broom is.' The compliment is here given, presumably, to Mona Laura and the Lady Plantagenet (or, in Provençal, *Planta genebres*), or it is, may be, only in homage to the loyalty of Richard himself. After seven centuries one cannot be too explicit in the unravelling of personal allusion. To be born a troubadour in Provence in the twelfth century was to be born, you would say, 'in one's due time'. It was to be born after two centuries of poetic tradition, of tradition that had run in one groove– to wit, the making of canzoni. The art might have, you would say, had time to come to flower, to perfect itself. Moreover, as an art it had few rivals; of painting and sculpture there was little or none. The art of song was to these people literature and opera: their books and their theatre. In the north of France the longer narrative poems held the field against it, but the two arts were fraternal, and one guild presided over them–not a formal guild, that is, but the same people purveyed them.

Now in the flower of this age, when many people were writing canzoni, or had just written them–Jaufre Rudel, Ventadorn, Borneilh, Marvoil, de Born–Arnaut discriminated between rhyme and rhyme.

He perceived, that is, that the beauty to be gotten from a similarity of line-terminations depends not upon their multiplicity, but upon their action the one upon the other; not upon frequency, but upon the manner of sequence and combination. The effect of 'lais' in monorhyme, or of a canzon in which a few rhymes appear too often, is monotonous, is monotonous beyond the point where monotony is charming or interesting. Arnaut uses what for want of a better term I call polyphonic rhyme.

At a time when both prose and poetry were loose-jointed, prolix, barbaric, he, to all intents and virtually, rediscovered 'style'. He conceived, that is, a manner of writing in which each word should bear some burden, should make some special contribution to the effect of the whole. The poem is an organism in which each part functions, gives to sound or to sense something–preferably to sound *and* sense gives something.

Thirdly, he discerns what Plato had discerned some time before, that μέλος is the union of words, rhythm, and music (i.e., that part of music which we do not perceive as rhythm). Intense hunger for a strict accord between these three has marked only the best lyric periods, and Arnaut felt this hunger more keenly and more precisely than his fellows or his forerunners.

He is significant for all these things. He bears to the technique of *accented* verse of Europe very much the same relation that Euclid does to our mathematics. For these things Dante honoured him in his 'Treatise on the Common Speech', and he honoured him in the 'Divina Commedia' for these three things and for perhaps one other– a matter of content, not of artistry, yet a thing intimate and bound in with the other three. For that fineness of Arnaut's senses which made him chary of his rhymes, impatient of tunes that would have distorted his language, fastidious of redundance, made him likewise accurate in his observation of Nature.

For long after him the poets of the North babbled of gardens where 'three birds sang on every bough' and where other things and creatures behaved as in nature they do not behave. And, apart from his rhyme, apart from the experiments in artistry which lead in so great part to the conclusions in the 'Treatise on the Common Tongue,'[1] it is this that Dante learns from him, this precision of observation and reference. '*Que jes Rozers*' sings Daniel, '*Dove l'Adige*' the other. And it will be difficult to prove that there is not some recognition and declaration of this in the passage in the Purgatorio (Canto XXVI), where Arnaut is made to reply–

> '*E vei jausen lo jorn qu'esper denan*' –
> 'I see rejoicing the day that is before.'

If this is not definite allegory, it is at least clearer than many allegories that tradition has brought to us, bound in through the Commedia. If Dante does not here use Arnaut as a symbol of perceptive

---

[1] I do not mean that Dante here accepts all Arnaut's forms and fashions. Arnaut's work as we have it shows constant search and rejection.

intelligence, sincere, making no pretence to powers beyond its own, but seeing out of its time and place, rejoicing in its perspicacity, we can at least, from our later vantage, find in this trait of Arnaut's some germ of the Renaissance, of the spirit which was to overthrow super-stition and dogma, of the 'scientific spirit' if you will, for science is unpoetic only to minds jaundiced with sentiment and romanticism—the great masters of the past boasted all they could of it and found it magical; of the spirit which finds itself most perfectly expressed and formulated in this speech which Merejkowski has set in the mouth of Leonardo da Vinci—I think on authority of the writings of the latter—when he is speaking of the artist, of the Greek and Roman classics, and of Nature: 'Few men will drink from the cup when they may drink from the fountain.'

ON VIRTUE

In an earlier chapter I said that interesting authors were either 'symp-tomatic' or 'donative'; permit me new diameters and a new circum-scription, even if I seem near to repetition.

As contemporary philosophy has so far resolved itself into a struggle to disagree as to the terms in which we shall define an indefinable something upon which we have previously agreed to agree, I ask the reader to regard what follows not as dogma, but as a metaphor which I find convenient to express certain relations.

The soul of each man is compounded of all the elements of the cosmos of souls, but in each soul there is some one element which predominates, which is in some peculiar and intense way the quality or *virtù* of the individual; in no two souls is this the same. It is by reason of this *virtù* that a given work of art persists. It is by reason of this *virtù* that we have one Catullus, one Villon; by reason of it that no amount of technical cleverness can produce a work having the same charm as the original, not though all progress in art is, in so great degree a progress through imitation.

This virtue is not a 'point of view', nor an 'attitude toward life'; nor is it the mental calibre or 'a way of thinking', but something more substantial which influences all these. We may as well agree, at this point, that we do not all of us think in at all the same sort of way or by the same sort of implements. Making a rough and incomplete category from personal experience I can say that certain people think with words, certain with, or in, objects; others realise nothing until they have pictured it; others progress by diagrams like those of the geometricians; some think, or construct, in rhythm, or by rhythms and sound; others, the unfortunate, move by words disconnected from the objects to which they might correspond, or more unfortun-ate still in blocks and *clichés* of words; some, favoured of Apollo, in words that hover above and cling close to the things they mean. And all these different sorts of people have most appalling difficulty in understanding each other.

It is the artist's business to find his own *virtù*. This virtue may be what you will:

> *Luteum pede soccum, . . .*
> > *Viden ut faces*
> *Splendidas quatiunt comas! . . .*
> *Luteumve papauer.*

It may be something which draws Catullus to write of scarlet poppies, of orange-yellow slippers, of the shaking, glorious hair of the torches; or Propertius to

> Quoscumque smaragdos
> Quosve dedit flavo lumine chrysolithos.[1]
> –'The honey-coloured light.'

Or it may be the so attractive, so nickel-plated neatness which brings Mr. Pope so to the quintessence of the obvious, with:

> 'Man is not a fly.'

So far as mortal immortality is concerned, the poet need only discover his *virtù* and survive the discovery long enough to write some few scant dozen verses– providing, that is, that he have acquired some reasonable technique, this latter being the matter of a lifetime–or not, according to the individual facility.

Beyond the discovery and expression of his virtue the artist may proceed to the erection of his microcosmos.

'Ego tamquam centrum circuli,[2] quae omnes circumferentiae partes habet equaliter, tu autem non sic'–'I am the centre of a circle which possesseth all parts of its circumference equally, but thou not so,' says the angel appearing to Dante ('Vita Nuova', XII).

Having discovered his own virtue the artist will be more likely to discern and allow for a peculiar *virtù* in others. The erection of the microcosmos consists in discriminating these other powers and in holding them in orderly arrangement about one's own. The process is uncommon. Dante, of all men, performed it in the most symmetrical and barefaced manner; yet I would for you–as I have done already for myself–stretch the fabric of my critique upon four great positions.

Among the poets there have been four men in especial virtuous, or, since virtues are so hard to define, let us say they represent four distinct phases of consciousness:

Homer of the Odyssey, man conscious of the world outside him: and if we accept the tradition of Homer's blindness, we may find in that

---

[1] Quoted in Canto VII. Ed.   [2] Quoted in Canto LXXXVII. Ed.

blindness the significant cause of his power; for him the outer world would have a place of mystery, of uncertainty, of things severed from their attendant trivialities, of acts, each one cloaked in some glamour of the inexperienced; his work, therefore, a work of imagination and not of observation;

Dante, in the 'Divina Commedia', man conscious of the world within him;

Chaucer, man conscious of the variety of persons about him, not so much of their acts and the outlines of their acts as of their character, their personalities; with the inception of this sort of interest any epic period comes to its end;

Shakespeare, man conscious of himself in the world about him—as Dante had been conscious of the spaces of the mind, its reach and its perspective.

I doubt not that a person of wider reading could make a better arrangement of names than this is, but I must talk from my corner of the things that I know; at any rate, each of these men constructed some sort of world into which we may plunge ourselves and find a life not glaringly incomplete. Of the last three we know definitely that each of them swept into his work the virtues of many forerunners and contemporaries, and that in no case do these obtrude or disturb the poise of the whole.

I believe sincerely that any man who has read these four authors with attention will find that a great many other works, now accepted as classic, rather bore him; he will understand their beauty, but with this understanding will come the memory of having met the same sort of beauty elsewhere in greater intensity. It will be said, rather, that he understands the books than that the books enlighten him. In the culture of the mind, as in the culture of fields, there is a law of diminishing return. If a book reveal to us something of which we were unconscious, it feeds us with its energy; if it reveal to us nothing but the fact that its author knew something which we knew, it draws energy from us.

Now it is inconceivable that any knowledge of Homer, Dante, Chaucer, and Shakespeare could ever diminish our enjoyment of Sappho, or of Villon, or of Heine, or of the 'Poema del Cid', or, perhaps, of Leopardi, though we would enjoy him in great part as a commentator, as a friend looking with us toward the classics and seeing, perhaps, into them further than we had seen.

The donative authors, or the real classics, inter-illuminate each other, and I should define a 'classic' as a book our enjoyment of which cannot be diminished by any amount of reading of other books, or even—and this is the fiercer test—by a first-hand knowledge of life.

Any author whose light remains visible in this place where the greater lamps are flashing back and forth upon each other is of no mean importance; of him it can be said without qualification that he has attained his own *virtù*. It is true that the results of Guido Cavalcanti and of Arnaut Daniel are in great measure included in the 'Divina Commedia', yet there remains over a portion not quite soluble, and in trying at this late date to reinstate them in our canon, I do nothing that Dante has not done before me; one reads their work, in fact, on his advice ('Purgatorio', XI and XXVI). In each case their virtue is a virtue of precision. In Arnaut, as I have said before, this fineness has its effect in his style, his form, the relation of his words and tune, and in his content.

ON TECHNIQUE

'Skill in technique,' says Joseph Conrad, 'is something more than honesty.' And if this is applicable to the racing of yachts it should be no less applicable to the writing of poetry.

We can imagine easily the delight of Ysaye and M. Nickisch on being invited, firstly to dinner and secondly to listen to your fourteen-year-old daughter play Beethoven; or lifting the parallel to more exact preciseness, let us suppose the child, never having taken a music lesson in her life, hears Busoni play Chopin, and on the spur of the moment, thinking to produce similar effect, hires a hall and produces what she thinks sounds somewhat the same. These things are in the realm of music mildly unthinkable; but then the ordinary piano teacher spends more thought on the art of music than does the average 'poet' on the art of poetry. No great composer has, so far as I know, boasted an ignorance of musical tradition or thought himself less a musician because he could play Mozart correctly. Yet it is not uncommon to hear practising 'poets' speak of 'technique' as if it were a thing antipathetic to 'poetry'. And they mean something that is more or less true. Likewise you will hear the people, one set of them, raging against form–by which they mean external symmetry–and another set against free verse. And it is quite certain that none of these people have any exact, effable concept of what they do mean; or if they have a definite dislike of something properly dislikable, they only succeeded in expressing a dislike for something not quite it and not quite not it.

As for the ancients, we say for them it was quite easy. There was then an interest in poetry. Homer had the advantage of writing for an audience each of whom knew something of a ship and of a sword. One could allude to things that all understood.

Let us imagine today a contest between Jack Johnson and the surviving 'White Hope'; let us imagine Court circles deeply interested; let us imagine Olympia filled half with the 'flower of the realm' and half with chieftains from Zlyzmmbaa; let us suppose that everyone had staked their last half-crown, and that the victors were going to rape all the wives and daughters of the vanquished, and there was a divorce scandal inextricably entangled in the affair; and that if the blacks won they were going to burn the National Gallery and the home of Sir Florence Tlallina-Lalina.

It is very hard to reproduce the simplicity of the epic period. Browning does, it is true, get at life almost as 'simply' as did Ovid and Catullus; but then he was one 'classicist' 'mid a host of Victorians. Even this is not Homer.

Let us return to our hypothetical prize-fight. In an account of the fight what details would we demand? Fine psychological analysis of the combatants? Character study? Or the sort of details that a sporting crowd want from a fight that they have stakes on? Left-lead for the jaw. Counter. If the fight were as important as the one mentioned they might even take it from one who called sacred things by uninitiated names: 'an almighty swat in the thorax', 'wot-for in the kisser', 'a resounding blow upon the optic'—bad, this last. Leave it in the hands of the 'descriptive writer'. *Qui sono io profano.*

The very existence of the 'descriptive writer' shows that the people are not without some vague, indefined hunger for euphues, for the decorated 'Elizabethan' speech And the 'descriptive writer' is so rare, I am told, that one 'great daily' had to have their 'coronation' done by an Italian and translated.

And as for poetry, for verse, and the people, I remember a series of 'poems' in a new form that ran long in the 'New York Journal,' and with acclaim, one a day. Alas! I can only remember two of them, as follows:

1. In the days of old Pompei
   Did the people get away?
   　　　　Nay! Nay!

2. In the days of Charlemagne
   Did the people get champagne?
   　　　　Guess again!

Yet even these verses will appeal only to 'certain classes', and our prize-fight is a phantom, Eheu fugaces! How, then, shall the poet in this dreary day attain universality, how write what will be understood of 'the many' and lauded of 'the few'?

What interest have all men in common? What forces play upon them all? Money and sex and tomorrow. And we have called money 'fate' until that game is played out. And sex? Well, poetry has been erotic, or amative, or something of that sort—at least, a vast deal of it has–ever since it stopped being epic–and this sort of thing interests the inexperienced. And tomorrow? We none of us agree about.

We are nevertheless one humanity, compounded of one mud and

of one aether; and every man who does his own job really well has a latent respect for every other man who does *his* own job really well; this is our lasting bond; whether it be a matter of buying up all the little brass farthings in Cuba and selling them at a quarter per cent. advance,[1] or of delivering steam-engines to King Menelek[2] across three rivers and one hundred and four ravines, or of conducting some new crotchety variety of employers' liability insurance, or of punching another man's head, the man who really does the thing well, if he be pleased afterwards to talk about it, gets always his auditors' attention; he gets his audience the moment he says something so intimate that it proves him the expert: he does not, as a rule, sling generalities; he gives the particular case for what it is worth; the truth is the individual.

As for the arts and their technique–technique is the means of conveying an exact impression of exactly what one means in such a way as to exhilarate.

When it comes to poetry, I hold no brief for any particular system of metric. Europe supplies us with three or five or perhaps more systems. The early Greek system of measure by quantity, which becomes the convention of later Greek and of Latin verse; the Provençal system, measure (*a*) by number of syllables, (*b*) by number of stressed syllables, which has become the convention of most European poetry; the Anglo-Saxon system of alliteration; these all concern the scansion. For terminations we have rhyme in various arrangements, blank verse, and the Spanish system of assonance. English is made up of Latin, French, and Anglo-Saxon, and it is probable that all these systems concern us. It is not beyond the pales of possibility that English verse of the future will be a sort of orchestration taking account of all these systems.

When I say above that technique is the means of conveying an exact impression of exactly what one means, I do not by any means mean that poetry is to be stripped of any of its powers of vague suggestion. Our life is, in so far as it is worth living, made up in great part of things indefinite, impalpable; and it is precisely because the arts present us these things that we–humanity–cannot get on without the arts. The picture that suggests indefinite poems, the line of verse that means a gallery of paintings, the modulation that suggests a score of metaphors and is contained in none: it is these things that touch us nearly that 'matter'.

The artist discriminates, that is, between one kind of indefinability and another, and poetry is a very complex art. Its media are on one hand the simplest, the least interesting, and on the other the most arcane, most fascinating. It is an art of pure sound bound in through an art of arbitrary and conventional symbols. In so far as it is an art of

---

[1] See Canto XII. Ed.   [2] See Canto XVIII. Ed.

pure sound, it is allied with music, painting, sculpture; in so far as it is an art of arbitrary symbols, it is allied to prose. A word exists when two or more people agree to mean the same thing by it.

Permit me one more cumbersome simile, for I am trying to say something about the masterly use of words, and it is not easy. Let us imagine that words are like great hollow cones of steel of different dullness and acuteness; I say great because I want them not too easy to move; they must be of different sizes. Let us imagine them charged with a force like electricity, or, rather, radiating a force from their apexes—some radiating, some sucking in. We must have a greater variety of activity than with electricity—not merely positive and negative; but let us say $+$, $-$, $\times$, $\div$, $+a$, $-a$, $\times a$, $\div a$, etc. Some of these kinds of force neutralise each other, some augment; but the only way any two cones can be got to act without waste is for them to be so placed that their apexes and a line of surface meet exactly. When this conjunction occurs let us say their force is not added one's to the other's, but multiplied the one's by the other's; thus three or four words in exact juxtaposition are capable of radiating this energy at a very high potentiality; mind you, the juxtaposition of their vertices must be exact and the angles or 'signs' of discharge must augment and not neutralise each other. This peculiar energy which fills the cones is the power of tradition, of centuries of race consciousness, of agreement, of association; and the control of it is the 'Technique of Content', which nothing short of genius understands.

There is the slighter 'technique of manner', a thing reducible almost to rules, a matter of 'j's' and 'd's', of order and sequence, a thing attenuable, a thing verging off until it degenerates into rhetoric; and this slighter technique is also a thing of price, notwithstanding that all the qualities which differentiate poetry from prose are things born before syntax; this technique of surface is valuable above its smoother virtues simply because it is technique, and because technique is the only gauge and test of a man's lasting sincerity.

Everyone, or nearly everyone, feels at one time or another poetic, and falls to writing verses; but only that man who cares and believes really in the pint of truth that is in him will work, year in and year out, to find the perfect expression.

If technique is thus the protection of the public, the sign manual by which it distinguishes between the serious artist and the disagreeable young person expressing its haedinus egotism, it is no less a protection to the artist himself during the most crucial period of his development. I speak now of technique seriously studied, of a searching into cause and effect, into the purposes of sound and rhythm as such, not—not by any means—of a conscientious and clever imitation of the master of the moment, of the poet in vogue.

How many have I seen, how many have we all of us known, young, with promising poetic insides, who produce one book and die of it? For in our time, at least, the little public that does read new poetry is not twice bored by the same aspirant, and if a man's first book has not in it some sign of a serious struggle with the bases of the art he has small likelihood of meeting them in a second. But the man who has some standard reasonably high–consider, says Longinus, in what mood Diogenes or Sophocles would have listened to your effusion– does, while he is striving to bring his work within reach of his own conception of it, get rid of the first froth of verse, which is in nearly every case quite like the first verse-froth of everyone else. He emerges decently clean after some reasonable purgation, not nearly a master, but licensed, an initiate, with some chance of conserving his will to speak and of seeing it mature and strengthen with the ripening and strengthening of the mind itself until, by the favour of the gods, he come upon some lasting excellence.

Let the poet who has been not too long ago born make very sure of this, that no one cares to hear, in strained iambics, that he feels sprightly in spring, is uncomfortable when his sexual desires are ungratified, and that he has read about human brotherhood in last year's magazines. But let a man once convince thirty people that he has some faint chance of finding, or that he, at least, is determined and ready to suffer all drudgery in attempting to find, some entanglement of words so subtle, so crafty that they can be read or heard without yawning, after the reading of Pindar and Meleager, and of 'As ye came from the holy land of Walsinghame' and 'Tamlin', and of a passage from John Keats–let thirty or a dozen people believe this, and the man of whom they believe it will find friendship where he had little expected it, and delightful things will befall him suddenly and with no other explanation.

ON MUSIC

The reasons why good description makes bad poetry, and why painters who insist on painting ideas instead of pictures offend so many, are not far to seek.

I am in sympathy equally with those who insist that there is *one* art and many media, and with those who cry out against the describing of work in any particular art by a terminology borrowed from all the others. This manner of description is objectionable, because it is, in most cases, a make-shift, a laziness. We talk of the odour of music and the timbre of a painting because we think we suggest what we mean and are too lazy to undertake the analysis necessary to find out exactly what we do mean. There is, perhaps, *one* art, but any given subject belongs to the artist, who must know that subject most intimately before he can express it through his particular medium.

Thus, it is bad poetry to talk much of the colours of the sunrise, though one may speak of our lady 'of rosy fingers' or 'in russet clad', invoking an image not present to the uninitiated; at this game the poet may surpass, but in the matter of the actual colour he is a bungler. The painter sees, or should see, half a hundred hues and varieties, where we see ten; or, granting we are ourselves skilled with the brush, how many hundred colours are there, where language has but a dozen crude names? Even if the poet understands the subtleties of gradation and juxtaposition, his medium refuses to convey them. He can say all his say while he is ignorant of the reality, and knowledge of the reality will not help him to say it better.

I express myself clumsily, but this much remains with me as certain: that any given work of art is bad when its content could have found more explicit and precise expression through some other medium, which the artist was, perhaps, too slothful to master.

This test should set to rest the vain disputes about 'psychological' and 'poetic' painting. If 'Beata Beatrix', which is more poetic than all Rossetti's poetry, could have occurred in any other medium but paint, then it was bad art to paint her, and the painters should stick to chromatic harmonies and proportional composition.

This principle of the profundity of apprehension is the only one which can guide us through mixed or compound media; and by it we must form our judgments as to the 'limitations of an art'.

After squandering a good deal of time and concentration on the question of the relation of poetry and music, it seems to me not only futile, but very nearly impossible, to lay down any principles whatever for the regulation of their conjunctions.

To join these two arts is in itself an art, and is no more capable of being reduced to formulae than are the others. It is all very well for Plato to tell us that μέλο is the accord of rhythm and words and music (i.e., varied pitch). We find ourselves in the same case as Aristotle when he set out to define poetics—and in view of the fact that 'The Stagirite' is, by reason of his admirers, become a Shavian holiday, let us observe that he–Aristotle–never attempts to restrict the working artist; he, and Dante after him, merely enumerate the means by which former artists have been successful.

Let us then catalogue, if possible, the simplest and briefest set of rules on which we may assume that intelligent musicians and poets are alike agreed:

First, that the words of a song sung should be intelligible.

Second, that words should not be unreasonably distorted.

Third, that the rhythm of poetry should not be unreasonably ruined by the musician setting it to music.

I say 'unreasonably' because it is quite certain that, however much this distortion may horrify the poet who, having built his words into a perfect rhythm and speech-melody, hears them sung with regard to neither and with outrage to one or both; still we do derive pleasure from songs which distort words most abominably. And we do this in obedience to aesthetic laws; do it because the sense of musical period is innate in us. And because of this instinct there is deadly strife between musicians, who are usually, in the poet's sense, fools, and poets who are usually, in the musician's sense, unmusical.

When, if it ever was so, the lyre was played before the poet began his rhapsody, quantity had some vital meaning in the work. The quantity of later Greek poetry and of Latin is a convention, an imitation of models, not an interpretation of speech. If certain of the troubadours did attend to the strict relation of word and tune—*motz el son*—it was because of the strict relation between poet and composer, when they were not one and the same person. And in many an envoi we find such boast as So-and-so 'made it, song and the words'.

It is my personal belief that the true economy lies in making the tune first. We all of us compose verse to some sort of a tune, and if the 'song' is to be sung we may as well compose to a 'musician's' tune straight away. Yet no musician comes to one with a melody, but rather he comes wishing to set our words to music. And this is a far more subtle manoeuvre. To set words to a tune one has but to let the musical accents fall upon words strong enough to bear them, to refrain from putting an over-long syllable under an over-short note, and to leave the word ligature rather loose; the singer does the rest quite well. One is spared all the finer workmanship which is requisite for good spoken verse. The stuff may not make good reading, but it is still finished art, suited to its purpose.

If, however, the verse is made to speak, it may have in it that sort of rhythm which not only makes music unnecessary, but which is repulsive to it; or it may have a rhythm which can, by some further mastery, be translated into a music subtler than either poetry or music would have separately attained. Or the poet may have felt a plucking of strings or a flurry of instrumental sound accompanying his words and been unable to record them, and be totally dependent on the musician for a completion of his work. And there may linger in his words some sign and trace of a hunger for this completion.

The musician working from here is apt to find barriers in the so-called 'laws' of music or of verse. The obvious answer is that none of these laws are yet absolutely discerned. We do not know whether the first neumes indicated a rise or fall of voice by definite gradations of pitch, or whether they indicate simply rise or fall. The music of the troubadour period is without bars in the modern sense. There are little lines like them, but they mean simply a pause, a rest; the notes do not register differences of duration—i.e., halves, wholes, quarters are written alike. One reads the words on which the notes indubitably depended; a rhythm comes to life—a rhythm which seems to explain the music and which is not a 'musician's' rhythm. Yet it is possible to set this rhythm in a musician's rhythm without, from the poet's feeling in the matter, harming it or even 'altering it', which means altering the part of it to which he is sensitive; which means, again, that both poet and musician 'feel around' the movement, 'feel at it' from different angles. Some people 'see colour' and some 'line'; very few are in any way conscious of just what it is they do see. I have no desire to set up a babel of 'post-impressionists in rhythm' by suggesting a kindred searching of hearts with regard to the perception of sound.

Yet it is quite certain that some people can hear and scan 'by quantity', and more can do so 'by stress', and fewer still feel rhythm by what I would call the inner form of the line. And it is this 'inner form', I think, which must be preserved in music; it is only by mastery of this inner form that the great masters of rhythm— Milton, Yeats, whoever you like—are masters of it.

'Nel mezzo del cammin di nostra vita.' Let me take this as an example. Some people will find the movement repeated in—
     'Eyes, dreams, lips and the night goes.'
And some will find it in—
     'If you fall off the roof you'll break your ankle.'
Some people will read it as if it were exactly the same 'shape' as the line which follows it—
     'Mi ritrovai per una selva oscura.'
So eminent a scholar and so noted a lover of poetry as Mr. Edmund Gardener reads the sonnets of the 'Vita Nuova' as if they were bad prose, and thinks me an outrageous liar for saying so. A certain Dalmation loose upon the town reads Dante with no sense of epic line and as if it were third-rate dramatic dialogue by the author of 'La Nave'. Any reporter feels at liberty to object to the way a great poet reads his verses, yet it is not reported that men tried to tell Bach or Wagner how to play their own music, or that they offer like suggestions to M. Debussy.

'Quo tandem abutere?' Can we have a more definite criterion of rhythm than we have of colour? Do we any of us really see or hear in the same register? Are we made in groups and species, some of us capable of sympathetic audition and vision? Or is Machiavelli right when he says: 'L'Uomo' or 'L'Umanità vive in pochi'?—'The life of the race is concentrated in a few individuals.'

PITCH

The preceding paragraphs have had to do with rhythm; the other limb of melody is the pitch and pitch-variation, and upon this our sole query is to be whether there is in speech, as there is in music, 'tone-leading'. We know that certain notes played in sequence call for other notes, for a 'resolution', for a 'close'; and in setting words to music it is often the hunger for this sort of musical apparatus that leads the musician away from the rhythm of the verse or makes him drag out the final syllables. What I want to get at is this: in the interpreting of the hidden melody of poetry into the more manifest melody of music, are there in the words themselves 'tone-leadings'? Granted a perfect accord of word and tune is attainable by singing a note to each syllable and a short or long note to short or long syllables respectively, and singing the syllable accented in verse on the note accented in the music, is there anything beyond this? Does, for instance, the voice really fall a little in speaking a vowel and nasal, and is a ligature of two notes one half-tone lower than the other and the first very short, a correct musical interpretation of such a sound as 'son', 'un', 'cham'? And are there other such cases where a ligature is not so much distortion as explication.

Song demands now and again passages of pure sound, of notes free from the bonds of speech, and good lyric masters have given the musicians this holiday with stray nonsense lines or with 'Hallelujah' and 'Alba' and 'Hey-nonny-nonny', asking in return that the rest of their words be left in statu.

No one man can set bounds to this sort of performance, and a full discussion of the case would fill a volume, which I have neither time nor inclination to write. The questions are, however, germane to the technique of our art.

A discussion of Arnaut Daniel's music—and Daniel is the particular slide in our microscope for the moment–would be, perhaps, too technical for these pages; but this much may be said, that his words, sung to the tunes he made for them, lose neither in beauty nor in intelligibility.

My questions may seem to be shot at random, but we are notably lacking in 'song-literature', and if it is at all important to make good this deficit we must have first some consideration of the basic questions of mediation between word and tune, some close attention to the quality of our audition, some reasoning parley between the two people most concerned–the poet and the musician.

*　　　*　　　*

I have been questioned, though rather in regard to 'The Seafarer' than to Arnaut, how much of this translation is mine and how much the original. 'The Seafarer' was as nearly literal, I think, as any translation can be. Nowhere in these poems of Arnaut's have I felt it my function to 'ornament' the text. Nevertheless, I may be able to show more precisely the style of his language–now that I have conveyed the nature of his rhyme schemes–by giving one translation in prose.

39

Beyond its external symmetry, every formal poem should have its internal thought-form, or, at least, thought progress. This form can, of course, be as well displayed in a prose version as in a metrical one. It is usually the last thing to be learned by a maker of canzoni. In the present example it is neither remarkable nor deficient.

EN BREU BRISARAL TEMPS BRAUS

I

Soon will the harsh time break upon us, the north wind hoot in the branches which all swish together with their closed-over boughs of leaves; no bird sings nor 'peeps' now, yet love teaches me to make a song that shall not be second nor third, but first for freeing the embittered heart.

II

Love is the garden-close of worth, a pool of prowess (i.e., low flooded land) whence all good fruits are born if there be one to gather them faithfully; for not one does ice or snow destroy while the good trunk nourisheth them; but, if knave or coward break it, the sap is lost between the loyal.

III

A fault mended is matter for praise; and I feel in both flanks that I have more love without thinking of it than have those who strut talking about it; it girds against my heart worse than a buckle. And as long as my lady shows her face angered against me, I'd rather bear pain in the desert where never bird hath eyrie.

IV

Good doctrine and gentle, and the body clear, subtle and frank, have led me to the sure hold of love of her whom I most wish to receive me; for if she was harsh and crabbed with me, now would we cut long time short with pleasure, for she is more fine in my eyes and I am more set toward her than were Atalanta and Meleagar, the one to the other.

V

I was so doubtful that for lack of daring I turned often from black to white, and desire so raids me and my mind that the heart knows not whether to dance or mourn; but Joy ,who gives me faith to hope, blames me for not calling to her, for I'm so skilled at praying and have such slight wish for aught else except her.

VI

It rests me to think of her, and I've both my eyes cankered when they're not looking at her; and think not that my heart turns from

40

her, for neither prayers (*orars*–I think perhaps here, 'prayers', ecclesiastical) nor jesting nor viol-playing can get me from her a reed's breadth. 'From her!' What have I said? God cover me, may I perish in the sea (for setting those words together).

Arnaut would have his song offered up somewhere where a sweet word ends in 'Agre'.

This song invites comparison, in its subtle diagnosis, to Sappho's

φαίνεταί μοι κῆνος ἴσος θέοισιν,

or to Catullus' version:

'Ille mi par esse deo videtur,'

and to Guido's lines near:

'Gli occhi orbati fa vedere scorto.'

I am not in the least sure that I have yet made clear the reasons for my writing these articles; one might conceivably translate a troubadour for one's own delectation, but explain him, never! Still, there is a unity of intention, not only in these rambling discourses, but in the translations of Arnaut and of the other poets.

As far as the 'living art' goes, I should like to break up *cliché*, to disintegrate these magnetised groups that stand between the reader of poetry and the drive of it, to escape from lines composed of two very nearly equal sections, each containing a noun and each noun decorously attended by a carefully selected epithet gleaned, apparently, from Shakespeare, Pope, or Horace. For it is not until poetry lives again 'close to the thing' that it will be a vital part of contemporary life. As long as the poet says not what he, at the very crux of a clarified conception, means, but is content to say something ornate and approximate, just so long will serious people, intently alive, consider poetry as balderdash–a sort of embroidery for dilettantes and women.

And the only way to escape from rhetoric and frilled paper decoration is through beauty–'beauty of the thing', certainly, but besides that, 'beauty of the means'. I mean by that that one must call a spade a spade in form so exactly adjusted, in a metric in itself so seductive, that the statement will not bore the auditor. Or again, since I seem to flounder in my attempt at utterance, we must have a simplicity and directness of utterance, which is different from the simplicity and directness of daily speech, which is more 'curial', more dignified. This difference, this dignity, cannot be conferred by florid adjectives or elaborate hyperbole; it must be conveyed by art, and by the art of the verse structure, by something which exalts the reader, making him feel that he is in contact with something arranged more finely than the commonplace.

There are few fallacies more common than the opinion that poetry should mimic the daily speech. Works of art attract by a resembling unlikeness. Colloquial poetry is to the real art as the barber's wax dummy is to sculpture. In every art I can think of we are dammed and clogged by the mimetic; dynamic acting is nearly forgotten; the painters of the moment escape through eccentricity.

The second question across my path is: Is my direction the right one? 'Technique', that much berated term, means not only suavity of exterior, but means the clinch of expression on the thing intended to be expressed. Through it alone has *the art*, as distinct from the work of the accidentally inspired genius, any chance for resurrection.

I have spent six months of my life translating fifteen experiments of a man living in what one of my more genial critics calls a 'very dead past'. Is this justifiable in anyone who is not purely a philologist?

Canello, who is a philologist, tells us that Arnaut used more different rhyme sounds than any other troubadour. I think it is ninety-two against Vidal's fifty-eight, and Vidal's work is far greater in bulk. I have forgotten the exact numbers. The statement is bare enough and sufficiently uninteresting.

I have no especial interest in rhyme. It tends to draw away the artist's attention from forty to ninety per cent of his syllables and concentrate it on the admittedly more prominent remainder. It tends to draw him into prolixity and pull him away from the thing. Nevertheless, it is one part, and a very small part of his technique. If he is to learn it with the least waste of energy, he might well study it in the work not of its greatest master, but of the man who first considered it critically, tried and tested it, and controlled it from the most diverse angles of attack. In a study of mathematics we pursue a course as sane as that which I here suggest.

I do not in the least wish to reinstate the Provençal canzon or to start a movement. The Italian canzone is in many ways more fit for general use, yet there are certain subjects which could be more aptly dealt with in the more centred Provençal forms.

This matter of rhyme may seem slight and far from life, yet out of the early study of Dante's writing there grew up the graceful legend that, while he was working at the 'Commedia', all the Italian rhymes appeared to him each one embodied as a woman, and that they all asked him the honour of being included in the masterpiece, and that he granted all their requests, as you may see today, for not one of them is forgotten.

Yet a study of Dante gives one less real grip on the problem of rhyming than a study of Daniel; for Daniel comes with an open mind, he looks about him in all directions; while Dante, out of the wealth of experiment at his disposal, chooses a certain few arrangements which best suit his immediate purpose.

As for the scholastic bearing, which matters much less than the artistic, if one wished an intimate acquaintance with the politics of England or Germany at certain periods, would one be wiser to read a book of generalities and then read at random through the archives, or to read through, let us say, first the State papers of Bismarck or Gladstone? Having become really conversant with the activities of either of these men, would not almost any document of the period fall, if we read it, into some sort of orderly arrangement? Would we not grasp its relation to the main stream of events?

Seeing that it is no mere predilection of my own, but an attempt to elucidate Dante's judgment, I am quite ready to hold the position that Arnaut is the finest of the troubadours against such modern scholars as happen to disagree.

I do not mean by that that he has written anything more poignant than de Born's 'Si tuit li dol el plor el marrimen',[1] or anything more haunting than Vidal's 'Ah l'alen tir vas me l'aire', or that his personality was more poetic than that of Arnaut de Marvoil, or his mind more subtle than that of Aimeric de Bellenoi; but simply that Arnaut's work as a whole is more interesting. They say that Marvoil is simpler; Daniel has his moments of simplicity.

'Pensar de lieis m'es repaus'[1]–'It rests me to think of her.' You cannot get statement simpler than that, or clearer, or less rhetorical. Still, this is a matter of aesthetic judgment, 'de gustibus'.

In this paragraph I wish to be strictly pedagogical. Arnaut was at the centre of the thing. So intimate a study of nearly any other troubadour would bore one, and might not throw much light on the work of the others; having analysed or even read an analysis of Arnaut, any other Provençal canzon is clearer to one. Knowing him, I mean, one can read the rest of Provençal poetry with as little need for special introductions and annotation as one has in reading the Victorians. We know in reading, let us say, de Born, what part is personal, what part is technical, how good it is in manner, how good in matter. And this method of study seems to me the one in which the critic or professor presents the energetic part of his knowledge, the method by which the audience becomes most intelligent of or the most sensitive to the subject or period discussed.

The virtue of Arnaut's poetry as art is not antipathetic to his value as a strategic point in scholarship; but the two things should be held very distinctly separate in the mind of the reader. The first might exist quite independently of the latter. Villon's relation to his contemporaries is, for instance, most dissimilar.

---

[1] Quoted Cantos LXXX and LXXX-IV. Ed.   [2] Quoted in Canto XCI, Ed.

PART TWO
Religio

To replace the marble goddess on her pedestal at Terracina is worth more than any metaphysical argument.

Aram nemus vult.

PART TWO

Religio[1]

or, The Child's Guide to Knowledge

What is a god?
   A god is an eternal state of mind.
   What is a faun?
A faun is an elemental creature.
What is a nymph?
A nymph is an elemental creature.
When is a god manifest?
When the states of mind take form.
When does a man become a god?
When he enters one of these states of mind.
What is the nature of the forms whereby a god is manifest?
They are variable but retain certain distinguishing characteristics.
Are all eternal states of mind gods?
We consider them so to be.
Are all durable states of mind gods?
They are not.
By what characteristic may we know the divine forms?
By beauty.
And if the presented forms are unbeautiful?
They are demons.
If they are grotesque?
They may be well-minded genii.
What are the kinds of knowledge?
There are immediate knowledge and hearsay.
Is hearsay of any value?
Of some.
What is the greatest hearsay?
The greatest hearsay is the tradition of the gods.
Of what use is this tradition?
It tells us to be ready to look.
In what manner do gods appear?
Formed and formlessly.

[1] *Pavannes & Divisions* (1918).

To what do they appear when formed?

To the sense of vision.

And when formless?

To the sense of knowledge.

May they when formed appear to anything save the sense of vision?

We may gain a sense of their presence as if they were standing behind us.

And in this case they may possess form?

We may feel that they do possess form.

Are there names for the gods?

The gods have many names. It is by names that they are handled in the tradition.

Is there harm in using these names?

There is no harm in thinking of the gods by their names.

How should one perceive a god, by his name?

It is better to perceive a god by form, or by the sense of knowledge, and, after perceiving him thus, to consider his name or to 'think what god it may be'.

Do we know the number of the gods?

It would be rash to say that we do. A man should be content with a reasonable number.

What are the gods of this rite?

Apollo, and in some sense Helios, Diana in some of her phases, also the Cytherean goddess.

To what other gods is it fitting, in harmony or in adjunction with these rites, to give incense?

To Koré and to Demeter, also to lares and to oreiads and to certain elemental creatures.

How is it fitting to please these lares and other creatures?

It is fitting to please and to nourish them with flowers.

Do they have need of such nutriment?

It would be foolish to believe that they have, nevertheless it bodes well for us that they should be pleased to appear.

Are these things so in the East?

This rite is made for the West.

Axiomata[1]

I

(1) The intimate essence of the universe is *not* of the same nature as our own consciousness.

(2) Our own consciousness is incapable of having produced the universe.

(3) God, therefore, exists. That is to say, there is no reason for not applying the term God, *Theos*, to the intimate essence.

(4) The universe exists. By exists we mean normally: is perceptible to our consciousness or deducible by human reason from data perceptible to our consciousness.

(5) Concerning the intimate essence of the universe we are utterly ignorant. We have no proof that this God, Theos, is one, or is many, or is divisible or indivisible, or is an ordered hierarchy culminating, or not culminating, in a unity.

(6) Not only is our consciousness, or any concentration or coagulation of such consciousness or consciousnesses, incapable of having produced the universe, it is incapable of accounting for how said universe has been and is.

(7) Dogma is bluff based upon ignorance.

(8) There is benevolent and malevolent dogma. Benevolent dogma is an attempt to 'save the world' by instigating it to accept certain propositions. Malevolent dogma is an attempt to gain control over others by persuading them to accept certain propositions.

There is also *nolent*, un-volent dogma, a sort of automatic reaction in the mind of the dogmatiser, who may have come to disaster by following certain propositions, and who, from this, becomes crampedly convinced that contrary propositions are true.

(9) Belief is a cramp, a paralysis, an atrophy of the mind in certain positions.

II

(1) It is as foolish to try to contain the *theos* in consciousness as to try to manage electricity according to the physics of water. It is as nonworkable as to think not only of our consciousness managing electricity according to the physics of water, but as to think of the water understanding the physics of electricity.

(2) All systems of philosophy fail when they attempt to set down

[1] *The New Age*, 13 January 1921.

axioms of the *theos* in terms of consciousness and of logic; similiter by the same figure that electricity escapes the physics of water.

(3) The selection of monotheism, polytheism, pluralism, dual, trinitarian god or gods, or hierarchies, is pure matter of individual temperament (in free minds), and of tradition in environment of discipular, bound minds.

(4) Historically the organisation of religions has usually been for some ulterior purpose, exploitation, control of the masses, etc.

III

(1) This is not to deny that the consciousness may be affected by the theos (remembering that we ascribe to this *theos* neither singular nor plural number).

(2) The theos may affect and may have affected the consciousness of individuals, but the consciousness is incapable of knowing why this occurs, or even in what manner it occurs, or whether it be the *theos*; though the consciousness may experience pleasant and possibly unpleasant sensations, or sensations partaking neither of pleasure or its opposite. Hence mysticism. If the consciousness receives or has received such effects from the theos, or from something not the theos yet which the consciousness has been incapable of understanding or classifying either as theos or a-theos, it is incapable of reducing these sensations to coherent sequence of cause and effect. The effects remain, so far as the consciousness is concerned, in the domain of experience, not differing intellectually from the taste of a lemon or the fragrance of violets or the aroma of dung-hills, or the feel of a stone or of tree-bark, or any other direct perception. As the consciousness observes the results of the senses, it observes also the mirage of the senses, or what may be a mirage of the senses, or an affect from the theos, the non-comprehensible.

(3) This is not to deny any of the visions or auditions or sensations of the mystics, Dante's rose or Theresa's walnut; but it is to affirm the propositions in Section I.

IV

(1) The consciousness may be aware of the effects of the unknown and of the non-knowable on the consciousness, but this does not affect the proposition that our consciousness is utterly ignorant of the nature of the intimate essence. For instance: a man may be hit by a bullet and not know its composition, nor the cause of its having been fired, nor its direction, nor that it is a bullet. He may die almost instantly, knowing only the sensation of shock. Thus consciousness may perfectly well register certain results, as sensation, without comprehending their nature. (I, (1).) He may even die of a long-considered disease without comprehending its bacillus.

(2) The thought here becomes clouded, and we see the tendency of logic to move in a circle. Confusion between a possibly discoverable bacillus and a non-knowable *theos*. Concerning the ultimate nature of the bacillus, however, no knowledge exists; but the consciousness may learn to deal with superficial effects of the bacillus, as with the directing of bullets. Confusion enters argument the moment one calls in analogy. We return to clarity of Section I (1–9).

(3) The introduction of analogy has not affected our proposition that the 'intimate essence' exists. It has muddied our conception of the non-knowability of the intimate essence.

[Speculation.—Religions have introduced analogy? Philosophies have attempted sometimes to do without it. This does not prove that religions have muddied all our concepts. There is no end to the variants one may draw out of the logical trick-hat.]

V

(1) It is, however, impossible to prove whether the theos be one or many.

(2) The greatest tyrannies have arisen from the dogma that the *theos* is one, or that there is a unity above various strata of theos which imposes its will upon the sub-strata, and thence upon human individuals.

(3) Certain beauties of fancy and of concept have arisen both from the proposition of many gods and from that of one god, or of an orderly arrangement of the theos.

(4) A choice of these fancies of the *theos* is a matter of taste; as the preference of Durer or Velasquez, or the Moscophorus, or Amen Hotep's effigy, or the marbles of Phidias.

(5) Religion usually holds that the theos can be, by its patent system, exploited.

(6) It is not known whether the theos may be or may not be exploited.

(7) Most religions offer a system or a few tips for exploiting the theos.

(8) Men often enjoy the feeling that they are performing this exploitation, or that they are on good terms with the theos.

(9) There is no harm in this, so long as they do not incommode anyone else.

(10) The reason why they should not incommode anyone else is not demonstrable; it belongs to that part of the concepts of consciousness which we call common decency.

(11) We do not quite know how we have come by these concepts of common decency, but one supposes it is our heritage from superior individuals of the past; that it is the treasure of tradition. Savages and professed believers in religion do not possess this concept of common

decency. They usually wish to interfere with us, and to get us to believe something 'for our good'.

(12) A belief is, as we have said, a cramp, and thence progressively a paralysis or atrophy of the mind in a given position.

A religion is damned, it confesses its own ultimate impotence, the day it burns its first heretic.

Pastiche the Regional VII, The New Age, August 21, 1919.

Inasmuch as the Jew has conducted no holy war for nearly two millenia, he is preferable to the Christian and the Mohammedan.

Pastiche the Regional XVII, The New Age, November 13, 1919.

Credo[1]

M r. Eliot who is at times an excellent poet and who has arrived at the supreme Eminence among English critics largely through disguising himself as a corpse once asked in the course of an amiable article what 'I believed'.

Having a strong disbelief in abstract and general statement as a means of conveying one's thought to others I have for a number of years answered such questions by telling the enquirer to read Confucius and Ovid. This can do no harm to the intelligent and the unintelligent may be damned.

Given the material means I would replace the statue of Venus on the cliffs of Terracina.[2] I would erect a temple to Artemis in Park Lane. I believe that a light from Eleusis persisted throughout the middle ages and set beauty in the song of Provence and of Italy.

I believe that postwar 'returns to christianity' (and its various subdivisions) have been merely the gran' rifiuto and, in general, signs of fatigue.

I do not expect science (mathematics, biology; etc.) to lead us back to the unwarrantable assumptions of theologians.

I do not expect the machine to dominate the human consciousness that created it.

[1] *Front* (I., 1), New Mexico, December 1930.

[2] See Cantos XXXIX, LXXIV and XCI. Ed.

Terra Italica[1]

S ome months ago and off and on for some time I tried and have tried to stimulate the publication in the outer occident of a series of brochures that would serve as communication between intelligent men, proposing to print such books in America! 'dollar impracticable' 'fifty cents impossible' undsoweiter can be imagined by 30 per cent of my readers; and the conclusion, i.e. that the idea that publishing is a profession not a trade, and the idea of using a publishing house as a focus of enlightenment are both alien to our national sensibility, will come as a surprise to, no one.

It is therefore with a certain pleasure that I observe the appearance of such a series in Italy (the country least known in American literary circles and most misrepresented by the lying Britannic press.) Edoardo Tinto, editore, publishes his series not at one dollar or half a dollar but at one lira a number (that is to say the nineteenth part of a dollar). Ogni fascicolo una lira. This is part of the Italian awakening. It is also the kind of publishing that must happen wherever people are indulging in a life of the understanding.

That is to say people engaged in the pleasures of thinking or in the search for answers to their curiosity both write and want to read *contemporary* information and formulation some of which is crystallized in chunks too long for magazine articles and too short for a book. (Both England and France show the ill-effect of brochures 'expanded' into books.)

The Italian awakening has shown the following phases. First 1919, travelling in a disturbed country, one felt a reserve of animal vigour and alertness, in contrast with England and France. In England the mental corpses lay about in the streets, no one desired to touch them but the general feeling was that they must be kept.

In France there was a great weariness but a general effort to get the carrion buried and to get the emptiness tidied up.

Second phase, the sudden change in Italian book store window. The intolerable monotony of Tasso, Ariosto, Petrarca gave place to the flood of translations of Dostoievsky, Kipling, etc.

I have yet to meet an Italian with any illusions concerning Italian contemporary literature, but one of them does occasionally murmur something about 'philosophy' or a movement. I have myself found several satisfactory volumes of history more or less specialised and

---

[1] *The New Review*. Winter 1931–2.

have been shocked, in contrast, by the appalling inaccuracy of a number of French works allegedly treating this subject.

There would be no point in my reviewing the separate brochures of Tinto's series, but I can at least indicate certain general conclusions. I do not mean to assert that he has performed a miracle by publishing half a hundred masterpieces in three years. I don't assert that most of information conveyed is not to be found elsewhere in voluminous works (Maspero, Frazer, etc.) or that a good deal of it could not be dug out of encyclopaedias circulated in England and America in 'sets'.

I do assert that a great deal of waste paper has been covered with print because of the lack of knowledge of what Tinto has printed in very convenient form. I also assert that comparison of No. 51 of his series with some of the earlier issues can be taken as indication of the value of this form of communication between a number of authors.

E.g. number twenty something or other is as stupid as if it had been printed in England. It contained one or two bits of information that make it worth reading. One accepts the information and thinks the author an ass. Several other numbers are merely good academic exposition. As the series proceeds there is a marked gain in simplicity, lucidity and directness of expression.

'Paganism, which at the base of its cosmogonic philosophy set the sexual phenomena whereby Life perpetuates itself mysteriously throughout the universe, not only did not disdain the erotic factor in its religious institutions but celebrated and exalted it, precisely because it encountered in it the marvellous vital principle infused by invisible Divinity into manifest nature.'

The clauses are too long and too many to give a perfect sentence in English, but the Italian sentence is quite clear and fluid.

The idea, like several intelligent ideas exposed by Confucius is too simple, too clear, and 'too well known' to cause admiration or comment. It is as a matter of fact not in the least well *known*. It is often heard and seldom expressed with either clarity, simplicity or moderation.

Our author is not discovering the moon or making this statement as revelation: it begins his third paragraph and is there to indicate the subject he is preparing to treat.

'and it was natural that the woman should have in the various rites the feminine role that holy nature had given her'.

This also is very simple but for lack of clear recognition of it thousands of pages of history have been confused and made unintelligible. Civilisations or cultures decay from the top. The loss of knowledge with the fall of Alexander's empire is not sufficiently recognised, we allow plenty for the fall of Rome, but we waste time in trying to understand the Middle Ages because we do not sufficiently dissociate the various strands that go to make up its culture: for example the difference between the Mithraic 'evil' and the light of Eleusis.

I know something about these confusions because I have been trying for three years to understand a mediaeval author's vocabulary. I am not the only man who has groped in this darkness. Luigi Valli has written a dozen fat books. I have commented on his *Linguaggio Segreto della Divina Commedia* in my notes on Cavalcanti. Some of these appeared in the *Dial* but the greater part were too highly specialised. Valli, I may say, ploughs through 450 pages, full of information and misunderstandings, for want of the lucidity which one finds in the 30 pages brochure.

Taken together the brochures 'Sacerdotesse' and 'Misteri di Mithra', will allow the reader to disentangle more confusions than any commentary on mediaeval poetry yet written.

For certain people the *pecten cteis* is the gate of wisdom. The glory of the polytheistic anschauung is that it never asserted a single and obligatory path for everyone. It never caused the assertion that everyone was fit for initiation and it never caused an attempt to force people into a path alien to their sensibilities.

Paganism never feared knowledge. It feared ignorance and under a flood of ignorance it was driven out of its temples.

In trying to untangle the confusion of history from the year 350 de l'era volgare to 350 or 1400 several dissociations are necessary.

The Pagan temples lost prestige either because they were overwhelmed by barbarian ignorance or because the priest caste had become a sort of exploiting Bloomsbury too much hokum, affectation, snobism, the various phenomena of decadent empires, etc. associated with the various cults. Probably le personnel manquait for a number of causes.

The Mithraic cult entered Rome with a paraphernalia still found almost intact in developed Xtian theology.

'Christianity' entered Rome about 100 years later. This 'christianity' took on most of the worst characteristics of Mithraism and appears to have lost a good many of its supposedly original own.

To understand this one must make a clear cleavage between 'religion' and 'administration'. The so called difficulties of penetrating the Eleusinian cult or of getting at the meaning of a 'religion' are due to the cult's indifference to empire.

The candidate is trying to understand something. Verbal manifestation is of very limited use to the candidate. Any intelligent man has understood a great deal more than he has ever read or ever written or ever pushed into verbal manifestation even in his own mind.

The minute a cult is associated with government a totally different set of problems and needs arises. The government must govern by formula. The unknown must be if not formulated at least concealed and treated by formula.

The adoption of Christianity as the Roman state religion had no more to do with the teaching of Christ or with a search for verity than the acquisition of a new well in Persia by the Standard Oil Co. has to do with Michaelson's ideas on the mathematics of the electromagnetic field.

Out of a need to administer arises or arose theology. The history of Byzantine intellectualism is theological history.

The desire of the candidate, or of the 'mystic' if one can still employ that much abused term, is to get something into his consciousness, as distinct from getting it into the vain locus of verbal exchanges.

If knowledge gets first into the vain locus of verbal exchanges, it is damnably and almost insuperably difficult to get it thence into the consciousness. Years afterwards one 'sees what the sentence means'.

Either by coincidence or causation the ancient wisdom seems to have disappeared when the mysteries entered the vain space of Christian theological discussion. The unity of God may be the supreme mystery beyond the multitudinous appearance of nature. But if you put a slab faced boob in the presence of the divine unity before he is well out of kindergarten you make it extremely unlikely that he will ever understand *anything*.

I take it that the Catholic Church broke from the top, as Paganism had possibly broken. I mean to say that the Church was no longer interested in theology, it no longer believed or even knew what it meant. Leo X was interested in administration, in culture, in building St. Peter's. It simply never occurred to him that anyone would take Luther seriously. No one in his set did take Luther seriously, I mean as a writer or thinker. He was merely a barbarian bore. Protestantism has no theology. By which I mean it has nothing that a well grounded theologian can possibly consider salonfähig.

Leibnitz and Bossuet managed to find the dividing line and this dividing line could not have existed, and did not exist as long as the College of Cardinals believed that an honest enquirer must, if he sought long enough, come into agreement with the orthodox faith. The history of mediaeval heresies is largely the history of fads and exaggerations corrected and restrained by the Church.

In the confusion of falling Rome certain elements have however a face value, or offer at least perceivably data for study. The gospels on the face of them are the story of a revolt in Judaea, that is to say the protagonist was trying to provide an antidote for Judaism. He attacks nearly every feature of it that he notices. Being himself a Jew, certain things escape his notice, or he takes them for granted. I have thought at times that these oversights provided the causes for Xtianity becoming unbearable.

The protagonist was not on the face of it constructing a code for the administrating empire but a *modus vivendi* for the individual. He invented no safeguard against fanaticism.

Our immediate point is that he was concerned with Jews and Judaism; he said no word against Eleusis or against Paganism, he told his students to attend first to the Jews, to enlighten them before they bothered about the Gentiles.

When this teaching or something bearing the same name arrives in Rome it is denatured or at least it is made to absorb a number of elements of which there is no gospel mention. But for the name, one might almost think it had itself *been absorbed* by the other elements.

Among the cults then pervasive in Rome Mithraism was of the strongest; it is for the modern mind the least interesting, is in fact thoroughly boring. It gave, so far as one can make out, nothing to civilization (the bullfight is an arguable exception but no one has proved that the features of bullfighting which Mr. Hemingway admires can be traced to Mithra. The killing is Mithraic but the pageantry is debatable property).

The mediaeval man would however have found the cult full of interest. The mediaeval frame of mind was in fact interested where we are bored. Aquinas and Co. received a great deal from Mithra or from some religion or religions to which the Mithraic celestial map bore marked resemblance. Even the more unpleasant type of present day Christian can be found admiring the ritual and the frame of the Mithraic mind.

'The celebrant immolated victims' would seem to be the main theme. It produced nothing to match the grace of the well-curb of Terracina.

For all its inclusiveness the new religion was for fifteen and more centuries troubled by heresies, mostly uninteresting and perhaps all of them traceable to some cult it had not included.

One cult that it had failed to include was that of Eleusis.

It may be arguable that Eleusinian elements persisted in the very early Church, and are responsible for some of the scandals. It is quite certain that the Church later emerges riddled with tendencies to fanaticism, with sadistic and masochistic tendencies that are in no way Eleusinian.

It is equally discernable upon study that some non-Christian and inextinguishable source of beauty persisted throughout the Middle Ages maintaining song in Provence, maintaining the grace of Kalenda Maya.[1]

And this force was the strongest counter force to the cult of Atys and asceticism. A great deal of obscurity has been made to encircle it. There are a few clear pages in Davidsohn's *Firenze ai Tempi di Dante*. The usual accusation against the Albigeois is that they were Mani-

---

[1] See Canto CXIII. Ed.

chaeans. This I believe after a long search to be pure bunkumb. The slanderers feared the truth. I mean they feared not only the force of a doctrine but they feared giving it even the publicity which a true bill against it would have required.

The best scholars do not believe there were any Manichaeans left in Europe at the time of the Albigensian Crusade. If there were any in Provence they have at any rate left no trace in troubadour art.

On the other hand the cult of Eleusis will explain not only general phenomena but particular beauties in Arnaut Daniel or in Guido Cavalcanti.

It will also shed a good deal of light on various passages of theology or of natural philosophy re the active and passive intellect (*possibile intelleto*, etc.).

I suggest that students trying to understand the poesy of southern Europe from 1050 to 1400 should try to open it with this key. It will perhaps save them reading Valli and my long arguments on that author.

The decline of the temples is I think understandable. Apart from bacteriological causes due to profanation the Eleusinian cult was obviously the most open to misunderstanding, the least possible to explain to barbarians.

The modern author can write 'aim the union with nature' or 'consciousness of the unity with nature'. This is at the root of any mystery and is a matter of the degree of comprehension, the personal inspection of the candidate being an infinitely more effective way of perceiving what he understands and to what degree he is capable of understanding than is communication in writing.

When this immediate sight is lacking the cult dilutes into verbal formulations; above the intuition in its varying profundity there arises a highly debatable intellectual paraphernalia usually without cultural force. Conjectures, possibilities, allegories, maps of a geocentric heaven, etc.

Wave after wave of ignorance, then an administrative system which gradually fears inquiry. In lieu of maintained tradition one has the half ignorant and more than half or nine-tenths ignorant folklore.

Farmer in Ireland burns wife as witch, not because he is superstitious but the superstes is insufficient. He ought only to have threatened her with burning. The history of thought, especially mediaeval thought, is full of such ergotisation based on half knowledge.

I am not separating all this from the present, the first disgusting or distressing, the second perhaps only curious or diverting, and the third extremely satisfactory.

That is to say you find in your newspapers horrible statistics of British lunatic asylums, amazing incidents, sadistic maniacs judging cases in British law courts, etc. hysterias, desiccations, pathologies, Freudian fringe undsoweiter.

Secondly you find an excited female in Foggia convinced that their own particular plaster of Paris Mater Dolorosa (apparently from the rue St. Sulpice) with upturned plaster eyes saved them from the plague. You learn that there is a gent in vicinity of Foggia who is still having stigmata. You find in the sacristy at Terracina a small barrocco angel, and the sacristan tells you that the bishop had it taken out of the church because the peasants insisted on worshipping it as Santa Lucia ('l'adoravano come Sta. Lucia') and the bishop didn't want the practice to continue.

All of which helps one to understand the Iconoclast shindies in Constantinople, the time of whatever their names were.

Thirdly you find Frobenius' profoundly satisfactory account of the old chief who 'was so foine and so healthy' that he was convinced that his soul would go into the soil of Africa and enrich the crops at his death. And you find Pitt-Rivers' account of the equally fine old Maori who would not have his people corrupted by the vile practices of British marriage, than which he could conceive nothing worse.

Ecclesiastical History[1]

Possum tree'd with a spellin' book?

All right. Fall of Church. Or, if the learned Christian prefer, we can call it a slide, supposing mama ecclesia to have slipped a few times while standing, recovered, but now to be finally slithering along on the more cushioned anatomical parts. Progressive stages.

Period when Scotus Erigina (spelled in Fr. Fiorentino's present edition with an extra *u*) said 'authority comes from right reason'. A time when, so far as we know, the Church authorities BELIEVED what they taught or were still searching for the truth.

Scandal of the Albigensian crusade. Economic corruption. Search for victim (common to all cowards).

Time when Church no longer had faith ENOUGH to believe that with proper instruction and argument the unbeliever or heretic could be made to see daylight. Invocation of authority to MAKE him believe. This runs up to debate (correspondence) between Leibnitz and Bossuet (Leibnitz can be spelled without the t if Mr. Eliot desire).

Concurrently: the decline of Christian ethics. The Middle Ages distinguished between SHARING and USURY. In theology, as Dante knew it, the usurer is damned with the sodomite. Usury judged with sodomy as 'contrary to natural increase', contrary to the nature of live things (animal and vegetable) to multiply. The mediaeval trading companies, beginning mainly with question of ship's cargoes; risk shared proportionally by all participants. A moral discrimination between, or dissociation of, what we would now call stocks and bonds (distinction obscured in certain forms of preferred stock, etc.).

Rise of banking. Banks of two sorts:

A. Gangs of creditors, organised to squeeze the last ounce out of debtors, conquered cities, etc.

B. Reconstruction banks. The great light among which was and is the Monte dei Paschi of Siena.[2]

The charter of this bank (ad. 1602) is a code of honesty that would crush 90 per cent of modern so-called bankers and, were they capable either of moral desire, intellectual courage, or of any shame for connivance with murder and prolongation of degrading conditions, CAUSED by their non-perception of relations, drive them into extreme expiation. (c.f., phenomena of 'religious conversion' recorded

[1] *The New English Weekly*, 5 July 1934.   [2] See Cantos XLII—LI. Ed.

in earlier stages of human history, tyrants and murderers having in earlier times had fits of revulsion and strong disgust with their OWN conduct.)

Coincidence of a banker Pope with the more virulent heretical break away. Leo X too 'civilised' to imagine that anyone would take Luther seriously. Luther clever enough to hitch his crude theology on to an economic grievance. Leo busy building a sort of Viennese Opera House and wanting ALL possible taxes.

Impossible to synchronise stages all over Europe, but a distinct difference observable between:

A. A period when Europe's best intellect and intelligence was IN the Church, best painting, architecture, etc. Ecclesiastical architecture expressed religion.

B. Period in which architecture obviously was an attempt to get back to Roman, Greek or Graeco-Roman or at any rate pre-Christian building.

C. The present century. 'Or la littérature religieuse est morte.'

Note: There *was* a period of religious wars, etc., great mass of people considering religious difference of some importance (even though economic element was often implicated in the conflicts).

But the Church by the time of Leo X was already ceasing to RULE. In her own domain, the spirit, she had abrogated her righteousness.

The interest in ETHICS was more and more degenerating into question of where and when, and subject to what documents people should copulate. What the Middle Ages had called venal sins came to the fore. The deeper evils were allowed to slither about in silence.

The normal man today will consider you completely insane if you suggest that there is a moral difference between a bond and a share certificate.

You have to come to Italy to find a man in high (not the highest) position who will write you:

'The two diseases of modern society are the legalisation of usury via the banks, and the legalisation of theft via the limited liability companies.'

Presidente D. who wrote that is almost the only man I know who really DOES believe his Catholicism. He believes that '*la povertà*' is holy, but does NOT believe that '*la miseria*' need be perpetuated. That is a lesson to the loose users of words. *Miseria* can be translated as EXCESSIVE shortage of purchasing power.

The fall of the Church is measured by the diminished degree in which she actually exercises a function, and the function in which this diminution is most flagrantly and disgustingly perceivable is that of enlightening ETHICS precisely in relation to ECONOMICS where the difference between seeing and doing RIGHT is or appears, to most ecclesiastics and controllers of finance, to be so inconvenient.

The Catholic Church (Roman) has a magnificent set of dissociations already available.

Apart from any inherited ethical culture, the following equations are offered for consideration.

I. The SOURCE of value is the CULTURAL HERITAGE, i.e.:

The aggregate of all mechanical inventions and correlations, improved seed and agricultural methods, selected habits of civilised life, the increment of association.

(Corollary: Values arising from these are in large part STATAL values, and exceed the boundaries of private ownership at many points.)

II. It is an infamy that the STATE in, and by reason of, the very act of creating material wealth should run into debt to individuals.

Perhaps those two ethical dissociations are all the Christian reader can digest before leaving for his secluded week-end. '*Aviation shares continue buoyant.*'

On the Degrees of Honesty in Various Occidental Religions[1]

It being impossible for me to speak in the abstract with finality, I can only offer the following paragraphs as certified data. It so happens that I have never met any one save an archbishop who ventured to defend *any* church as such, I mean as an organism.

I have more than once been visited by members of the lower clergy, or received from them denunciations of the insincerity of their superiors. I know of no officially Christian publication of *any* sect which stands up and answers a theological question, however soberly put. You might as well expect a straight answer from a banker's son-in-law about money, or from a hired professor about economics!

Taking the more prevalent creeds in order and with respect to their scriptures, I think no impartial examiner will deny that the ethics of the Old Testament are merely squalid. The two-standards system of Geneva cannot be blamed on the Semites, but the Semitic avoidance of their own law on usury while wishing to be accepted as neighbours is on a par with Geneva, and Geneva is at heart (in soul and to the uttermost atom) the frontage of Basel and the international bank of that usurers' stronghold.

The Protestant almost invariably accuses the Catholic of lack of downright honesty. But I cannot see that this is done on comparative grounds.

No Protestant sect is honest *by programme* about money. After Anthony Trollope's careful analysis it seems mere waste of time to try to state the case against the Church of England in mere general statement.

A noted Dean, as disgusted as I am with his superior and just as far as I am from suspecting his immediate overlords of sincerity or real honesty, yet after preaching peace merely relapses into silence when I suggest that he meet some one from the other side to see if two men not immediately embroiled in a present war can agree on just terms of settlement.

A parson in the antipodes writes to me denouncing his archbishop almost as the incarnation of evil and as the most evil man who has occupied a given see for the past thirteen centuries.

[1] *Aryan Path*, October 1939. See Cantos LX—LXI. Ed.

It is quite certain that Christianity appears or has in known instances appeared both immoral and anti-statal to the serious Chinese literate. He saw it as such when the Jesuits were inserting it into China in the seventeenth and eighteenth centuries. Disruptive of family life, disturbing to the quiet and order of the empire, inducing disrespect to the dead and destructive to Confucian ethics.

Under stress the Christians promptly lied, and caused themselves thereby great inconvenience. They claimed that their churches were built by an Emperor's order, whereas no such order existed, and this fact was perfectly demonstrable by documentary proof.

The whole story is in many ways typically Christian in its inconsequence. A few most admirable Jesuits carried in Western science, something totally dissociated from their religion. In fact there had been that little case against Galileo, and it was Galileo's mathematics that gained them their favour, along with a dash of quinine and an aptitude in the founding of cannon (military not ecclesiastic).

An Emperor finally ousted 'em with an answer full of sobriety.

If any Christian writer or controversialist ever faced a question or answered it, I should like to know whether he thinks or they think the New Testament is or is not anti-Semitic in the sense that it is a repudiation of a great deal of pre-Nazarene teaching.

It has long appeared to me that the protagonist of those very peculiar documents, the Evangels or Gospels, disliked Semitism very intensely and set about reversing its attitude, but, being partially Semite, several items escaped his notice. He merely took 'em for granted, and they have infested his sect until now. It is in many ways a sect headed for disorder, and does not conduce to a very developed sense of responsibility.

Under stress of emotion, the Jew seems to lose his sense of reality. When a causal sequence would result to his personal disadvantage, he is not alone in losing his sense of causality. Example *re neschek*. During the past three years I have found very few Jews who would follow me through a discussion of *neschek*, either from the point of view of the Mosaic code or of the social consequence of this evil. Dante, Shakespeare and, I am told, the earlier Elizabethans were interested in the problem. Since the time of Claudius Salmasius historians have been very weak in their treatment of it. Most of them are headed for the ash-can because they did *not* analyse monetary pressures. You can't on this ground blame the church fathers; there exists a canonist tradition worthy of study and not the least out of date. What is out of date is the ignorantism coming from Calvin, Cromwell, Baxter, and persisting through the mercantilist era.

In trying to get a focus, or to see whether race comes into the problem of ethics, one sees empirically that Anglo- (so called) Saxons do not cling to their Wode epoch. They do not howl for a return to the ethos of their more savage days. In fact you can see only the Jew proclaiming the ethos of a nomadic era (unless the *Koran* does).

I don't see that the erudite Jesuits came out very well against Yong Tching in the 1720's. Both this emperor and his father seem to have acted 'in malice toward none', and with impeccable frankness, recognizing services rendered, writing without heat and with personal appreciation of the high personal merits of the individual Jesuits. These latter could not deny certain known facts nor could they claim absolute singleness of intention, though they objected to being mixed up with dirty Dutch traders and masters of frigates.

From the Confucian base, as I understand it, one wants to see the actual texts of their accusers. Were they accused of being exiles from Europe, or do the texts simply mean that they had left their own countries, meaning that they had left them *before* using their utmost efforts to improve them, to set up within them (as a basis for world peace or peace over more of the planet) a social order worthy of being copied by others or such as would conduce to such imitation.

The state of Europe in 1725 was no more fit to be imitated by any foreign man or nation than it was under the grilling heel of international filth and usury in 1925.

The problem of missions is difficult, but it is inherent in the looseness of the Christian programme, and shows a sketchiness in the disordered (often brilliant and lofty) injunctions huddled together in the curious Greek of the Early 'Church'.

One sees utterly illiterate Occidentals rushing into the Orient to teach savants. True they go often to the outcast, to the lower people, and it seems undeniable that in many cases they have exercised what George Washington called 'benign influence'.

But in the matter of proportion, in a sense of the relative weight, is this tendency to go off half-cocked of as much ethical weight as the conviction *that order should be promoted from where one is; that order should start inside one's own cerebrum*, in the *directio voluntatis*?

On the supposition that my infant mind was attracted to or distracted by Christianity at a tender age and in Sunday School, I might almost say that for a period of nearly fifty years I have never met Christian FAITH. I have heard faith once over the radio, and it was concentrated in the two syllables *Schicksal*, uttered in a context that might have been taken from the testament of Kang Hi.

Confucian faith I can conceive. I can conceive of a man's believing that if, and in measure as, he brings order into his own consciousness (his own 'innermost') that order will emanate from him. The cycle of Chinese history, the reception of the 'mandate' (called the mandate of heaven) by various dynasties, seems to offer demonstrable evidence of this process.

In the present very imperfect state of half-knowledge I fail to see that the history of China, or Chinese historic process, suffers a dichotomy or split into two opposite forces, as does that of Europe. Not, that is, unless you want to set Buddhism and Taoism together as a sort of Guelf Party. And even then that wouldn't be a decent analogy.

The Papacy *as ideal* is, in this dimension, equivalent to the ideal of the empire. It is a Roman ideal of order and subordination, and *inside* itself has always shown us a spectacle similar to that of Hochang and Taoist struggling against the order of Empire.

As I see it, the literate Christian explorer found nothing in Confucius to object to; there was nothing that the most sincere Catholic missionary could wish to remove from Confucius' teaching. They were reduced to asking about the technical meaning of the Lord of Heaven and as to how far Kung was, or was not, incarnate or inpietrate or present in the cartouche or tablet.

So far as I make out, Christianity did not ask the Chinese to assume any new responsibility; it only offered him relaxation from various duties.

This is quite possibly too rough a statement. Obviously the missionary is convinced, or the first few missionaries and martyrs are and must be convinced and oblivious of minor objections. It is their method of implementing their fervour that I would bring up for examination.

Modern Europe has merely dumped mediaeval thought about *la vita contemplativa*. That doesn't mean that there are no Western mystics, but again the European schizophrenia has split their being. Instead of the *vita contemplativa* being conceived as the dynamo of the active life, it is merely sidetracked, and commonly regarded as 'useless'.

I am aware that no mystic, no recluse, no Hindoo would say that it is so. I am stating a general contingency. The Occident regards the contemplative as a do-nothing. An empiric test would probably 'give him reason', if it did not prove that his estimate was correct in ninety-eight per cent of all cases. This is a very sad state of affairs, at least from some angles.

How far are religions honest? How far have they ever been honest in Europe?

In the condemnation of Scotus Erigena? In the wrangle of Bossuet's correspondence with Leibnitz? How far can any man today who wants a straight answer to *any* ethical query (let alone a query about a vital and demonstrable infamy such as the monopoly of money or the frauds of international exchange) expect to get that answer from Christian, Jew, Protestant, Catholic, Quaker or any minor sect in the Occident?

A most valuable study of usury in India could and should be written by some one with knowledge of Hindoo theologians. So far one has heard little about it save picturesque details of vicarious penances for this prevalent sin.

The Nordic will, I think, always want to know from the Indian: how far is religion effective? One of the widest gulfs between East and West might be bridged if some sort of survey and mensuration were set up to take this dimension.

From what history I have been able to learn, it appears to me that Confucius has in his dimension a pre-eminence over other founders of ethical systems; while yielding nothing to any of them in other domains. (By which I don't mean to offer any homage at all to academics who have exploited the label Confucian without meditating the texts, or even to bright young Chinese journalists who have a merely superficial notion of the text of the *King*, the accepted Confucian books.)

Were we in a meeting I should rise to express my doubts as to the spiritual value of the *Koran* in relation to the philosophy of the Arab philosophers, with Avicenna at the apex. I see almost no spiritual elevation in the *Old Testament*, and the *Talmud*, if one is to judge by current quotations, is not an ethical volume at all but a species of gangster's handbook. After the loss of faith in the Roman Church, the Christian sectaries produced no first-rate theology and little that can be considered intellectually serious.

I defy any Christian to produce more than *one* element in Christianity, if that, which is not anticipated in the cult practised by the Chinese literati. I leave it to their ingenuity to discover what I consider the basic intuition of Nazarene genius. When you find the Emperor Yong Tching spending all his efforts to govern well that he might bring comfort to the soul of his father, 'deceased emperor now in heaven', you have at least a savour of piety. Research might well be directed to how much of whatever Christianity has brought us, including some of its ceremonial gestures, pre-existed in China.

As to sacrifices, I think the body of notes on this subject, everything that has ever come to my attention, is just plain stupid to the point of imbecility. 'Pleasing to heaven', etc. Various ideas of pleasing the spirits are all very well, but there could still be a lesson in animal sacrifice for any group that had evolved beyond primitive stages. Animals are killed now in abattoirs; the sight of a killing can remind us, in the midst of our normal semi-consciousness of all that goes on in our vile and degraded mercantilist ambience, that life exists by destruction of other life. The sight of one day's hecatomb might even cause thought in the midst of our democracy and usuriocracy.

In praise of the Christian religion, despite its manifest incompetence to maintain decency or even any strong tendency toward economic justice in any Occidental country, I can at least say this. In favourable circumstances Christianity or several of its ideals could and should conduce to a deeper understanding of the cult of the Chinese literati than is prevalent among half-educated Chinese. Both Confucianism and Christianity propose a state of sincerity which is almost unattainable, but the Christian proposals are mixed with all sorts of disorder, whereas a Confucian progress offers chance for a steady rise, and defects either in conduct or in theory are in plain violation of its simple and central doctrine.

Religio[1]

Paganism included a certain attitude toward; a certain understanding of, coitus, which is the mysterium.

The other rites are the festivals of fecundity of the grain and the sun festivals, without revival of which religion can not return to the hearts of the people.

[1] *The Townsman,* November 1939.

Statues of Gods[1]

We want an European religion. Christianity is verminous with semitic infections. What we really believe is the pre-Christian element which Christianity has not stamped out. The only Christian festivals having any vitality are welded to sun festivals, the spring solstice, the Corpus and St. John's eve, registering the turn of the sun, the crying of 'Ligo' in Lithuania, the people rushing down into the sea in Rapallo on Easter morning, the gardens of Adonis carried to Church on the Thursday.

The peasant women carrying silk cucoons to Church carefully hidden in their clasped hands, cannot be, we suppose, European, but at any rate it is real, if almost unknown to the reading world.[2]

The cult was of the few. The evil came perhaps with the invasion of temple enclosures. Un-understanding and incapable of understanding what went on in temples, the gross apes destroyed them. At any rate you can get money for any fool oriental flummery, anything tinged with fanaticism or hypocrisy gets an endowment. The mystery is, or is not, that the believed cults, the cults of Aphrodite and Helios have no temples in our day, whereas the hang-overs of all varieties of the utterly nonsensical and unbelieved are upheld.

From now on statues should be statues of gods.

The unshakable wisdom of Confucius and Mencius in comparison with which Christianity is a fad.

[1] *The Townsman*, August 1939.   [2] See Canto XCI. Ed.

Deus est Amor[1]

The idea that the love of god for human beings is a Christian invention is sheer hokum, part and parcel of the vast impertinence of the Christers. The Greek gods loved, I admit, select individuals, either for reasons of kinship or because of particular merits of the individual. It was more humanly comprehensible than the abstract love of mankind at large regardless of his abstract and collective infamies and imbecilities. The loved were the elect, or you might say, the hand picked. It becomes ridiculous and infantile in the writings of Nonnus.

Calvin's god and the god of all writers leading to and descending from Calvin is a maniac sadist, one would prefer other qualities in one's immediate parenthood. French good sense, that is european good sense dealt with the matter:

> Pere eternal vous avez tort
> Et ben devetz avoir vergogne,
> Vestre fils bien amis est mort
> Et vous dormez comme un ivrogne.

The religious man communes every time his teeth sink into a bread crust.

If a race NEGLECTS to create its own gods, it gets the bump.

The essence of religion is the *present* tense.

[1] *The Townsman*, June 1940.

Quotations from Richard of St. Victor[1]

Incipit quaedam familiaritas inter Deum et animam fieri.
A certain familiarity begins to sprout between God and the soul.

Felicem cui datum est dispersiones cordis in unum colligere.
Happy who can gather the heart's fragmentations into unity.

Amare videre est.
To love is to perceive.

Oportet eam tam gratuito quam debito amore abundare.
There should be abundance of gratuitous love, as well as what is merely owed.

Anima formosa est aut deformis ex voluntate sua.
The soul is beautiful or deformed from its own will.

Plenitudo legis est charitas; legem continet et prophetas . . . dilapsa reformans, consumpta restaurans, implere non cessat; nomen diffi-cultatis ignorat.
The plenitude of the law is charity; it contains the law and the prophets . . . Remaking what has fallen, restoring what is worn away, it ceases not to fill; it ignores the word difficulty.

Qui secundum quod cor dictat, verba componit.
Who composes words, as the heart dictates.

Bona voluntatis per quam in nobis divinae similitudinis imago reperietur.
The good things of will, through which an image of the divine likeness will be found in us.

Nisi bona intentio, mens moritur.
Without good intention, the mind dies.

Posse, sapientia, bonitas vel charitas. Trinitatis imago.
The being able, the wisdom, the goodness or charity. Image of Trinity.

In avibus intellige studia spiritualia, in animalibus exercitia corporalia.
Watch birds to understand how spiritual things move, animals to understand physical motion.

[1] Selected and translated 1956.   [2] Quoted Canto XC. Ed.

73

Ne simplicitas nostra sit frigida.
Our simplicity should not be frigid.

Ignis quidquid in nobis est.
There is a certain fire within us.
  OVID: . . . est Deus in nobis[1], agitante calescemus illo.[2]

Cum hic Spiritus spiritum rationalem intrat, ipsius affectum divino amore inflammat, et ad proprietatis suae similitudinem transformat, ut auctori suo amorem quem debet exhibeat.
When this Spirit enters the rational spirit, it inflames it with its own divine ardour and transforms its qualities into its own likeness, so that it shows forth the love of its author, as is fitting.

[1] Quoted Canto XCVIII. Ed.   [2] Quoted Canto XCIII. Ed.

PART THREE
The Treatise on Harmony

*Celui qui se trompe est des nôtres ;
celui qui ajoute ou retranche dans une
mélodie est des nôtres ; mais celui
qui s'ecarte du temps sans s'en rendre
compte ne peut pas être des nôtres.*
Ishac ben Ibrahim El Mossuli
cited by
M. Jules Rouanet.

Rattle snakes are almost totally deaf
Paris Times, 8 July 1924, p. 4.
col. 3.

PART THREE

The Treatise on Harmony

'**W**hat, mon élève, is the element grossly omitted from all treatises on *harmony* . . .'
at this point the élève looks up brightly . . .
'except the treatise now being composed' . . .? the élève continues to regard me brightly . . . and blankly. No answer is offered me.

The answer, mon élève, is:

The element most grossly omitted from treatises on harmony up to the present is the element of *time*. The question of the time-interval that must elapse between one sound and another if the two sounds are to produce a pleasing consonance or an *interesting* relation, has been avoided.

And yet the simplest consideration of the physics of the matter by almost the simplest mathematician, should lead to equations showing that

A sound of any pitch, or any combination of such sounds, may be followed by a sound of any other pitch, or any combination of such sounds, providing the time-interval between them is properly gauged; and this is true for *any series of sounds, chords or arpeggios*.

The limits for the practical purposes of music depend solely on our capacity to produce a sound that will last long enough, i.e. remain audible long enough, for the succeeding sound or sounds to catch up, traverse, intersect it.

Why is this question of time-intervals omitted from all other treatises on harmony?

Parenthesis for historic survey.

1. Musical theoricians are exceedingly conventional, for centuries they went on quoting Franco of Cologne instead of listening to sound.

2. Harmony in Bach's time was a vigorous and interesting matter. Why?

The answer to this question and to the main question of this section, is:

The early students of harmony were so accustomed to think of music as something with a strong lateral or horizontal motion that they never imagined any one, *any one* could be stupid enough to think of it as static; it never entered their heads that people would make music like steam ascending from a morass.

They thought of music as travelling rhythm going through points or barriers of pitch and pitch-combinations.

They had this concept in their blood, as the oriental has his raga and his tala. It simply never occurred to them that people would start with static harmony and stick in that stationary position.

Hence it has arrived that the term 'Harmony' is applied to the science of chords that can be struck simultaneously; and the directions for modulations have been worked out for chords that can follow each other without demanding a strict or even interesting time-interval between their emission.

In short, Mr. Joseph Corfe produced his
thoroughbass
simplified
and laid open to the meanest capacity;
he did that over a century ago, and no one detected the fact till this year (A.D. 1923).

I am told that even Mr. Corfe's work contains errors.

But far be it, far, afar from me to contradict Mr. Corfe, or that still more illustrious professor, Dr. Schönberg. All that they have said is, or may be true, and lacking in interest.

Ernst Friederich Richter has said:

'Pure theory can not and should not concern itself with practice, for it has as sole aim the definition of the nature of the divers constituent elements of the art, without ever treating the special and particular cases which result from the employment of personal procedures'.

Observation:
Aristotle was not a pure theorist.
Sauzay
'Il faut se borner à penser que J-S. Bach écrivait la musique par certains procédés dont la loi générale nous échappe.'

(Sauzay, *Le Violon Harmonique*, p. 217)

The secret or part of it probably is that Bach, consciously or unconsciously, never thought of using two chords except as parts, integral parts, of a progression, a rhythmic progression.
Credo

I believe in an absolute rhythm. E.P. 1910 with explanations.[1]

In 1910 I was working with monolinear verbal rhythm but one had already an adumbration that the bits of rhythm used in verse were capable of being used in musical structure, even with other dimensions.

Treatises on harmony give you all sorts of recipes for getting from one chord to another (this is more or less reduced to a few simple mechanisms) they do not stop to enquire whether the transit by these means is interesting, or, in a given situation, expressive.

That is supposed to be a matter of creative genius. It is.

Any series of chords can follow any other, provided the right time-interval is discovered. The interesting sequences are probably those that *demand* very set and definite intervals.

That is probably all we have to say in this chapter.

Given proper approach, the progression

is probably perfectly sound. I mean from the point of view of mathematics.

Fortunately this theory of harmony can never be reduced to an academicism. At least it seems unlikely that any mathematician will bother. The mathematics of the case might prove discouraging.

You can reduce the line composition of *La Nascita di Venere* to trigonometric equations; it would make a long charming series. The results might be interesting but they would not help you to draw.

'How did you find those four notes?' said X ... in undisguised admiration. 'Gee, I wish I had found those four notes.'

Answer: By listening to the sound that they made, a thing no pyanist has ever done.

That is perhaps all we have to say in this chapter.

And possibly the last; for we have probably said about all we have to say. The former treatises on harmony dealt with static harmony, they may have defined harmony as 'simultaneous melody' or they may have sought some other definition, but they did not consider that lateral motion, the horizontal motion, and the time-interval between

[1] Preface to translation of Guido Cavalcanti.

succeeding sounds *must* affect the human ear, and not only the ear but the absolute physics of the matter. The question of where one wave-node meets another, or where it banks against the course of another wave to strengthen or weaken its action, must be considered.

The harmony for one instrument is *by no means* necessarily the harmony for another. Good players have always '*got the most out of*' the compositions they played by their subtle seizing of this gaya scienca, and we have said 'he has a sense of rhythm' or she 'has a sense of rhythm'.

And again Sauzay:[1] Le fameux Durante, que a fait tant d'élèves célèbres, ne leur donnait jamais les raisons des règles qu'il formulait. Naturally. When Harmony was alive it was merely a personal give away, it was a bundle of tricks of the trade, the fruit of personal experience, it was A way of getting over a difficulty or managing a turn of expression; it wasn't intended to cramp anyone's style: It was pragmatic, it worked, and each school worked its trade secrets to death with the magnificence of Bel Canto, of music up to Johann Sebastien. The mechanism was a plus thing, it worked in an open field.

The mess came when it was set up as a fence, and everyone tried to walk on the rails or climb over it.

They rotted their melodies by trying to find schemes which 'harmonize' according to a concept of 'harmony' in which the tendency to lifelessness was inherent.

COROLLARIES AND COMPLICATIONS

Continuing, mon élève; you will probably have noticed by now a glaring omission on my part.

A sound of any pitch etc. . . . .

any chord may be followed by any other provided the right time-interval be placed between them.

The duration of the resolving chord must also be considered; and the duration of the various chords in a sequence will be subject to mathematical computations, if people prefer mathematics to judging the sounds by ear.

The harmony for one instrument may not be the harmony for another.

Again the competent mathematician could show us that the vibrations of a 'cello where the sound is steadily produced by a drawn bow will combine in a different way from those of a horn, a plucked string or an instrument of percussion.

Everybody knows this; but the time is over when we can give more

[1] *Violon harmonique*, p. 69.

reverence to a person who can detect slight variations of pitch, than to one who can detect the difference between

and

It will make a difference what instrument the sounds are played on; it will make a difference if one note or several notes are played louder in the chord; it will make a difference if the next chord strikes the precedent chord while that chord is still being propelled from the instruments or if the second chord strike the other chord as it fades;

and all these things are really in the domain of harmony, that is of active, not static, harmony;

and as for the workings of the latter; this time element may upset them or reinforce them in given circumstance.

The so called 'laws' of harmony were useful when they were a bag of handy tools; but if one tries to carry the whole machine shop; one's mobility will probably suffer.

To the above treatise I received four answers;

1. Antheil: had known for some time that the duration of the notes and the duration of the time-intervals between them made a difference to the way the harmony sounded.

2. A violinist: had not thought of the matter but tried various combinations of notes and found that my statement applied.

3. Author of a work on Einstein: approved the treatise; thought it ought to be longer; doubted whether the statement was true for *all* possible combinations of notes.

(This, I take it, was due to his overlooking my restrictive clause.)

Perhaps I might better my statement. Perhaps I should say: There are no two chords which may not follow each other, if the sequence of time-intervals and durations is correct.

4. Then there was the gent who found the treatise interesting but who (as who should prefer to study the circulation of the blood from corpses exclusively) preferred to study his harmony 'separate', i.e. static.

Which might be very nice if it could be done or if there were any essential difference between one part of harmony and the other.

PROLEGOMENA

To make my simple statement even simpler; let us consider the nature of the ear, and of sound.

81

Sound, we are told, consists of vibrations of from 16 to 36,000 per second.

The ear is an organ for the detection of frequency.

To the best of my knowledge I have always heard the lower notes of the pipe-organ not as pitch but as a series of separate woof-woofs. I don't want to insist on what may be a personal idiosyncrasy due to my being so excessively quick on the uptake. The point is that *up* to 16 items per second we notice the separate shocks; after that we notice a synthesis of frequency.

Animals probably notice frequencies favourable and unfavourable to their existence. Hence the powers of Orpheus.

Music as the ancient philosophers say, arises from number.

Let us say that music is a composition of frequencies.

That definition covers all possible forms of music; harmony, melody, counterpoint, form in the fugue, etc.

Some of these combinations of frequency, very simple ones, are academically considered pleasant.

Raphael Socius in A.D. 1556 catalogues a number of them, that had long been considered respectable.

When the frequency of vibration of one note bears the relation of 3 to 2 to the frequency of vibration of another, the combination is considered respectable.

Academicism is not excess of knowledge; it is the possession of *idées fixes* as to how one shall make use of one's data.

The time element affects harmony [*sic*].

You can hear a note which has 16 vibrations per second.

But

You can also beat (on a drum head or other object) 16 times per second.

The ear measures frequency.

If you sound a note whose frequency is 16 per second and start beating, tap, tap, etc. exactly half way between the nodes of your note 16, you will produce a combined frequency of 32, i.e. equivalent to the octave above 16.

If your beats fall $\frac{2}{3}$ of a wave behind the inception of the note 16, you will get alternate periods, some belonging to the series 24, i.e. the fifth above the note 16; and others belonging to the series 48, i.e. the octave above that fifth.

So the Negroes in darkest Africa are probably right when they say that from simple beating of their drums they can imagine other instruments.

And the proportions, even very complicated proportions can be established by simple percussion.

I have taken a very simple and understandable case of a note vibrating 16, the number low enough to be thought of easily.

The stiff-necked will say: Oh but for higher notes this beating can't matter; you can't beat 3,000 times per second, or even 256 times per second.

Responsus est:

The consonances of counterpoint as outlined by comrade Raphael, or of harmony as meant by Dr. Schönberg apply to simple combinations of frequency. Obviously if one note is vibrating 600 per second, and another 1,200 there can be six hundred coincidences per second, and you can not strike your drum as often as that.

(There is nothing sacred about the duration of the second, it is merely a convenient and current measure. A note vibrating 221 and $\frac{1}{2}$ times per second is just as conceivable as one vibrating 221 or 222.)

If three notes are sounded at once, the complete coincidences of their wave-nodes may be considerably rarer than when only two of them are sounded. You may beat with or against the coincidence; with, to clarify; against, to complicate.

You can use your beat as a third or fourth or Nth note in the harmony.

To put it another way; the percussion of the rhythm can enter the harmony exactly as another note would. It enters usually as a Bassus, a still deeper bassus; giving the main form to the sound.

It may be convenient to call these different degrees of the scale the megaphonic and microphonic parts of the harmony.

Rhythm is nothing but the division of frequency plus an emphasis or phrasing of that division.

Why, mon contradicteur, have masters of music specified that certain compositions be played at a certain speed?

(Example, in my copy of Le Nozze, one finds: Presto; half note equals 84; Allegro, black equals 144, etc.)

If anyone is interested, or cares to speculate upon Mozart's indubitable comprehension of the matter, they might do worse than study the time proportions in the opening of the Concerto in A major.

DISSOCIATION A

Percussion can enter:

1. At unison, i.e. at each incidence of nodes of the lower notes.
2. At bassus, i.e. on octaves, double octaves, 12th, etc., below the more frequent incidences of nodes of the higher notes.
3. (As afore noted), against the incidences, thereby complicating the harmony rather than emphasizing some other element or elements.

There is no fundamental difference between the first two manners, or even between them and the third.

The more complicated the incidences the more interesting the arrangement of percussion may be.

The arrangement of the percussion is probably more important, or more effectively or interestingly employable in a sequence of 2nds, and 7ths than in the simpler relations (listed by comrade Raphael as safe for contrapunto).

Naturally percussion in unison can be used higher in the scale for less simple proportions, than for more simple proportions of pitch-intervals.

If I can only get the mathematics of these relations so complicated that composers will become discouraged; give up trying to compose by half-remembered rules, and really listen to sound, I shall have performed no inconsiderable service to music.

NEXT SECTION

Or:

various inconvenient items which the bud should consider before becoming too fixed in its opinions.

What applies to the harmony, or the 'perpendicular' or simultaneous melody 'microphonically', applies also to the melody, i.e. the succeeding notes of a series, to the interceptions of counterpoint, to the statement and answer in the fugue.

There is nothing whatever in music but a composition of frequencies, microphonic and macrophonic.

There are 40,360 possible sequences of the eight notes in the single octave, regardless of their duration; if you take eight half notes and add a quarter note, there are nine times as many combinations.

The modern musician says he can't hear a melody till it's harmonised.

This is utter atrophy.

Dom Nicholas, inventor of the archicembalo, thought the ear could distinguish difference up to the proportion of 80 to 81 per second, but that its power of synthesis stopped there.

It would notice a difference of 80 to 82, i.e. the proportion of 40 to 41.

The academic musician prides himself on his sense of pitch. Sir X. X. of the Royal, etc., sat next to H. in the Albert Hall, the singer sang E. 'Ah C,' said Sir X. X. 'No, E,' said H.

A little later the singer sang B. 'E,' again said Sir X. X.

So let us refrain from vainglory.

Some people have a sense of absolute frequency, others of proportional frequency.

i.e. some recognise the number of vibrations of the note.

Others recognise only the proportion of vibrations of a note to some other note (pitch) already given.

This proportional sensitivity is called having a musical ear.

And the fight between these two kinds of auditives has been going on from the time of Aristotle and Ptolemy to the present. Thank heaven.

That is to say one party (mine) says: You can *not* transpose. That is to say you can transpose till you are blue in the face, but the thing after transposition is *not* the same, i.e. does *not* sound the same as it did before.

Doni in the *Trattato de'modi veri* says that if 'I Modi si pratichino separati da una certa e determinata tensione, perdono la meta della loro efficacita, ed anco piu'.

(I beg the reader, at this point, to consider that M. Antheil and I have heard all about superpartient sesqui octaval proportion, etc. If anyone wants more mathematics let me refer him to Lemme Rossi's *Sistema Musico overo Musica Speculativa*. [Perugia 1666.])

170 pages of mathematics are of less value than a little curiosity and a willingness to listen to the sound that actually proceeds from an instrument.

Singers transpose because they are thinking of their own throats, not of their ears, or of the ears of their auditors. Pianists think of their fingers, of the gymnastic excitement of their adrenals.

You may reduce the line composition of Botticelli's Nascita to the algebraic equations of analytics, without learning how to paint.

After Dolmetsch tunes a clavicord he has slightly to untune it. Why? That is to say, the proportion of the different notes remain correct but each note is sounded on two strings, and these must *not* be in absolute accord. He says the waves 'cut' each other and ruin the resonance.

One may either graph this by picturing two sound waves, the crests of which mutually bump and depress each other, or you may say that the nodes need a certain width, they must meet, but they must meet as if on the knife's back not on the razor's edge.

These prolegomena are not intended as the complete whifflepink to deaf musicians. They are a statement of points that should be considered before contradicting the author.

And to hot tempered sticklers, could we recommend dear old Lavignac's temperance:

'Nous n'entendons pas dire que ce système a été organisé par les mathématiciens ou d'après leurs calculs; il a été crée empiriquement par les musiciens, sans autre guide que leur instinct.'

(P. 55, 18th edtn. *La Musique et les Musiciens.*)

P. 52. Discussing some chanting he had heard one Easter: Le résultat était atroce *pour mes oreilles*. Words of a savant.

PART FOUR
Confucius and Mencius

PART FOUR

Immediate need of Confucius[1]

In considering a value already age-old, and never to end while men are, I prefer not to write 'to the modern world'. The *Ta Hio* stands, and the commentator were better advised to sweep a few leaves from the temple steps. This is no shrine for the hurried tourist or for the conductor with: 'One moment, and now for the alligator tanks so that we can catch the Bombay Express at 8.47.'

Dante for a reason wrote *De Vulgari Eloquio*—On the Common Tongue—and in each age there is need to write De Vulgari Eloquio, that is, to insist on *seeing* the words daily in use and to know the *why* of their usage.

No man has ever known enough about words. The greatest teachers have been content to use a few of them justly.

If my version of the *Ta Hio* is the most valuable work I have done in three decades I can only wait for the reader to see it. And for each to discover its 'value' to the 'modern world' for himself.

Mr. S. V. V. (*The Aryan Path*, December 1936) has indicated the parallels in Indian teaching, but the Western reader will first see the antithesis to the general impression of Indian thought now clouding Occidental attention. This cloud exists, and until some light or lightning disrupts it, many of the better minds in the West will be suspicious of all Eastern teaching.

It is 'our' impression that an Indian begins all talk with an allusion to the Infinite and that the Ultimate Unity appears four times on every Indian page.

I am not saying what ought to be. I am not expounding Indian thought, but indicating a misapprehension. It is in the opinion of the hard-headed, as distinct from the bone-headed, West that Westerners who are drawn to Indian thought are Westerners in search of an escape mechanism, Westerners who dare face neither the rigours of mediaeval dialectic nor the concrete and often exhausting detail of the twentieth-century material sciences.

Writing, which is communications service, should be held distinct from the production of merchandise for the book trade. And the

[1] *Aryan Path*, August 1937.

89

measure of communication was defined by Leo Frobenius when he said:

'It is not what a man says but the part of it which his auditor considers important that determines the amount of the communication.'

In considering the Occident the Oriental should allow for a fact that I have not yet seen printed. Western contact with the Far East was made in an era of Western degradation. American contact with Japan was forced in the very middle of 'the century of usury.' Western ethics were a consummate filth in the middle of the last century.

You can probably date any Western work of art by reference to the ethical estimate of usury prevalent at the time of that work's composition; the greater the component of tolerance for usury the more blobby and messy the work of art. The kind of thought which distinguishes good from evil, down into the details of commerce, rises into the quality of line in paintings and into the clear definition of the word written.

If the editors complain that I am not confining my essay to Confucius, I reply that I am writing on the 'need for Confucius'. I am trying to diagnose Western disease. Western disease has raged for over two centuries. Western disease shows in sixty per cent racket on ink money. That is a *symptom* of moral obtuseness.

The Oriental looking at the West should try more often to look at the total West over a longer period than is usually drawn to his attention.

For over a thousand years the acute intellectual labour of Europe was done *inside* the Catholic Church. The readers of *The Aryan Path* (December 1936) were reminded a few months ago that Scotus Erigena was a layman. A 'movement' or an institution lives while it searches for truth. It dies with its own curiosity. *Vide* the death of Moslem civilisation. *Vide* the very rapid withering of Marxist determinism. Yeats burbles when he talks of 'withering into the truth'. You *wither* into non-curiosity.

Catholicism led Europe as long as Erigena, Grosseteste and their fellows struggled for definitions of words.

Today the whole Occident is bathed daily in mental sewage, that is, the 'morning paper' in ten millions of copies rouses the Western brain daily. Bunkus is called a philosopher, Puley an economist, and a hundred lesser vermin swarm daily over acres of print.

Ex diffinientium cognitione diffiniti resultat cognitio—'Knowledge of a definite thing comes from a knowledge of things defined,' wrote Dante, rubbing it in. You can't know a canzone, which is a structure of strophes, until you know strophes.

'Man triplex, seeks the useful, this in common with vegetables; the delectable, in common with animals; the *honestum*; and here he is alone; vel angelicae naturae sociatur.'

This kind of dissociation and tidiness is 'mediaeval'.

When the experimental method came into material science giving a *defined* knowledge in realms whereto verbal distinctions had not then penetrated, and where they probably never will penetrate, the Occident lost the habit of verbal definition.

The Church had lost its faith anyhow, and mess, unholy and slithering mess, supervened.[1] Curiosity deserted almost all realms save those of physiology, chemistry and kindred material sciences.

A tolerance of the most ungodly indistinctness supervened. The life of Occidental mind fell apart into progressively stupider and still more stupid segregations. The Church of England for example remained a bulwark of usury and/or a concatenation of sinecures, for the holding whereof neither courage, character nor intelligence was required or even wanted.

Hence (leaping over a certain amount of barbed wire, and intermediary gradations), hence the Western need of Confucius, and specifically of the *Ta Hio*, and more specifically of the *first chapter* of the *Ta Hio*; which you may treat as a *mantram*, or as a *mantram* reinforced, a *mantram* elaborated so that the meditation may gradually be concentrated into contemplation. (Keeping those two grades of life separate as they are defined in the Benjamin Minor of R. St. Victor.)

There is respectable Western thought. There is Western thought that conforms to Confucius just as S. V. V. in December reminded you that there is in Indian Scripture a stress on Confucian 'self-examination etc., with emphasis on action'. Yet I fail to understand S. V. V. when he adds 'without concern for its fruits'. This phrase of his seems to me capable of grave misinterpretation. Does he mean 'profits'? Does he mean 'material profits'?

In any case the *need* is a matter of emphasis. We in the West *need* to begin with the first chapter of the *Ta Hio*, not merely to grant a casual admission of it in some out-house of our ethics or of our speculations.

There is nothing in this chapter that destroys the best that has been thought in the Occident. The Occident has already done its apparent utmost to destroy the best Western perceptions. Official Christianity is a sink. Catholicism reached nadir, let us say, with Antonelli in the

---

[1] Mr. Eliot's *Primer of Heresy* (*After Strange Gods*) was not examined with sufficient care, nor did the present author chew on it sufficiently, especially in regard to the distinction between A Church, an orthodoxy, and a collection of intelligent observations by individual theologians, however brilliant. Eliot's use of Confucius in *The Rock* (section 5), is worth noting. E.P., 1959.

eighteen hundred and fifties. It has started a new ascension with the encyclicals, Rerum Novarum and Quadrigesimo Anno. But the whole of Western idealism is a jungle. Christian theology is a jungle. To think through it, to reduce it to some semblance of order, there is no better axe than the *Ta Hio*.

I, personally, want a revision of the trial of Scotus Erigena. If 'authority comes from right reason' the shindy between Leibniz and Bossuet was unnecessary.

Ernest Fenollosa emphasised a difference between the approach of logic and that of science. Confucius left his record in ideogram. I do not wish to confuse the ideogramic method with the specific and basic teaching of the *Ta Hio*, first chapter.

There are here two related matters. The good scholastic (mediaeval) or good canonist recognised the limits of knowledge transmissible by verbal definitions:

> Scientes quia rationale animal homo est, et quia sensibilis anima et corpus est animal, et *ignorantes* de hac anima quid ea sit, vel de ipso corpore, perfectam hominis cognitionem habere non possumus; quia cognitionis perfectio uniuscuiusque terminatur ad ultima elementa.
>
> [Knowing because man is a rational animal, and because a sensible soul and body is animal, and *ignorant* what this soul is, or what this body is, we cannot have complete (perfect) cognition of man, because the completeness of cognition of anything in particular ends with the ultimate element.]

Fenollosa accented the Western need of ideogramic thinking. Get your 'red' down to rose, rust, cherry, if you want to know what you are talking about. We have too much of this talk about vibrations and infinites.

There is here a common element with the Confucian method of getting in to one's own 'intentions'.

Naturally there is nothing in this which is hostile to Dante's concept of the 'directio voluntatis'. There exists passage after passage in our serious mediaeval thinkers which contains the terms 'virtu', *virtus*, with vivid and dynamic meaning. But it is precisely the *kind* of thought that is now atrophied in the Occident. This is precisely how we do *not* now think.

It is for these values that we have need of *Ta Hio*, and as S. V. V., approaching the work from so different a background, agrees, 'here is a very treasury of wisdom'.

S. V. V. did not, I take it, awaken to consciousness in McKinley's America, his early boyhood was not adorned with the bustuous noises of Kipling and the first Mr. Roosevelt. Apparently the *Ta Hio* offers us a meeting-place, a field of agreement.

IMMEDIATE NEED OF CONFUCIUS

In so far as 'at the centre of every movement for order or reconstruction in China you will find a Confucian' (this referring to the
procession of centuries) in so far as my own knowledge of Kung has
come *via* Tokio, there appears to be here a common field not only for
men of Bombay and London, but for pilgrims from an even wider
circumference. To my mind there is need, very great need of such
common *locus* of mutual comprehension.

The late A. R. Orage claimed to have read the *Mahabharata*. Very few
Occidentals *can* read it. It is manifestly *not* the possible meeting ground
for Eastern and Western man in our era.

Suma Gengi has just been televisioned from London. The news reaches
me between one page and another of this essay. There are common
denominators. There are points and lines wherein the East can make
contact with us Occidentals.

But the 'need of Confucius'. Let me try to get this as clear as possible.
A 'need' implies a lack, a sick man has 'need'. Something he has not.
Kung as medicine?

In every cranny of the West there is mildew of books that start from
nowhere. There is a marasmus of books that start 'treating of this,
that and the other' without defining their terminology, let alone their
terms, or circle, of reference. A thousand infernal self-styled economists start off without even defining 'money' (which is a *measured* claim,
transferable from any one to any one else, and which does not bear
interest as does a bond or a share-certificate).

I take that as example. These filthy writers then go on to muddle
their readers with discussion of 'systems' of inflation, of cancellation,
of credit problems. And naturally their work is useless and merely
spreads ignorance. Think, gentle reader, if the greasy fog in so concrete a science as economics is thus dense, what density is it likely to
attain in metaphysics. Where is ethical discrimination to end or begin
among us?

If only for the sake of understanding and valuating our own European past, we have need of the Master Kung.

And that is by no means our whole need. The fact that we have
such a past, is but an encouragement. It is perhaps but a tentative
reassurance that we have a chance of understanding part of the
Orient.

The 'value' of Confucius to the Modern World is not, I think we
agree, limited to medicinal value for the Occident. There is visible and
raging need of the *Ta Hio* in barbarous countries like Spain and Russia,
but above all questions of emergency, of hypodermic injection or
strait-jacket for fever patients and lunatics, there is also a question of
milder and continuous hygiene.

No one has ever yet exhausted the wisdom of the forty-six ideograms
of the first chapter. No one has ever yet attained so complete a wisdom

93

that he can find no further nutriment in this *mantram*. And no one, least of all a twentieth-century American with only a superficial acquaintance with Oriental intuition and language, should aspire to emit the 'last word' on this subject. I certainly cannot condense the *Ta Hio*. I have tried to present as much of it as I understand, free from needless clutteration of dead verbiage.

I am ready to wrestle in friendly manner over the words used even by S. V. V., but such contest would at this point obscure my main meaning. I hope some day to see a proper bilingual text, each ideogram with full explanation so that the American reader may have not merely the one side of the meaning which seems to one translator most imperative in a given passage, but one full meaning held in such restraint that a hierarchy of imperatives be not lost.

In the Dantescan symbol for the universe truth is not lost with velocity. An age-old intelligence is not lost in an era of speed. We are bedevilled with false diagnoses. We are obfuscated with the noise of those who attribute all troubles to irrelevant symptoms of evil. We are oppressed by powerful persons who lie, who have no curiosity, who smear the world and their high offices with Ersatz sincerity. His grace the Wubbok of the Wok dare not investigate this, that and the other, and so forth. . . . Neither does so-and-so nor his colleague (protected by libel laws) *dare* read the *Ta Hio*.

Name, nomen, cognomen etc., dare not be left alone in a lighted room with this document. They cannot face the forty-six characters in the solitude of their library. All this testifies to the strength of the chapter and to their need of it. Men suffer malnutrition by millions because their overlords dare not read the *Ta Hio*.

子孟

Mang Tsze[1]
(The Ethics of Mencius)

I am convinced that the most fantastically foolish or at best crassly
inadequate notions both of Kungfutsu and of Mang Tsze are current
not only among the weak minded but among that class which, if it
can't quite be considered an intelligentsia, has at least a greater domesticity with books than has the average reader.

A Chinese female in the U.S. has been lamenting in print that although Chinamen greatly outnumber the Chinese girls in America
these girls have the deuce of a time finding husbands. The men go
back to China for wives, they say the girls with an American 'education' are brainless.

And this I take it arises from our occidental habit of never looking
at anything. I may be inattentive. I have no doubt whatsoever that my
long-suffering friends consider me inattentive, but on the other hand
I am not a distracted infant, and I have on occasion seen more than
was meant for me, or even, in the case of Gaudier's sculpture and
Wyndham Lewis's drawings back in 1911 to 1914 more than some
others did.

Nevertheless we occidentals do not see when we look.

Kim had an education. I doubt if we occidentals ever receive one.
Having drawn an ideogram, quite a simple one, three times WRONG,
I am humbled but not in any dust of the occident. It was a simple
picture, a bureaucrat (or minister) faced by a member of the public,
thereby forming the verb 'to sleep', occurring in the sentence: Mencius
put his head on his stool (or head rest) and slept. It was not difficult to
write, and it looked wrong when done wrong. I committed the same
error three times running before I found out what was wrong, and
whatever be my 'low' for idiocy I find traces of at least similar failure
in sinologues. This note is the result of an experiment, necessarily
personal but which I must describe if the reader is to judge its results.

[1] *The Criterion*, July 1938.

During August and the first half of September 1937, I isolated myself with the Chinese text of the three books of Confucius, Ta Hio, Analects and the Unwavering Middle, and that of Mencius, together with an enormously learned crib but no dictionary. You can't pack Morrison or Giles in a suit case.

When I disagreed with the crib or was puzzled by it I had only the look of the characters and the radicals to go on from. And my contention is that the learned have known too much and seen a little too little. Such of 'em as knew Fenollosa profited nothing.

Without knowing at least the nature of ideogram I don't think anyone can suspect what is wrong with their current translations. Even with what I have known for some time I did not sufficiently ponder it. The Ta Hio is of textures far more mixed than Pauthier's version. I see no reason to doubt the statement that it was a family possession, and that the actual bamboo tablets had got out of order and some of them lost, any more than I doubt the ethnographic evidence of the portrait of Confucius, as likely to be authentic as any bust of a Caesar.

This diversity is not due to any failure of unity in the meaning of the Ta Hio. No one has brought out the contrasts of style from the magnificence of citation to the terseness and lucidity of Kung's statements. Kung was an anthologist and a shortener.

With Pauthier under my hand for 23 or more years and the Confucian matter in that form long familiar I had never read through Pauthier's Mencius. In the French he seemed merely prolix and inferior. The original gives ample reason for the four books appearing together, and my title is for a reason. Mencius nowhere turns against Kung, all of Mencius is implicit in Kung's doctrine. This doctrine is one, indivisible, a nature extending to every detail as the nature of being oak or maple extends to every part of the oak tree or maple. Mencius has gone into detail as, let us say, Van Buren goes into detail from a Jeffersonian basis.

By taking the 'ethics of Mencius' I include the ethics of Kung. Yet if I tried to ascribe some of the opinions here about to be exposed, to Kungfutsu I might be accused of trying to modernise them or of seeing too much in the original text. In Mencius several cardinal lines are explicit, the most squirmy Ersatz-monger will have difficulty in worming away from them.

What I mean by not looking at the text can be shown by the very nice little story of Kung in discouragement saying–'It's no go. We aren't getting anywhere. I think I'll get a raft and float about at sea for a little. And the one of you chaps who will go along, will be Yu.'

The elected disciple throws out his chest at the compliment, and Kung continues, 'Yu likes danger better than I do. But he wouldn't bother about getting the logs.'

Implying I think that logs are used to make rafts. Nevertheless the translator in question talks about 'exercise of judgment', losing we believe the simple and Lincoln-like humour of the original. (2)

For the LOGS are there in the ideogram very clearly. Whatever later centuries may have done about political platforms etc., and the raft ideogram appears to show a log and claw and a child, (3)

hinting sylvan (if riparian) origin.

I am not denying certain ambiguities in the text or in certain statements in ideogram but there are also certain utterly unambiguous uses of ideogram. You must distinguish between the inclusive and the ambiguous.

Ambiguity and inclusiveness are far from the same.

The specialist will often want a more particular statement inside the inclusive one, but the including statement can be perfectly categoric, in the sense of having its frontiers clearly defined. And this is not in the least the same as straddling the category's fence.

In ascribing ideas to Mang Tsze I shall limit myself to what seem to me utterly clear cases of statement. Any borderline cases will be noted as such, and where I am stumped I shall ascribe no meaning.

I do, on the other hand, object to under-translation. I do *not* think that I have a better mind than Confucius. Mencius' great merit is that *he* did not think he had a better mind than Confucius. (There are numerous cases recorded of Confucians refusing to be had by such suggestions re themselves.) When I get a good idea from the ideograms I do not think it is my idea. If by any chance my ideas are better than those of the Man of Tsau's offspring, then, of course, my tablet should be placed in the Temple and my views replace those of earlier sages. But I consider it unlikely that occasion for this will arise. What matters is the true view. If my views are better than those in the ideogram, pray do accept them, but accept also the burden of proving it.

The ethics of Mencius are Confucian. The spelling *Mencius* is all right if you take count of the way some people pronounce latin. Kung-fu-tsu. Chung Ne, Kung, Confucius all refer to the man of Tsau's son. Nobody now in Anglo-Saxon countries pronounces a *c* as *tsz*.

Serious approach to Chinese doctrines must start with wiping off any idea that they are all merely chinese. Mencius had an holy fear

---

[1] Note similar process in meaning in the Greek ὕλη uncut forest, and the stuff of which a thing is made, matter as a principle of being.

of cranks and idiots, and nearly all the most recent forms of idiocy had already pullulated in his time, among sectaries of one sort or another. As to subversiveness, the editor of the *Criterion* may for all I know still be waiting for me to review a volume of Chinese philosophy which I found too rancid to mention. After finding the text too rancid for use I turned to the introduction. (The translator has merits of efficiency, his English must have been as slippery as the original, and in this introduction he delighted me with the statement that all except the most hard-boiled Confucians had swallowed his author.)

Thanks to nature, destiny, or Kung fu tsu, I did not swallow him.

Nevertheless before we can have any serious discussion of Chinese philosophy we must agree on terminology. We must decide more clearly than has, I think, yet been done, which ideograms correspond to what terms of good Latin. *Directio voluntatis.* Dante's view upon rectitude rimes certainly with that of Mencius.

Here (Analects IV, IV) is luminous doctrine reiterated in Mencius.

4

Tsin Sin, part 1, XXXIII, 3.

I cannot think that the translators have been careful enough in correlating their terms either with those having great contents and elaborate precisions in Christian (catholic) theology,[1] or with those of Greek philosophy. Apart from Latin (and Greek) theologians I doubt if we have any occidental theologians. We have a word 'sincere', said to date from Roman luxury trade in faked marble. The Chinese have a sign which is translated by this word of English. But the Chinese sign implicates quite definitely naming the emotion or condition.

5

Which you can tie up if you like to the first chapter of Leone Vivante's *Originalità nel pensiero.* There are two ideograms, one middle-heart,

[1] Since writing this, though not necessarily altering the mentioned condition of things, Routledge announces 'Soothill and Hedous' Dictionary of Chinese-Buddhist terms', and Motoschiro's Greek-Japanese dictionary has been published.

which might be translatable by sincere in its now current meaning, and this other sign: the *word* and the action of fixing or *perfecting* (just given, ideogram 5).

All of which comes out of the Confucian answer when asked about the first act of government: 'call things by their right names'.

There is a third sign recurring and again recurring, of the man who stands by his word.

The conditions of my experiment, if you will consider them implied not being distracted or led off into the mazes of the dictionary with its infinite (i.e. unbounded) interest and interests. Having been three times through the whole text and having perforce to look at the ideograms and try to work out the unfamiliar ones from their bases, I should have now a better idea of the whole and the unity of the doctrine, at any rate I believe that I have, and that the constants have been impressed on my eye.

Clearly what they translate virtue is the greek *arete*

it is not mediaeval *virtu*, though it is radically *virtus* from *vir*. It is, in Chinese, the whole man and the whole man's contents. This is or should be impressed on the eye.

The sick part of our philosophy is 'Greek splitting', a term which I will shortly re-explain. The Confucian is totalitarian. When the aims of Shun and Wan were set together, though after a thousand years interval, they were as two halves of a tally stick.[1] (Even the greatly learned translator has translated this 'seal' in the text with a foot-note to say 'tally-stick'.)

[1] See Canto LXXVII. Ed.

10

That things can be known a hundred generations distant, implied no supernatural powers, it did imply the durability of natural process which alone gives a possibility for science.

I take it the Mencian affirmation is of a permanent human process. There is no reason for me to tone that down with the phrase 'I take it'. The doctrine is clear. But the effects of the doctrine are startling when Mr. D. tells me he suspects Soothill of modernising his version of Analects.

Mencius distinguishes a tax from a share, he is for an economy of abundance. Riches are due to exchange. The man who wants to lower the standard of living should end as an earthworm. Simple-lifers are half-wits. All this is perfectly clear and utterly non-semitic in the original text.

The semitic is excess. The semitic is against ANY scale of values. The Church in the middle ages evolved an hierarchy of values.

It is mere shouting for the home team to pretend that the so-called Christian virtues were invented A.D. 1 to A.D. 32 in Judea.

'If a man died in a ditch Shun felt it as if he had killed him.' This of the Emperor Shun.

'Is there', said Mang Tsze, 'any difference between killing a man with a club and a sword?'

'No,' said King Hwuy.

'Is there any difference between killing him with a sword and with a system of government?'

This is not the Chemin de Velours. There are perfectly good reasons why this philosophy does not get more publicity.

The cabinet ministers who can face it? I know of none in London or Paris.

Greek philosophy was almost an attack upon nature. That sentence cannot stand as it is, but may serve to disturb excessive complacencies.

The school of Kung included intelligence without cutting it from its base.

You can no more fake in this company than you can fake in a science laboratory. But you are not split into fragments. The curse of European thought appeared between the Nichomachean notes and the Magna Moralia. Aristotle (as recorded in the earlier record) began his list of mental processes with TeXne, $\tau\acute{\epsilon}\chi\nu\eta$, and the damned college parrots omitted it. This was done almost before the poor bloke was cold in his coffin.

Greek philosophy, and European in its wake, degenerated into an attack on mythology and mythology is, perforce, totalitarian. I mean that it tries to find an expression for reality without over-simplification, and without scission, you can examine a living animal, but at a certain point dissection is compatible only with death. I believe Leibniz felt this, and that Gemisto Pleton felt it.

Without knowing the Book of Rites it would be foolish to talk on Mencius' position in this regard further than to note what is actually said in his writing. There is an allusion to banishing the spirits of the fields and grain and electing others. I doubt if this is compatible with pejorative superstition. The point relevant to my title is that at no point does the Confucio-Mencian ethic or philosophy splinter and split away from organic nature. The man who pulled up his corn because it didn't grow fast enough, and then told his family he had assisted the grain, is Mencius' parable. The nature of things is good. The *way* is the process of nature, *one*, in the sense that the chemist and biologist so find it. Any attempt to to deal with it as split, is due to ignorance and a failure in the direction of the will.

Whence the Mencian does not try to avoid concrete application. Marx and Hegel break down when their ideas come to be worked out in conduct. My contention is that you can quite clearly judge what Mencius would have thought of specific situations in our time, and to support this I shall now quote, first from his talks with King Hwuy of Leang:

> Your dogs and swine eat the food of men and you do not make any restrictive arrangements.
> Your people are dying from famine on the roads and you do not know how to issue stores for them. When they die you say it is owing to the year. How does this differ from killing a man and saying it was not I but the weapon?

and a few lines lower:

> Is there any difference between killing a man with the sword or with a system of government? Beasts devour one another . . . there are fat horses in your stables (while people die of famine) . . . this is called leading on beasts to devour men.

In another place he defines 'leading on the earth to devour men', that is in a prince's wars for more territory. 'In the *Spring and Autumn* there are no righteous wars, some are better than others.' Spring and Autumn is the title of Confucius' history text book.

I have found very curious opinions as to Kung's formalism. L. Vivante recently showed me 'a horrible reference book' as he called it, where the condensing ass had cited nothing but details of Kung's behaviour and several rules of formality.

CONFUCIUS AND MENCIUS

Anyone who had read the text of Kung and Mencius in even a passable translation would know that at no point and on no occasion do such rules ask one to overstep common sense. There are times for politeness and times for prompt action. Discretion in perceiving the when is basic in Confucianism.

There are two elements in the 'rules of propriety'.

A. the expression of finer feelings and a resultant standard of behaviour on occasions when no graver and more impelling circumstance demands their abrogation. This is the permanent part. There is (B) the part relative to the times of Confucius. Certain ceremonies served, I think, as passports, such as the complicated Guard's salute. Today a man not a guardsman would give himself away if he tried it without preparation.

When you hadn't a telegraph, some of these ceremonies would have served to show the authenticity and also the nature of the man who turned up at the frontier.

The three years mourning is scarcely in the New England blood. It was not universal in China. Mencius justifies it as being more civil and human than allowing one's dead to lie in ditches and be chewed by stray animals. From which he dates the idea of having any burial customs at all. There is no doubt that Latins and Nordics differ greatly in their feeling for funerals. This is not my prime concern, nor do I introduce it save to protest against taking the Chinese texts on the subject out of focus and out of the Mencian sense of their origin. His ideas on where to begin improving the social order are more to my point and our time.

> Therefore an intelligent ruler will regulate the livelihood of the people, so as to make sure that they shall have sufficient to serve their parents, and sufficient wherewith to support their wives and children: that in good years they shall be abundantly satisfied, and in bad years shall escape danger of perishing.
>
> Only men of education can maintain a steady heart without a fixed livelihood.

The steady or fixed heart is part of the *directio voluntatis*. The commendable have it, and work inside themselves, the uncommendable look out for lucky chances. Permit me a longer quotation from (Book VII) *Tsin Sin*, i, Chapter 22 and 23.

> At fifty warmth cannot be maintained without silks and at seventy flesh is necessary to satisfy the appetite. Persons not kept warm and supplied with food are said to be starved and famished, but among the people of King Wan there were no aged who were starved and famished.
>
> Let it be seen to that their fields of grain and hemp are well culti-

vated, and make the taxes on them light . . . so that the people may be made rich.

Let it be seen that the people USE (caps. mine) their resources of food seasonably and expend their wealth on the ceremonies, and they won't be able to exhaust it at that.

The 'ceremonies' here would cover the equivalents for Greek drama, and the outlay for Latin processions at the feast of the Madonna, etc. They are of the amenities.

People cannot live without water and fire. Knock at a door in the dusk of evening no one will deny you water and fire. . . .

When pulse and grain are as abundant as water and fire, how shall the people be other than humane.

(Here the ideogram for ARETE, entire man.)

 9

The question of tax is here specified. Other passages clearly define the root difference between share and impost. 'Nothing is worse than a fixed tax.' A fixed tax on grain is in bad years a tyranny, a tithe proper, no tyranny. If, as he brings out against the simple lifers, a country cannot do without potters it certainly cannot do without governors. As for an emperor tilling his fields, it is mere shop front, no one ever expected him to make his own clothes as well, in fact, 'is', he asks, 'the imperial function the only business compatible with doing one's ploughing, potters and carpenters being exempt?'

In the conditions of 500 and 400 B.C. if you cut the tithe lower than 10 per cent you could live only as the 'dog and camp-fire people'. If you raised it above 10 per cent for traders and people in the centre of empire and above the NINE FIELDS share system for rurals and border folk, you would have tyranny.

The analogy of the nine fields system to Rossoni's *ammassi* in present-day Italy is notable.

It is OF the permanence of nature that honest men, even if endowed with no special brilliance, with no talents above those of straightness and honesty, come repeatedly to the same answers in ethics, without need of borrowing each other's ideas.

Shun and Wan had a thousand years between them and when their wills were compared they were as two halves of a tally stick.

 11   10

From Kung to Mencius a century, and to St. Ambrose another six or so hundred years, and a thousand years to St. Antonino, and they are as parts of one pattern, as wood of a single tree.

The 'Christian virtues' are THERE in the emperors who had responsibility in their hearts and willed the good of the people; who saw that starvation can gnaw through more than the body and eat into the spirit; who saw, above all, that in so far as governing the people went, it begins with a livelihood, and that all talk of morals before that livelihood is attained, is sheer bunkum and rotten hypocrisy.

The level of civilisation recorded in these ideograms is higher than anything in the near eastern tradition.

It is only in the evolved Roman sense of proportion that we find equal sanity.

There is a root difference between an immoderate demand or a law which takes no account of the nature of things and the Mencian hierarchy of values.

'Our' hierarchy of values shines from the Divina Commedia, or one can at least use that work as a convenient indicator of it. Both the catholic mediaeval and the Chinese hierarchies and senses of proportion are infinitely removed from semitic immoderation. When Europe flopped from the state of mind of St. Ambrose and St. Antonino into pre-Christian barbarisms we suffered a not inconsiderable setback. The thing we flopped back to is unpleasant. It was and still filthily is usurer's measure. Let us try to avoid words that could give rise to partisanship and say, you can no more consider Western civilisation without the Roman component than you can consider the Orient and leave out the Chinese Imperial order, which already in Kung's time recognised an historic process, including the alternating periods of order and of confusion.

The ethic of Kung and Mencius is not registered in words of irresponsible fanatics. The semitic component in Christianity is anarchic and irresponsible. Take the record on its face value, it is of a sect in a rebellious and irresponsible province, and for a kingdom, specifically in the words of its founder, not of this world but the next.

The Christian ideal has been recognised as something different, something NOT evolved without Constantine and Justinian and those who built it with them. Civilisation consists in the establishment of an hierarchy of values, it cannot remain as a mere division between the damned and the saved ... with alternate wailing and hysterical merriment.

Mencius' sense of responsibility is omnipresent. It is in man to himself. Governing of the Empire was specifically NOT among the sage's desires, or at least not regarded by him as a simple pleasure. Out of office he attends to his own internal order, in office to that of as much of the state as is entrusted to him. But at no moment is he irresponsible. His desideratum: to gather and teach the most intelligent of his contemporaries, unless by good fortune he find a sage from whom he can learn, but in any case not to start teaching prematurely and not to teach his own ignorance.

The alibi of the irresponsible is often a false one, those who say they can do nothing because they lack talent, could at least refrain from deleterious action. This phase of Mencian doctrine has, I think, been grossly exaggerated in our superstition as to the nature of Confucianism. It is set out as the MINIMUM and universal requirement, not as a maximum.

The earlier *politica* of *ammassi* was as follows: in a square divided in nine equal parts, the central one was cultivated by the eight surrounding families, and its produce went to the administration, this was commuted to a ten per cent on central or as you might say in the metropolitan areas where 'things aren't as simple as all that'. In irregular country a just equivalence of what would be equal measuring of flat acreage.

Marketing customs similarly equitable. The profit motive is specifically denounced. I mean that you will get no more accurate translation of the ideograms in Mencius' talk with King Hwey than 'profit-motive'.

Mercantilism is incompatible with Mencius. Cheap evasion and evasiveness are impossible anywhere near him.

Naturally men love life. Mencius professes a taste for fish and bears' trotters, but there is an order of preference. Some things are worth more than others. Life is not above rectitude.

If anyone in calm mind will compare the Four Classics with the greatly publicised Hebrew scriptures he will find that the former are a record of civilised men, the latter the annals of a servile and nomadic tribe that had not evolved into agricultural order. It is with the greatest and most tortuous difficulty that the Sunday School has got a moral teaching out of these sordid accounts of lechery, trickery and isolated acts of courage, very fine and such as could be paralleled in the annals of Mohawks and Iroquois. Any sort of objectivity, taking the record as it stands, must arrive at something like this conclusion.

Jehovah is a semitic cuckoo's egg laid in the European nest. He has no connection with Dante's god. That later concept of supreme Love and Intelligence is certainly not derived from the Old Testament.

Numerous invasions of China have destroyed several strata of civilisation, but this in no way detracts from the Mencian wisdom, nor does even Mr. Lin Yutang's brilliant picture of Chinese folly, which latter is a portrayal of universal stupidity.

In every country idiots treat the branch as the root. If you deprive Confucianism of its essentials among which are the sense of proportion and timeliness, if you take isolated remarks and cut them off wholly and utterly from the rest of the four books, naturally the text can be quoted in defence of five hundred follies.

The Rules of Propriety are to be observed under certain circumstances and at the proper times, obedience and respect have their limits.

Some sort of time focus must be applied.

It may quite well be that Confucius and Mencius are a hormone that could be more vitally effective in the West today than in a China busily engaged in livening up the business of the Acceptance Houses. Apropos which I understand that a living Kung has stated in private conversation that his Most Illustrious Ancestor is now more regarded here than in Pekin. Foreign loans for munitions do not enter the Analects.

When Pih Kwei stated that his irrigation system was better than the Emperor Yu's, Mencius pointed out that the latter had led off the excessive flood water to the sea 'according to the natural law of waters', whereas Pih Kwei had merely dumped his into a neighbouring state. Mencius declined to regard this bit of *scaltrezza* as an improvement.

I have no doubt that if the Acceptance Houses succeed in piling up a sufficiency of Chinese debt to Europe and then induce hefty or half-starved occidentals to try to collect it, even China might wake and the great final and definitive armageddon, yellow peril, etc. become as actual as our American civil war was, because of the South's debts to our (N.Y.) city.

Naturally if you neglect the root of the Doctrine the rest will wither, and a neglect of its basic wisdom is undoubtedly apparent among the less wise Chinese.

Neither that country nor any other has ever suffered a glut of sages.

'Dead!' said Mencius on hearing that P'wan-shing Kwoh had received a high government post in Ts'e. After execution, a disciple asked M. 'How did you know this would happen?' 'He was a busy fellow,' said Mencius, 'with a little talent. Just enough to get himself condemned to the scaffold.'

The 'busy' exists in the four classics with just the shade that has given it a derogative sense in the argot of Edgar Wallace's crooks. Not meaning 'cop' in Chinese but indicating why the crook calls the policeman a busy. A better word than busybody and more aromatic.

If the reader jumps every verb meaning CHANGE or MOVE, if he remains blind to the verbs meaning RENEWAL and neglects every allusion to 'changing what is not good', naturally he can reduce the rest of

Mencius and Confucius to a static and inactive doctrine, inactive enough to please even the bank of Basel and our western monopolists. But this would mean excising a great deal of the original text.

In fact it can't be done. You cannot so ignore the bright ideogram for the highest music,

 12[1]

the sign of metamorphosis,  13

or the constantly recurring symbol which looks to me like the back of boat with rudder,

 14[2]

and might lead one to think that it emerged from association with river traffic. Danger ever present to the autodidact as it comes from representation of a foot with footprints.

This constant pageant of the sun, of process, of the tree with its 'small, white, small' (ideogram 12) does not give any clear-headed spectator the feeling of deadness and stasis.

There are categories of ideogram not indicated as such in the dictionaries, but divided really by the feel of their forms, the twisted as evil, the stunted, the radiant.

The mountain itself has a 'nature' and that nature is to come forth in trees, though men cut and sheep nibble.

Tsin Sin, pt. 1, xxxiii, 2, is our solidest join with Dante. 'What is the scholar's aim?' (Scholar here being also officer.) There follows one of the shortest verses, '*Mang tse said*', then the sign for '*raise*' and the sign for '*will*'.

(vide ideogram 4.)

They translate it 'exalt the aim'. This is definitely Dante's *directio voluntatis*, with no ambiguity possible. The top of the *will* sign is the scholar-officer sign, and its base the heart. The lifting up is structural.

---

[1] The central stroke in lower half of this ideogram should be straight not hooked.

[2] Used in composition as part of a sign.

Nevertheless Dante's 'god above' exists in an ideogram. No one with any visual sense can fail to be affected by the way the strokes move in these characters.

The 'above', Plato's power above the heaven; lateral motion; the tree trunks; the man who stands by his word; the qualities of these signs are basic and no one who does not pereceive them can read ideogram save as an ape.

Man, man, man, humanity all over the page, land and trees.

The people who take up one point and spoil the totality 'neglecting a hundred other points' are un-Mencian. They 'lift up and grind one, and hang up and cover a hundred'.

Condensing from the Third book of Mencius (the T'ang Wan Kung) and from other passages, I find the belief that 'without government services distribution and use of resources will be insufficient'. I find definite statement as to what conduces to borrowing, and its results. I find an interesting series of five characters, the meaning of which someone may say that I force.

The first contains the knife radical, plus pearls or precious shell, and certainly means draw an outline, make a pattern of (it is used also as a particle 'derivative from that'). It is followed by wealth, use, not enough.

It might apply to production, but it appears to me to apply equally to the distribution. The 'use' is utterly undodgeable. It does not mean exhaust.

'If he levy a ground tax and *do not* tax goods or enforce proper regulations *without* levying tax. . . . Merchants will store goods in his market.' I.e. one OR the other not both.

All through there is the sense of need of a proper (not an improper) income for administrative expenses.

'No tax out of season.' 'No better system than mutual aid, none WORSE than a fixed tax.' A tithe is another matter.

Government's job is to feed the people, that is its FIRST job. (This not to be confused with Kung's 'get the right names'. That 'Ch'ing Ming' is the first step toward conditioning the government to do its work.)

Anyone who mistakes Kung or Mencius for a materialist is a plain unadulterated idiot. Their philosophy is not in the least materialist, it is volitionist.

(1) Arms and defences, (2) food, (3) the faith of the people, if they must be given up, be it in this order.

'Let Mulberry trees be planted about the homesteads with their five *mow* (land measure) and persons of fifty may be clothed with silk. In keeping fowls pigs and swine let not their times of breeding be neglected, and persons of seventy may eat flesh. Let there not be taken away the time that is proper for the cultivation of the farm with its hundred mow, and the family of 8 mouths that is supported by it shall not suffer from hunger. Let there be careful attention to education in schools. . . .'

All this is on an infinitely higher level than Mosaic *lex talionis*. It is all out, over, and above the balderdash that was inflicted on my generation of christians.

I am not inveighing against the best Christian ethic or against the quality of Western mind shown in Bishop Grosseteste's treatise on light. I am against the disorderly tendencies, the anarchy and barbarism which appear in poor christian teaching, fanaticism and superstition; against the lack of proportion and failure of objectivity when dealing with texts extant, and, naturally, against the insularity which credits Byron with having invented a kind of writing that had been used by Pulci.

But if we are ever to communicate with the orient, or cohabit a planet rapidly becoming more quickly circumnavigable, had we not better try to find the proportions, try perhaps to collect some of our own better writers (of the ages) to present to our oriental contemporaries, rather than offer them an unmixed export of grossness, barbarities, stove pipes and machine guns? Several young men in Tokio seem pleased to meet Cavalcanti. I have no doubt that even the Ten Remnants[1] could have found something admirable in our tradition had it been more tactfully shown them.

Lady Hosie's introduction to a recent reprint tells us that the Four Classics 'have been relegated to University study and are no longer the main preoccupation of Chinese schools'. She dates the essay 1937, which year has brought the natural consequence of unusual idiocy in the form of Japanese invasion. If China had got to this point, naturally there would be an invasion, and quite naturally some Chinese would, as they do, hold the view that such an invasion is to be welcomed.

Lady Hosie, M.A. Cantab., regards the degradation as temporary. Tuan Szetsun is old. Certainly a nucleus of sanity exists in China. The West needs the Confucian injection.

The Four Books have survived Ch'in Shih Huang (the gorilla who ordered these books to be destroyed) and China was not effaced by that pimple.

The blots of my correction are not dry on this quotation from Lady Hosie before a still later bulletin confirms an old belief to the effect that any order in China proceeds from a Confucian centre. Chiang Kai Shek 'the Christian general' and the one man who got a little order out of chaos took to using Confucian slogans a little too late, thereby confirming another text of the philosopher.

---

[1] (Ten remnants. A title given to several elderly gentlemen of the Empress Dowager's time, now, alas, disappearing.)

I am not in this essay trying to give a modern Chinese feeling about the effects of such Confucianism as survived in China in 1900, and Mr. Lin Yutang will probably admit that the citizen of a chaos which has long lacked a certain code of ideas and perceptions is bound to see that code differently from the citizen of a chaos wherein such ideas have long been abused.

I am putting the original text against semitic insanity and against Socrates. If the shoving of it into University study in China were intended to bring it with fresh impact on to more thoughtful minds? ... if ... but was it? and is, in any case, the adolescent any fitter to receive it than the child?

Obviously Mr. Yutang knows its worst side–Obviously certain practices come to US dated China 500 B.C. and we brush very lightly over them. They have not affected our lives and cannot. Seven inch planks for one's coffin or cremation is all pretty much one to us.

In any case there are or were practices. Soaking our occidental selves in the quite clearly illuminated principles of Confucius would hardly bring *us* out into certain Chinese forms. In fact, for us to take up odd rites would be, as it were 'sacrificing to a spirit which does not belong to us', and therefore against Mencian and Confucian good taste, anyhow.

I do not see the abuse as inherent in the principle of Confucius, whereas the semitic is schizophrenic essentially. People who talk about 'something deeper in their nature' which laid the Chinese open to Buddhism, seem to me to have failed lamentably to LOOK at the Mencian text.

In any case I am dealing with ethics and not with cosmology, imaginary, pneumatic, or 'scientific', granting that Mencius hadn't the Western female to deal with and that the captious may think he over simplifies in this domain, or rather avoids it, though he can't be said to deny its importance. But the abuses of the 'system', mentioned by descriptive writers, are incompatible with the root. This I don't propose to argue save with someone who has passed the Pythagorean time of silence. The putting order inside oneself first, cannot be omitted from Confucian-Mencian practice if that is to be valid. Any other course is sheer fake.

Faith without works is fake, and the Mencian suggestion is that one should act right before formulating the axiom tried in act, and thereafter follow it.

The ethic of Confucius and Mencius is a Nordic ethic, a Nordic morale, if it has been boggit in *laissez faire* and tropical indolence that cannot be blamed on its shape. It is not quietistic. It is concentrated in the Mencian parable: 'An Archer having missed the bullseye does NOT turn round and blame someone else. He seeks the cause in himself.'[1]

MANG TSZE

Mencius is very difficult to summarise, yet as Legge cannot be suspected of collusion with credit cranks and new orthologic economists I add a few sentences and phrases from his version:

'Resources arising from government,' that is to say the increment of association. So far as I know this is the earliest clear formulation of it.

'If a man can prevent the evils of hunger and thirst from being any evils to his mind . . .'

'Hostile states do not correct one another.'

'The way of the people is this: if they have a certain livelihood they will have a fixed heart. If they have not a fixed livelihood . . . there is nothing they will not do in the way of . . . moral deflection.'

'What leisure have they to cultivate propriety and righteousness?'

'Only men of education are able to maintain a fixed heart without a certain livelihood.'

To treat the needy as criminals is not governing decently, it is merely trapping them.

PART FIVE
America

PART FIVE

'What I feel about Walt Whitman'[1]

From this side of the Atlantic I am for the first time able to read Whitman, and from the vantage of my education and–if it be permitted a man of my scant years – my world citizenship: I see him America's poet. The only Poet before the artists of the Carmen-Hovey period, or better, the only one of the conventionally recognised 'American Poets' who is worth reading.

He *is* America. His crudity is an exceeding great stench, but it *is* America. He is the hollow place in the rock that echoes with his time. He *does* 'chant the crucial stage' and he is the 'voice triumphant'. He is disgusting. He is an exceedingly nauseating pill, but he accomplishes his mission.

Entirely free from the renaissance humanist ideal of the complete man or from the Greek idealism, he is content to be what he is, and he is his time and his people. He is a genius because he has vision of what he is and of his function. He knows that he is a beginning and not a classically finished work.

I honour him for he prophesied me while I can only recognise him as a forebear of whom I ought to be proud.

In America there is much for the healing of the nations, but woe unto him of the cultured palate who attempts the dose.

As for Whitman, I read him (in many parts) with acute pain, but when I write of certain things I find myself using his rhythms. The expression of certain things related to cosmic consciousness seems tainted with this maramis.

I am (in common with every educated man) an heir of the ages and I demand my birth-right. Yet if Whitman represented his time in language acceptable to one accustomed to my standard of intellectual-artistic living he would belie his time and nation. And yet I am but one of his 'ages and ages' encrustations' or to be exact an encrustation of the next age. The vital part of my message, taken from the sap and fibre of America, is the same as his.

Mentally I am a Walt Whitman who has learned to wear a collar and a dress shirt (although at times inimical to both). Personally I might be very glad to conceal my relationship to my spiritual father and brag

[1] 1909.

about my more congenial ancestry–Dante, Shakespeare, Theocritus, Villon, but the descent is a bit difficult to establish. And, to be frank, Whitman is to my fatherland (*Patriam quam odi et amo* for no uncertain reasons) what Dante is to Italy and I at my best can only be a strife for a renaissance in America of all the lost or temporarily mislaid beauty, truth, valour, glory of Greece, Italy, England and all the rest of it.

And yet if a man has written lines like Whitman's to the *Sunset Breeze* one has to love him. I think we have not yet paid enough attention to the deliberate artistry of the man, not in details but in the large.

I am immortal even as he is, yet with a lesser vitality as I am the more in love with beauty (If I really do love it more than he did). Like Dante he wrote in the 'vulgar tongue', in a new metric. The first great man to write in the language of his people.

Et ego Petrarca in lingua vetera scribo, and in a tongue my people understood not.

It seems to me I should like to drive Whitman into the old world. I sledge, he drill–and to scourge America with all the old beauty. (For Beauty *is* an accusation) and with a thousand thongs from Homer to Yeats, from Theocritus to Marcel Schwob. This desire is because I am young and impatient, were I old and wise I should content myself in seeing and saying that these things will come. But now, since I am by no means sure it would be true prophecy, I am fain set my own hand to the labour.

It is a great thing, reading a man to know, not 'His Tricks are not as yet my Tricks, but I can easily make them mine' but 'His message is my message. We will see that men hear it.'

The Jefferson–Adams Letters as a
Shrine and a Monument[1]

O ur national life might, at least provisorily, be divided into
four periods:
    1. American civilisation, 1760 to 1830.
  2. The period of thinning, of mental impoverishment, scission between life of the mind and life of the nation, say 1830 to 1860.
  3. The period of despair, civil war as hiatus, 1870 to 1930. The division
between the temper, thickness, richness of the mental life of Henry
Adams, and Henry James, and that of say U. S. Grant, McKinley,
Harding, Coolidge, and Hoover.
  4. The possibilities of revival, starting perhaps with a valorisation
of our cultural heritage, not merely as something lost in dim retrospect, a tombstone, tastily carved, whereon to shed dry tears or upon
which to lay a few withered violets, in the manner of, let us say, the
late Henry (aforementioned) Adams. The query being: should we lose
or go on losing our own revolution (of 1776–1830) by whoring after
exotics, Muscovite or European?

'As monument' or I should prefer to say as a still workable dynamo,
left us from the real period, nothing surpasses the Jefferson correspondence. Or to reduce it to convenient bulk concentrating on the
best of it, and its fullest implications, nothing surpasses the evidence
that CIVILISATION WAS in America, than the series of letters exchanged
between Jefferson and John Adams, during the decade of reconciliation after their disagreements.

It is probable that I could pick one crow a week with the American
university system 'for the rest of my natural', but two immediate
crows are quite obvious, one with the modus of teaching history
omitting the most significant documents, and second the mode of
teaching literature and/or 'American literature', omitting the most
significant documents, and assuming that the life of a nation's letters
is restricted mostly to second-rate fiction.

From 1760 to 1826 two civilised men lived and to a considerable
extent reigned in America. They did not feel themselves isolated
phenomena. They were not by any means shrunk into a clique or
dependent on mutual admiration, or on clique estimation. They both

---

[1] *North American Review* (Winter 1937–1938).

wrote an excellent prose which has not, so far as I know, been surpassed in our fatherland, though Henry James had a style of his own (narrative) which was fit for a different purpose.

For the purpose and/or duration of this essay I shall define a civilised man as one who can give a serious answer to a serious question and whose circle of mental reference is not limited to mere acquisition of profit. The degree of his civilisation will depend both on the depth of his thought and on the spread of his curiosity. He may have made absolutely no special study of anything outside his profession, but his thoughts on that profession will have been such that his thoughts about anything else will not be completely inane.

In 170 years the United States have at no time contained a more civilised 'world' than that comprised by the men to whom Adams and Jefferson wrote and from whom they received private correspondence. A history of American Literature that omits the letters of the founders and memoirs or diaries of J. Q. Adams and Martin Van Buren is merely nonsense. Without competence in matters pertaining to Benjamin Franklin, I should nevertheless hazard the opinion that his public writing will be found slithery and perhaps cheap in comparison. He had not integrity of the word. At least on occasions it deserted him.

From early 'bending of the twig' it is impossible for me to think of certain books save as parts of curricula. Certain books should not be in curricula. Other books belong in curricula. The Adams-Jefferson writings ought to be in curricula.

If we are a nation, we must have a national mind. Frobenius escaped both the fiddling term 'culture' and rigid 'Kultur' by recourse to Greek, he used 'Paideuma' with a meaning that is necessary to almost all serious discussion of such subjects as that now under discussion. His 'Paideuma' means the mental formation, the inherited habits of thought, the conditionings, aptitudes of a given race or time.

In Italy there is current the adjective 'anti-storico' to describe unlikely proposals; ideologies hung in a vacuum or contrary to the natural order of events as conditioned by race, time and geography.

Without Frobenius north of the Alps and the Mediterranean sanity south of them our thoughts would, I heartily believe, lack some of its pleasantest pastures.

As Americans we are neither Teutonic nor in any strict sense Mediterranean, though we should be fools to neglect either element of private nutrition.

As far as I remember U.S. school histories, they start with Columbus and/or in another sense with the Pilgrims. None of them starts with the Encyclopaedists. Is the term heard even by University Undergraduates?

Our national culture can be perhaps better defined from the Jefferson letters than from any other three sources, and mainly to its bene-fice. I don't think they have been analysed very clearly in themselves, and I am not sure that anyone has tried very coherently to relate them to anything else.

No one has thought them perfection. Jefferson has been abused as an incredible optimist. I am not going to concede much to these possible accusations.

Henry Adams with a familial and inherited, but very very discrete chip on his somewhat feminine shoulder lacked, on his own implicit, but never explicit confession, the one quality needful for judging action. Adams never guessed right. Take him in London during his father's embassy. He never foresaw.

It was not for nothing that Quincy Adams took up astrology, not anthropology. The discrete descendant wanted a science, almost a mathematical science of history—overlooking, or does he specifically say he didn't overlook, the impossibility of laboratory methods. Take it that he saw the shallowness of historic aimlessness in his time, his first urge is to rectify it by mathematical measurement. And thereby he loses the chance of examining a great many phenomena which were and still are available for any patient man's contemplation.

I am not leaving my subject. You can not 'place' the Jefferson correspondence save by postulating some axes of reference, and by some defined method of mensuration.

Frobenius outrages the English because he agrees with Aquinas that nothing is without efficient cause.

Before trying to establish type-cycles and accelerated rhythms in history it is advisable to gather at least a few data, and if the urge towards rhythmic analysis obsesses one, it might even be possible to study certain recurrences.

Nevertheless, the Flaubertian concept of 'l'histoire morale contem-poraine' arose not from mathematics but from a perception of paucity. A perception of the paucity registered in historians, the shallowness of their analysis of motivation, their inadequate measure-ments of causality.

Stendhal, Michelet, Flaubert, the Goncourts differ as individuals, but they were all of them on a trail, they wanted to set down an intelligible record of life in which things happened.

The mere statement that so and so made a war, or so and so re-formed or extended an empire is much too much in the vague.

Frobenius taking things back to supposedly 'simpler' conditions does try to sort out tendencies and predispositions. He dissociates modes of living. There are twenty volumes waiting translation. The patient reader must allow me to have them there as possible footnote; per-mitting me for a moment an anthropologist's dissociation of two systems which have functioned in Europe. Without which dissociation

one can not 'place' the Encyclopaedists or 'come to Jefferson', save as
isolated phenomenon sprung versatile, voluble, out of chaos. Polu-
metis, many-minded, distracting, discussable, but minus origins.

A Mediterranean state of mind, state of intelligence, modus of order
'arose' out of Sparta perhaps more than from Athens, it developed a
system of graduations, an hierarchy of values among which was, perhaps above all other, 'order'. As a mental and intellectual filing system
it certainly did not fall with Romulus Augustulus in A.D. 476.

In fact the earlier parts of it we know almost as palimpsest. We begin
to find it in Constantine, after A.D. 300, and we can carry on via Justinian, after 500, Charlemagne, Gratian, in St. Ambrose, and Duns
Scotus. This, you see, is by no means confusing a paideuma or mental
growth with an empire, such as Propertius debunked under Augustus,
slitting out its blah and its rhetoric. Say that this civilisation lasted
down to Leo the Tenth. And that its clearest formulation (along my
present line of measurement) is Dante's 'in una parte piu e meno
altrove'.

Which detached phrase I had best translate by explaining that I take
it to mean *a sense of gradations*. Things neither perfect nor utterly
wrong, but arranged in a cosmos, an order, stratified, having relations
one with another.

This means 'the money that built the cathedrals', it means very
great care in terminology because the 'word' is 'holy'.

I will take these last terms out of any possible jargon. Translate it,
for present emergency, words, an exact terminology, are an effective
means of communication, an efficient *modus operandi* ONLY if they do
retain meanings.

This Mediterranean paideuma fell before, or coincident with, the
onslaught of brute disorder of taboo. The grossness of incult thought
came into Europe simultaneously with manifestations called 'renaissance', 'restoration' and muddled in our time with a good deal of
newspaper yawp about puritans.

Certain things were 'forbidden'. Specifically, on parchment, they
were forbidden to Hebrews. The bible emerged and broke the Church
Fathers, who had for centuries quoted the bible. All sense of fine assay
seemed to decline in Europe.

A whole table of values was lost, but it wasn't just dropped overboard. A confusion which has lasted for several centuries will not be
wholly untangled even by this essay. I don't expect to get 500 years onto a shingle.

Lorenzo Valla extended, in one sense, the propaganda for the RIGHT
WORD, but at the same time the cult of terminology lost its grip on
general life.

Bayle and Voltaire spent their lives battling against 'superstition', and something escaped them. The process of impoverishment had set in, analagous in long curve, to the short curve I have given for America 1830 to 60. There are no exact historical parallels. I don't want to be held to strict analogy. For the moment all I can do is to *dissociate* a graduated concept of say good and evil from an incult and gross paideuma. The former created by a series of men following one on another, not neglecting original examination of fact, but not thinking each one in turn that the moon and sea were discovered first by him.

Anybody who has read a labour paper, or reform party propaganda will grasp what I mean by the second crass mode of mentality.

There can be no doubt that the renaissance was born of wide awake curiosity, and that from Italy in the Quattrocento, straight down through Bayle and Voltaire the LIVE men were actuated by a new urge toward veracity.

There can I think, be equally little doubt, that the Church, as bureaucracy and as vested interest was the worst enemy of 'faith', of 'christianity', of mental order? And yet that doesn't quite cover it either.

Something did *not* hit plumb on the nail. Without saying that anyone was dead wrong, and without committing me to a statement, can we find some sort of split, some scission or lesion in the mental working of Europe? Didn't the mental integrity of the Encyclopaedists dwindle into bare intellect by dropping that ETHICAL simplicity which makes the canonists, say any canonist so much more 'modern', more scientific, than any eighteenth-century 'intellectual'?

All I want to do for the moment is to set up two poles of reference. One: a graduated system in which all actions were relative good or evil, according to almost millimetric measurement, but in the absolute. Two, a system in which everything was good or bad without any graduation, but as taboo, though the system itself was continually modified in action by contingencies.

When this second system emerged from low life into high life, when it took over vast stretches of already acquired knowledge, it produced the Encyclopedists. Things were so or not so. You had 'Candide', you had writers of maxims, you had 'analysis', and you evolved into the Declaration of Les Droits de l'Homme which attained a fineness so near to that of the canonists that no one, so far as I know, has thought much of comparing them.

Out of intellectual revolt. Out of, (perhaps unwittingly) Pico on Human Dignity there proliferated Bobby Burns and to hell with the Duke and the parson ...

At which point the elder Adams had the puritanical stubbornness to stand up against popular clamour and to question the omniscience of Mr. Jefferson. It cost him four years in the Executive Mansion.

But America was a civilised land in those days. Jefferson could imagine no man leaving it for the pleasures of Europe. He and Adams had been there and met Europeans.

It is only in our time that anyone has, with any shadow of right, questioned the presuppositions on which the U.S. is founded. If we are off that base, why are we off it? Jefferson's America was civilised while because its chief men were social. It is only in our gormy and squalid day that the chief American powers have been, and are, anti-social.

Has any public man in our lifetime dared to say without a sneer or without fear of ridicule that Liberty is the right to do 'ce que ne nuit pas aux autres'? That was, past tense, a definition of civic and social concept. Such liberty was, at least by programme guaranteed the American citizen, but no other was offered him.

Jefferson and Adams were responsible. I mean they both were and FELT responsible. *Their* equals felt with them. The oath of allegiance implies this responsibility but it isn't printed in capitals, it passes in an unheeded phrase.

Two methods of turning in the evidence of the Adams letters are open. I could quote fragments and thereby be inadequate. The letters are printed. Or I could assert the implications, or at least the chief implications. The MAIN implication is that they stand for a life not split into bits.

Neither of these two men would have thought of literature as something having nothing to do with life, the nation, the organisation of government. Of course no first-rate author ever did think of his books in this manner. If he was lyrist, he was crushed under a system; or he was speaking of every man's life in its depth; if he was Trollope or Flaubert he was thinking of history without the defects of generic books by historians which miss the pith and point of the story. The pith and point of Jefferson's story is in a letter to Crawford (1816) ... 'and if the national bills issued be bottomed (as is indispensable) on pledges of specific taxes for their redemption within certain and moderate epochs, and be of *proper denominations* for *circulation*, no interest on them would be necessary or just, because they would answer to every one of the purposes of the metallic money withdrawn and replaced by them.'

I do not expect one reader in even 600 to believe me when I say these are eight of the most significant lines ever written.

It may take another twenty years' education to give that passage a meaning.[1] People quite often think me crazy when I make a jump

---

[1] Give 'em another 20 or 40. E.P., 1959.

instead of a step, just as if all jumps were unsound and never carried one anywhere.

From that take off I land on the Walter Page correspondence, one hundred or one hundred and one or two years after the Jefferson letter. Page went to Washington and found (verbatim) 'men about him (Wilson) nearly all very small fry or worse, narrowest two penny lot I've ever come across . . . never knew quite such a condition in American life.'

The colouring there being that Page has a memorial tablet in Westminster Abbey. He cut no ice in European intellectual life. He earned the gratitude of the British. He and Grey passed through those years of racking anxiety, and Page was refined from a perhaps gawky provincial into a character by that anxiety, WITHOUT either of them ever having any idea of what started the war. Page saw things Wilson didn't. He had detailed news of appalling results; but even Wilson saw things that Page didn't. But Europe went blind into that war because mankind had not digested Jefferson's knowledge. They went into that war because the canon law had been buried, because all general knowledge had been split up into useless or incompetent fragments. Because literature no longer bothered about the language 'of law and of the state' because the state and plutocracy cared less than a damn about letters. If I say those eight lines of Jefferson should be cut in brass and nailed to the door of Monticello the reader will think me eccentric. Let it pass as a picturesque fantasy.

And literature in the meanwhile? Goes to p-o-t, pot. Steadily it gets duller and duller, steadily it runs into neologism in contravention to T. J.'s moderate precept of style, namely that any man has the right to a new word when it can make his meaning more clear than an old one. Literature gets duller and duller by limitation of subject. Balzac, Trollope and Henry James extended the subject. EXTENDED the subject, they as Dante before them and as every real writer before them or since, extended the domain of their treatment.

Up till 1820 people read Latin. Your Jefferson-Adams correspondence shows acquaintance with Latin, note the line of impoverishment. The University of today does not communicate to the student the idea of Latin as a window. It instills the idea of 'the classics', certain books often of very limited scope, to be read in the acquisition of culture. At some point the whole fact that Berkeley, Hume, whatever serious thought had been printed in English, came in part out of books printed in Latin, has just gone by the board. If anyone had told me or any student of my undergraduate time that I would extend my Greek vocabulary because I have been infuriated to a curiosity as to the nature of money they would have been greeted by (let us hope at least bland) amazement.

There is nothing more firmly rooted in young America's mind than the belief that certain subjects are dull, there is nothing further from the spirit of American University education than the perception that subjects that have interested the best minds for three, five or twenty-five centuries are not perhaps very dull. There must have been something in them to attract recurrent unstill curiosities.

The historic process is continuous. Or 'the historic process is probably continuous'. Apparent breaks are probably due to laziness of historians who haven't dug down into causality. When you find two men as different as Marx and M. le Marquis de la Tour du Pin blind in the same spot, there is a chance to use curiosity.

In an age beset with cranks we have I suppose heard of Freud. For every man with an anxiety state due to sex, there are nine and ninety with an anxiety state due to lack of purchasing power, or anticipation of same. It is typical of a bewildered society that it should erect a pathology into a system.

The sanity and civilisation of Adams-Jefferson stems from the Encyclopaedists. You find in their letters a varied culture, and an omniverous (or apparently so) curiosity. And yet the 'thinning', the impoverishment of mental life shows in the decades after their death, and not, I think, without cause.

The Aquinian universe, the grades of divine intelligence and/or goodness or goodwill present in graduated degrees throughout this universe gave the thinker, any thinker something to measure by. What was lost or mislaid in the succeeding centuries, or what at least went out of the limelight may have been belief in 'God', but it most certainly was the HABIT of thinking of things in general as set in an orderly universe.

The laws of material science presuppose uniformity throughout the cosmos, but they do not offer an hierarchy of anything like the earlier coherence. Call it an hierarchy of evaluation.

The Encyclopaedists have a rich culture. What is the Dictionnaire de Bayle? As an arrangement it treats topics ALPHABETICALLY. Voltaire's Dictionnaire is hardly more than a slight addendum. Bayle has Moreri to make fun of, but they all have an ORDER to criticise. They go over the Accepted Aquinian universe with a set of measuring tools, *reductio ad absurdum* etc. The multifarious nature of cognisance remains, but they have only the Alphabet for a filing system.

They are brilliant. Bayle is robust with the heritage of Rabelais and Brantome, Voltaire a bit finer, down almost to silver point. But the idea and/or habit of gradations of value, and the infinitely more vital custom of digging down into principles gradually fade out of the picture. The degrees of light and motion, the whole metaphoric richness begin to perish. From a musical concept of man they dwindle downward to a mathematical concept.

Fontenelle notices it but attributes natural human resistance to abstraction to a hunger for ERROR. I don't think Chesterton ever quite formulated an epigram in reply, but the whole of his life was a protest against this impoverishment.

In fact the whole of Flaubert, the whole of the fight for the novel as 'histoire morale contemporaine' was a fight against maxims, against abstractions, a fight back toward a human and/or total conception.

Flaubert, Trollope, and toward the last Henry James got through to money. Marx and La Tour du Pin, not working on total problem, but on a special problem which one would have thought of necessity would have concentrated their attention on money, merely go blind at the crucial point.

In totalitarian writings before Voltaire one does not find this blind spot. The Church Fathers think down to detail, Duns Scotus has no cloudy obsession on this point. There is a great deal of Latin on Intrinsic and Extrinsic value of money.

Jefferson is still lucid. Gallatin found banks useful, as T. J. says, because they 'gave ubiquity to his money'.

Does the historian stop for such details? I mean the pestilent variety of historian who has filled 97 per cent of the shelves in our libraries (historical alcoves)? Venice took over private banking but it took decades to persuade the normal Venetian to keep books, to get down to the office to see whether his butler did the job for him, let alone having the addition correct.

There is a continuity of historic process. The imaginary speech of Q. Xtius Decimus after the battle of Bogoluz or the steaming open of despatches by Metternich is not the whole of the story.

In American history as professed the monetary factor has been left to the LAST. Van Buren's memoirs stays six decades in manuscript. How you expect to have a nation with no national culture beats me.

'Congress will then be paying six per cent on twenty millions, and receiving seven per cent on ten millions, being its third of the institution; so that on the ten millions cash which they receive from the States and individuals, they will, in fact, have to pay but 5 per cent interest. This is the bait.' (Monticello, 6 November 1813.)

The idea, put about I know not why, by I know not whom, that Jefferson was an imprecise rhetorician disappears in a thorough perusal of his letters.

There may be a defect in the 'decline and fall' method in writing history. There is certainly a defect in it if the analyst persists in assuming that this or that institution (say the Church) 'fell' merely because some other paideuma or activity (organised formally, or sporadic and informal) arises, overcrowds, overshadows it, or merely gets greater publicity.

The Church may not have fallen. The steady building up of social and economic criteria, ever with a tendency to control, via Constantine, Justinian, Charlemagne is still there in the records. It is still there as thought and discrimination for anyone who chooses to look at it.

Leibnitz was possibly the last prominent thinker who worried about 'reconciliation', about getting all the best European thought 'back into' the Church, but one might note that it is not merely theology but philosophy that STOPS with Herr Leibnitz. By that I mean that since his correspondence with Bossuet 'philosophy', general ideation, has been merely a squib and trailer, correlated to material particular sciences, from which it has had its starts, shoves, incentives. Often splurging in the vaguest analogies.

' "The same political parties which now agitate the United States, have existed through all time"; precisely. And this is precisely the complaint in the first volume of my defence.' (John Adams quoting Priestley to Jefferson, 9 July 1813.)

'By comparing the first and the last of these articles' (this follows a table of figures) 'we see that if the United States were in possession of the circulating medium, as they ought to be, they cd. redeem what they cd. borrow from that, dollar for dollar, and in ten annual installments; whereas usurpation of that fund by bank paper, obliging them to borrow elsewhere at $7\frac{1}{2}\%$, two dollars are required to reimburse one.' (T. J. from Poplar Forest, 11 September 1813.)

I am not offering proof, because full proof will not go onto ten pages. I am offering indications, which the reader can follow for himself, but which will I think lead to perception:

That Adams and Jefferson exist in a full world. They are NOT a province of England. The letters abound in consciousness of Europe, that is of France, Holland, Spain, Russia, Italy. The truly appalling suburbanism that set in after the civil war, partly from our exhaustion, partly from the oedematous bulging of the British Empire, our relapse into cerebral tutelage, our suburbanism did not afflict Adams and Jefferson. Not only were they level and (with emphasis) CONTEMPORARY with the best minds of Europe but they entered into the making of that mind. Chateaubriand did not come to Philadelphia to lecture, he came to learn.

I do not believe that either public men or American writers for the past forty years have dared to face the implications of the Adams-Jefferson volumes. Henry James would have, had he been aware of such works existing.

I doubt if they can be adduced to back up any particular theory, unless you call it a theory to hold that one should look at the totality of the facts or at least at as many as are thrust under your observation and as many more as you can dig out for yourselves.

The first quotation of Jefferson here used, could lead to Gesell. Chemistry and Physics are not mutually contradictory. Faddists and the incult are perpetually trying to refute one set of ideas with other ideas that are sometimes unrelated, sometimes complementary. The just price is a canonist concept. The order of the Roman empire, the possibility of organising such an empire is indissolubly bound up with reduction of usury rates, with disentanglement of the notion of usury from that of marine insurance (hence the scandal of Cato the censor).

An idea or ideal of order developed with the Roman empire, but it was not the empire. It was an ideal of justice that penetrated down, out, through, into marketing. The idea that you can tax idle money dates back through a number of centuries. These questions have intrigued the best human minds, Hume, Berkeley, a whole line of Catholic writers, and a whole congeries of late Latin writers. You can not write or understand any history, and you can not write or understand any serious 'history of contemporary customs' in the form of Goncourt and Flaubert novels if you persist in staving off all enquiry into the most vital phenomena, e.g. such as search into the nature and source of the 'carrier', of the agent and implement of transference.

A total culture such as that of Adams and Jefferson does not dodge such investigation. A history of literature which refuses to look at such matters remains merely a shell and a sham.

Adams was anti-clerical (at least I suppose one would call it that), they are both of them heritors of encyclopaedism, but they inherit that *forma mentis* in an active state where definition of terms and ideas has not been lost. I mean liberty is still the right to do ANYTHING that harms no one else. For seventy years it has been boomed mainly as effrenis in faenerando licentia, alias to hell with the public.

They both had a wide circle of reference, of knowledge, of ideas, with the acid test for hoakum, and no economic inhibitions. The growth of economic inhibition, I mean specifically in the domain of THOUGHT, is a nineteenth-century phenomenon to a degree that I believe inhered in no other century. Edward Grey and Page were sincerely unconscious. They 'didn't see things that way'. There was a vast penumbra about their excitement, and penumbra is the mother of bogies.

Jefferson specifically wanted a civilisation in Virginia. Van Buren was at work from very early years. He was servant of the public, and during his public life had, so far as one makes out, time only for good manners. Heaven knows how he spent his time after he was defeated. His memoirs are very well written.

After the death of Van Buren the desire for civilization was limited you might almost say to professional writers, to a very few professional writers and an ineffective minority of the electorate. You have a definite opposition between public life and such men as H. James and H. Adams which you can not ascribe *wholly* to their individual temperaments.

A totalitarian state uses the best of its human components. Shakespeare and Chaucer did not think of emigrating. Landor, Shelley, Keats, Browning, Beddoes did emigrate, and Bobby Burns thought of it. Something had happened in and to England. An historian, if he were real, would want to pry into it.

And the lesson is, if, heaven help us, I am supposed to be teaching anyone anything in this article–the lesson is against raw ideology, which Napoleon, Adams, Jefferson were all up against, and whereto, as Adams remarked, Napoleon had, in those days, given a name.

The lesson is or might be against peripheric acid as distinct from Confucian building of ideogram and search into motivation, or 'principle'.

If you want certain results, you must as scientist examine a great many phenomena. If you won't admit what you are driving at, even to yourself, you remain in penumbra. Adams did not keep himself in penumbra, he believed in a responsible class. He wanted safeguards and precautions and thereby attained unpopularity.

'You and I ought not to die before we have explained ourselves to each other.' (Adams to Jefferson, 15 July 1813.) Did Rousseau or Montaigne ever write anything to equal that sentence, given the context (1760 to 1813)?

Introductory Textbook[1]

CHAPTER I

'All the perplexities, confusion, and distress in America arise, not from defects in their constitution or confederation, not from want of honour and virtue, so much as from downright ignorance of the nature of coin, credit, and circulation.'

John Adams.

CHAPTER II

'... and if the national bills issued, be bottomed (as is indispensable) on pledges of specific taxes for their redemption within certain and moderate epochs, and be of *proper denomination* for *circulation*, no interest on them would be necessary or just, because they would answer to every one of the purposes of the metallic money withdrawn and replaced by them.'

Thomas Jefferson (1816, letter to Crawford).

CHAPTER III

'... and gave to the people of this Republic THE GREATEST BLESSING THEY EVER HAD—THEIR OWN PAPER TO PAY THEIR OWN DEBTS.

Abraham Lincoln.

CHAPTER IV

The Congress shall have power; To coin money, regulate the value thereof and of foreign coin and to fix the standards of weights and measures.'

Constitution of the United States, Article I Legislative Department, Section 8, page 5.

Done in the convention by the unanimous consent of the States, 7 September 1787, and of the Independence of the United States the twelfth. In witness whereof we have hereunto subscribed our names.

George Washington.
President and Deputy from Virginia

[1] 1938.

NOTE

The abrogation of this last mentioned power derives from the ignorance mentioned in my first quotation. Of the three preceding citations, Lincoln's has become the text of Willis Overholser's recent 'History of Money in the U.S.', the first citation was taken as opening text by Jerry Voorhis in his speech in the House of Representatives, 6 June 1938, and the passage from Jefferson is the nucleus of my 'Jefferson and/or Mussolini'.

Douglas' proposals are a sub-head under the main idea in Lincoln's sentence, Gesell's 'invention' is a special case under Jefferson's general law. I have done my best to make simple summaries and clear definitions in various books and pamphlets, and recommend as *introductory* study, apart from C. H. Douglas' 'Economic Democracy' and Gesell's 'Natural Economic Order', Chris. Hollis' 'Two Nations', McNair Wilson's 'Promise to Pay', Larranaga's 'Gold, Glut and Government' and M. Butchart's compendium of three centuries thought, that is an anthology of what has been said, in 'Money'. (Originally published by Nott.)

National Culture[1]

A Manifesto 1938

A national or racial culture exists when the works (art, letters) of that nation do not and do not need to ask favours because they have been produced by a member of that particular nation or race. A national American culture existed from 1770 till at least 1861. Jefferson could not imagine an American going voluntarily to inhabit Europe. After the debacle of American culture individuals had to emigrate in order to conserve such fragments of American culture as had survived. It was perhaps no less American but it was in a distinct sense less *nationally* American as the usurocracy came into steadily more filthy and damnable control of the Union.

The distinction between nationalism and non-absorbency needs stressing. Our revolutionary culture was critical and not monolingual. A national culture can exist so long as it *chooses* between other cultures. It obviously descends to the swamps when it degenerates into a snobism, when it accepts from abroad instead of selecting. There is no inferiority sense in the Jefferson-Adams letters. Till at least 1850 the U.S. was respected. The American as such was not at a disadvantage. Europe looked *to* America; not as to a rich cheese but as to a model and example.

An American culture has existed and exists in any American work that imposes itself on foreign judgment, and the quality of its existence is measured by the quality of that judgment.

A distinction exists between a national (or racial) culture and a metropolitan market. The criteria of quick sales, speedy profit etc., belong to Broadway hair oil. The fact that there is more lucre in shoddy and Ersatz is often a mere sign of provincialism. All of which remarks are probably platitude, but are necessary for clearing the ground.

There exist means to reconstruct or coordinate such American culture as is available.

It is possible to learn and apply high and international criteria. It should be possible to establish a communications service between individual components of such culture-containers and engines as humanly exist. One can not create by fiat a phalanx of great writers, or men of genius. One could however establish a certain degree of

First published *Impact*, 1960.

131

mental integrity, and an utter and blistering intolerance of certain present habits of sloppiness and bad faith.

Certain inaccuracies (now serving ill will) could be eliminated.

Efforts could be made to establish committees of correspondence between men, in America, who produce or prefer good writing to bad.

There is at the moment no periodical giving even rudimentary information on American thought, let alone correlating that thought with live thought in other countries. To shun such correlation is cowardice. It is also the habit of the American mercantilist age, as indeed of the mercantilist age anywhere.

I do not see a regeneration of American culture while Marx and Lenin are reprinted at 10 cents and 25 cents in editions of 100,000 and Adams' and Jefferson's thought is kept out of the plain man's reach, and out of my reach considering that for three years I have in vain tried to buy John Adams' letters.

Men who impede the examination of the monetary and financial causes of historic events are a seething corruption. Whether one start that examination before the collapse of our civilization in the war of the 1860's or before the last war that study is to be made. We physicians of the mind can not rest until we have discovered a serum which will make impossible the existence on the American scene of the persons who have impeded this study, wilfully or in abuleia. In most cases the obstruction is a compost of sloth, fear and greed.

The befouling of terminology should be put an end to. It is a time for clear definition of terms. Immediately, of economic terms, but ultimately of all terms. It is not a revolution of the word but a castigation of the word. And that castigation must precede any reform.

An administration that can not or dare not define money, credit, debt, property, capital, is unlikely to provide a durable solution of national chaos or evolve a durable system of national order.

In aiming this manifesto at a few dozen just men I am trying to find out whether they want anything better than the present circumjacent fugg and moral morass.

Do six dozen or six hundred Americans value 'a national culture' sufficiently to conserve it

A. By correlated reprint of proofs of its earlier existence?
B. By periodical bulletin of its present products?
C. By keeping sharp the criteria which would prevent a relapse into the narcissism of the U.S. of the late nineteenth century?

What other measures are they concretely prepared to take for its maintenance? Jefferson and Adams were in position to decide whether the English or French view or idea in a given case were preferable. The snob or member of Harvey's generation or the later derivers are merely there to assure the boob that London says this or the other.

The hair oil boys, out for quick profit and exploitation of a fad or fashion.

The degradation of American publishing was nowhere more manifest in that from 1917 to 1919 the actual centre of activity in printing work in English was transferred from London to New York. Later it hovered over Paris. Then for the rest of a decade New York did nothing and the centre of publishing live work flopped back to London. This shows contempt for and oblivion of whatever national culture exists. Culture is individual and not national so long as the individual having unusual capacity is forced OUT of his native milieu by material (i.e. economic) conditions and the imbecility or incapacity of the milieu to sustain and coordinate effort.

Concretely, *if* American individuals have to communicate via Europe the national culture will not function to its own best advantage. Provincialism shows equally in four ways.

One, the absurd aping of foreign modes.

Two, the absurd timidity and fear of accepting foreign work in an unknown mode.

Three, neglect of high-grade work done at home.

Four, back-scratching and boosting of tosh *because* it is produced at home.

A national culture has a minimum of components. If the production be simply unconscious we are in a state of folk culture only. Any more developed phase must of necessity include criteria which are, as criteria, capable of comparison with the best alien criteria.

In one sense it can almost be said: there are no alien criteria.

The hair oil boys of course could not sustain foreign criteria for a week. The 'bright and slick' goes *once* with the European. The seventh issue of any of the hair oil organs is identical with the first. The issues of a serious periodical are all different, one from the others. *Cantleman's Spring Mate* is not confoundable with a chapter from *Ulysses*.

It is or should be obvious that H. James asked no favours of French and English contemporaries. He was sold in French in the 1880's, and his later small sales were due not to inferiority but to his superiority to the foreign reader's capacity.

I suppose in the long run Jimmy Whistler was not so good a painter as Manet but he had a damn good run for his money. I don't recall any British painter of his time cropping up in a poem by Mallarmé.

In our own day and vocation it can't be said that either Mr. Eliot nor the undersigned have exactly looked UP to British contemporaries. It can't be said that an alteration on Mr. Eliot's passport has altered the essential Americanness of his work. H. James' death-bed change of citizenship was the one last and possible defiance that he could hurl at the scum in the White House.

Eliot's real criticism of England was written some years before he committed the technical change.

> crawls between dry ribs
> To keep our metaphysics warm.

Out of Gautier and the Bay State Hymn Book, but no soft Victorian slither converging.

Williams is American by programme, and in so far as his nationality is factitious it has an immediate local appeal. His verity, despite a provincial top-dressing, has driven in, even into some silly young Britons. You have here some of the best work done on the ground, but you have also the proof that race is stronger than programme.

The American culture is Franco-English, it is at the start the culture in the bone of the one English segment that ever in all history threw off the tyranny of the conquerors of the Island. And it is then lightened, brought into clearer demarcation by a French ideation plus, for all I know, climate.

Henry James is as New England as Henry Adams because of the same racial origins and mixed by education with the same other chemical. The national culture was there in Jefferson-Adams. Van Buren was too busy on necessary public jobs to *learn* much of it. If you can conceive an idle Van Buren I suspect he might have imbibed quite a good deal of it.

Whitman was neglected by prigs, and then the snobs overlooked the part of him which was quite simply exotic.

Williams is international. Cummings on the other hand who has been driven abroad for his two major subjects (*Enormous Room* and the Russia of *Eimi*) is indelibly New England. And, though it be almost axymoron to say so, 'Whitman's one living descendant.'

There is I think little doubt that I should have more quickly attained a unity of expression had I been also New England without disorderly trek of four or five generations across the whole teeming continent.

Zukofsky is in the American vein in his essays on Henry Adams, and *Meet Baruch Spinoza*.

AS TO ERSATZ AND MARGARINE

The pseudoculture insists on staying twenty years or so behind Europe. I have always advised against this. The press is always all for it. Nothing will induce the American press to print contemporary news of Europe.

In closing and before I divagate, I should advise

ONE: a decision as to the bases of our national culture.

TWO: a serious constructive programme, complete with possible methods of organization before I hear any more about destructive programmes.

134

I mean to say there is one point in the constitution which has not been tried and which the infamies infesting the White House for the past decades do not and dare not try: namely the right of congress to determine the value of money.

We had a basis for civic order in the time of Jackson and Van Buren. A new order must at least incorporate that base. Once that is done we can consider modernisation of other components and decide whether and/or how far a more modern articulation is possible or desirable. By possible, I mean initiable in time and in our time, without loose analogies to European needs and possibilities. An ORDER yes, but per force an American order. A *directio voluntatis* certainly, but in writing the details of a programme this directio must take count both of its own driving force and material obstacles.

The excuse for materialism exists only when the sane man is faced by doctrinaires who do not see the reality of these obstacles. As the worship of inertia it is not even a philosophy, it is merely sub-human. Though it is a quite natural excess of a short-distance thinker suffering from irritation. Even poor Charlie Marx couldn't carry it into his theory of values, and as a working system Russia knows it's a wash-out.

The total democracy bilge, by which I mean the clichés, the assumptions, the current cant about 'the people' arose from sheer misunderstanding or perversion. Perversion of ideas by means and by misuse of words.

The disequality of human beings can be observed, if you take long enough, from the reports in the English Journal (organ of teaching in secondary schools). There is no more equality between men than between animals. Jefferson never thought that there was. I say 'Jefferson' because J. Adams might be abused as a monarchist, which he wasn't. I say Jefferson because I want the extreme case, the inventor or impresario of our democracy.

Equality before the law courts, equality in the sense of there being no insurmountable obstacles imposed by arbitrary classification and arbitrary limits of categories. Liberty: to do that which harms not another.

To ORGANISE in our barbarism, in our utter and rabbity inconsequence, an hierarchy and order is not an affair of decades. We can not, or at any rate we have not organised one clean book club, we have not organised even committees of communication, we have not one publication that serves as postal system for ideas between the few hundred top-notch (however low the top be) intelligentsia. And until a selection of the intelligentsia can organise something, until they can set up at least a model they can not expect the 120 or whatever million to copy it.

We have, god pity us, an 'Institute'. Is it organised? Has it a status official or other? Can even a member of it ascertain what it has done? Has it even a bulletin? Has it records?

Flaubert cannot meet Turgenev at the Goncourts in every decade, and 30 or 200 men of talent can not be created on demand, but at least standards of intellectual probity COULD be observed. At least protests could be registered against the more flagrant rackets, against the worst malpractices of the press and the book trade, and more violent inaccuracies of so-called books of reference.

Thirty or 200 persons 'elected' because of superior services to American letters could were they not a farce demand and obtain the publication of essential parts of our heritage.

Were there any general spirit among them their recommendation of such publication would also place the publication on a perfectly practical level. The umpteen hundred dead libraries in the umpteen etc. pseudo-universities and travesties, plus the public (so) libraries (called) would absorb (that is the just word) enough copies to cover the printing expenses.

Until you root out the mercantilist morale by acid you will have no decent America. Ivar Kreuger was boomed in the *Saturday Evening Post* as more than a financial titan. And that state of belly tickling sycophancy still festers.

FOR A NATIONAL CULTURE the first step is stocktaking: what is there of it *solid*. The second step is to make this available and to facilitate access to it.

An Introduction to the Economic
Nature of the United States[1]

THE TITLE

This is not a SHORT History of the Economy of the United States. For forty years I have schooled myself, not to write an economic history of the U.S. or any other country, but to write an epic poem which begins 'In the Dark Forest' crosses the Purgatory of human error, and ends in the light, and 'fra i maestri di color che sanno'. For this reason I have had to understand the NATURE of error. But I don't think it necessary to refer to each particular case of error.

I do not believe that the method of historiography has progressed much since the days when Confucius selected the documents of the old kingdoms, and condensed his conclusions in the Testament. Aristotle toward the end of his life arrived at a similar method, in his collection of Greek State Constitutions. Voltaire used the 'human' method which hinges on chance and the personal element. A prince eats a pudding and dies of acute indigestion at a critical moment. Caesar Borgia said: 'I had anticipated everything except being bedridden the day my father died.' Michelet analyses the motives of different social groups and tells us that the manual labourer wants to own a shop because he thinks shop-keepers don't work. Another method consists in analysing certain mechanisms invented to humbug the public. Perhaps it is the renewal of an Aristotelian tendency but, in any event, it is suitable for the present narrative, and I am following it in this essay or definition, of the struggle between the people and the usurers, or financiers, in the colonies, and then in the United States of North America.

Towards the end of the eighteenth century the settlers, having been driven by the desire for Freedom of Conscience, hardened by privations, favoured and betrayed, reached a certain degree of prosperity, thanks to their own hard work and to a sane system of using paper money as a means of exchange that freed them, temporarily, from the clutches of the Bank of England.

The Settlers, or Colonizers, in Pennsylvania and in other colonies, irritated by the disappearance of metal money, understood that any

[1] 1944. Translated from the original Italian by Carmine Amore. Translation revised by John Drummond, 1971. English translation first published by Peter Russell in 1950.

other document could be used for book-keeping and as a certificate of what the bearer was entitled to receive in the market. The agriculturists who arrived in the new country, while they cleared the forests and prepared their camps, lacked the power to buy what was necessary to build houses, to buy ploughs, and to live. So the governments of several colonies began to loan paper-money for these purposes. Pennsylvania chose the best method adapted to the conditions—repayment in ten or twelve years, and loaning amounts up to one half of the value of the farm. Those who loaned the money, living near to those who had received the loan, could judge the character of the borrowers. This arcadian simplicity displeased the London monopolists and the suppression of this competition, together with other irritants, provoked the 1776 'Revolution'.

The clearness of comprehension on the part of the revolutionary leaders is registered in diaries and 'memoirs' of the times, and particularly in the notes of John Adams who, among other things, had been sent to Europe to organise the credit for the new State, and who secured the first loan from Holland.

It is to be understood that the experience of John Adams was neither theoretical nor abstract. Firmly convinced of the capacity of the Americans to produce farm products and merchandise, he met and overcame, all the insidiousness of Europe. He convinced the Hollanders of the solidarity of the American guarantees by comparing the insignificant debt of the United States to the great debt of England.

I repeat: His notes are neither abstract nor theoretical. It was a question of paying the war expenditures with tobacco. The intimate letters and conversations, between Adams and his friends contain concrete concepts as, for example: 'It is necessary to keep up the idea that this paper is good for something', meaning that the note can be exchanged for actual goods.

It was understood that the Navy depended on iron, timber and tar, and not on the manoeuvers of a false finance.

Some time later the bankers perpetrated projects for the extension of credit, 'funding', or the institution of a public debit. Adams met the terrors of inflation by stating that a diminishing buying power of the paper money functioned as an unevenly distributed tax, a tax that hit those with a fixed salary, or living on an income; that the merchants would have the best of it; and that, in any event, an inflation of this kind would *not* have created a public debt WITH INTEREST.

It was understood that credit is Paul's supposition that Peter will pay. It was understood that the real base of credit of the thirteen colonies was their capacity to work, taken together with the truly great possibility of future production limited then, not by nature, fields, vegetation, but only by the number of the inhabitants.

Washington was able to win in the war because he resisted to the bitter end. Washington won, but not without indebtedness to the tenacity and good sense of Adams – the Negotiator.

History, as seen by a Monetary Economist, is a continuous struggle between producers, and those who try to make a living by inserting a false system of book-keeping between the producers and their just recompense.

The Bank of England was based on the discovery that instead of loaning money, the Bank's paper could be put out on loan. The Philadelphia financiers, not entirely severed from their friends in foreign countries, saw the possibility of speculation and the mono-polisers of money tried their usual tricks on a thick-headed public.

'Financiers and Congressmen bought a great quantity of soldier's pay certificates which had been issued during the war. The certificates were simply printing press money without anything of value behind them. Years had passed since their date of issue and, as their hope for redemption went down, their value went down, and down. In 1789 they could be bought for 10 or 15 cents to the dollar. Alexander Hamilton proposed that the Continental certificates be redeemed at par.'[1] And then the nation 'assumed' the responsibility of paying them as proposed. *These were the famous certificates of pay due to the veterans. This constituted the 'Scandal of the Assumption'.*

England was trying diverse methods of usury and sanctions. The lack of caution on the part of the great property owners of the South, led them into indebtedness. Slavery became less profitable than the new industrial system, in which the owner did not have to take care of his employees.

Let us note that at the beginning of the nineteenth century the 'Mercantile' concept still retained traces of decency. Adams judged it 'hardly mercantile' to do trade on borrowed capital. At that time individualism had its own probity, a modest but secure income was called an '*independence*'.

History taken as a lesson, and taking into account the difference between certainty and supposition, would be an *exposition of the nature of events*, rather than a chronicle of names.

Some events can be known only after centuries. We know, for example, that Parisina d'Este[1] incurred certain expenditures which were paid from the Ducal Treasury of Ferrara, and we also know the date of these payments. Other deeds are never explained and must remain enigmas of the participants. A signed letter proves what the writer wanted the recipient to believe on such and such a day. But the clarity of an idea remains among the ASCERTAINED facts. The

[1] Quotation from *A New American History* by W. E. Woodward.

[2] Parisina d'Este was the wife of Niccolo III of Ferrara. She was exe-cuted after the discovery of her adultery with Niccolo's son Ugo. Peter Russell.

definition of an idea, as observed by someone who understands the events of the day, may shed more light on the historical process than many volumes.

SOURCES

The true history of the economy of the United States, as I see it, is to be found in the correspondence between Adams and Jefferson, in the writings of Van Buren, and in quotations from the intimate letters of the Fathers of the Republic. The elements remain the same: debts, altering the value of monetary units, and the attempts, and triumphs of usury, due to monopolies, or to a 'Corner'.

In order to please those who love to gamble, the Exchange permits Mr. A to sell to Mr. B what Mr. A does not possess; on condition that Mr. A succeeds in buying it and consigning it to Mr. B within a determined time.

The Americans have chosen this game instead of bull-fighting. And naturally, if a group of financiers succeeds in inducing simpletons to sell more than actually exists, or to sell more than is available, the late-comers find themselves left in the lurch. In 1869, Gould, Fisk and others almost succeeded in monopolising the available gold in New York. Roosevelt followed Jim Fisk.

The speculators boast about their courage or temerity, but this courage is a different kind of courage from that displayed at the Roulette, or other games of chance; for, by speculating on wheat and other commodities these gamblers are not just gambling among themselves, they are affecting the prices the public must pay for its necessities. *Civic conscience has not developed in America. It seems to me that this conscience was higher during the first years of the Republic, or, at least, the heroes of that era have left to us monuments of their personal consciences, which are higher than those in the publications of today.*

From the War of Secession up to now, the economic history, I might almost say *the* history, of the United States has consisted in a series of stock exchange manoeuvres in New York and in Chicago; attempts to impose monopolies, corners, variations in the prices of the shares of new industries, and of the means of transportation. In the beginning they speculated on the value of land. An inflation in its value was stimulated without bothering about the difficulty, or the impossibility of transporting products from remote areas to the market. Then they speculated on the values of the railroads.

If it is in the interest of the common worker, producer, or citizen to have an equitable and fixed price, this is not at all in the interest of the speculator or broker. 'Hell', he says, 'I don't want a still market. I couldn't make any money.'

Like a patient angler, the broker waits for the rise or fall of even $\frac{1}{4}$ or $\frac{1}{8}$ per cent, and there is his fifty or one hundred dollars.

ECONOMIC NATURE OF THE UNITED STATES

He waits for a 'break'. It may come once in a life time. It may be the starting point to a fortune. The great Morgan, during the Civil War, bought on credit a certain quantity of damaged rifles from the War Department in Washington, and sold them to a Military Command in Texas, and was paid by the latter before he had to pay the former. He made $75,000.00 profit. Later he was even tried and convicted, but that did not prevent his becoming the great Mahatma of Wall Street, and a world politico-economical power. Such is the material of which the economic and human history of the United States is made.

STRATAGEMS AND ILLUSIONS

The Morgan affair, or trial, will be classified perhaps as one of the normal exploits of finance and could have happened anywhere in the old world. But the new land, because of the new conditions, offered several kinds of opportunity for fraud. In order to display the problem of the American mentality and its development, or perversion, as a component in the historical process, these frauds should be classified. Take for example, the concession to construct the Northern Pacific Railroad. This concession had a clause in it which conferred on the constructors the right to all the lumber cleared during the construction. The route went through the virgin forest and the trees were destined to be used as crossties, but the clause did not specify the width of the road to be cut and the company, with perfect legality, cut for itself a strip of land two miles wide. The land and the forests were the property of the nation, but no private citizen felt that he had been swindled.

Similar things are the basis of American humour. They are a matter of pride and tradition. The fight against the forest, and the difficulties of the desert was hard. Craftiness as well as marksmanship was being developed. A man in Connecticut succeeded in manufacturing imitation nutmegs out of plain wood and selling them at a profit. This trick sent the whole country into peals of laughter. The Centenary of this trick was commemorated at the St. Louis Exposition. Imitation nutmegs were made and sold at 5 cents each. One day, when the stock of these souvenirs ran out, the man in charge, a true son of Connecticut, pure-blooded yankee, did not hesitate one instant to substitute real nutmegs, at the same price. The public heard it, and roared again.

Since the days of the California Gold Rush there have been men who have specialised in 'Gold Bricks', that is, a lead brick covered with a layer of gold, or even solid gold in some parts so that the seller can bore through it at known points and show it to be solid gold. After the Alaskan Gold Rush the 'gold brick' made its reappearance. The majority of those who had been duped brought their bricks to my father who was an assayer at the Mint. This was the period of free coining of gold, and any one had the right to have his own metal coined. So, the stories of these dupes have been familiar to me, through personal experience, since I was five years old.

I should like to differentiate between two kinds of dishonesty: (1) that of financial frauds and book-keeping; and (2) that arising from particular material opportunities, as in the case of the Northern Pacific.

TRADITION

The usual frauds of book-keeping, monopoly, etc., have been known since the beginning of history, and it is precisely for this reason that the usurers are opposed to classical studies. Aristotle, in his POLITICS 1. 4/5, relates how Thales, wishing to show that a philosopher could easily 'make money' if he had nothing better to do, foreseeing a bumper crop of olives, hired by paying a small deposit, all the olive presses on the islands of Miletus and Chios. When the abundant harvest arrived, everybody went to see Thales. Aristotle remarks that this is a common business practice.[1] And the Exchange frauds are, nearly all of them, variants on this theme–artificial scarcity of grain and of merchandise, artificial scarcity of money, that is, scarcity of the key to all the other exchanges.

PROVERBS AND WISDOM

The struggle between the Producers and the Falsifiers of Book-keeping was clearly seen and understood by the Fathers of the Republic. Their wisdom was recorded in pungent phrases: 'The safest place of deposit is in the pants of the people.' 'Every Bank of Discount is downright iniquity, robbing the public for individuals' gain.' An insurance agent once asked a banker why the railroad companies, which are privately owned, must run to him, a banker, in order to sell their bonds. The banker, with ironic sadness, whispered: 'Hush'.

THE PATTERN

To understand the pattern of the American historical process, it is necessary to consider the successive waves of immigration.

1. Those who came through a spirit of adventure or, because of religious convictions and the desire for freedom of conscience and who were willing to face the difficulties of a savage and uncultivated country;

2. The slaves;

3. and those who arrived when the machinery was already beginning to function.

The class struggle in the United States did not follow the European

[1] Quoted Canto XCII. Ed.

pattern. It is a recent and an almost exotic problem, in the sense that it does not derive from the Founders. Let us take a 'typical American family'. Two Wadsworth brothers, or two men of that name, arrived in Massachusetts in 1632. In 1882 their descendants had a family reunion and published the history of their family. In the eight generations we find all sort and conditions–rich and poor. One, at the age of sixteen, sold his hair for a shilling, and 'this was the first money he ever did see'. Another fitted out a ship with his own money, during the Civil War. On the 250th Anniversary the participants presented equal variety and extremes among them–members of the Stock Exchange, travelling salesmen, doctors, a telegraph operator and two old women for whom a collection was taken up. Under these conditions class warfare, in the true sense of the word, does not exist, even though the differences in wealth and position are undeniably visible.

COLONIAL TENDENCIES

The Fathers of the Republic revolted against the English ruling class, the younger brothers against the first-born. Popular hatred of the monarchist idea hampered Adams throughout his life. And all because, at the age of seventeen, he had written a letter in which he foresaw the possibility of an American Kingdom capable of resisting any European force. Demagogy seized this phrase to insist that Adams had never been anti-monarchist, but preferred the House of Braintree, namely, his own, to that of the Hanover. His father held the plough. His son, John Q. Adams, awaited the results of a presidential election at the plough. Perhaps a classical pose, but he was capable of holding the plough, and was not doing it for the first time in his life.

Let us compare a score of personal cases in order to understand the pattern of American economic history. In the docket of a great-grandfather, Justice of the Peace, in New York State, the fines run from $1.30 to about $25.00, and the Court's expenses from 8c to $1.30.

His daughter, at least once in her life, went to work in a factory, married a man who became a Congressman, helped in the kitchen, not as a spectator, but in order to prepare the meals for about forty lumbermen. At the time of her separation she had $100,000.00 in the bank, but the bank failed. My father, the first white man to be born in that part of Wisconsin, was looked after by a male redskin instead of a nurse. He inspected mines in Idaho, and got a job in the Land Office. One week he had his kindling wood sawn by a certain man for a dollar. Ten days later he asked the man if he wanted to saw a little more wood. 'Saw wood? Saw Wood? Say Homer do you want to go East and sell a mine? I got $10,000.00 in the bank.'

In 1919 I met in Paris a quiet little man, Ambassador at the time, whom my father remembered thirty-five years before in the act of reaching for a revolver to help out his partner. American distances are different from the European, and the statistics do not record all the nuances.

WAVES

Religious convictions, anarchic tendencies, love of adventure and then laziness. The American tragedy, in a certain sense, is the tragedy of laziness. The sense of justice gave way to the sense of laziness. Justice was limited first to the whites, and then to the bosses.

From Europe a flood of workers poured in. The national type was formed from a similarity of tastes and temperaments and not on a racial basis. Those who wanted material gain emigrated to America. Those of a milder nature, the more contemplative, who were fond of beauty, who were more attached to their soil and home, remained in Europe. The strong, the restless, the malcontents, the misfits went. The younger sons of the English went in the 1600's, but after 1800 emigrants from England diminished.

The Puritans were somewhat Bible-crazy, but they did not bring the Hebrew Scriptures only. The culture of Adams and Jefferson is a Latin culture with a mixture of Greek. Otis wrote a Greek Grammar which he destroyed, or which was lost for the lack of a competent printer. During the prosperous colonial era the arts of silversmithing, furniture making, and architecture developed. The houses of white-painted wood, were a Greek dream. Numbers of them burned down. From Germany came groups of religious sectarians. They brought with them the art of glassmaking, and organised, at least once a year, a Bach Festival. Monticello is full of refinement. The polygrapher[1] longed for a complete civilisation equal to that of an Italian Court, ceremonies omitted, of the fourteenth century. He got into debt.

Adams was frugal, and used the weather-boards of his attic study as a handy file for his correspondence. For at least a century New England took the slogan: 'Low Living High Thinking' seriously.

Usury ruined the Republic. Usury has been defined as too high an interest on money. The word finance became fashionable in the bank-paper era. And it is to this that Jefferson alludes in the phrase: 'No one has a natural right to be money-lender save him who has it to lend.' With the 'financial' era the word usury disappeared from polite conversation.

There is no greater imbecility than to leave one's own bank-account or one's own sources of information in the hands of an enemy, or an irresponsible man.

[1] Thomas Jefferson, the architect of Monticello, his own home. Peter Russell.

ECONOMIC NATURE OF THE UNITED STATES

The struggle between the people and the exploiters, in America, was waged around these forms of imbecility.

A handful of people, who lived on little and did not run into debit brought to, and preserved in America, a rather high, severe culture, and a civic sense nourished by the traditions of English legal liberty, that is, by a centuries-long conquest in which the traditions of North European tribes and Roman Law converge.

The Republic was started with a limited suffrage which was gradually extended from the love of justice and because of the good sense of the common people. The frontier aristocracy was, of necessity, a physical aristocracy. The others either died or weakened. My grandfather used to wrestle with his lumberjacks not only for sport, but to maintain his prestige. Lincoln was the last president of this race and of this tradition. For two centuries the frontier required daring. With the danger gone came the people who know how to suffer and to endure; or those who merely subside.

Up to the time of the Civil War the public seems to have taken some interest in the Congressional debates. The Congressional Record at least might nourish a civic sense, and the names of the protagonists are remembered. Even today it is possible to tell some truths in Congress, but the public's attention has been diverted.

The 'Economic' history of the United States is, in a sense, the history of enormous waste of the immense natural resources, waste that took place because no immediate need for conservation was apparent and, in many instances, did not exist.

Land was given to whomsoever wished to settle on it, but no provisions were taken to protect the nation or the people from the hazards of resale. Often resold for a trifle, it went to form large landed estates which for a long time, and perhaps even today, have not injured anyone.

THE TREASURE OF A NATION IS ITS HONESTY

The following phases follow one another: Open Country. The need of manpower. Slaves. Debts. 'Free' craftsmanship in competition with the slave system. In the beginning personal commerce without indebtedness to finance. In many cases direct superintendence by the owners.

No man could be a director of the Salem Museum who had not sailed round both the Cape of Good Hope and the Horn. The construction of fast clippers was New England's glory a century ago. These clippers had brought the kind of wealth that follows the exchange of goods with the Orient and the entire world. Even if economic, the history of the United States was, up to the year 1860, romantic. It was the period of the cult of business which continued an Italic tradition, the tradition of the great City Republics of Venice and Genoa, the Superba and the Dominante. Economic affairs were not wholly sordid. Usury however is a cancer, Finance a disease.

Paterson, who invented the system of the Bank of England, that is, the system of loaning promissory notes, died poor, outcast by his early colleagues. California gold was discovered on the land of a man who did not profit by it. On the contrary, his farm was ruined and he got no protection from law.

The American tragedy is a continuous history of waste – waste of the natural abundance first, then waste of the new abundance offered by the machine, and then by machines, no longer isolated, but correlated and centuplicating the creative power of human labour.

The improvident Americans killed bison without thought of protecting them. Forests were cut down without thought of conservation. This had no immediate effect on the prosperity of the inhabitants, because of nature's abundance. The usurers, now called financiers, plotted against abundance. To understand the effect of the American system, it is necessary to go back to the monopoly of Thales and then take up the thread of the so-called Reformation, or protestant schism, seen from the economic angle. The Protestants did not wish to pay ecclesiastical taxes to Rome, and to the priests for their rites. The Bible was invented as a substitute-Priest. The Canonical prohibition against usury disappeared. Polite society did not consider usury as Dante did, that is, damned to the same circle of Hell as the sodomites, both acting against the potential abundance of nature.

The Catholic economy had proclaimed the doctrine of the just price. Monopoly is a manœuvre against the just price. To be able to speculate one needs a fluctuating market.

The employers naturally tried to get their work done for the least possible price. The working-men, in self-defence, asked for the suffrage. The people won the war against the Bank of the U.S. between 1830 and 1840 but, with the new waves of European work hands, the quality of the electorate declined, and demagogy undertook to corrupt it. The Press misled, or distracted, the people from the nature of the economic problem.

Toward the end of the eighteenth century the Republic was in revolt against the privileges of 'birth', and the whole democratic movement was in revolt against the monopolies held by the guilds; monopolies of the opportunity of working. This explains the bearing of Adam Smith's phrase: 'Men of the same trade never gather together without a conspiracy against the general public.'

But the monopolies, the sanctions, the restrictions imposed by the guilds were, at least, monopolies of *producers*. The various monopolies which culminate in the monopoly of money itself, key to all the other monopolies were, and are, monopolies of *exploiters*.

146

The situation is complicated when the same man has his hand both in production and in finance as the cleverest men have today. Henry Ford found himself forced into this situation in order to defend himself against Wall Street.

To understand the development of economic ideas in America, it is useful to know European precedents, even if these are little known in Europe itself.

The traces of the Leopoldine Reforms have been lost, as far as I know, but the analogy remains. It can be said with certainty that the same current towards the liberation from the shackles of the guilds made its appearance in Tuscany and in the American Colonies. The return to a controlled economy in Tuscany was wrecked by the Napoleonic Wars, and nothing was heard of it in Europe for years. As far as I can discover, it had no echo in America.

John Quincy Adams, almost alone and smeared as an eccentric, supported a doctrine giving more authority to the state. He wanted to conserve the national lands as property of the nation.

The romance of the covered waggon, clipper of the prairies, finds its analogy in the Italian colonization in Africa. All this emigration had some resemblance to what Italy was doing on her Fourth Shore, but the former was done without the state's doing anything save granting the land without foresight.

The natural abundance existed, but it was wasted. Today, among the few merits of F. D. R. stands, perhaps, a vague idea of reforestation. But he was scared into it by the dust bowl of the west.

BANKS

The trap of the banking system has always worked in the same way—some case of abundance is used to create optimism. This optimism is exaggerated, usually with the help of propaganda. Sales increase; prices of land, or of shares, rise beyond the possibility of material revenue. The banks had favoured exaggerated loans, in order to manoeuvre the increase, restrict, recall their loans, and presently panic overtakes the people.

Toward the end of the First World War, C. H. Douglas insisted on the possibility of great potential abundance and demanded national dividends, that is, a distribution of family or individual allowances so as to permit the public to buy what the public was producing.

Naturally all that was called insane. The London *Times*, and other newspapers, in the hands of financiers opposed this suggestion.

The justice of Major Douglas's views was confirmed by the Loeb Report (Report of the National Survey of Potential Product Capacity, New York City Housing Authority, 1935). No one has been willing to dispute these statistics. Before entering this war every family of four persons in the United States could have had a $4,000.00 to $5,000.00 Standard-of-Living. Only the iniquity, the imbecility of the monetary-financial system prevented the realisation of this material welfare.

War was brought about to impede the utilisation of this abundance. Without scarcity unjust prices cannot be imposed through mono-polies.

American money was not socialized. American money had not been democratic for eighty years, as Lincoln had democratised it tempor-arily, and as Jackson had democratised it, even succeeding in extirpat-ing the national debt.

The American people as late as 1939 had not yet learned the lesson taught by American history and, much less, by world history.

It is idiotic to leave the pocket-book of the nation in the hands of private and, perhaps foreign, irresponsible individuals.

It is idiotic to leave the nation's sources of information in the hands of irresponsible individuals and, sometimes, in foreign hands.

This ruin has its roots in the greed for lucre, a greed which abandons all common-sense and every sense of proportion, and blindly creates its own undoing.

Man has been reduced not even to a digestive tube, but to a bag of money that gradually is losing its value. This cycle has lasted three centuries; from the arrival of the Pilgrims who sought freedom of worship, to the Cult of Lucre dominating today. This is both econo-mic history and the history of a spiritual decadence. Part of the story is technical, part monetary, and part financial.

The aim of finance is to profit by others' labour. In the last four decades, the aim of finance, in order that the gains of a small group be greater, has been the retention of all the benefits of mechanical inventions and the lowering to a minimum the workers' rewards. And this was done in the open market through free competition.

Now-a-days, in normal times, the necessity of working as formerly does not exist. Van Buren, a century ago, was interested in reducing the working-day to ten hours. The working-day could be limited to four hours now, and everybody could have the opportunity of work-ing. But humanity, or, I should say, the working class, is not lazy. The great mass is not touched by an appeal to laziness.

Only the artist, for centuries, has succeeded in detaching the idea of work from the idea of profit, and not all artists have been capable of this dissociation of concepts.

I do not know whether or not I should cull long or brief citations in regard to the financial technique. The former would be a bore, the latter may be incomprehensible.

Van Buren was opposed to imprisoning debtors. The manoeuvres of finance are registered in phrases such as the following: . . . 'it [the Bank of the United States] increased the amount of the discounts. . . .

In the month of October, 1830, they were forty millions, and in May, 1832, seventy millions. Mr. Webster said: 'They must be decreased by thirty million dollars in states along the Mississippi.'

'The Bank received 341 millions and six millions from the Government. The funds under the control of the President of the Republic (Jackson) amounted to something between fifteen and twenty thousand." (Note: the President controlled THOUSANDS not millions.)

'. . . by using the methods of the bank in order to disorientate credit within the country, by creating panic so as to dominate the mind of the public . . .' '. . . Government members excluded from the real committee of the Bank Directors . . .' '. . . The Bank President controlling the government funds to betray the nation . . . "greasing" the Press by making nominal loans to non-existing bailsmen.' '. . . The Bank restricted seventeen millions of the sixty-four million dollar credit . . .' 'If Mr. Taney (Treasury) has not prevented the Bank's New York branch from collecting $8,700,000, and had not armed our city with nine million to defend ourselves (i.e. the nation) in this war on our commerce.'[1]

Van Buren had the transitory honour of being called THE LIBERATOR OF THE TREASURY. But his decade has disappeared from American memory.

After the assassination of Lincoln, President Johnson did not have the means to maintain fiscal liberty. In 1878 a Congressman expressed, or explained, his position by saying that he wanted to keep at least a part of the national debt in circulation as non-interest-bearing currency.

The 'free-silver' movement tried to oppose the interests of the silver owners to the gold interests, but did not go to the root. William Jennings Bryan headed this movement, and a few oldsters remember it even now. Once in a while an idealist plays up to the Silver men, or is started on his career by them. A Silverite, privately, will sometimes confess the truth as, in fact, Bryan confessed it to Kitson. At the moment I don't remember if Kitson published the details of the interview or communicated them in a personal letter to the undersigned. Though I have the impression that I have seen these details in print. Bryan, knowing that he was continuing an honest tradition, or striving to do so, fought vigorously, taking advantage of the means that were available to him.

---

[1] The source of these quotations is Van Buren's *Autobiography* ('Annual Report of the American Historical Association for the Year 1918', Vol. II, Govt. Printing Office, Washington, 1920). Mr. Pound has used the paraphrases of this book which he made in Canto XXXVII as the basis for his Italian text. Ed.

AMERICA

CHRONOLOGICAL OUTLINE

The chronology of American economic events is, roughly, as follows:

1620–1750–Beginning and development of colonial prosperity based finally, upon a system of loans by some of the Colonial Governments to those who tilled the land. This prosperity whetted the appetite of the London financiers who tried to impose their monetary monopoly;

1750–1776–1788– Preparation for the Revolution, Formation of the American System;

1789–Washington President. Struggle between Hamilton, conservative agent of finance and Jefferson's democratisation. 'Fraud of the Assumption'.

1801–1825–Jefferson and his disciples in the White House. The Louisiana Purchase. Second war against England;

1829–1841–Jackson and Van Buren in the White House. Fight between the Banks and the people. The people won;

1841–1861–Gold discovered in California, in 1849. Debts contracted by the 'South' to New York Bankers, and elsewhere. Negro Slavery. Symptoms of the Civil War;

from 1861 War of Secession. Triumph of Finance;

1869–1877–Grant President. Scandals. Gold against the people;

1890–The silver question. Trusts;

1914–Industrial development. Technocracy. The menace of Abundance.

1935–Chart of Potential Product Capacity;

1939–'War is his only way out,' phrase pronounced by a Congressman to signify that Roosevelt had made such a mess of things that war was his only way of escape. In other words, the only way to hide his past and to maintain his political power.

ROTTENNESS

From the Annual Reports of the Secretary of the Treasury, from June 1932 to June 1939, it can be learned that the Treasury of the United States bought ten billion dollars of gold at thirty-five dollars per ounce instead of $21.65 as in former times. The Treasury does not issue any reports regarding the source of this gold and, even if the Secretary of the Treasury himself wanted to find out where the gold came from, all he could find in his files, would be the names of the last sellers. This means that the government, or the American people, paid ten billion dollars for gold that, before the change in price, could have been bought for six billions. This amounted to a gift of four billion dollars to gold merchants irrespective of their nationality, many of them in fact being foreigners.

Only God knows how much gold the people have bought during

the war, from 1939 to the present time. The trick is simple. Whenever the Rothschild and other gents in the gold business have gold to sell, they raise the price. The public is fooled by propagandising the devaluation of the dollar, or other monetary unit according to the country chosen to be victimised. The argument is that the high price of the monetary unit is injurious to the nation's commerce.

But when the nation, that is, the people of that nation, own the gold and the financiers own the dollars or other monetary units, the gold standard is restored. This raises the value of the dollar and the citizens of 'rich' nations, as well as citizens of other nations, are diddled.

The manipulation of silver follows simple lines. It's all part of what Aristotle calls the 'common practice of commerce'. (Politics 1.4/5 Thales.) The silver merchants are less important than the merchants of gold. Other metals are monopolised but they do not enter directly into the monetary game. With these keys you can open the records, or the Congressional Record, wherever you wish, and you will find attempts to resist these swindles though they are getting weaker and weaker.

REMEDIES

Words fade. Facts repeat themselves. Truth makes an appearance at times, but it is misunderstood and exposed to ridicule. Economists do not see what stands right in front of their own eyes. Nine years ago a well-known and able Italian sociologist had not looked at the inscriptions on either Italian Bank or State notes. These economists carry on an immemorial tradition.

People do not look at plain common objects. A professor from the London School of Economics once sent me three satirical post cards. One of these was furnished with a sort of bellows so that when the card was pressed between the fingers it squeaked. He had bought these cards with a metal 'bon' issued by the French United Chambers of Commerce that had no value outside of France. He sent me these cards, nevertheless, to deny the possibility of having one kind of money valid everywhere and, at the same time, another kind valid only within the country of origin.

The diverse groups of monetary rebels and reformers, lacking a knowledge of tradition and possessing only a part of the truth, contradict one another and do not understand their different terminologies.

Fernando Ritter is perfectly right in insisting that the farmer who consigns his wheat to the pool must be guaranteed the supply of fertilisers etc., necessary for future cultivation. He echoes the statement of Zublay at the time of the formation of the United States:

'It is necessary to have the public believe that this paper is good for something.' (That is, exchangeable for agricultural products or other goods.) It is necessary that money be a guarantee of future exchange. This is in line with the commodity dollar fight, and for a just price-index.

Against these just proposals Wall Street roared: 'Rubber Dollar'. The usurers, naturally, oppose any control on the part of the public or of a state that pretends to represent the public's interests. The usurers want the control to remain entirely in their hands.

The whole history of the United States oscillates between these two camps. The people rebelled against the London usurers and instituted a government in America. This government fell prey to the resident usurers who kept in touch with the arch-usurers in the mother-country. Belmont used to represent the Rothschild, etc. Today the Main Office is in New York, the Branch Office is in London. The ubicity of the victims does not matter, and the headquarters maintains a high degree of mobility.

The usurers act through fraud, falsehood and by taking advantage of habits and superstitions of accounting, and, when these methods do not function, they let loose a war. Everything hinges on monopoly, and the particular monopolies hinge on the great delusive monopoly of money.

BIBLIOGRAPHY

No vast reading is needed to understand this phase of history, if the reader begins from the beginning, that is, with the POLITICS and ECONOMICS of Aristotle, and the Orations of Demosthenes, that against Dionysius, for example. The case of the United States, in particular, has been exposed in the books here below listed. As a beginning read the writings of John Adams and of Jefferson.

C. BOWERS: JEFFERSON AND HAMILTON, for the Scandal of the Assumption.

VAN BUREN: Autobiography.

HENRY ADAMS: Four volumes on the Administration of Jefferson and of Madison. Less interesting for a specifically Economico-Monetary study.

Novelists and playwrights, once in a while, give one a clearer idea than professors. One can learn more from Ernest Poole's THE HARBOUR about fast clippers; and from William Mahl's TWO PLAYS OF THE SOCIAL COMEDY about the attempt of monopolising the gold in 1869, than he is likely to learn from historiographers.

I have already mentioned the REPORT OF THE NATIONAL SURVEY OF POTENTIAL PRODUCT CAPACITY, 1935, New York City Housing Authority.

Irving Fisher was the first man to publish, in America, STAMP SCRIP, a book that clearly treats the Gesellist proposed currency system. The basic book of this school is THE NATURAL ECONOMIC ORDER, by Silvio Gesell.

H. A. Fack of Los Angeles, California, is its American publisher. For years he has been publishing an idealistic monthly THE WAY OUT.

The Alberta (Canada) revolt proceeded from the theories of C. H. Douglas mixed with Gesellism.

To get acquainted with the Technocrats' tendencies Dexter Kimball's INDUSTRIAL ECONOMICS would be useful.

D. R. Dewey's FINANCIAL HISTORY OF THE UNITED STATES could be of help to students already prepared to understand the significance of the facts listed in it. This book lacks, perhaps, total candour. It has been reprinted in various editions beyond the twelfth, and it is a favourite text-book in Universities. If my memory serves me right, Dewey does not mention any of the above-mentioned writers, except Henry Adams, who is not dangerous.

The students' lack of preparation these days, this modern schizophrenia called demo-liberal, derives from the neglect in the study of the Classics, and from the erroneous idea that Greek is a dead language, and that it is of no help in our preparing ourselves for the modern way of life. We begin with Adam Smith instead of beginning with Aristotle. Or the student is beclouded with the Ethics, Poetics, and Metaphysics. Commercial schools would profit, if not by the complete text, by studying, at least, some good edition of selected passages of translations. Those who consider this arrangement scandalous and want to be erudite, could be provided with a full text and a special index of passages that have an immediate and direct importance for the affairs of today. This could serve as true teaching for life, and this second arrangement would not harm any man of good will.

CHRONOLOGICAL TABLE

regarding other facts, plus a few indications as to the degree of perspicacity existing during the diverse epochs in America.

1684–England suppresses the Mint of Massachusetts which had coined a little silver.
1814–Calhoun opposed the process in which the government was forced to get its own credit on loan.
1819–Crawford issued Treasury bills bearing no interest.
1825–The industrial crisis in England led to dumping on the American market, glutting it with merchandise at bankrupt prices.
1832–Jackson: 'THE REAL VALUE OF LAND IS DUE TO LABOUR'.
1834-5–Jackson eliminates the national debt. The United States was left with no debt whatever.

Upon examining the receipts and the expenditures of the government between 1816 and 1833, even Dewey admits that the great decrease of expenditure was due to the reduction and, finally, to the elimination of the payments of interest on public debt.

BRIEFLY:

1816–Receipts $47,677,000.00
      Expenditure $31,196,000.00
1833–Receipts $33,948,000.00
      Expenditure $23,017,000.00

Interest on the Public Debt. In 1816 $7,823,000.00; in 1833 $303,000.00, and later ZERO.

1836–The National Treasury, having an active balance, distributed this money to the different states.

Without going back to the legendary Mohammedan Calif, those who, because of ignorance, shouted that C. H. Douglas's proposal of a National Dividend was a scandal and a novelty, may consider the following facts: Massachusetts distributed its share of the money to the various cities and towns; Boston used it for current expenses; Salem built a Town Hall; Groton repaired a bridge, and Maine made a *per capita* distribution.

1863–4–Chase favoured the maximum distribution of the National Loan among the people instead of trafficking with the banks.

1878–The Greenback Party, was in favour of the National Bills and against the bankers' monopoly. This party received a million votes.

1884–The end of the Greenback Party.

NOTE: I should not wish to appear unjust to D. R. Dewey when I say that he lacks candour. He has, perhaps, deceived himself by his own viscid terminology. For example, credit is not directly transformed into wealth. No paper operation can effect such a change, but credit can easily be transformed into buying power with varying terminologies printed on any subject, or substance.

A perfect example of instinctive monetary good sense is met today in this small town. The newsvendor, Mr. Baffico, certainly not an erudite man, because he lacked the necessary small change, and not wanting to use postage stamps as they lose their freshness and gum in a series of exchanges, has had some little tags printed which he now gives to his patrons as change. I found Signor Baffico indignant because other merchants had begun to accept his tags as money and he had to incur the expense of having another supply printed.

Any form of Transferable memory-aid serves, and has served, to simplify book-keeping, and to liberate us from the necessity of keeping every debit and every credit written in a ledger.

In order that money, admonitions, symbols, or certificates of debt become valid means of exchange, all that is necessary is that whoever issues them have the means to honour them.

F. Ritter, in a recent article, insists on the convertibility of money. His pessimism does not lean at all on the possibility, or advisibility of using labour as a MEASURE OF THE VALUES of the goods to be delivered.

PART SIX
Civilisation, Money and History

Bellum cano perenne . . .
> *. . . between the usurer and any*
> *man who*
> *wants to do a good job*
> *(perenne)*
without regard to production—
> *a charge*
for the use of money or credit.

Cantos 86/87.

PART SIX

Provincialism the Enemy[1]

I

If they had read my 'Education Sentimentale' these things would not have happened.

GUSTAVE FLAUBERT

PROVINCIALISM consists in:

(a) An ignorance of the manners, customs and nature of people living outside one's own village, parish, or nation.

(b) A desire to coerce others into uniformity.

Galdos, Turgenev, Flaubert, Henry James, the whole fight of modern enlightenment is against this. It is not of any one country. I name four great modern novelists because, perhaps, the best of their work has been an analysis, a diagnosis of this disease. In Galdos it is almost diagrammatic: a young civil engineer from Madrid is ultimately done to death by the bigots of 'Orbajosa', solely because he is from the Capital, and possessed of an education. His own relatives lead in the intrigue for his suppression. Turgenev in 'Fumée' and in the 'Nichée de Gentilshommes' digging out the stupidity of the Russian. Flaubert in his treatment of last century France. Henry James in his unending endeavour to provide a common language, an idiom of manners and meanings for the three nations, England, America, France. Henry James was, despite any literary detachments, the crusader, both in this internationalism, and in his constant propaganda against personal tyranny, against the hundred subtle forms of personal oppressions and coercions.

Idiots said he was untouched by emotion.

This in the face, or probably in their ignorance, of the outbursts in 'The Tragic Muse', or the meaning of the 'Turn of the Screw'. Human liberty, personal liberty, underlay all of his work, a life-long, unchangeable passion; and with it the sense of national differences, the small and the large misunderstanding, the slight difference in tone, and the greater national 'trend'. For example, this from 'A Bundle of Letters'. His Dr. Rudolph Staub writes from Paris:

'You will, I think, hold me warranted in believing that between

---

[1] *The New Age*, 12 July 1917.

159

precipitate decay and internecine enmities the English-speaking family is destined to consume itself, and that with its decline the prospect of general pervasiveness, to which I alluded above, will brighten for the deep-lunged children of the fatherland.'

'Universal pervasiveness.' We have heard a lot of this sort of thing during the last three years. My edition of the 'Bundle of Letters' was, however, printed in '83, thirty-one years before Armageddon. It had been written before that. However, the lords of the temporal world never will take an artist with any seriousness. Flaubert and Henry James had their previsions almost in vain.

Provincialism is more than an ignorance, it is ignorance plus a lust after uniformity. It is a latent malevolence, often an active malevolence. The odium theologicum is only one phase of it. It is very insidious, even with eyes open one can scarcely keep free of it. (Example, I have been delighted with the detection of Gerlach. All the morning I have been muttering, a priest and a burglar; Italy has scored by setting two burglars to deal with one clerical.)

Religious dogma is a set of arbitrary, unprovable statements about the unknown.

A clergy, any clergy, is an organised set of men using these arbitrary statements to further their own designs. There is no room for such among people of any enlightenment.

England and France are civilisation. They are civilisation because they have not given way to the yelp of 'nationality'. That, of course, is a debatable statement. All the same, they have not, at bottom, given way to the yelp of 'nationality', for all their 'Little England', 'La France', 'Imperialism', etc.

More profoundly they have not given way to the yelp of 'race'. France is so many races that she has had to settle things by appeal to reason. England is so many races, even 'Little England', that she has kept some real respect for personality, for the outline of the individual.

This is modern civilisation. Neither nation has been coercible into a Kultur; into a damnable holy Roman Empire, holy Roman Church orthodoxy, obedience, Deutschland über Alles, infallibility, mouse-trap.

There has been no single bait that the whole of either nation would swallow. It has been possible to cook up for 'the German' so tempting a stew of anaesthetics that the whole nation was 'fetched'. A certain uniform lurability could be counted on.

America has been hauled out by the scruff of her neck. She had imbibed a good deal of the poison. Her universities were tainted. Race, her original ideas, i.e., those taken over from France, and her customs, imported from England, won out in the end. Until they had done so it was very difficult to get any American periodical to print an attack on Kultur, Kultur which will still be found lurking by the grave of Munsterburg in the cemetery of the American universities.

I still find among educated people an ignorance of 'kultur', that is, of all save its overt manifestations, the bombing of infant schools, etc.

Distress over a system of education and of 'higher education' remains as much a mystery to people with whom I converse as was my disgust with the system, to my professors, fifteen years ago. People see no connection between 'philology' and the Junker.

Now, apart from intensive national propaganda, quite apart from German national propaganda, the 'university system' of Germany is evil. It is evil wherever it penetrates. Its 'universal pervasiveness' is a poisonous and most pestilent sort of pervasiveness. The drug is insidious and attractive.

It is, as Verhaeren said, the only system whereby every local nobody is able to imagine himself a somebody. It is in essence a provincialism. It is the 'single' bait which caught all the German intellectuals, and which had hooked many of their American confrères (even before 'exchange professorships' had set in).

Its action in Germany was perfectly simple. Every man of intelligence had that intelligence nicely switched on to some particular problem, some minute particular problem *unconnected* with life, *unconnected* with main principles (to use a detestable, much abused phrase). By confining his attention to *ablauts*, hair-length, foraminifera, he could become at small price an 'authority', a celebrity. I myself am an 'authority', I was limed to that extent. It takes some time to get clean.

Entirely apart from any willingness to preach history according to the ideas of the Berlin party, or to turn the class room into a hall of propaganda, the whole method of this German and American higher education was, is, evil, a perversion.

It is evil because it holds up an ideal of 'scholarship', not an ideal of humanity. It says in effect: you are to acquire knowledge in order that knowledge may be acquired. Metaphorically, you are to build up a dam'd and useless pyramid which will be no use to you or to anyone else, but which will serve as a 'monument'. To this end you are to sacrifice your mind and vitality.

The system has fought tooth and nail against the humanist belief that a man acquires knowledge in order that he may be a more complete man, a finer individual, a fuller, more able, more interesting companion for other men.

Knowledge as the adornment of the mind, the enrichment of the personality, has been cried down in every educational establishment where the Germano-American 'university' ideal has reached. The student as the bondslave of his subject, the gelded ant, the compiler of data, has been preached as a *summum bonum*.

This is the bone of the mastadon, this is the symptom of the disease;

it is all one with the idea that the man is the slave of the State, the 'unit', the piece of the machine.

Where the other phase of the idea, the slave of the State (i.e., of the emperor) idea has worked on the masses, the idea of the scholar as the slave of learning has worked on the 'intellectual'. It still works on him.

No one who has not been caught young and pitchforked into a 'graduate school' knows anything of the fascination of being about to 'know more than anyone else' about the sex of oysters, or the tonic accents in Aramaic. No one who has not been one of a gang of young men all heading for scholastic 'honours' knows how easy it is to have the mind switched off all general considerations, all considerations of the values of life, and switched on to some minute, unvital detail.

This has nothing whatever to do with the 'progress of modern science'. There is no contradicting the fact that science has been advanced, greatly advanced, by a system which divides the labour of research, and gives each student a minute detail to investigate.

But this division of the subject has not been the sole means of advance, and by itself it would have been useless. And *in any case* it is not the crux of the matter.

The crux of the matter is that the student, burying himself in detail, has not done so with the understanding of his act. He has not done it as a necessary sacrifice in order that he may emerge.

In the study of literature he has buried himself in questions of morphology, without ever thinking of being able to know good literature from bad. In all studies he has buried himself in 'problems', and completely turned away from any sense of proportion between the 'problems' and vital values.

In most cases the experiment has been merely blind experiment along a main line, in accord with a main idea *dictated by someone else*.

The student has become accustomed first to *receiving* his main ideas without question; then to being indifferent to them. In this state he has accepted the Deutschland über Alles idea, in this state he has accepted the idea that he is an ant, not a human being. He has become impotent, and quite pliable. This state of things has gone on long enough already.

It is time the American college president, indifferent to the curricula of his college or university, and anxious only 'to erect a memorial to his father' (as an American provost once said to me), it is time that he and his like awoke from their nap, and turned out the ideal of philology in favour of something human and cleanly.

II[1]

> Provincialism: an ignorance of the customs of other peoples,
> a desire to control the acts of other people.

Nothing 'matters' till some fool starts resorting to force. To prevent that initial insanity is the goal, and always has been, of intelligent political effort.

The provincialism of Darius led him to desire the subjugation of the Greeks, and his ignorance of the Greeks led him to think they would put up with him. There is no 'getting back to the beginning' of the matter. The fundamental 'philosophical' error or shortcoming is in Christianity itself. I think the world can well dispense with the Christian religion, and certainly with all paid and banded together ministers of religion. But I think also that 'Christ', as presented in the New Testament (real or fictitious personage, it is no matter), is a most profound philosophic genius, and one credible in the stated surroundings; an intuitive, inexperienced man, dying before middle age. The things unthought of in his philosophy are precisely the things that would be unthought in the philosophy of a provincial genius, a man of a subject nation. The whole sense of social order is absent.

The things neglected are precisely the things so well thought in the philosophy of Confucius, a minister high in the State, and living to his full age, and also a man of great genius.

There is no disagreement. There is a difference in emphasis. Confucius' emphasis is on conduct. 'Fraternal deference' is his phrase. If a man have 'fraternal deference' his character and his opinions will not be a nuisance to his friends and a peril to the community.

It is a statesman's way of thinking. The thought is for the community. Confucius' constant emphasis is on the value of personality, on the outlines of personality, on the man's right to preserve the outlines of his personality, and of his duty not to interfere with the personalities of others.

The irresponsible Galilean is profounder: 'As a man thinketh in his heart,' 'What shall it profit to gain the world and lose your own soul.' A man of decent character will not injure his neighbours. That is all very well. But there are no safeguards.

And Christianity has become the slogan of every oppression, of every iniquity. From saving your own soul, you progress to thinking it your duty or right to save other people's souls, and to burn them if they object to your method of doing it.

The profound intuitions are too incoherent in their expression, too much mixed with irrelevancies, the ironies misunderstood and mistranslated by cheats. The provincial has not guarded against provincialism. He has been the seed of fanatics. I doubt if Confucius has ever been the seed of fanatics. After his death his country was cursed with Buddhism, which is very much the same as part of the pest which spread over mediaeval Europe, clothed in the lamb's wool of Christ. It showed in China many resembling symptoms. But this had nothing to do with Confucius, 'the first man who did not receive a divine inspiration'.

Christ's cross was not so much on Calvary as in His lamentable lack of foresight. Had He possessed this faculty we might imagine His having dictated to His disciples some such text as 'Thou shalt not "save" thy neighbour's soul by any patent panacea or kultur. And especially thou shalt not "save" it against his will.'

In such case the passage would either have been deleted by His 'followers', or the Church of Rome would have founded itself on Mohammed. The contest for 'rights', democracy, etc., in the West, has been little concerned with personality. If personality has been thought of, it was taken for granted. Tyranny had to be got rid of. So little time has passed since 'slavery' was abolished, that one need not greatly despond; that is, slavery *to* an individual owner.

I think the work of the subtlest thinkers for the last thirty years has been a tentative exploration for means to prevent slavery to a 'State' or a 'democracy', or some such corporation, though this exploration has not been 'organised', or 'systematised', or coherent, or even very articulate in its utterance.

Undoubtedly, we must have something at least as good as socialism. The whole body of the Allies is presumably united in demanding something at least as good as socialism. The only demand for something definitely and uncompromisingly worse than socialism, worse than democracy, more anthropoid, comes from the Central Powers.

The arts, explorative, 'creative', the 'real arts', literature, are always too far ahead of any general consciousness to be of the slightest contemporary use. A coal strike, with 2,000,000 orderly strikers happens half a century after the artistic act, half a century after the 'creator's', or discoverer's concept of labour in orderly organisation.

When, in the foregoing paragraph, I talk about the few subtle thinkers, I talk of those whose undogmatic speculations will be the bases of 'parties' some time after present 'political' issues, and 'social' issues have been settled.

While half the world is struggling to maintain certain rights which every thinking man has long recognised as just, a few, a very few 'unpractical', or, rather, unexecutive men have been trying to 'carry the matter further'; to prevent a new form of tyranny succeeding in the place of an old form.

Modern thought is trying to kill not merely slavery but the desire to enslave; the desire to maintain an enslavement. This concept is a long way ahead of any actuality, it is a long way ahead of any working economic system that any of our contemporaries will be able to devise or to operate. But the desire for cannibalism is very largely extinct, and in the realm of reason there is nothing to prevent the conception of other barbaric ideas and desires entering equal extinction.

The desire to coerce the acts of another is evil. Every ethical thought is of slow growth; it has taken at least thirty years to suggest the thought that the desire to coerce the acts of others is evil. The thought belongs to only a few hundreds of people. Humanity is hardly out of the thought that you may have inquisitions and burn people at stakes.

To come back to where I started this brief series of essays: The bulk of the work in Henry James' novels is precisely an analysis of, and thence a protest against, all sorts of petty tyrannies and petty coercions, at close range. And this protest is knit into and made part of his analysis of the habits of mind of three nations at least. And Galdos, Flaubert, Turgenev, despite any proclamations about artistic detachment or any theories of writing, are all absorbed in this struggle. It is a struggle against provincialism, a struggle for the rights of personality; and the weapon of these authors has largely been a presentation of human variety. The German university system has been the antagonist, i.e., off the the plane of force and of politics, and in the 'intellectual field'.

Narrowing the discussion to university educations, for the moment; meeting the philological boasts of efficiency and of 'results produced', there is a perfectly good antidote, there is no need of any powers of invention or of careful devising. A Germany of happier era provided the term 'Wanderjahr', and the humanist ideals of the Renaissance are sounder than any that have been evolved in an attempt to raise 'monuments' of scholarship; of hammering the student into a piece of mechanism for the accretion of details, and of habituating men to consider themselves as bits of mechanism for one use or another: in contrast to considering first what use they are in being.

The bulk of scholarship has gone under completely; the fascinations of technical and mechanical education have been extremely seductive (I mean definitely the study of machines, the association with engines of all sorts, the inebriety of mechanical efficiency, in all the excitement of its very rapid evolution).

The social theorist, springing, alas, a good deal from Germany, has not been careful enough to emphasise that no man is merely a unit. He 'knows' the fact well enough, perhaps. But the error of his propagandist literature is that it does not sufficiently dwell on this matter.

Tyranny is always a matter of course. Only as a 'matter of course', as a thing that 'has been', as a 'custom' can it exist. It exists unnoticed, or commended. When I say that these novelists have worked against it, I do not mean they have worked in platitude, their writing has been a delineation as tyranny of many things that had passed for 'custom' or 'duty'. They alone have refrained from creating catchwords, phrases for the magnetising and mechanising of men.

Shaw slips into the kultur error (I think it is in some preface or other), where he speaks of a man being no use until you put an idea inside him. The idea that man should be used 'like a spindle', instead of existing 'like a tree or a calf' is very insidious. These two analogies do not present a dilemma. There is no reason why we should accept either Smiles or Rousseau, or utilitarianism, on any plane, or utopic stagnation. But if we did away with analogies and false dilemmas, 'causes' and mob orators would have a very poor time.

III[1]

> Fifty graduated grunts and as many representative signs will serve for all needful communication between thoroughly socialised men. REMY DE GOURMONT

De Gourmont's jibe sums up the intellectual opposition to socialism. The good socialist will say it is only a jibe and that socialism offers as much protection to the individual as any other known system. This is not quite the point, and it is not enough for the 'inventor', under which term I include artists and projective thinkers of all sorts. Rightly or wrongly, the 'inventor' is apt to consider the general tone of socialist propaganda, and to find it prone to emphasise the idea of man as a unit, society as a thing of 'component parts', each capable of an assignable 'function'.

When socialism can free itself from the suspicion of this heresy, the intellectual opposition to it will, presumably, go to pieces, capitulate, be converted.

The denuded or mechanised life lacks attraction. No intelligent man goes toward it with his eyes open–whether it means a mechanical simplification, or a mechanical complication. 'Kultur' has propounded a mechanical complication for the deadening of the faculties.

The 'State' forgot the 'use' of 'man'; 'scholarship', as a 'function of the State', forgot the use of the individual, or, at least, mislaid it, secreted it for its own purpose. 'Philology' laid hold of the arts, and did its best to make them knuckle under. Kunstwissenschaft was exalted. The arts also were to become a function of the State, duly ordered and controlled. It is all exceedingly plausible. Germany was so provincial that she supposed the rest of the world would swallow the bait and submit. American was so provincial that it took her

[1] *The New Age*, 26 July 1917.

several years to understand that militarism must be put down. Even now, she does not much understand; she is stampeded, thank God, in the right direction, towards the annihilation of Kaisers.

America has as yet no notion of reforming her universities. The connection between the destruction of Rheims, the massacres of near-Eastern populations, etc., and a peculiar tone of study, is not too clearly apparent. Provincialism I have defined as an ignorance of the nature and custom of foreign peoples, a desire to coerce others, a desire for uniformity–uniformity always based on the temperament of the particular provincial desiring it.

The moment you teach a man to study literature not for his own delight, but for some exterior reason, a reason hidden in vague and cloudy words such as 'monuments of scholarships', 'exactness', 'soundness', etc., 'service to scholarship', you begin his destruction, you begin to prepare his mind for all sorts of acts to be undertaken for exterior reasons 'of State', etc., without regard to their merit.

The right in the 'Lusitania' matter is not a question of 'military necessity' . . . or of whether the Germans gave a sporting warning . . ., etc.; it is simply that 'this kind of thing must not happen'. The human value as against the rationalistic explanation is always the weightier.

Take a man's mind off the human value of the poem he is reading (and in this case the human value is the art value), switch it on to some question of grammar and you begin his dehumanisation.

Such dehumanisation went on in the universities of Deutschland, subtly and with many exterior hues. There appeared to be no harm in it so long as it produced nothing more appalling than 'grundrissen' and 'Zeitschrifts für blankische philologie':–parts of which might conceivably be of some use and facilitate the reading of lost literatures. I know at least one German professor who has produced a dictionary and remained delightfully human at the age of about sixty-five. His abridgment would have helped me to read troubadours if I had not learned to read them before I found it.

I have no objection to any man making himself into a tank or refrigerator for as much exact information as he enjoys holding. There may even be a sensuous pleasure in such entanking. But a system which makes this entanking not only a *sine qua non*, but a fetish, is pernicious.

The uncritical habit of mind spreads from the university to the Press and to the people. I am well aware that this uncritical habit of mind is hidden by an apparatus criticus, and by more kinds of 'criticism' and criteria, and talk about criticism than the man in the street has heard of. But it is for all that uncritical. It divides facts into the known and the unknown, the arranged and the unarranged. It talks about the advancement of learning and demands 'original research', i.e., a re-tabulation of data, and a retabulation of tables already retabulated.

The 'State' and the 'universities' which are its bacilli work in a uniform way. In scholarship it leads to the connoisseur of sculpture who tells you, re the early Greek work, that your values are 'merely aesthetic values', and, therefore, of no importance; he being intent only on archaeological values. (This is not fanciful but an actual incident.) It leads, in the general, to an uncritical acceptance of any schematised plan laid down by higher commands of one sort or another. These things have their relative 'use' or convenience, or efficiency, but their ultimate human use is nil, or it is pernicious.

The ultimate goal of scholarship is popularisation. (Groans from the scholar, the aesthete, the connoisseur!) I admit that 'popularisation' of a sort is impossible. You cannot make a man enjoy Campion's quality by setting a book in front of him. You cannot make a bred-in-the-bone philologist enjoy the quality of an author's style rather than the peculiarity of his morphological forms. That sort of popularisation is not quite what I mean. Popularisation in its decent and respectable sense means simply that the scholar's ultimate end is to put the greatest amount of the best literature (i.e., if that is his subject) within the easiest reach of the public; free literature, as a whole, from the stultified taste of a particular generation. This usually means, from the taste of the generation which has just preceded him, and which is always engaged in warping the mass humanity of Welt literature into the peculiar modality of its own needs or preferences; needs or preferences often of a transient value which is quite real and often obscured and unduly derided by later eras. He is, or should be, engaged in an attack on provincialism of time, as the realist author is engaged in an attack on a provincialism of place. His job is much more to dig out the fine thing forgotten, than to write huge tomes 'about' this, that, and the other.

Fitzgerald's 'Omar' is worth all the Persian scholarship of a century. Yet, in my undergraduate days I was accustomed to hear England damned as an unscholarly country, and to be told that practically no authoritative books on any subject had come out of England for many decades. This may, for all I know, be, from some angles, true, but a harping on this point of view shows an ill-sense of proportion. I am not saying that nine hundred small philologists and researchers should all of them have been trying to be second and third Fitzgeralds. I do say that all literary research should look toward and long for some such consummation, and that only with such a hope can it be healthy and properly oriented. And in every department of scholarship or of life I demand a similar orientation. One does not make steel rails in order that steel rails shall be made. Industrialism propagates this heresy with some vigour. Without steel rails international communication would suffer, and 'intercommunication is civilisation'. That has nothing to do with the matter.

Civilisation means the enrichment of life and the abolition of violence; the man with this before him can indubitably make steel rails, and, in doing so, be alive. The man who makes steel rails in order that steel rails shall be made is little better than the mechanism he works with. He is no safeguard against Kaiserism; he is as dangerous and as impotent as a chemical. He is as much a sink of prejudice as of energy, he is a breeding ground of provincialism.

The history of the world is the history of temperaments in opposition. A sane historian will recognise this, a sane sociologist will recognise the value of 'temperament'. I am not afraid to use a word made ridiculous by its association with freaks and Bohemians. France and England are civilisation, and they are civilisation because they, more than other nations, do recognise such diversity. Modern civilisation comes out of Italy, out of renaissance Italy, the first nation which broke away from Aquinian dogmatism, and proclaimed the individual; respected the personality. That enlightenment still gleams in the common Italian's 'Cosi son io!' when asked for the cause of his acts.

IV[1]

'Transportation is civilisation.' Whatever literary precocity may have led people to object to Kipling, or to 'the later Kipling' *as art*, there is meat in this sentence from *The Night Mail*. It is about the last word in the matter. Whatever interferes with the 'traffic and all that it implies' is evil. A tunnel is worth more than a dynasty.

A tunnel would almost be worth part of this war, or, at least, a resultant tunnel would leave the war with some constructiveness indirectly to its credit, and no single act of any of the Allies would have so inhibitive an effect on all war parties whatsoever. There is something sinister in the way *the* tunnel disappears from discussion every now and again. I dare say it is not the supreme issue of the war. It may not be the millennium, but it is one, and, perhaps, *the* one firm step that can definitely be taken, if not toward a perpetual peace, at least toward a greater peace probability.

Zola saw 'one country: Europe, with Paris as its capital.' I do not see this, though if I care for anything in politics I care for a coalition of England, France and America. And after years of anxiety, one sees the beginning of, or, at least, an approach to some such combination: America, who owes all that she has to French thought and English customs, is at last beginning to take up her share in the contest.

Fundamentally, I do not care 'politically', I care for civilisation, and I do not care who collects the taxes, or who polices the thoroughfares.

[1] *The New Age*, 2 August 1917.

Humanity is a collection of individuals, not a *whole* divided into segments or units. The only things that matter are the things which make individual life more interesting.

Ultimately, all these things proceed from a metropolis. Peace, our ideas of justice, of liberty, of as much of these as are feasible, the immaterial, as well as material things, proceed from a metropolis. Athens, Rome, the Cities of the Italian Renaissance, London, Paris, make and have made us our lives. New York distributes to America. It is conceivable that in a few centuries the centre may have shifted to the west side of the Atlantic, but that is not for our time.

At present the centre of the world is somewhere on an imaginary line between London and Paris, the sooner that line is shortened, the better for all of us, the richer the life of the world. I mean this both 'intellectually' and 'politically'. France and England have always been at their best when knit closest. Our literature is always in full bloom after contact with France. Chaucer, the Elizabethans, both built on French stock. Translations of Villon revived our poetry in the midst of the mid-Victorian desiccation.

Contrariwise, the best of French prose, let us say the most 'typical', the vaunted Voltairian clarity is built on England, on Voltaire's admiration of English freedom and English writers.

And the disease of both England and America during the last century is due precisely to a stoppage of circulation. Note that just at the time when Voltaire would normally have been reaching the English public and being translated, the Napoleonic wars intervened, communication was stopped. There has never been a complete or adequate English translation of Voltaire, not even of representative selections. England and America have brushed about in a dust-heap of bigotry for decades. No one has pointed out why. France went on to Stendhal and Flaubert. England declined from the glorious clarity of Fielding. She underwent an inferior century, lacking an essential chemical in her thought. Her anaemia contaminated America.

Even Landor was almost suppressed, not officially and by edict, but left unobtainable, or 'selected' by Colvin.

Even before the war what sort of communication had we with France? Who, in any way, realised the Celt, and the Pict in France, or the Charente stock among the English? Who but a solitary crank would look into a south French town called 'Gourdon', with a street of 'Fourgous', and note the flaming red hair of its denizens? This is a long way from Brittany, and that more generally recognised racial kinship.

I do not wish to sentimentalise. My sole intent is to point out that England had forgotten a number of bonds with France, and that there may remain still more which even war rhetoric has not brought to the surface.

Wars are not ended by theorising. Burckhardt notes as the highest point of renaissance civilisation the date when Milan refused to make war on Venice because a 'war between buyer and seller could be profitable to neither'. The 'Peace of *Dives*' was recognised for an instant and forgotten. Historically, peace has not been doctrinaire. It has been not unlike a rolled snowball. Burgundy and Aquitaine no longer make war on each other. England and Scotland no longer make war on each other. Dante propounded a general central judiciary for all Europe, a sort of Hague tribunal to judge and decide between nations. His work remains as a treatise. What peace Europe acquired she acquired by an enlargement of nations, by coalitions, such as that of Castille, Leon and Aragon.

The closer these unions the greater the area in which a lasting peace is made possible. And against this moves the ever damned spirit of provincialism. Napoleon was its incarnation. Only a backwoods hell like Corsica could have produced him.

He was simply a belated condottiere working on a much greater scale. The Italian Renaissance cities had produced his type by the hundred.

Coming from a barbarous island he arrived with a form of ambition two centuries behind the times, and wrecks incalculable mischief. He came with an idiotic form of ambition which had been civilised out of his more intelligent, more urban contemporaries.

The same can be said of the Hohenzollern bred in a mediaeval sink like North Germany, fed on rhetoric and on allegory. They had a mediaeval decor, a mediaeval lack of bath-tubs (indeed, this is a slur on some mediaeval castles), they had about them a learning which furnishes a parallel to the elaborate scholarship of the schoolmen, and was as fundamentally vain. They desired an isolation. All reactionaries desire an isolation. The project for a means of communication is a wound. A definite start, to be quite concrete for the moment, a definite start on the Channel Tunnel would be worth many German defeats. It belongs to a world and an order of things in which local princes with the right of life and death over their subjects do not exist, and wherein many other mediaeval malpractices pass into desuetude.

As for decentralisation, does the general English reader know that the City of New York proposed to secede from the State of New York at the time of the Southern Secession? It is the best parallel I know for the situation of Ulster (? Belfast). We may take it that Ulster is Belfast. As an American I may be permitted to be glad that the United States were not sub-divided; that some trace of civilisation has been permitted to remain in them, and, despite many of their faults, to continue, if not to progress.

Among the present sub-sectional criers within your Islands I hear no voice raised on behalf of civilisation. I hear many howling for a literal and meticulous application of political doctrine; for a doctrinaire application, for a carrying *ad absurdum* of a doctrine that is good enough as a general principle. Neither from South Ireland nor from Ulster has anyone spoken on behalf of civilisation, or spoken with any concern for humanity as a whole. And because of this the 'outer world' not only has no sympathy, but is bored, definitely bored sick with the whole Irish business, and in particular with the Ulster dog-in-the-manger. No man with any care for civilisation as a whole can care a damn who taxes a few hucksters in Belfast, or what rhetorical cry about local rights they lift up as a defence against taxes. As for religion, that is a hoax, and a circulation of education would end it. But a nation which protects its bigotry by the propagation of ignorance must pay the cost in one way or another. Provincialism is the enemy.

And again for the tunnel which means union and not disseverance. 'It would suck the guts out of Paris in a few years, in less than no time.' Would it? There are perhaps few people in this island who would stop for such consideration. There are French who would mock the idea, and still more intelligent French who would accept it, *and* desire the tunnel.

The point is *not* would the tunnel turn Paris into a sort of Newport, into a sort of swell suburb of London. (Which it very conceivably might.) The question is, does a closer union of the two capitals make for a richer civilisation, for a completer human life for the individual? And to this question there is only one overwhelmingly affirmative answer.

Not only would it do this, but it would, I think, tend not to making the two cities alike, but to accentuate their difference. Nothing is more valuable than just this amicable accentuation of difference, and of complementary values.

It is a waste of time to arrange one's study of a literary period anywhere save in the British Museum. (No one who has not tried to start the examination of a period elsewhere can fully appreciate this.) I am taking a perhaps trifling illustration, but I wish to avoid ambiguity. It is a waste of time for a painter not to have both the Louvre and the National Gallery (and the Prado, for that matter) 'under his thumb'. Artists are not the only men to whom a metropolis is of value. They are not an isolated exception. I but take my illustration from the things most familiar to me. To put it another way: Civilisation is made by men of unusual intelligence. It is their product. And what man of unusual intelligence in our day, or in any day, has been content to live away from, or out of touch with, the biggest metropolis he could get to?

PROVINCIALISM THE ENEMY

A lumping of Paris and London into one, or anything which approximates such a lumping, doubles all the faculties and facilities. Anything which stands in the way of this combination is a reaction and evil. And any man who does not do his part toward bringing the two cities together has set his hand against the best of humanity.

Kublai Khan and his Currency[1]

The gentleman who said 'Veritas praevalebit' was careful to put his verb in the future tense and to affix no date to his prophecy. Truth sticks her nose out of the water-butt at rare intervals and then ducks beneath the shower of butt-lids hurled upon her. There is enough theological sense in Rabelais to blast all the bloated bishops and bell-clanging vicars in England to reduce them to fine malodorous powder, yet, as no multitude is paid annually to spread Rabelais or Bayle or Voltaire, the obscurity of the populace is undiminished, the same wheezes work age in and age out; Chaucer's pardoner, the party who plays with peas and shells at the country fair, and the makers of currency are still with us.

Apropos of Professor Pigou and his salary, we turn to Yule's edition of 'The Travels of Marco Polo' (Vol. I, pp. 423 ff.):

> The Emperor's Mint then is in this same City of Cambaluc, and the way it is wrought is such that you might say he hath the Secret of Alchemy in perfection, and you would be right! For he makes his money after this fashion.
>
> He makes them take the bark of a certain tree, in fact the Mulberry Tree, the leaves of which are the food of the silkworms–these trees being so numerous that whole districts are full of them. What they take is a certain fine white bast or skin which lies between the wood of the tree and the thick outer bark, and this they make into something resembling sheets of paper, but black. When these sheets have been prepared they are cut up into pieces of different sizes. The smallest of these is worth half a tornesel; the next, a little larger, one tornesel; one, a little larger still, is worth half a silver groat of Venice; another, a whole groat; others yet two groats, five groats, and ten groats. There is also a kind worth one Bezant of gold, etc.
>
> All these pieces of paper are issued with as much solemnity as if they were of pure gold or silver; and on every piece a variety of officials . . . have to write their names and to put their seals, etc.

Forgery was punished; every year 'the Khan causes to be made such a vast quantity of this money which costs him nothing that it must equal in amount all the treasure in the world.' All the Khan's debts were paid in paper, which he made current legal tender throughout his dominions. Merchants arriving from foreign countries were not

---

[1] *The New Age*, 20 May 1920. See Canto XVIII. Ed.

allowed to sell gold, silver or gems to anyone but the Emperor. Twelve experts did the buying. The Emperor paid a 'liberal price' in paper, which the merchants took, knowing they could not get so good a price from anyone else (i.e., anyone who did not have a printing press). Proclamations were also issued several times a year invited anyone who had gold, pearls, etc., to bring them to the Mint and receive paper for them.

Old and worn notes were redeemed at 97 per cent face value.

And if any Baron, or any one else soever, hath need of gold or silver or gems or pearls, in order to make plates, or girdles, or the like (i.e., luxury products), he goes to the Mint and buys as much as he list, paying in this paper money.

Now you have heard the ways and means whereby the Great Khan may have, and, in fact, has, more treasure than all the Kings in the World; and you know all about it and the reason why.

The learned notes on this passage tell us that the issue of paper money began in China in the ninth century; that by 1160 the country was flooded with paper, to the nominal value of 43,600,000 ounces of silver, exclusive of local notes. The Kin dynasty issued notes which were current for seven years, and then redeemable in new notes at 15 per cent loss. Kublai began his issue in 1260. By 1287 he had to issue a new currency, redeeming the old with one new note against *five* of the preceding issues.

The annotations to Polo continue with various details concerning successful and unsuccessful attempts to impose paper in Persia, China, and India.

We must in fairness admit that when the Khan finally allowed Polo to return to Venice he redeemed a good deal of Polo's paper, and that the Venetians returned to their native city with a more universal medium of exchange; but then, Polo had been quite useful to the Khan, and may certainly be regarded as an insider.

Kublai was indubitably an able administrator; and democratic notions had not penetrated the best circles of Cambaluc. Polo's account of him was greeted as the accounts of other explorers, though Columbus read him with interest.

What we see on closer examination of the text is that Polo regarded the issue of paper money as a sort of clever hoax, backed up by tyrannic power. The real tyranny resided, of course, in the Khan's control of credit. The parallels are fairly obvious.

Paper money in Europe, as in the Orient, seems to have been regarded either as a perquisite of tyrants or as an expedient. Frederic II honourably redeemed' the leather coinage issued during the siege of Faenza. Paper and even leather coinage were certainly a convenience on the ground of portability. We have ceased to regard the issue of paper as a hoax, yet Polo smelled a rat, and a real rat; but when he says, 'Now you know all about it,' he over-estimated the intelligence of his readers. After six centuries the number of readers who 'know all about it' on a single reading of Polo's paragraphs is still exceedingly few.

It was not the bureaucratic solemnity of the officials 'whose duty it was' to write their names on the paper and affix the imperial seals; it was in credit-control. The unification of the function with the other functions of tyranny is very simple. It is so simple indeed that chairs of economics have to be founded with increasing frequency to keep the fact from becoming apparent.

As for administrative efficiency, the ages have gained little. Kublai's post-riders with their coats buttoned behind and *sealed* with official seals so that there should be no question of their having dallied by the way-side, or reclined upon alien couches, are sufficient memorial to his insight into man's character.

'Probari Ratio'[1]

The orthodox church of Economics finds itself increasingly prey to suspicions, some worthy no doubt, and others doubtless unworthy; the Roscelins and Abelards are few, the chief haeresiarchs, in the main, unattractive; the permitted fads are presumably 'warranted harmless'. Mr. J. M. Keynes may deplore the poverty of our late enemies from a more humanitarian angle than those who merely regret an unlikelihood of ultimate payment; Nationalisation and Communism are no more likely to become world systems than were the various panaceas of Anabaptists and Mammillaires to become worldwide spiritual nostrums. And yet scepticism grows under the post-war pressure, sometimes half-conscious, sometimes as polished as that in which the Medici pontiff may have indulged himself between high masses and banquets.

Fabianism and Prussianism alike give grounds for what Major Douglas has ably synthesized as 'a claim for the complete subjection of the individual to an objective which is externally imposed on him; which it is not necessary or even desirable that he should understand in full.' Even if one cannot accept the detail of Major Douglas' thesis one is compelled to sympathise with the humanism of his approach to the problems of disguised Prussianism and of the high cost of living; if one sees no such Utopias as he vaguely adumbrates, one can but admire his very sincere protest against the wastage of human material under the present system of wage-tyranny and his instinctive revolt against any system of ratiocination which treats a man as a 'unit'.

The 'button-moulder' of Ibsenian drama has long since passed from the supernatural to the mundane; uniforming Death has donned the robe of the social theorist, and, not content to wait extreme unctions, has encroached upon the purlieus of the living. Major Douglas' realism begins with a fundamental denial that man with his moods and hypostases is or can decently ever become a 'unit'; in this underlying, implicit and hardly elaborated contention lies the philosophic value of his treatise. He is for a free exercise of the will, and his paragraphs arouse and rearouse one to a sense of how far we have given up our individual wills in all matters of economics.

The second strand of this author's realism is his perception, very clear and hard-headed, that the ultimate control of industry is financial control. There are the makers of credit, and into their hands do

[1] *The Athenaeum*, 2 April 1920.

we commit our trust, rather against Major Douglas' judgment; for he would have us retain, we think, some sort of string-end or chain-end. 'Real credit' is, in his definition, 'a measure of the reserve of energy belonging to a community', and 'in consequence drafts of this reserve should be accounted for by a financial system which reflects that fact'. 'The State should lend, not borrow . . . in this respect, as in others, the Capitalist usurps the function of the State.' This latter proposition is perhaps the most 'revolutionary' in the book, that is to say it is almost the only complete reversal of present custom which the author advocates; in the rest he offers modifications and makes rather startling promises.

His remedy, for those who no longer regard the present system as the best possible modus in the best of Candidian worlds, is neither a sharing of goods, nor a nationalisation of coal-mines, nor a complete preliminary metamorphosis of human nature, nor the capital levy recommended by Mr. Keynes, but simply

> the administration of credit by a decentralised local authority; the placing of the control of process entirely in the hands of the organised producer (and this in the broadest sense of the evolution of goods and services) and the fixing of prices on the broad principles of use value, by the community as a whole operating by the most flexible representation possible.

Various further mechanisms are by this entailed, but we are insured against an increase of bureaucracy. Given the feasibility of such placing and fixing, we are, by the author, assured, if not of millennial happiness, at any rate of a much chastened Mammon, whose bonds are not to incommode his utility.

The formula is certainly not framed to stir street-corner enthusiasms, it is proposed in very moderate if not very comprehensible terms; and by reason of their moderation one is left with the question, 'If it will not do any good, this decentralisation of the credit-administration, will it, could it, on the contrary do very much harm, and to whom?' It would be carping to point out that the author is not very definite about the composition of his 'decentralized local authority'; in so brief a book something must be left, we presume, to the reader's constructive imagination.

The author tries with undeniable honesty to solve the vicious-circle riddle; he writes with sufficient precision of phrase to command a certain respect for his mental capacity. Surrounded on all sides by confessions of helplessness and appeals to the better nature of abstract competitive bodies, one cannot abruptly reject the calculations of any man who has succeeded in convincing himself of the existence of a remedy; moreover the book, sound or unsound, is a mental stimulant. Present conditions cannot be laid wholly to the war; one remembers the spring of 1914. The Trade Unions are naïve seekers of plunder offering no solution, but presenting rather an extended demonstration of Adam Smith's basis of 'Economics' to the effect that 'Men of the same trade never meet together without a conspiracy against the public'; but in the other camp even *The Times* lifts up a protest against Messrs. Coates, and the dodge of increasing a company's capital is too transparent for any but the most obtuse among laymen.

Economic treatises, in the main, neglect human values; they content themselves with tables of statistics, which from the general-readers' viewpoint might often be interchanged or turned upside down without much affecting the argument. Major Douglas is at least philosophically wholesome, and if his forebodings are exaggerated they at any rate show what kind of perils he would teach his audience to avoid:

> The danger which at the moment threatens individual liberty far more than any extension of individual enterprise is the Servile State; the erection of an irresistible and impersonal organisation through which the ambition of able men, animated consciously or unconsciously by the lust of domination, may operate to the enslavement of their fellows.

The State exists for mankind, ideas exist for mankind, and lastly–and here is the rub of his treatise–credit exists for mankind; or, in Major Douglas' words, 'The administration of real capital, i.e., the power to draw on the collective potential capacity to do work, is clearly subject to the control of its real owners through the agency of credit.'

It is extremely difficult to find a flaw in this doctrine on the basis of ethics or equity, as for the practical workings of any system which attempts to put this poetic justice into action we must await the event. Major Douglas does not, apparently, contemplate Soviets or red shirts or polygamy or free beer or free divorce or guillotines, or any of the more decorative paraphernalia of ancient and modern revolution; we are to be saved by a few hundred chartered, but honest accountants working in a plate-glass room under communal supervision, which, if we are, alas! destined for salvation despite our natural inclinations, may be as good a method as any.

Economic Democracy[1]

The science of political economy as distinct from the theology of the subject may be said to begin with Adam Smith's dictum that 'men of the same trade never meet together without a conspiracy against the public'. With Messrs. Coates in one part of the foreground, and trade unions, associations for plunder, in another and with 'the great financiers' ever present (save in the 'Black List'), the above axiom needs little defence. For two decades the intelligentsia has made its own brand of poison, the Fabians and persons of Webbian temperament have put forward the ideal: man as a social unit. German philology with sacrifice of individual intelligence to the Moloch of 'Scholarship'; Shaw, being notably of his period, with his assertion of man's inferiority to an idea, are all part of one masochistic curse. And in a 'world' resulting from these things one may advisedly welcome a Don Quixote desiring to '*Make democracy safe for the individual.*'

But few Englishmen in each generation can understand the statement that 'Le style c'est l'homme'; the manner in which Wilson's uncolloquial early paragraphs bamboozled the British public, not merely the outer public but the inner public, is a fairly fresh example of the folly of trusting wholly to what Sir Henry Newbolt designates as the 'political rather than literary' genius of this nation; but, with that example before one, it is almost hopeless to attempt to prove the validity of Major C. H. Douglas' mental processes by giving examples of his rugged and unpolished but clean hitting prose. Universitaire economics hold the field as non-experimental science and catholicism held the fields in Bacon's day and in Voltaire's, and I have no doubt that the opposition to Major Douglas' statements will take the tack of making him out a mere Luther. Humanism came to the surface in the renaissance and the succeeding centuries have laboured, not always in vain, to crush it down.

Le style c'est l'homme; and a chinaman has written 'A man's character is known from his brush-strokes.' The clarity of some of Major Douglas' statements should show the more intelligent reader, and show him almost instantly, that he has here to deal with a genius as valid in its own specialty as any we can point to in the arts. What we all have to face, what Douglas is combatting is:

'a claim for the complete subjugation of the individual to an

---

[1] *The Little Review*, April 1920.

objective which is externally imposed on him; which it is not necessary or even desirable that he should understand in full.'

It is impossible to condense Douglas' arguments into the scope of a review, one can at most indicate his main tendencies and the temper and tonality of his mind. He is humanist, which is a blessed relief after humanitarians; he is emphatically and repeatedly against the 'demand to subordinate the individuality to the need of some external organisation, the exaltation of the State into an authority from which there is no appeal.'

'Centralisation is the way to do it, but is neither the correct method of deciding what to do nor of selecting the individual who is to do it.'

He is realist in his perception that the concentration of credit-capital into a few hands means the concentration of directive power into those same few hands, and that 'current methods of finance far from offering maximum distribution are decreasingly capable of meeting any requirements of society fully.' Sentences and definitions apart from context may sound like sentences from any other book on economics; it is in the underflow of protest against the wastage of human beings that we find the author's true motive power. His new declaration of independence is perhaps compressed into a few paragraphs [sic]:

'The administration of real capital, i.e. the power to draw on the collective potential capacity to do work, is clearly subject to the control of its owners through the agency of credit.'
'Real credit is a measure of the reserve of energy belonging to a community and in consequence drafts on this reserve should be accounted for by a financial system which reflects that fact.'
'It must be perfectly obvious to anyone who seriously considers the matter that the State should lend, not borrow . . . in this respect as in others the Capitalist usurps the function of the State.'

The argument for remedying present conditions is closely woven, conviction or doubt must be based on the author's text itself and not on summary indications.

There is exposure of industrial sabotage, suggestion for a new and just mode of estimating real costs, attack upon the 'creation and approximation of credits *at the expense of the community*'. All of which is, for the reader, an old story or a new story or a fatras of technical jargon, according as the reader has read many books or no books on economics, or is capable or incapable of close thought; but whatever else, whatever mental stimulus or detailed economic conviction the book conveys, any reader of intelligence must be aware, at the end of

181

it, of a new and definite force in economic thought, and, moreover, of a force well employed and well directed, that is to say directed toward a more humane standard of life; directed to the prevention of new wars, wars blown up out of economic villainies at the whim and instigation of small bodies of irresponsible individuals. In this Major Douglas must command the unqualified respect of all save those few cliques of the irresponsible and the economically guilty.

So much for the book's character; as for the intellectual details, one can only add one's personal approbation for what it may or may not be worth; one has at least honest thinking, no festoons of ecclesiastical verbiage, no weak arguments covered with sentimentalism; no appeals to the 'trend of events', no pretence that mankind is not what it is but what it ought to be. All of which is a comfort.

The political issue in these matters is perfectly clear, not only in England but in every 'civilised' country; it consists in dividing society at a level just below the great banks and controllers of loan-credit, i.e., along the line of real interest. In England at this moment the whole of political jugglery is expended upon an effort to divide society just above the Trade Unions, the poor old-fashioned trade unions which are plunder associations too naïve to survive keen analysis.

Douglas' book offers an alternative to bloody and violent revolutions, and might on that account be more welcomed than it will be, but perspicacity is not given to all men, and many have in abuleia gone to their doom.

The work is radical in the true sense, trenchant but without a trace of fanaticism.

Definitions[1]

1. A good state is one which impinges least upon the peripheries of its citizens.

2. The function of the state is to facilitate the traffic, i.e. the circulation of goods, air, water, heat, coal (black or white), power, and even thought;

and to prevent the citizens from impinging on each other.

3. The aim of state education has been (historically) to prevent people from discovering that the classics are worth reading. In this endeavour it has been almost wholly successful.

4. Politicians: fahrts of the multitude.

Nature of war depends entirely on the state of civilisation of the parties contending. Nature of social revolution depends entirely on state of ignorance and barbarism of elements cast to the TOP.

The only way a nation can render itself safe is by civilizing its neighbours. The duty of an aristocracy is to educate its plebs; failure in this simple precaution means its own bloody destruction. History presents no more imbecile a series of spectacles than the conduct of aristocracies. Without whom civilisation is impossible. And after one imbecile lot of these lepidoptera is destroyed the whole of woodenheaded humanity has to concentrate its efforts on production of another lot, equally piffling and light headed.

[1] *Der Querschnitt*, January 1925.

The State[1]

The republic, the *res publica* means, or ought to mean 'the public
convenience'. When it does not, it is an evil, to be ameliorated
or amended out of, or into decent, existence. Detailed emend-
ment is usually easier, and we await proof that any other course is
necessary. But in so far as America is concerned, we should like to
know whether there is *any* mental activity outside the so-called
'revolutionary elements', the communescents, etc.

At present, in that distressed country, it would seem that neither
side ever answers the other; such ignoring, leading, in both cases, to
ignorance. I should like a small open forum in which the virtues or
faults of *either* side might be mentioned without excessive animus.

Both Fascio and the Russian revolution are interesting phenomena;
beyond which there is the historic perspective. Herrin and Passaic are
also phenomena, and indictments.

The capitalist imperialist state must be judged not only in comparison with unrealised utopias, but with past forms of the state; if it will
not bear comparison with the feudal order; with the small city states
both republican and despotic; either as to its 'social justice' *or* as to its
permanent products, art, science, literature, the onus of proof goes
against it.

The contemporary mind will have to digest this concept: the state
as convenience.

The antithesis is: the state as an infernal nuisance.

As to our 'joining revolutions' etc. It is unlikely. The artist is concerned with producing something that will be enjoyable even after
a successful revolution. So far as we know even the most violent
bolshevik has never abolished electric light globes merely because
they were invented under another régime, and by a man intent rather
on his own job than on particular propaganda.

(Parenthesis: a great deal of rubbish is emitted by 'economists' who
fail to distinguish between transient and permanent goods. Between
these there are graduations.

1. Transient: fresh vegetables
             luxuries
             jerry-built houses
             fake art,
             pseudo books
             battleships.

[1] *The Exile*, Spring, 1927.

184

2. Durable: well constructed buildings, roads, public works, canals,
           intelligent afforestation.
3. Permanent: scientific discoveries
               works of art
               classics

That is to say these latter can be put in a class by themselves, as they are always in use and never consumed; or they are, in jargon, 'consumed' but not destroyed by consumption.

Note: the shyster is always trying to pass off class 1 for class 2 or 3. This is, naturally, bad economics. Just as the writings of Keynes, Pigou, and the rest of their tribe are bad economics.

    end of parenthesis.)

The artist, the maker is always too far ahead of any revolution, or reaction, or counter-revolution or counter-reaction for his vote to have any immediate result; and no party programme ever contains enough of his programme to give him the least satisfaction. The party that follows him wins; and the speed with which they set about it, is the measure of their practical capacity and intelligence. Blessed are they who pick the right artists and makers.

Prolegomena[1]

The drear horror of American life can be traced to two damnable roots, or perhaps it is only one root: 1. The loss of *all* distinction between public and private affairs. 2. The tendency to mess into other peoples' affairs before establishing order in one's own affairs, and in one's thought. To which one might perhaps add the lack in America of any habit of connecting or correlating *any* act or thought to *any* main principle whatsoever; the ineffable rudderlessness of that people. The principle of good is enunciated by Confucius; it consists in establishing order within oneself. This order or harmony spreads by a sort of contagion without specific effort. The principle of evil consists in messing into other peoples' affairs. Against this principle of evil no adequate precaution is taken by Christianity, Moslemism, Judaism, nor, so far as I know, by *any* monotheistic religion. Many 'mystics' do not even aim at the principle of good; they seek merely establishment of a parasitic relationship with the unknown. The original Quakers may have had some adumbration of the good principle. (But no early Quaker texts are available in this village.)

[1] *The Exile*, 2, Autumn 1927.

Bureaucracy the Flail of Jehovah[1]

Bureaucrats are a pox. They are supposed to be *necessary*. Certain chemicals in the body are supposed to be necessary to life, but cause death the moment they increase beyond a suitable limit.

The time has come when we should begin to study Lenin qualitatively and analytically, and not merely polemically. He is, after all, an historic figure, and we should consider him calmly, as we consider Cardinal Richelieu, or Mazarin, or any other man indubitably effective in public action. It is highly probable that we will find him a more interesting and far less disagreeable character than either of these so distinguished French prelates.

And it now begins to appear that, considering his setting, Lenin was a very moderate person . . . surrounded by fanatical and emotionally excitable persons–swayed often by aimless bitterness. Apart from the social aspect he was of interest, technically, to serious writers. He never wrote a sentence that has any interest in itself, but he evolved almost a new medium, a sort of expression half way between writing and action. This was a definite creation, as the Napoleonic code was creation. Lenin observed that bureaucracy was an evil, and 'meant' to eliminate it as fast as possible. Giving it as nearly as possible in the words Steffens used on his return from Russia, Lenin had said: 'All that is the political department, and it is to be got rid of as soon as we can.'

No country produces two Napoleons or two Lenins in succession; so we may expect Russia to be reasonably slow in producing Utopia, but we have fairly straight testimony as to one man's perception of a law of state. That is: as soon as any group of men found a government, or an order, bureaucrats begin to destroy it.

It makes no difference whether it is an autocracy, tyranny, democracy, or even one of these projected horrors based on the mutually merging imbecility of the stupidest; the minute the state exists the bureaucrat begins parasitic action for himself and against the general public. He is in perpetual session, he acts continuously. And 'men of the same trade', as Adam Smith has remarked, 'never meet together without a conspiracy against the general public'.

America is acephalous, and things recognised elsewhere penetrate our consciousness very slowly. The French have long since begun serious study of the habits of one bureaucrat and 'the fonctionnaire'.

[1] *The Exile*, Autumn, 1928.

But France is, unfortunately, in her dotage. In the century before last such an analysis would have been a prelude to action; now the French while making analytic research into the tropisms of this disagreeable fauna merely tend toward observation, or towards finding excuses for the matoid who takes eight minutes to sell a 25 centime stamp, or who causes queues to stand twenty minutes at the railway ticket window in Toulouse.

It is a weak nation, that having existed intellectually, and with most laudable activity, from 1830 straight down to 1918 feels it has earned its rest. If it dies it will die at a respectable age. We, on the contrary, not having yet produced a civilisation, must guard against premature death. At present even the name of the disease is unfamiliar to our general public, the disease is, heaven knows, rampant enough, but the patient is so young and distracted that no one takes any notice.

The Fall-Sinclair case is treated, in every American journal I have seen, as if it were something discrete, and separate from everything else. How anyone can suppose that this case can occur without there being a vast mass of cognate and allied torpidity all through the Washington bureaus is beyond me. The answer is 'they don't suppose', if thinking at all they are thinking of something else.

The English theory (I mean among the 'high up'), the theory of the actual rulers of England, is that theories of government are of no importance, and that the form of government is absolutely unimportant, and that the whole and maximum governing talent and energy of any actual or possible nation is required to keep its legislature and bureaucracy honest. Hence their utter indifference to the 'anachronism of a monarchy'. Hence their huge salaries paid to judges, their heavy pensions to government servants of all kinds.

In all of which things, form or no form, they set a most admirable example to our skinflint dealings with public servants, to the bullying of them by senators, etc., to the tardiness of state pensions and to the general lack of *demand* for the best possible government service.

The U.S. government can no longer compete with even third rate mercantile companies in buying its labour. The result is what one would expect: rotten service, bureaucratic scheming, the multiplication of jobs. I mean if a man can't get pay and a pension, he can manage to get a secretary, a few flapper typists, etc., and the more he gets the more he must justify their existence.

That is perhaps a new phase, due to the efficiency mania brought in under President Taft.

The ideal bureaucracy is the smallest possible one, and one with functions reduced to a minimum. Kipling in his third intelligent moment defined proper function of government as 'dealing with the traffic, and all that it implies'.

This obviously is as far as it is possible to get from the degrading concepts of government practised by Wilson, Harding, Bryan, Volstead, the pork-boys, theologians, and other plagues of our capital.

Parenthesis, I know I am expected to be factual, but one must occasionally stop to define an idea, or to ascertain the lines along which one means to assemble one's facts, and the sort of interpretative value one can give them when marshalled.

One can cite delightful anecdotes of the incompetence of Taft's efficiency experts, but the point is that this idea of activity as a merit is, when applied to bureaucrats, as deadly as the idea of activity among tuberculous bacillae. Whereas in time past they slacked and left the nation in comparative peace, they, under Taft, began to justify their existence by working, and by discovering things to work on. The necessity being to work, as distinct from finding work which was of use to the public or which contributes to the general convenience. Work to protect oneself from the danger of being caught with a sinecure.

Then came Wilson, and give him all the 'credit' you wish, all the servile adulation of Mr. Baker will not be enough to hide, ultimately, the fact that Wilson's reign was a period of almost continuous misfortune to the organism of official life in America.

Came the war, the ultimate stupidity of Europe, the slow breaking of ignorance in America, the immense engulfments of bunk and sentiment, that would have been spared us, perhaps by an immediate Rooseveltian Fourth of July celebration in 1914. Came the creation of a vast number of offices, functions, furies, etc., and the never to be sufficiently damned, blasted, and reviled substitution of the attitude of professor to undergrad for that of elected official to electors, in our ill-starred jejune republic.

The *res republica* means the public thing, the public convenience.

It is not convenient to have one's nose blown by another, and we therefore blow our own noses, after the age of two.

That is the view point of the sane citizen. But the point of view of the fonctionnaire is: I must have a function. I must do something I must keep busy. And moving along that line there is absolutely nothing he is not ready to do to or for the 'people', regardless absolutely and utterly of whether the 'peepul' want it done, or derive any benefit or any augmented convenience from it.

Hence he, the fonctionnaire, becomes first a mild nuisance, then an aggravated nuisance, and finally an unending curse, everywhere present, nowhere desirable, and daily increasing in pomposity, stupidity, ingenuity and a conviction of the divinity of his mission he becomes, in his own eye, the lifeblood of the state. Without him no state would exist. Men would be an herd without law (by this time he no longer distinguishes between law, and government), and, horror of untimely horrors, each man would blow his own nose, and no official nose blowers would receive a salary as nose blowers, with a small extra commission per nose.

As to the ingenuity in inutility to which bureaucracy can attain in well bureau'd states, one has the incident reported to us by Mr. Antheil: before the war all foreigners were registered in Germany. Wanting to find a friend who had changed his address Mr. A. was told that 'they' would know at the Stadtsverwhichumwhach, whither he repaired. Oh yes they were all registered, there were slips for everyone who had come to the city since 1813, but the records had only been *made up* as far as A.D. 1848. That is to say there were slips, all right enough, for everyone who had come to the town, but those that could be found without having to examine each slip of the myriad stopped in that year, A.D. 1848.

That is the type of harmless bureaucracy, under tyranny. It corresponds with pre-Taft America where the treasury still bought wads of red string of a given length for the purpose of tying up the sacks of two cent pieces. No two cent pieces having been made since, let us say some time in the sixties. Let us say government waste of about 60 dollars a year. That is innocuous.

The actions of one efficiency expert inebriated by the above discovery, take me into pure comedy and away from my subject. They are perfectly factual. Old and wise governments recognise the uses of sinecure, small simple sinecures, and the uses of fidelity. Governments based on injustice, or on some ludicrous principle like the divine right of kings aim, per force, at smooth functioning of the governmental machinery, at the suavity of official 'servants', etc.

That is why 'mature' men hesitate about revoluting, hesitate about busting up some government founded on comic opera theory, in favour of some form of government based on high sounding cliché, and unassailable rectitude of professions.

It is because the inspectors in the port of New York are told that they represent justice that they behave like gorillas. Strong in the might of the Lord, burning with righteousness, etc. crusading ever in the name of one Highest. They keep watch for the possible victim, their natural enemy, not an official but the public.

It is a choice of evils.

In a rotten tyranny these men would share possibly the humanity of the victim, i.e., part of the time; the rest they would be engaged in accepting petty bribes.

The point or corollary here is that theoretical perfection in a government impels it ineluctably toward tyranny. In ancient days it was the divine descent of the ruler; in our time it is the theoretical justice or perfection of the organism, the to, for and by the plebs, etc. that puts this more moral fervour and confidence in so dangerous a place, i.e., as powder in the cannon, and behind the projectile.

190

BUREAUCRACY THE FLAIL OF JEHOVAH

All it comes to is that everyone must observe constant vigilance; knowing that the official is paid 'by the people', that he is definitely their employee, they must insist on his behaving with the same sort of servicibility that a waiter shows when bringing their dinner.

There must be no ambiguity whatsoever in this matter. The waiter is not there to juggle plates, to wash the dishes in the dining-room, to bring dishwater for soup, etc. or to inspect the private lives of the clientèle.

You don't, on the other hand, expect a good waiter at half price.

We must have bureaucrats? If we must have bureaucrats by all means let us treat them humanely; let us increase their salaries, let us give them comforting pensions; let them be employed making concordances to Hiawatha, or in computing the number of sand-fleas to every mile of beach at Cape May, but under no circumstances allow them to do anything what bloody ever that brings them into contact with the citizen. The citizen should never meet or see an official in the exercise of its functions. Treat the bureaucrat with every consideration, and when he ultimately dies do not replace him.

The job of America for the next twenty years will be to drive back the government into its proper place, i.e., to force it to occupy itself solely with things which are the proper functions of government.

Twenty years ago most of the American writing talent was drawn off onto writing about civic affairs. The present crop of young writers, with perhaps no more talent, are too lazy to occupy themselves with civic affairs, even when these impinge on the writers' own. There are 600 young, who are not yet able to do anything in literature who could occupy themselves writing articles against contemporary idiocies in administration until such time as they are ripe for original composition.

The qualifications of the ideal fonctionnaire, customs official or other are that he should be lazy, timid, have nice manners, no power, and a good deal of intelligence. The higher bureaucrats should be grounded in the TA HIO and in the analects of Confucius, apart from which they need only a specialist's 'education'. In the ideal state no Christian should ever be permitted to hold executive office. If this last proposition is not self-evident I am perfectly willing to debate it.

Peace[1]

There are certain *known* causes of war, or let us say there are certain perfectly well-known forces that constantly work toward war. 'Foundations' etc. supposed to be labouring for peace would do well to stop studying the 'effects of war' (e.g., 'Early Effects of the European War upon the Finance, Commerce and Industry of Chile'. List of Publications Carnegie Endowment for International Peace, 1 September 1927, p. 17) and study the causes.

The known causes of war are:
1. Manufacture and high pressure salesmanship of munitions, armaments etc.
2. Overproduction and dumping, leading to trade friction, etc. strife for markets etc.
3. The works of interested cliques, commercial, dynastic and bureaucratic.

The useful research, in fact the only research that is not almost a sabotage of intentions of peace foundations would consist in contemporary (not retrospective) i.e., up to the minute gathering and distribution of information re. these activities– through commercial channels or through any other.

Where retrospection is necessary or commodious, the life of Sir Basil Zaharoff would be a fascinating document, any well informed record of the exact procedures followed by Vickers or Krupp in getting off their products onto 'les nations jeunes', of passing the guns into China or other areas of absorbtion would not need painful distribution; [*sic*] 'sales, 2 copies, $1.68; sales, 2 copies, $2.52; distributed gratis, 48.' (Annual report of the secretary, Carnegie endowment, 1927 Year Book.)

Needless to say the individual unsubsidised author is in less advantageous position to gather such data than a whole staff of paid researchers with a ten million dollar endowment behind them.

Probably we need a repentant Machiavelli, a private secretary to Messrs. Creusot to tell how the wiggle is waggled.

Too bad Carnegie is dead, *he* might have seen the point of this argument, as it is we must depend for action on Dr. Nicholas Butler, Dr. Nicholas Murray Butler.

Or perhaps as Mr. Magnus for the ultimate degradation of British letters, we shall find a guide for munitions-salesmen, printed in good

[1] *The Exile*, Autumn 1928.

192

faith by an enthusiast, who being unable to do it himself, is anxious to tell the secret to others. At any rate the book is much needed, whether it proceed from pocket of the ploot or the vanity of the knowing author.

As to effective distribution of the information I can only comply with the Carnegie Endowment Committee's request: pages 66–7 of their Year Book for 1927, and suggest that they compare their distribution report with the article in the 'NATION' for May 16th of this year, 'The Million Dollar Lobby', which article ought to be quoted in full for the light it throws on American life and in particular the government and 'education'.

From the 'Nation's' Article

The lobby paid $7,500 to Richard Washburn Child, former United States Ambassador to Italy, to prepare an unsigned 'booklet' opposing federal development of Boulder Dam. It paid Ernest Greenwood, former American agent of the League of Nations Labour Office, an 'initial fee' of $5,000 to write a propaganda book, 'Aladdin, U.S.A.', published by Harpers. It paid ex-Senator Lenroot of Wisconsin at least two fees of $10,000 each to lobby for it among his former colleagues. It paid the law firm of Meechem and Vellacott of Albuquerque, New Mexico, $5,299.66 to 'report' the Governors' Conference on Boulder Dam at a time when Merritt Meechem, former Governor of New Mexico, was supposed to be representing the State of New Mexico at that conference. It paid the General Federation of Women's Clubs $30,000 for an 'urban and rural home survey'. It paid the Harvard Graduate School, in three years, $62,000 for 'research' which, after study of the views of the responsible professors, it felt safe; and after equally careful study of the professorial field it contributed at least $62,500 (perhaps $95,000) to Northwestern University, $12,249.37 to the University of Michigan, $3,000 to the Massachusetts Institute of Technology, $5,000 to Johns Hopkins University, and $33,000 to Howard University. It has twenty-eight committees working in thirty-eight States, teaching that 'government ownership is the masked advance agent of communism'.

'We have located,' the industrious committee reported, 'practically every textbook and also have found the textbooks in course of preparation, and have been able to be of considerable assistance to the writers of these books in providing them with reliable data.'

That article is full of good nutritive matter. It shows what Mr. L. meant when he spoke to me years ago of the 'Text-book ring' (*vide* my 'How to Read' if that admirable brochure ever gets printed). It shows what at least one of our 'diplomats' was doing when he should have been serving the public and eliminating the visa infamy.

The City[1]

Mr. Edison has been reported as turning loose on the perfect city of the future with such phrases as: 'nerves to toughen', and: 'the loss of acute hearing will be a benefit rather than a handicap to the city-dweller'.

Either Mr. Edison is gaga or he was pullin' the reporter's leg.

We will not sacrifice our ears in favour of idiotic noise, and we will not cut off our right feet so as to make more room in the bottoms of automobiles. We have five senses and we are not going to put out our eyes in favour of acetylene glare.

The city of today is picturesque, and demoded, it belongs to the gothic phase of our cycle. All our cities exist on pre-automobile and pre-airplane plans. Anyone with an eye for proportion can see that the narrowness of their streets is in ratio to their buildings as the narrowness of alleys in Tangier or in the oldest ghettos of Europe, not in the post-Napoleonic proportions of Baron Haussmann's designing.

Our chequer-board ground plans are inefficient, stupidly so. The wiggly and twisty streets of the garden suburb are equally silly, a product of reaction and dilettantism, conducive to no convenience.

All great changes are simple, and the changes to To-morrow's city will obey a very few and very simple laws. First: the streets will follow the stream line or speed line, not a set of blocking and checking right-angles, but a sweep rather like the curves in a rail-road siding.

Towns with 'natural advantages', convenient rivers and hills will take more conscious advantage of these set features, but natural advantages really count for very little in the making of larger cities. A small town like Orvieto shows the character of the underlying geology, Rome does not, its picturesque crags lie under two millennia of human construction.

The one natural advantage no future and conscious town or great annex will neglect is the simple solar advantage. On a group of speed-ways, that will at first seem very wide, bunched in their stem and gradually diverging, we will build not dominos glued one to the other but L-shaped blocks, separate, and with the convex angle headed somewhere to North by East by North. That will give one sun and light in the concave angle.

The smoke nuisance goes. I mean it is eliminated. Ruskin was well-meaning but a goose. The remedy for machines is not pastoral retro-

[1] *The Exile*, Autumn 1928.

gression. The remedy for the locomotive belching soft-coal smoke is not the stage coach, but the electric locomotive, such as we now use on that picturesque old-world run: Spezia, Genova, Pavia, Torino. The engineer's cab is clean as a porcelain bath-tub. His job is not a white-collar job, if you mean a starched collar job.

The smoke-nuisance having been eliminated we revive the loggia, the open-arched or at any rate open porch taking the afternoon sun. The loggia means the reintegration of the arts, place for sculpture etc. as reader may figure out for himself.

The ground-space in the concave side of the L, of apartments is large enough for a tennis court, and one does not propose to be inconveniently separated from such simple convenience. One's tennis is in the front yard, one's bath is reached by the elevator. The Ls are not so ubiquitous that small boys have to go to some distant vacant lot for their baseball or football.

Our towers are the great Ls grouped at the apex of the city, sheer steel to some harmonious average, of 30 and 40 stories, with here and there a high tower. Incline-plane cellar parking throughout. That is to say a normal office building 50 offices or rooms to a floor, 40 stories, meaning a minimum place for 20,000 autos in the basements. Our homes are in the ten and twelve storey Ls. Open loggia to each floor.

To the North side of the city is the great wind-wall, open in summer like the slats of a blind, closed in winter, made of some light vitreous matter, possibly enforced with steel fibre or some metallic filament giving it toughness.

And by this wall, the still wider boulevard or takeoff for air planes, stretching the full length of the city. I see the city longish rather than square, for sake both of air and convenience.

Lacking sea-water or clean flowing river, a river, that is, without industrial dumping or unhealthy mud-bottom, one places open baths to the south, cleaned electrically or charged with chemical antiseptics, sulphur and sea-salt.

The whole thing is extremely simple, air, sun and freedom from traffic blocks.

Solving this perfectly clear engineering problem the beauty comes of itself. Take any 'old and picturesque bit of Europe', say the old houses east of the Ponte Vecchio in Florence–they are in simple lines, all made for utility, and they attain extreme beauty. The horror of Florence is in the wilfully ornate sections. (This is not the place to insert a discourse on the incapacity of the Florentines to make use of their city–in which there is no place to walk, sit or stand.)

In the new city there will be an occasional building of sheer beauty, neither church nor museum. Not covered with pastry-cook gothic. It will be perhaps the frame for one picture, or there will be in it a dozen fine paintings, and a segment of library, grouped for some special purpose—a place for quiet, and for intellectual pleasure.

I take it golf and polo will be imagined to the north of the wind-wall, but all of these things will be of easy lateral access. The number of 'fans' will diminish, fewer people will be content to freeze or swelter on benches while someone else has the fun.

The government will be reduced to a minimum. The more intelligent people are, the less organised government will they tolerate; the fewer pompous officials and busy bodies will be allowed to stand about clogging the circulation. Even the need of the traffic cop will be diminished by the open nature of the roadways. I mean the main routes and speedways through the high buildings will be as wide as the Place de la Concorde, and between the chief towers there will be light steel footbridges at every tenth or fifteenth level. But all of it airy.

The nightmare of triple subways and overhead railways is all buncombe. Intelligent man will not stifle in a mole-hole twice daily. A tunnel may possibly serve for eliminating the English Channel or the Straits of Gibraltar, but not for getting from 10th Street to 87th. The traffic cop gives way in any case to the automatic light signal.

The first error they will make will be to scamp the aviation fair-way. However, all people make blunders. No sane man will have an elevated train shaking dirt down his collar.

New York is already quaint, picturesque and very old fashioned. Parts of it will be kept on as specimens, as they keep the old houses in Holborn, London, a monument of their epoch.

The right-angle street plan has lost its use. The new city is built on stream line and follows the natural flow of the traffic.

Murder by Capital[1]

Twenty-five years ago 'one' came to England to escape Ersatz; that is to say, whenever a British half-wit expressed an opinion, some American quarter-wit rehashed it in one of the 'respectable' American organs. Disease is more contagious than health. England may be growing American in the worst sense of that term. The flagrant example is that of receiving Spengler instead of Frobenius. I can't conceive of Spengler's being the faintest possible *use* in any constructive endeavour. Frobenius is a bitter pill for the Anglo-Saxon. He believes that when a thing exists it probably has a cause. He has lately been very un-archaeological in his exploration of the Tripolitan Sahara, etc., for the Italian Government. He noticed (vide *London Illustrated News*) that where the cliffs were ornamented, water could be found fairly near the surface.

But his most annoying tendency is to believe that bad art indicates something more than just bad art.

Twenty years ago, before 'one', 'we', 'the present writer' or his acquaintances had begun to think about 'cold subjects like economics' one began to notice that the social order hated *any* art of maximum intensity and preferred dilutations. The best artists were unemployed, they were unemployed long before, or at any rate appreciably before, the unemployment crises began to make the front page in the newspapers.

Capitalist society, or whatever you choose to call the social organisation of 1905 to 1915 was *not* getting the most out of its available artistic 'plant'.

'I give *myself* Work,' said Epstein when he was asked if he had any.

The best writers of my generation got into print or into books mainly *via* small organisations initiated for that purpose and in defiance of the established publishing business of their time. This is true of Joyce, Eliot, Wyndham Lewis (the original as distinct from the 'Blue Moon') and of the present writer, from the moment his intention of break with the immediate past was apparent. My one modern volume issued by Mathews was sent to the ineffable printer before dear old Elkin had read it. He wanted a 'book by' me. In the case of '*Quia Pauper Amavi*', he again wanted a book by me, and suggested that I omit the '*Propertius*' and the '*Moeurs Contemporaines*'.

The story of getting '*Lustra*' into print is beyond the scope of this

[1] *The Criterion*, July 1933.

essay, it belongs to stage comedy not even to memoirs. If a new England or a new generation is being born, it can only know the wholly incredible island of those years *if* some genius who remembers them can be persuaded to devote himself wholly and exclusively to developing a comic technique. The young gentlemen who write to me: 'I was eight years old at the time' will have, for the moment, to take it on faith, that England in those years was very funny, much funnier than Mr. Belcher's drawings or Mr. Bateman's, unless one had the unfortunate habit of looking at the serious side.

You might put the question in the following form: What drives, or what can drive a man interested almost exclusively in the arts, into social theory or into a study of the 'gross material aspects' videlicet economic aspects of the present? What causes the ferocity and bad manners of revolutionaries?

We know that Lenin was annoyed by the execution of his older, admired brother. We mostly do not know or remember that George Washington greatly admired an elder brother who was, roughly speaking, sacrificed to official imbecility and ultimately died of it, i.e., after-effects of the 'war of Jenkins's ear'.

Why should a peace-loving writer of Quaker descent be quite ready to shoot certain persons whom he never laid eyes on? I mean to say, if it ever should come to the barricades in America (as England is not my specific business).

What specific wrong has the present order done to writers and artists *as such*, not as an economic class or category, but specifically *as artists*? And why should some of them be 'driven' to all sorts of excessive opinion, or 'into the arms of' groups who are highly unlikely to be of use to them? If Frobenius ever saw the inside of Schönbrun he was not surprised by the fall of the Habsburgs.

I do not believe that any oligarchy can indefinitely survive continuous sin against the best art of its time. I certainly did not look forward to the Russian Revolution when I wrote my monograph on Gaudier-Brzeska, but I pointed out that the best conversation was to be found, 1912 to 1914, in *quadriviis et angiportis*, under a railway arch out by Putney, in cheap restaurants and not in official circles or in the offices of rich periodicals. The cleverness and quickness 'in society' was probably even then limited to the small segment actually concerned in governing. I mean to say that those who govern, govern *on condition* of being a *beau monde* of one sort or another. Their rule cannot indefinitely survive their abrogation of 'culture' in the decent sense of that word, if any decent sense still remain in it.

In 1915 good art could occasionally appear in high places for a moment, like Jocanahan sticking his head up from the cellarage.

Hatred can be bred in the mind, it need not of necessity rise from the 'heart'. Head-born hate is possibly the most virulent. Leaving aside my present belief that economic order is possible and that the way to a commonly decent economic order is known. What has capital done that I should hate Andy Mellon as a symbol or as a reality?

This article is *'per far ridere i polli'* among our Bolshevik friends. Many of them are, alas, as far from an understanding as are the decadents.

I have grown, if not fat under the existing order, at least dangerously near it. I have no personal grievance. They tried to break me and didn't or couldn't or, at any rate, chance and destiny, etc., gave me 'a fairly good break'. I was tough enough to escape or to stand the pressure. Personally. Why, then, have I blood lust?

I have blood lust because of what I have seen done to, and attempted against, the arts in my time.

A publishing system existed and was tolerated almost without a murmur, and its effect, whether due to conscious aim or blind muddling fear, was to erect barriers against the best writing. Concurrently, there rose barriers against the best sculpture, painting and music. Toward the end of my sojourn in London even an outcast editor of a rebellious paper, Mr. Orage of the *New Age*, as it then was, had to limit me to criticism of music as no other topic was safe. Contrary to general belief I did not arrive hastily at conclusions, but I observed facts with a patience that I can now regard as little short of miraculous. As a music critic I saw the best performers gradually driven off the platform. I saw a few desperate attempts and a still smaller number of successful attempts to put over something a bit better than was 'wanted'. A few years later the French musicians were parading the streets wanting work. This is not due to radio, and it was still less due to radio a decade and more ago.

It is perhaps only now that all these disagreeable phenomena can be traced to maladministration of credit. Artists are the race's antennae. The effects of social evil show first in the arts. Most social evils are at root economic. I, personally, know of no social evil that cannot be cured, or very largely cured, economically.

The lack of printed and exchangeable slips of paper corresponding to extant goods is at the root of bad taste, it is at the root not of *bad* musical composition, but at the root of the non-performance of the best music, ancient, modern and contemporary; it is at the root of the difficulty in printing good books *when* written.

The fear of change is very possibly a contributing cause. I don't mean an honest and perspicacious fear of change, but a love of lolling and a cerebral fixation. But with a decent fiscal system the few hundred people who want work of first intensity could at any rate have it, whether it were supposed to leaven the mass or not.

CIVILIZATION, MONEY AND HISTORY

THE UNEMPLOYMENT PROBLEM

Mussolini is the first head of a state in our time to perceive and to proclaim *quality* as a dimension in national production. He is the first man in power to publish any such recognition *since*, since whom?– since Sigismond Malatesta, since Cosimo, since what's-his-name, the Elector of Hanover or wherever it was, who was friendly with Leibnitz?

The unemployment problem that I have been faced with, for a quarter of a century, is not or has not been the unemployment of nine million or five million, or whatever I might be supposed to contemplate as a problem for those in authority or those responsible, etc., it has been the problem of the unemployment of Gaudier-Brzeska, T. S. Eliot, Wyndham Lewis the painter, E.P. the present writer, and of twenty or thirty musicians, and fifty or more other makers in stone, in paint, in verbal composition.

If there was (and I admit that there was) a time when I thought this problem could be solved without regard to the common man, humanity in general, the man in the street, the average citizen, etc., I retract, I sing palinode, I apologise.

One intelligent millionaire *might* have done a good deal–several people of moderate means have done 'something'; i.e., a poultice or two and bit of plaster hither or yon.

The stupidity of great and much-advertised efforts and donations and endowments is now blatant and visible to anyone who has the patience to look at the facts. The 'patron' must be a live and knowledgeable patron, the entrusting of patronage to a group of boneheaded professors ignorant of art and writing, is and has been a most manifest failure. There is no reason to pity anyone. Millions of American dollars have been entrusted to incompetent persons, whose crime may not be incompetence but consists, definitely, in their failure to recognise their incompetence. I suppose no pig has ever felt the circumscription of pig-ness and that even the career of an Aydelotte cannot be ascribed to other than natural causes.

This is what American capitalism has offered us, and by its works stands condemned. The British parallel is probably that lord and publisher, X, who objected to colloquial language.

For the purpose of, and the duration of, this essay I am trying to dissociate an objection or a hate based on specific effects of a system *on* a specific and limited area–i.e., I am examining the effects on art, in its social aspect; i.e., the opportunity given the artist to exist and practise his artistry *in* a given social order, as distinct from all questions of general social justice, economic justice, etc.

Autobiography if you like. Slovinsky looked at me in 1912: 'Boundt haff you gno bolidigal basshuntz?' Whatever economic passions I now

200

have, began *ab initio* from having crimes against living art thrust under my perceptions.

It is no answer to say that Tauchnitz can at last gratify their avarice by printing books that one had to fight to get printed in the decade before last. It is no answer to say that 'my' programme in art and letters has gradually been forced through, has, to some extent, grabbed its place in the sun. For one thing, I don't care about 'minority culture'. I have never cared a damn about snobbisms or for writing *ultimately* for the few. Perhaps that is an exaggeration. Perhaps I was a worse young man than I think I was.

Serious art is unpopular at its birth. But it ultimately forms the mass culture. Not perhaps at full strength? Perhaps at full strength. Yatter about art does *not* become a part of mass culture. Mass culture insists on the fundamental virtues which are common to Edgar Wallace and to Homer. It insists on the part of technique which is germane to both these authors. I believe that mass culture does not *ultimately* resist a great deal that Mr. Wallace omitted. I think it ultimately sifts out and consigns to the ash-can a great deal that the generation of accepted authors of Mr. Arnold Bennett's period put in. I do not believe mass culture makes any such specific and tenacious attack on good art as that which has been maintained during the last forty years of 'capitalist, or whatever you call it', ci–or whatever you call it–vilization.

Mass culture probably contains an element present also in Christianity, I mean the demand for that which is hidden. This sometimes pans out as a demand for colloquial; i.e., living language as distinct from the ridiculous dialect of the present Cambridge school of 'critics' who believe that their books about books about writing will breed a 'better taste' than would a familiarity with the great poets.

You can probably do nothing for a man who has arrived at the cardboard cerebration of supposing that you read Homer and Villon in order to 'collect a bag of tricks', or that you 'train a sensibility' by reading a book about Villon rather than by reading Villon himself. And when such men write criticism and tell you to read other critics we are carried back to the scarcity economist Mr. Smith, who remarked that men of the same trade never gather together without a conspiracy against the general public.

The bureaucracy of letters is no better than any other bureaucracy, it injects its poison nearer to the vital nerves of the State.

Mr. Yeats's criticism is so mixed up with his Celticism that it may be more confusing to cite it than not, but he gave a better reason for reading great poets.

When you read Homer you do not read him for tricks, but if you are engaged in the secondary activity of building up a critical faculty you might read him in order not to be fooled by tricks, by second-hand sleight of hand derivations.

TO RECAPITULATE

The effects of capitalism on art and letters, apart from all questions of the relations of either capitalism, art, or letters, to the general public or the mass, have been: (1) the non-employment of the best artists and writers; (2) the erection of an enormous and horrible bureaucracy of letters, supposed to act as curators, etc., which bureaucracy has almost uninterruptedly sabotaged intellectual life, obscuring the memory of the best work of the past and doing its villainous utmost to impede the work of contemporary creators.

As for proposed remedies, C. H. Douglas is the first economist to include creative art and writing in an economic scheme, and the first to give the painter or sculptor or poet a definite reason for being interested in economics; namely, that a better economic system would release more energy for invention and design.

Mussolini has emphasised the dimension of quality. (*En passant*, it is monstrous or ridiculous to suppose that Lloyd George or Mr. Churchill are either of them capable of understanding Fascism. If either of them has spoken in its favour, it is only because they do not understand it).

A B C of Economics[1]

The aim of this brochure is to express the fundamentals of economics so simply and clearly that even people of different economic schools and factions will be able to understand each other when they discuss them.

After about forty pages I shall not 'descend', but I shall certainly go into, 'go down into' repetitions and restatements in the hope of reaching this clarity and simplicity.

PART ONE

I shall have no peace until I get the subject off my chest, and there is no other way of protecting myself against charges of unsystematised, uncorrelated thought, dilettantism, idle eclecticism, etc., than to write a brief formal treatise.

1. *Dissociations: Or preliminary clearance of the ground.*

I beg the reader not to seek implications. When I express a belief I will say so. When I am trying to prove something, I will say so. At the start I am attempting merely to get the reader to distinguish between certain things, for the sake of his own mental clarity, before he attempts to solve anything.

I shall use the term *property* as distinct from the term *capital*.

'Capital' for the duration of this treatise implies a sort of claim on others, a sort of right to make others work. Property does not.

For example. My bust by Gaudier is my property. Nobody is expected to do anything about it.

My bond of the X and Y railroad is capital. Somebody is supposed to earn at least 60 dollars a year and pay it to me because I own such a bond.

Therefore: it would be possible to attack the 'rights' or 'privileges' of capital without attacking the rights or privileges of property.

Once again, please do not imply. Please do not think I mean one whit more than what I have written. When I want to mean something further I will say it.

Dissociation 2. Overproduction did not begin with the industrial system. Nature habitually overproduces. Chestnuts go to waste on the the mountain side, and it has never yet caused a world crisis.

[1] Faber, 1933.

203

Sane engineers and wise men tell us that the question of production is solved. The world's producing plant can produce everything the world needs.

There is not the faintest reason to doubt this.

2. As mechanical efficiency increases, the above-mentioned production will require progressively less human time and effort.

3. Sane economy demands that this effort should be, for various reasons, apportioned to a very considerable number of people. This is not absolutely necessary, but it is advisable. It is not necessary, since a few million slaves or temperamentally busy human beings could indubitably do the whole work for the lot of us. They did it for the Roman Empire and nobody objected save an occasional slave.

4. Objections to slavery are in part ideal and sentimental. Openly avowed slavery has nevertheless gone out of fashion.

5. It is pure dogma to assert that an adult human being should be ready to do a reasonable amount of work for his keep. It is empiric opinion that a man who is constantly trying to sponge on others and who is unwilling to do anything whatever conducive to the general comfort or to the maintenance of civilisation is a mere skunk and that he ultimately becomes a blasted bore not only to others but to his own blasted self.

6. I assert a simple dogma: Man should have some sense of responsibility to the human congeries.

7. As a matter of observation, very few men have any such sense.

8. No social order can exist very long unless a few, at least a few, men have such a sense.

Democracy implies that the man must take the responsibility for choosing his rulers and representatives, and for the maintenance of his own 'rights' against the possible and probable encroachments of the government which he has sanctioned to act for him in public matters.

9. These encroachments in so far as they were political; in so far as they were special privileges handed down from mediaeval chaos and feudal arrangements have been from time to time more or less put in order. Jefferson and John Adams observed that in their young days very few men had thought about 'government'. There were very few writers on 'government'. The study of economics is a later arrival. An economic library in 1800 could have been packed in a trunk.

10. Some economic problems could perhaps be considered *via* political analogy, but a greater number cannot.

Probably the only economic problem needing emergency solution in our time is the problem of distribution. There are enough goods, there is superabundant capacity to produce goods in superabundance. Why should anyone starve?

204

That is the crude and rhetorical question. It is as much our question as Hamlet's melancholy was the problem of the renaissance dyspeptic.

And the answer is that nobody should. The 'science' or study of economics is intended to make sure no one does.

There is Enough

How are you going to get it from where it is, or can be, to where it is not and is needed?

I spare the reader the old history of barter, etc. Apples for rabbits; slips of paper from the owner ordering his servants to give to the bearer two barrels of beer; generalised tokens of gold, leather; paper inscribed with a 'value' as of 16 ounces of copper; metal by weight; cheques with fantastic figures; all serve or have served to shift wealth, wheat and beef from one place to another or to move wool cloth from Flanders to Italy.

Who is to have these Tokens?

Obviously certain men deserve well of humanity or of other limited numbers of men.

Those who grow wheat, those who make cloth and harness, those who carry these things from where they are in superfluity to where they are needed, by pushcarts and airplanes, etc.

AND ALSO THOSE who know where things are, or who discover new and easier means of getting them 'out', coal from the earth, energy from an explosion of gasoline.

Makers, transporters, facilitators and those who contribute to their pleasure or comfort or whom it pleases them favour . . . usual sequence of children, if they have or want children, aged parents who have earned their affection.

All of which would seem perfectly simple and idyllic, but then we come to the jam.

Some of these people who work or who could and would work are left without paper tokens.

Someone else has got all the tokens; or someone else has done all the work 'needed'.

CURIOUSLY ENOUGH, despite the long howls of those who used to complain about being oppressed and overworked, the last thing human beings appear to wish to share is WORK.

The last thing the exploiters want to let their employees divide is labour.

IT IS NEVERTHELESS UNDENIABLE that if no one were allowed to work (this year 1933) more than five (5) hours a day, there would be hardly anyone out of a job and no family without paper tokens potent enough to permit them to eat.

The objections to this solution are very mysterious. I have never yet seen a valid one, though I have seen some very complicated 'explanations' about increase in costs.

I would be willing to set it out as simple dogma that the shortening of the working day (day of paid labour) is the first clean cut to be made. I admit it is not the whole answer, but it would go a long way to keep credit distributed among a great part of the population (of any country whatsoever), and thereby to keep goods, necessities, luxuries, comforts, distributed and in circulation.

It is not the whole answer; not the whole answer to the present emergency nor does it constitute the whole science of economics.

When goods are produced, some recognition of that fact must be made, let us say in the certificates of goods in existence.

Can we say that perfect money consists in true certificates of goods extant?

Or must we limit that statement?

Does perfect money consist in a potent order: Deliver these goods?

Or is it a conditional? A compromise between a certificate of existence and a request or a promise of proportional concession?

Or is it an abracadabra? A fake having no strict correspondence with goods extant?

Excursus

A hard-headed Scotchman has for some years been telling us that money (credit) as we actually find it at present is a more or less irrelevant product; that it acts as a very strong imperative: Have thou the weight of wheat at such and such a place and deliver it!

But an increasingly large proportion of goods produced never gets its certificate. Some fool or some skunk plays mean, out of stupidity, out of fear, out of craven and cringing malice.

We artists have known this for a long time, and laughed. We took it as our punishment for being artists, we expected nothing else, but now it occurs to the artisan, and there being a lot of artisans, clerks, etc., this devilment has led the world into misery. There was room for the artist to dodge through the cracks, a few thousand artists could wangle or make a haul now and then, but the cracks won't pass men by the million.

So there has got to be some fairness in the issuing of certificates, or at any rate something has got to be 'done' to keep people from, etc. . . .

CALL IT A DOLLAR, or a quid or ten shillings or anything else you like. If a quid is a certificate of work done (goods produced) and if you produce twice as much as you did yesterday, you have either got to have more quids OR you have got to agree, all of you, that the quid that meant one bushel now means two bushels. That is to say if you, in any sense, mean to play fair.

To put it another way, if money is scarce and an ox sells at four pence you can conceivably have economic justice at four pence per ox. But you can not have social justice at four pence per *ox* and ten shillings per beefsteak.

If ox is four pence, beefsteak must be some small fraction of a farden.

At some agreed ratio the certificate must function. From 1914 to '24 bar chocolate remained, as nearly as I can remember, stationary in respect to gold. Nations rose and fell, currencies and commodities became dearer or cheaper. We have had fifteen or more prime years for empiric observation. Nobody remembers the 1830s' (Eighteen-thirties), anything men learned then in America has been long since forgotten. The civil war wiped it out.

Inflation and Deflation

I am all for controlled inflation, if by that you allow me to mean that more certificates must be granted when more goods are produced.

All the inflation wangles and all the official governmental schemes for inflations yet proposed, leave out the question of control. That is to say, the place of control is a dark room back of a bank, hung with deep purple curtains. No one must see what happens. What happened in the Bank of the U.S.A. before Mr. Van Buren set up an Independent government treasury? What happened?

Inflation for the benefit of the few.

Every economist has to start somewhere. I start on the proposition that every man who is decent enough to be willing to work for his keep or that of his helpless dependents (immature or senescent) ought to have the chance of doing a reasonable amount of work. This is highly American and anti-English.

THE FIRST STEP is to keep the working day short enough to prevent any one man doing two or three men's paid work.

THE SECOND STEP is the provision of honest certificates of work done (goods produced, or transported, discoveries, facilitations, etc.).

Nobody can be left free to fill in cheques with large figures regardless of services rendered.

Yes, yes, I have a cheque book but if I get fanciful the bank doesn't pay for my cheque.

But there be some, alas my brother there be some who can write cheques for great figures and for mysterious reasons. Who, my brother, controlleth the bank?

In one country the east wind, and in another country the west wind. In England a private firm has for so long done it so quietly that the world has forgotten it. All that our great grandfathers did for the liberation of the American treasury before our fathers were yet in the egg, has been allowed to slip into oblivion, and we are so little taught economics (a dry, dull and damned subject) that there are not ten thousand Americans who are the least aware that a similar movement, a similar step toward liberty or democracy or individual responsibility and state control of the national finances simply never occurred in England. So clever was the British clique, so astute and so prudent that the 'issue has never arisen'. The American in the street knows that England has a 'curious old institution called royalty' [funny old thing out of the poker deck], but he supposes that the two nations have the same fiscal system (that is, if he ever stops to consider it).

It may not be a matter of names. A free private company may administer a nation's credit as justly and with as little graft as a board nominally of government officials, bribed or 'influenced' by cliques of friends and acquaintances.

The economist is the man who knows WHAT the board, official or unofficial SHOULD do for the continued well-being of the nation. In other words, where and how it should allocate its certificates of work done or its orders to do further work and to deliver such and such products.

PART TWO

On Volition

It will be objected that I am trying to base a system on will, not on intellect. And that is one of the main reasons for my writing this treatise.

The criminal classes have no intellectual interests. In proportion as people are without intellectual interests they approach the criminal classes, and approach criminal psychology.

No economic system is worth a hoot without 'good will'. No intellectual system of economics will function unless people are prepared to act on their understanding.

People indifferent to the definition of liberty as '*le droit de faire tout ce qui ne nuit pas aux autres*' will not DO anything about their economic knowledge, whatever be the degree of that knowledge.

People with no sense of responsibility fall under despotism, and they deserve all the possible castigations and afflictions that the worst forms of despotism provide.

No economic system can be effective until a reasonable number of people are *interested* in economics; interested, I should say, in economics as part of the problem: what does and what does not injure others. That the answer to this is probably identical with the answer to: what is the most enlightened form of egotism, does not affect the matter.

No egoist has the energy to attain the maximum of egoistic enlightenment.

Marx has aroused interest far less than the importance of his thought might seem to have warranted. He knew, but forgot or at any rate failed to make clear, the limits of his economics. That is to say, Marxian economics deal with goods for sale, goods in the shop. The minute I cook my own dinner or nail four boards together into a chair, I escape from the whole cycle of Marxian economics.

'Can't move 'em with a cold thing like economics,' said Mr. Griffiths, the inventor of Sinn Fein.

Not one man in a thousand can be aroused to an interest in economics until he definitely suffers from the effects of an evil system. I know no subject in which it is harder to arouse any interest whatsoever. The cost of things which really interest human beings has nothing whatever to do with their quality. A pleasant woman costs no more than an unpleasant one, in fact, she probably costs infinitely less.

It costs no more to cook a dinner well than to cook it badly. You can, I admit, probably pay more for a good dinner than for a bad one, but what you get is due to your knowledge and not to the category of the hotel.

The *arts* of commerce are built on personal application of the laws of value (Marxian metaphysics and the 'psychology' of American business ballyhoo).

You will get no further with economics *as a science* until you are ready to mark out the scope of that science, as you do in the study of chemistry, physics, mathematics.

Goods in the window are worth more than the goods in the basement.

The art of commerce whereby the proprietor of one café acquires a clientele and his neighbour does not.

The luxury of the poor, the luxuriousness of the poor which has for ages sanctioned the small shop and the middleman. The saving of steps, I buy my coffee at my front door, not at the large shop 40 yards off. The same applies to my tailor (?), cobbler and butter merchant.

Over a decade ago, Major Douglas admitted that I had made a contribution to the subject when I pointed out that my grandfather had built a railroad probably less from a desire to make money or an illusion that he could make more that way than some other, than from inherent activity, artist's desire to MAKE something, the fun of constructing and the play of outwitting and overcoming obstruction.

Very well, I am not proceeding according to Aristotelian logic but according to the ideogramic method of first heaping together the necessary components of thought.

None of these 'incoherent' or contradictory facts can be omitted. A problem in the resolution of forces can only be solved when all the forces are taken count of. If there be any of them whose variants we cannot reduce to an equation, that one must remain at least temporarily outside our 'science'.

If I remember it correctly my 'Part One' was concerned mainly with science.

The science of economics will not get very far until it grants the existence of will as a component; i.e. will toward order, will toward 'justice' or fairness, desire for civilisation, amenities included. The intensity of that will is definitely a component in any solution.

Objections
The certificate of work done must equal that work
BUT
when it is certified that too much corn has been grown the certificates of its growth, or orders to deliver it, will be less prized. That is to say, the ticket for some particular substance depreciates in relation to the general ticket (money). The finance of financiers is largely the juggling of general tickets against specific tickets. As, per example, decline of price in the wheat pit. All of which would seem to have been worked out and to be fairly familiar.

When the certificate is not 'money' or *common carrier*, but a particularized certificate, it is 'just' in the sense that the order to deliver so many bushels already 'paid for' implies many bushels.

A certificate made out in 'common carrier' will not automatically stabilise currency or produce justice, unless some common sense is used in the production of goods (food, etc.). Hence the cries for planning, etc. I mean to say all the objections, etc., to my main thesis lead us back into familiar phenomena.

Either the individual must use his intelligence, or some congeries of individuals (state or whatever) must persuade or foresee or advise or control.

Nature overproduces. Overproduction does no harm until you over-market (dump).

In politics *the* problem of our time is to find the border between public and private affairs.

In economics: to find a means whereby the common-carrier may be in such way kept in circulation that the individual's demand, or at any rate his necessary requirement, shall not exceed the amount of common-carrier in his pocket at any moment, or at his proximate disposal.

A new school of economists says it *should be put* into his pocket (every week, every morning, every six months?).

And old type of mentality asks whether this would maintain the said individual's sense of responsibility, and answers the question very emphatically in the negative.

I fall back on a profession of faith. The simplest *starting-point* appears to me to be the individual's willingness to work four hours a day between the ages of twenty and forty.

There are doubtless, in modern industry, various directive jobs, etc., that need more prolonged attention, but very few in which an equivalent stint would not serve. Ten years at eight hours a day, as proportionate.

Counting money as certificate of work done, the simplest means of keeping money distributed (in legal-tender credit-slips) is to keep work distributed. I do not say it is the only conceivable means, but I definitely assert that it is the most available means, the simplest, the one requiring least bureaucracy and supervision and interference.

As for over-time.

Let it mean over-time. Let the man work four hours for pay, and if he still wants to work after that, let him work as any artist or poet works, let him embellish his home or his garden, or stretch his legs in some form of exercise, or crook his back over a pool-table or sit on his rump and smoke. He would get a great deal more out of life, and, supposing him to have any rudiments of intelligence, he would be infinitely more likely to use it and let it grow, and in any case he would 'get a great deal more for his money'.

I know, not from theory but from practice, that you can live infinitely better with a very little money and a lot of spare time, than with more money and less time. Time is not money, but it is almost everything else.

Even suppose that the wage for a four-hour day should be 'cut' to half the wage of an eight-hour day (which is for various simple reasons unnecessary), but even supposing it were necessary and were done. The man on that wage, once he were assured of its continuance, once he had 'arranged his life' in accordance, and organised his other four hours for private activity, could have a damn sight better life than he now gets.

I say 'which is for various reasons unnecessary' because the 'wage' is now measured in currency which is merely a convention, and a bit of paper with 10 on it is no more difficult to provide than a bit of paper with 5 or with 20.

There are various credit schemes which could take care of the problem of leaving the figure 10 on the bit of paper, even though the day's work were cut in half.

Douglas would pass out slips to the middleman. I have outlined a scheme for passing them out *via* the factory. Neither scheme is necessary. A few months ago the German government proposed an inflation without, apparently, any control.

The 'need' of such a scheme is possibly due more to the strength of habits of mind, to conventionality in the populace's thoughts about money, than to anything else.

Freedom from worry, inherent in the reasonable certainty of keeping one's job, must be worth at least 25 per cent of ANY income.

NOTE that this reasonable certainty can only exist when the necessity of progressively shortening the working day, *pari passu* with mechanical invention, is generally recognised.

No arbitrary number of hours set for 1933 will be valid in 1987, let alone in 2043.

Over and above which we come upon Major Douglas's equations *re*–superstition in costing.

PART THREE

Costing

I don't quite see how anyone is going to dodge (for ever) the Major's equations.

There are various verbal manifestations and various terminologies and various approaches to the problem.

I have begun with distribution of work. A point at which the Douglasites dislike to begin. I have gone on to the demand for justice in the distribution of credit slips, but that does not invalidate the Major's contention that *under the present system* there are never enough credit slips to deal with the product; to distribute the product; to purchase the product; to conjugate ANY of the necessary verbs of sane economics or of a decent and agreeable life.

The Major has pointed out the superstition in the computation of costs. The reader can look up the details in a number of contemporary works.

He will not find a simpler statement than Douglas's: You pay for the tree every time you buy a bit of the fruit.

Obviously the tree has to be maintained, some fraction over and above the worth of the fruit must be added, but the computation of that fraction can and should be free from gross error.

Gross error here could undoubtedly undo the good effects of a short working day. As a patient may easily die of one disease after you have cured him of another.

The requirements so far on our list are:

(1) 'Money' as certificate of work done.

(2) 'Work done' to be in a sense 'inside a system', that is to say, it must be 'necessary' or at any rate it must be work that someone WANTS

done. The product must be what someone lacks. [*sic*]–I lack half a loaf of bread daily or thereabouts. I lack a few suits of clothes per annum, etc.

(3) There must be some way for everyone to get enough money or common-carrier to satisfy a reasonable number of lacks.

The simplest road is *via* work, and I suspect any other. This is also the first instinctive outcry. It is empirically observable that the first thing men ask for is work; and only after refusal do they cry out for free food. If this statement indicates a great naïve trust in humanity I am willing to stand the charge.

(4) Fairness in the issuance of certificates. (I think the various Douglas plans fall mainly under this heading.)

Time is Not Money

Time is not money, but it is nearly everything else. That is to say. . . . It is not money, food, raw materials, women or various fundamental necessities which I cannot at the moment remember, including possibly health, but it is a very important lever to most of them.

'Nobody, but socialists', reads Marx, and there is consequently little enlightened discussion of either his history or his 'errors'.

I have never, so far as I can recall, seen a contemporary recognition of the plain fact that a man with a lot of spare time can get a great deal more out of life with a very little money, than an overworked man with a great deal. I mean apart from polyana.

Leisure is not gained by simply being out of work. Leisure is spare time *free from anxiety*.

Any spare time not absolutely obsessed by worry can be made the means to a 'better life'.

Marx deals with goods in the shop window or the shop basement. The minute I cook my own dinner or make the chair that I sit on I escape from the whole cycle of Marxian economics. In consideration of which fact I remain a Jeffersonian republican, and I believe the present troubles, or at any rate the present U.S. American or English troubles, can be treated from a Jeffersonian angle.

You can throw in Confucius and Van Buren, but you must distinguish between 1820 and 1930, you must bring your Jefferson up to date. T. J. had already seen that agriculture would in great measure give way to manufacturing, etc.

All American and republican principles were lost during the damnable reign of the infamous Woodrow, but even Woodrow did not favour the XVIII amendment. Despite 'liberty unions', etc., it is almost impossible to discover any sense of American principles in contemporary American writing, apart from editorials in one or two newspapers which naturally are not read by highbrows.

One commissioner of labour whose name I have forgotten, did

definitely advocate a shorter working day. No one has raised any coherent or even publicly avowable objection.

No one has ventured to say that a shorter day would not decrease the number of totally unemployed.

No one has claimed that it would lead to the creation of more 'bureaus' and more bureaucrats, and more sassy typists to take notes of vacuous commissioners and sit on their obese laps in government offices.

Naturally there is no very clear outcry for shorter hours from the workmen themselves. The labour party in America is not rich in economists. You can't arouse any very fiery passion on the bare plea of less work. It spells less pay to most hearers.

By simple extensions of credit (paper credit) it would probably be possible to leave the nominal pay exactly where it is, but it requires an almost transcendent comprehension of credit to understand this.

The plain man cannot in any way comprehend that the accelerated movement of money when everybody has a little means greater comfort than the constipated state of things when a lot of people have none.

The fiery labourite wants the unemployed paid out of the rich man's pocket. The rich man's pocket happens to be a mere pipe and not an inexhaustible upspringing fountain.

Naturally all men desire to pass the buck. The immediate effect of distributing work, under the present system, means that working men would have to divide with working men. It cannot, therefore, be a very popular cause.

The benefits of a shorter day would be diffused, everyone would in a few months RECEIVE them, but it would take probably longer to PERceive them. Annoyances strike more quickly than comforts.

Tell any man that he can live better on 40 shillings a week and an extra two hours per day to himself, than he can on 50 shillings without the two hours and see how little he believes you.

The idea that prices would come down sounds like a pipe dream. Prices have always adjusted themselves to the current spending powers of the general public, but that again is a general idea.

Two hours more per day to loaf, to think, to keep fit by exercise of a different set of muscles, as distinct from overwork and the spectacle of several millions in idleness... !

I am an expert. I have lived nearly all my life, at any rate all my adult life, among the unemployed. All the arts have been unemployed in my time.

Free Trade

Free Trade might be possible between two countries if they had for each other a full and wholly enlightened good will, provided they had first attained an almost perfect adjustment of their own internal affairs.

It need hardly be said that for the last century or more, the practice of governments has been to neglect internal economy; to commit every conceivable villainy, devilry and idiocy and to employ foreign affairs, conquests, dumpings, exploitations as a means of distracting attention from conditions at home, or to use the spoils of savages as palliatives to domestic sores or in producing an eyewash of 'prosperity'. In the sense that such prosperity is useful as 'bait'; as spectacular fortunes; as 'the chance' of getting rich.

Malthus

In practice it has been shown that families who do not overproduce, that is, who beget no more children than they can support, have been able to maintain decent standards of living, and that other families do not.

It is probably useless to propound theories of perfect government or of perfect economics for human beings who are too demnition stupid and too ignorant to acquire so rudimentary a perception of cause and effect.

Objections to this system are raised and are conceivably raisable on the score of national greatness, etc. . . . . Nevertheless we are told that Holland has maintained decent standards of living, etc., by not over populating herself. The system is supposed (for wholly arcane reasons) to work for a small nation and not for a large.

It would work. The only objection to it is that curtailment of the philoprogenitive instinct may not be necessary. Or possibly on practical grounds, that the present state of bigotry and idiocy prevent the curtailment, and that the inadequate progress of education is not able to achieve it. Yet sparsely populated districts are not necessarily the most prosperous. The remedy is to be recommended only at close range for the individual family living in a bad economic system. It cannot be made the backbone of enlightened economics on the grand scale. Such economics, now, being little more than a study of how we can USE our resources, not how we can refrain from employing them.

Until we have decent economics the sane man will refuse to overbreed. And pity for the large poor family will continue to be pity for idiotic lack of prevision.

It may be that all, or most, sciences start from suffering or from pity; but once a science is started these emotions have no place in that science.

Give a people an almost perfect government, and in two generations they will let it run to rot from sheer laziness (*vide* the U.S.A. where not one person in ten exercises his rights and not one person in ten thousand has the faintest idea of the aims and ambitions of the country's great founders and lawmakers. Their dung has covered their heads.).

It is nevertheless one's duty to try to think out a sane economics, and to try to enforce it by that most violent of all means, the attempting to make people think.

Proof of this last statement is very obscure. I suppose the only warrant for it is the capacity to think and the sense of obligation thereby conferred.

Self-Help

The foregoing is not mere nihilism, or mere in-vain-ism or mere quietism, nor is it so far off the subject as it might seem; the point is that NO ONE in any society has the right to blame his troubles on any one else. Liberals and liberal thought so-called have been a mess of mush because of this unacknowledged assumption, and a tendency to breed this state of mind.

The law of nature is that the animal must either adapt itself to environment or overcome that environment – soft life and decadence.

Decline of the American type, often bewailed! First the pioneer, then the boob and the soft-head! Flooding of peasant type, without peasant perseverance and peasant patience in face of low return!

Ability to think, part of the adaptation to environment!

Laziness of whole generations! All the back-bone of Jefferson's thought and of Van Buren's forgotten! Benefits of the latter, lost in civil war and post civil war finance!

All of which is not wholly alien to my subject.

All questions of *how* measures can be taken, how enforced, are questions of politics.

ECONOMICS is concerned with determining WHAT financial measures, what methods or regulations of trade, etc., must be taken, or can most advantageously be taken or decreed by government whatever its nature, or by whatever elected or haphazard or private or dictatorial bodies or individuals control trade, credit, money, etc.

Certain things are wise, let us say, for the governors of the Bank of England (a private corporation) and wise for the U.S. Federal Board, appointed by an elected president, and would be equally wise or equally foolish for a body directly elected by the people.

England, as we have remarked, gave herself to a gang of bankers ages ago. No one remembers why. It is no concern of a foreigner. The British wished it or at least some British wished it, and now the rest don't, apparently, mind.

All these things are part of politics. Economics is concerned with what should be done, not with how you are going to get a controlling group of men to carry out an idea; but with the idea, with the proper equations. As you might say the Baldwin Locomotive Works are concerned with making engines that will pull trains, not with which direction they are to run.

Good economics are as sound for Russia as for the U.S.A.

There may even be several economic solutions to any problem. Gasoline and coal both serve as fuel.

PART FOUR

Politics, A Necessary Digression

Science or no science an economic system or lack-of-system is bound to be affected by the political system in which or beside which it exists, and more especially by the preconceptions or prejudices or pre-dispositions and attitudes implied in the political system.

The preconception of democracy, let us say at its best, democracy as it existed in the minds of Jefferson and Van Buren, is that the best men, kaloikagathoi, etc., WILL TAKE THE TROUBLE to place their ideas and policies before the majority with such clarity and persuasiveness that the majority will accept their guidance, i.e. 'be right'.

The preconception of let us say the Adamses, or aristodemocratic parties is that privilege, a little of it, will breed a sense of responsibility.

The further Toryism is that the best should be served.

In practice it is claimed that the best get tired or fail to exert themselves to the necessary degree.

It seems fairly proved that privilege does NOT breed a sense of responsibility. Individuals, let us say exceptional individuals in privileged classes, maintain the sense of responsibility, but the general ruck, namely 95 per cent of all privileged classes, seem to believe that the main use of privileges is to be exempt from responsibility, from responsibilities of every possible kind.

This is as true of financial privilege as of political privilege.

The apparent exception seems to occur at the birth of any new privileged class, which amounts to saying that any new governing class is bound to be composed of exceptional men, or at any rate of men having more energy and being therefore more fit (apt) to govern than their fellows.

The dross of the intelligentsia, lacking the force to govern, constantly try to spread the belief that THEY are the 'best', the agathoi, etc.

Obviously no best, no even good, governing class can be spineless; this applies even to an administrative class, or people administering economics. The term 'good' in either case must include a capacity for action; some sense of relation between action and mere thought or talk.

A lot of rot is talked and written on the assumption of political and economic laws existing *in vacuo*.

I go on writing because it appears to me that no thoughtful man can in our time avoid trying to arrange those things in his own mind in an orderly fashion, or shirk coming to conclusions about them, i.e. as man living perforce among other men, affected by their actions, and by his affecting them.

To separate ideas that are not identical and to determine their relations.

As to the history of the subject, a fig for that history save in so far as it applies to the present and to the day after tomorrow.

A democracy, the majority which 'decides' in a democracy functioning as such, would presumably choose sound economics shortly after it had learned to distinguish the sound from the unsound. Subjects of an autocrat would obey, and continue obeying the economic decisions of their ruler or rulers as long as the orders were economically sound, and for a considerable period after those orders were unsound. Various durations of patience in intermediate forms of government.

A break, revolution, chaos, need not imply any new discovery or ambition or new form of soundness; it is, nevertheless, usually engineered in the name of some form of justice, or some social belief with economic implications.

The point is that the orders of an omniscient despot and of an intelligent democracy would be very much alike in so far as they affected the main body of the country's economics. Whether as independent citizens, individuals, etc., or as pack animals, the nutrition of the population would have its importance.

For any particular country, the most immediate road thereto has a good deal to be said in its favour, and that road would start FROM the conditions in which the said country finds itself at the moment.

The present moment, the moment under consideration.

Capital is generally considered as perdurable, eternal and indestructible. This is probably an error. Gold coin in circulation wears down, whence paper currency, to save attrition. Paper has to be renewed. The expense is trifling but mathematically extant.

Jewels might seem to be property and not capital. They or precious metal can be buried in cellars. Whence they work as a magnet.

Observe the magnetism of a man reputed to be wealthy. The force of this rumour on those about him.

Observe the force of the wildest and mildest hopes of profit, and consider the imponderabilia that enter into any consideration of credit ('the expectation that the other man will pay').

A further point is that not only particular masses of credit may rot, but that the credit of ANY economic system, qua system, may rot.

Not only may a year's crop fail, but the tree itself may.

There have been so-called systems based not on any sound thought or equation but on nothing more than a temporary accident; as say the chance of swapping glass beads to the heathen, or the monopoly of a trade route, or the willingness of Indians to swap forty square miles of land for a rifle.

Some of these systems have lasted for at least three hundred years. Nile tolls are at the beginning of history. Kublai understood paper currency. The Mantuans in the quatrocento considered a cloth pool on the lines of the Hoover government's buying of wheat. There is probably no inventable scheme or measure that can't be upholstered with historic background.

In 1933 Where are We?

For civilised countries the problem of production is solved. There are doubtless particular products not producible in particular geographic areas, and particular uncivilised areas where industrialisation, improved methods of production would solve the local troubles, but for the 'great powers' etc., the problem is not production.

2. The shortening of the working day (say to five or four hours) would so aid the general distribution in all civilised countries that they could carry on without other change for a considerable period.

3. But this would not in the long run permit them perpetually to dodge the problem of a fair and/or adequate distribution of credit slips. Called the problem of money or of the fiduciary system.

That is the main question and the overwhelming question of economic science. It is, I should assert, open to permanent solution. Scientific solution.

4. But a permanent and scientific solution of it would still leave us with the necessity of practising the ART of economics; that is to say, we should still have to exercise constant vigilance with the same caginess that the peasant shows in selecting his next crop. There is no way of dispensing with the perceptive faculties. Five year planners, ten year planners, clever men, etc., will for ever have to guess and to try to guess right re-what is to be produced and how much and when.

Make fair the distribution of paper slips certifying work done, keep the work distributed among a sufficient proportion of the people, and you still must have constant caginess not to find yourself in October with nothing but wheat, or nothing but aluminium frying pans.

And toward this end, there is probably no equation other than the greatest watchfulness of the greatest number of the most competent.

One man asleep at a switch can very greatly discommode quite a good railway.

In a world of Kreugers and Mellons you might say the switch-boards are enveloped (on purpose) in darkness. What I am getting at is, that with all the solvable problems solved, clear and in the open, there will still be 'opportunity', there will still be need to use wits.

Inflation (Science as possibly distinct from art in economics)
Inflation was said to be 'understood' in Germany after the war. There
are now almost universal cries for inflation (Germany, U.S.A., and
elsewhere).

There are very few demands for *control* of inflation.

Inflation is perhaps the ambiguous or camouflaging homonym for
a dozen or more manoeuvres.

Dissociate what we can. For many people it means merely abandoning the gold standard. Merely having certificates for something other
than precious metal.

The banks (the bogy men) inflate and deflate at will, or appear to.

We are told that the tariffs on money are too high, and the tellers
are answered that the bank rates on overnight money are almost *nil*.
So that is not the real crux. The banks possibly use their freedom to
inflate and deflate to their own disproportionate advantage.

*TWO sorts of nations exist: those which control their finances and those which 'are
financed'.*

There are, I take it, intermediate degrees, nations that try more or
less to control part of their finances, or that exercise a semi-conscious
control over their finances, or have an unconscious influence on
them.

The American (U.S.) treasury was 'freed' about a century ago. It was
somewhat confused by the civil war, etc.

Once again we are not even concerned with HOW a people or nation
is to get control of its economics but with WHAT it ought to do with
them if it did get control.

Another form of the question is: what price should it insist on getting from the present controllers if it continues to tolerate their
control, i.e. what is the minimum (or maximum) of intelligence and
of intelligent measures it should demand of its 'owners' or financiers.

We have stated at least part of this in the formula.

ADEQUATE (and more or less just) distribution of credit slips
(certificates of work done, etc.).

I have put 'ADEQUATE' in capitals and 'just' in lower case because
that is the order of their importance.

There is a very great margin of error, a very great coefficient of
injustice possible in a quite workable and quite comfortable economic
system. The Miller of Dee and the rest of it. Once a human being is
comfortable, even tolerably comfortable, without actual suffering
and free, more or less, from IMMEDIATE worry, he will not bother (to
an almost incredible degree he will refuse to bother) about economics.

But an *inadequate* distribution of credit slips will upset the whole
system, any system; it will heap up obstacles before anyone is aware,
it will heap them up all over the place and without ascribing responsibility to anyone in particular, and without offering handy solutions.

'Adequate' with Queries about Solutions
The Mahometans ran on a share-out system.

I forget whether every fanatic got an equal share. It don't much matter, it was so long ago, but at any rate they had national dividends, at least as long as they continued to conquest.

It is difficult to conceive national dividends in our day and in our countries without a noisome increase in bureaucracy.

National dividends have worked in the past. Undoubtedly most people would like to receive ten guineas a month in crisp bills from the postman or other trusted minion of officialdom.

It sounds so easy, so easy that hardly anyone (including the author) can believe it.

It seems as if the recipients ought at least to go through the motions, or to hold themselves ready to do something useful in return for the bonanza, or at least to keep awake and make sure that something was being done, that the greenbacks or Bradbury's or whatever, meant and continued to mean something other than greenbacks.

I seem to remember a time when Major Douglas wrote books without mention of national dividends.

I am now making simply a catalogue or list of offered 'solutions'. I am inclined to leave the national dividendists to show HOW they will insure the perennial delivery of needed goods against distributed greenbacks. I am not denying the possibility. I merely await fuller enlightenment.

As nearly as I can recall Douglas's early expositions, he claimed that in the present system a certain proportion of the credit-slips, or what should be the quantity of same, were sucked up or absorbed or caused to disappear.

I am purposely putting this the 'other way on' to see whether the idea is sufficiently well constructed to stand being joggled about.

In the 'present industrial system', work is done, goods produced, and the manufacturers, owners, traders, etc., demand from the public more credit-slips than the work is worth, or at any rate more credit-slips than the governments and banks will permit to be available against that work.

And the effect is cumulative. There are constantly more goods and constantly fewer and fewer valid certificates, which same leads to constipation.

And again, if I remember rightly, Major Douglas explained how the wangle was wangled. According to him, if I translate correctly, a certain part of the credit-slips received by the *entrepreneurs* was wormed down a sort of tube, i.e. instead of equalling the cost of the thing made and given for it, it equalled that cost plus part of the machinery used in producing the article (part of the plant).

And nothing was done against this amount of credit taken in from the public and hidden. It flowed continually down into the ground, down into somebody's pocket.

Result – constantly more and more goods for sale – constantly fewer certificates of work done.

So that to keep things even, one would have either to print more slips, or to compute the cost in some other way, i.e. to distinguish between real costs and costs according to the traditional book-keeping.

According to traditional book-keeping the Major's requirements would have meant that impossible thing: sales under cost. But he figured that they would not be less than the real cost, and that the paradox was all on paper.

All of which requires a bit of thinking.

Manifestly we have seen companies building new plants out of 'profits'. Manifestly we have seen crises.

The foregoing is perhaps very confusing. I state in one place the maker ought to get a certificate of work done, a fair certificate equivalent TO the work done.

Then I appear (to some readers) to say that he gets too much. When I ought apparently to say that he gets too little.

There is no contradiction. He gets too much, or asks too much for some of his product, and is unable to get anything for the rest.

Let us say he makes one million brooms that really cost him 3d. each.

He asserts (in accordance to inherited beliefs of his accountants) that they cost him 5d. and must be sold for 6d.

He sells 400,000 for 6d., has 600,000 left on his hands, and ultimately goes bust. Despite the fact that five hundred or seven hundred thousand people could use the brooms.

That is an 'impossible case'. Or rather it is a crude statement, and there are various intermediate conditions.

Say he drops his price to 1d. and sells his six hundred thousand spare brooms, and thereby ruins some other manufacturer, etc.

My imaginary example is merely to show that high price needn't ensure perpetual success, and needn't be the best possible commerce.

The issue of credit (or money) must be just, i.e. neither too much nor too little.

Against every hour's work (human or kilowatt hour), an hour's certificate. That can be the first step. That can be scientific. Ultimately it must be scientific.

But it will not get you out of the necessity of using intelligence re – what and how much you produce.

What? can be answered by 'Everything useful or desirable'.

And the how much can be answered by 'all that is wanted' with allowance over for accidents.

That may sound very vague, but it is nevertheless reducible to mathematical equations and can be scientifically treated.

The equations (algebraic equations) *will not mean* merely any old quantity turned out haphazard.

Their answer will govern the length of the working day. By which I still mean the number of hours' work per day for which a man is *paid*. Over and above which, he can paint pictures on his wall, stuff his armchairs, breed fighting cocks, buy lottery tickets, or indulge in any form of frugality or wastefulness that suits his temperament (so long as he confines his action to his own *property* (*vide* definition in Part I).

So long as his action is confined to his own home and front yard.

Digression Perhaps Unnecessary
Personally I favour a home for each individual, in the sense that I think each individual should have a certain amount of cubic space into which he or she can retire and be exempt from any outside interference what so damn ever.

From that I should build individual rights, and as they move out from that cubicle or inverted trapezoid they should be modified by balancing and counterpoise of the same-sprung rights of others, up to the rights of the state or the congeries.

Parallels political and economic.

Economics
There would seem to be the following kinds of error or crime in the issuance of credit-slips against work.

1. The issuers may refuse to issue any slips, or adequate slips against the work.

2. They may issue too many.

3. They may issue them in such a way that for products produced and distributed in a complicated manner too much of the credit goes to some, or some kind of the labour, and not enough to some other.

The terms 'labour', 'work', throughout this discussion apply to the man with a shovel, the clerk, the transporter, the *entrepreneur*, etc. Everyone who acts in the transposition of the article from mother earth to the eater (eye of beholder, hand of user).

I know of no alphabetic or primer simplification of the questions of *de-* and *in-*flation. I mean nothing easier to comprehend than the history of some particular instance, say the story of Van Buren *versus* Biddle in the 1830's.

At the other end of the scale, Doughty's *Arabia Deserta* or Leo's history of the eighth and ninth centuries can illumine the reader *re*–what occurs when there is NO production.

The point is that in any system, in any conceivable system, there arise similar problems, whether under Soviet or Florentine Banker.

The goods needed,

The transport,

The use or consumption. The necessity of motion, which means both of goods and of the 'carrier',

Monetary carrier.

The clarity of mind that understands that one hundred gallons a minute through an inch pipe at one speed can equal one hundred gallons through a different pipe at another speed–the bigger the slower, the faster the smaller, etc.

A small amount of 'money' changing hands rapidly will do the work of a lot moving slowly, etc.

As in mechanics some sizes of machine are found fit for some work, etc., detailed applications without change of principle. Fruits of experience *as to detail*: ideas as to main causes.

This looks like a mare's nest or like wilful confusion! What the Major said fifteen years ago matters less than getting a valid and clear statement.

The manufacturer is 'paid' in two ways under the present system. He gets 'money' or 'is owed' money for what he sells, and he gets ability to borrow from banks, i.e. his action and potentiality to produce enable him to get credit as well as payments (cash and deferred) and the banks get more credit than they give HIM, i.e. he has to hand part of it back to them, and for the part he hands back he gets no direct credit, though he may get the ability to have more (on similar terms).

Perhaps the only value of these statements is a test value. I mean that I am merely saying 5 and 2 make 7 in place of the other economists' statements that 2 and 5 make 7, to see whether either they or their readers understand their previous statements.

After all, this is a very rudimentary treatise.

By the time the banks have got more credit than they gave the manufacturer, the potential consumer hasn't enough credit to purchase the needed goods. Where would he get it? The banks will always give him less than he has to give them. They are not there for their health.

The book-keeping cost of the goods is the cost (real) of the goods plus the cost of the money, or the rent of the money.

I take it that in the perfect economic state the cost of the money is reduced almost to nothing, to something like the mere cost of postage, and that this cost is borne by the state, i.e. distributed so as to be a burden on no one in particular.

Once that end is attained, the general intelligence can apply itself to the problem of what and how much to produce.

The state conceived as the public convenience. Money conceived as a public convenience. Neither as private bonanza.

Novelties

The possibility of novelties in economics is probably somewhat exaggerated. Hume by 1750 is already talking of paper credit and cites someone or other to the effect that the great amount of gold coin in Athens seemed to be no use to the Athenians save in facilitating arithmetic.

Twenty years ago we were asked to think that someone was being a 'modern' with a large 'M' economist because he 'left out money'.

Some know and many fail to state or keep clearly in mind the need of money, which is the need of a common denominator FOR THE SAKE OF ACCOUNTING, so as not to send book-keepers crazy with columns of ten horses, twelve cows, nine locomotives. Consider the chips in a poker game, more convenient than to have each man betting his shirt, watch and cuff-links.

A GRAVER FAILURE to dissociate: is in the nature of wealth. Crises in the sheik and sheep trade seldom occur. I mean that the primitive grazer counts his property in sheep and is not continually worried if he cannot sell out his whole herd.

Half the modern trouble is the mania or hallucination or *idée fixe* of MARKET and market value. The fundamental difference in wealth is that of animal, vegetable and mineral kingdoms.

All manufactured articles partake of the main property of the latter, namely, they do not increase and multiply.

The shepherd's sheep multiply, the crops that are sown multiply, and neither requires much work. I mean the shepherd sits around, with a boy and a dog. The dangers from bears and wolves and other incidents of primitive shepherd's life have been diminished. In legendary countries he may still do odd jobs of knitting.

The sheep supply clothing (Jefferson's calculation was that one sheep per person gave sufficient wool). The meat is disagreeable but nutritive. There is no question of keeping the shepherd FULLY employed.

Crops demand work (too much) at special seasons.

But with a minimum of care crops and sheep multiply.

Your possessions and mine do not multiply. Your tables, pianos, etc., remain set as a mineral, but you can't get more by digging up the floor of your cellar.

Hume already saw that 'the increase and *consumption* (italics mine) of all the commodities, which serve to the ornament and pleasure of life, are advantages to society; because at the same time they multiply those innocent gratifications to individuals, they are a kind of *storehouse* (italics his) of labour ... which in the exigencies of the state, may be turned to the public service'.

Hume might have served as a warning; for his 'exigencies of state' are mainly war, which fact ought to have made people think a bit more deeply. I suggest that it didn't, for the simple reason that they didn't in the least understand his first proposition.

No book can do ALL a man's thinking for him. The utility of any statement is limited by the willingness of the receiver to think.

The practices of rent and interest arise out of the natural disposition of grain and animals to multiply. The sense of right and justice which has sustained the main practice of rent and interest through the ages, *despite* countless instances of particular injustice in the application, is inherent in the nature of animal and vegetable.

There is no need to postulate any greater perversion than natural indolence, and that in itself is insufficient as postulate. There has always been a supply of lackers, members of less civilised tribes, or non-possidentes ready and glad to watch sheep for part of the wool. The impulse of the French in our day to get work out of the Congo is wholly traditional and 'normal'.

As for selling children into servitude, etc., the whole problem is no longer–but at many periods of history has been hardly more than–the duration of mortmain. How long shall the dead hand rule, and to what extent?

The two extremes: superstitious sacrosanctity of 'property' *versus* Jefferson's 'The earth belongs to the living', which was part dogma, and part observation of a fact so obvious that it took a man of genius to perceive it.

It led Jefferson to the belief that no nation has the right to contract debts not payable within the lifetime of the contractors, which he interpreted to mean the lifetime of the majority of the contractors who were of age at the date of contract. So that from a first estimate of thirty-five years, he finally fixed on nineteen years as the limit of validity of such debts.

By the light of his intelligence American economics improved from the time of the revolution till the confusion of the U.S. civil war.

No system of economics can be valid unless it take count of this inherence in vegetable and animal nature (which inherence includes or extends to overproduction).

The term 'over-production' usually means 'more of a thing than will sell'.[1]

---

[1] After the last war Henry Ford as an experiment broke up a number of armoured vessels. He made no money profit, he got back what it cost him, and he was left with a great number of engines, which, for all I know, he still has. There is no reason to suppose that these engines do any harm, any more than the ruins of Aigues Mortes or Carcassonne.

Yes, they occupy space. You don't want 'em in Piccadilly Circus. I have also seen a sign translatable as: 'Mountain to let, capable of enalping 30,000 muttons.' There is still room to breathe and walk about the face of the planet.

Dissociate Permanence from Permanence

Dissociate the perdurability of granite from the perdurability of grain or of a species of animals. Some people seem to demand the same kind of durability from a germinating organism as they do from the lump of rock.

At the other end of the scale they say: A bank manager need know nothing save the difference between a bill and a mortgage. Several 'great financiers' and prize-receiving 'economists' in our time fail to make this distinction.

Economic habits arise from the nature of things (animal, mineral, vegetable). Economic mess, evil theories are due to failure to keep the different nature of different things clearly distinct in the mind.

The economic 'revolution' or an economic revolution occurred when raw supply ceased to be limited to *static* mineral matter (plus animal and vegetable increases).

The minute work began to be in great measure 'raw supply' the need for a change in economic concepts arose.

The minute you have practically unlimited stores of work at your disposal, (by the simple device of letting water run down hill through a pipe onto a turbine, or any other device), you have got to begin to readjust your mental derivatives.

Not only will sheep go on begetting each other, without much attention from the shepherd, but lights will shine, stoves give heat, trains move, etc., while a couple of men watch a dynamo.

The cattle drover fed his family. The turbine can work for the group. Even the idea of national dividends (which I dislike) seems less goofy from this angle.

It is as idiotic to expect members of a civilized twentieth-century community to go on working eight hours a day as it would be to expect the shepherd to try to grow wool on his sheep by hand; the farmer to blow with his own breath on each buried seed to warm it; the poulterer to sit on his hens' eggs.

People are so little used, or shall we say the readers of books and papers are so little used to using their eyes, or so little travelled as never to have seen simple phenomena.

Has the reader ever seen women at a well curb, or at a public spigot or pump?

Kitchen plumbing, the spigot in the home, means half an hour's idleness (or leisure) per day to every female member of the community. (Civilized community as compared with the savage and with many very far from savage communities.)

This is not a theory of the leisure class. It is a fact of leisure humanity (i.e. civilised human life).

227

PART FIVE

Minor Addenda and Varia

I have never met a gambler with an ounce of intelligence, but the prejudice against lotteries is in the category of superstitions, totemism and taboo. Lotteries can harm only the imbeciles who buy tickets, but these imbeciles appear to be wholly in their own right. As a means of collecting money for state purposes no sound reason has ever been adduced against this sane safety valve.

The instinct has been romanticised, doubtless in special cases it is the only danger some men can incur and the only chance of adventure they get. I doubt if it would greatly survive in a sane commonwealth, but the world has not yet seen such a commonwealth. The prejudice is part of the puritan imbecility, which is at root a disease, begotten of the worst in nature.

There is, however, every reason why the imbecile pastime should be isolated, i.e. confined in its effects to those who voluntarily gamble, and that it should not be allowed to affect the price of foodstuffs and necessities.

The whinings of a Whitney and the yowls of stock jobbers are no better than any other form of gangster's sobstuff.

The purpose of an act is one of its dimensions; is a component of its specific gravity, and no one ever yet claimed to have sold short, or rigged the stock market, save in the hope of picking other men's pockets.

There is nothing to be said against any gang of thieves playing poker except that they are playing with other men's money. When members of a stock exchange play against each other without affecting the food and welfare of members of the community who have no chance of profiting by the play and in any case no voice in the laying of the bets, the said brokers, etc., cannot make much showing as sportsmen.

They have had a fair amount of time to show what they have done for their countries and so far haven't been able to dig up even a journalist liar to write them a tombstone. As a public utility they are not a success.

It is perfectly easy to dissociate investment from speculation; it is fairly easy to spin cobwebs over the borders of the dissociation. A stock exchange confined to the buying and selling for real investors would doubtless be very very dull, and many of the present practitioners and scoundrels would take to golf and chicken-farming in preference to such ovine tranquillity, but we are not out to guarantee the private amusements of a few hundred or a few thousand barons.

It would be much better from the *bono publico* standpoint if they were to kill themselves racing motor-boats, get their kicks playing the races,

228

and leave the small fry to roulette and the lotteries. Economics, as a science, has no messianic call to alter the instincts.

Short of an absolute state ownership of all property there will always be plenty of chance for men to 'make fortunes' with serious construction in industry. The fewer fake diamond mines, the more likely new inventions and amplifications will be to find support.

NOTE. The printing of fine books improved greatly after the late war. Because a great number of people had no confidence in the value of money.

I am aware that I am here in a risky position, and that an attempt to dogmatise might jeopard my credit, nevertheless I should hazard a guess that a definite good or gain occurred because of a definite state of intelligence. The good occurred not because money was unstable, which I don't think anyone can regard as a desirable state of things, but because these people were freed from the *idée fixe* of money as the one and only fixed value.

I admit they were only half free and mostly bought *de luxe* editions because they hoped to be able to sell them later at a profit, but at any rate it was the 'thin end of the wedge'; they had at least for ten minutes got their eye on to something concrete. A few honest consumers and a few of the better producers reaped a benefit.

Check Up

The remarks foregoing, even though they are in some cases my own, have no claim to be novelties. Any man reading or re-reading a classic will be affected by what he agrees with, but probably respect the ancient author in proportion as he seems sound or as he seems to have ante-dated modernity.

Thus in Hume, 'Prices do not so much depend on the absolute quantity of commodities and that of money which are in a nation, as on that of the commodities which come or may come to market, and that of the money which circulates' (D. Hume, b. 1711, d. 1776. *Essay on Money*).

The error of America in the 1830's was to bull the land market as if unworked land far from railways could 'yield'.

The analogy in the 1930's is that the American fool has repeated himself, putting 'industry' in the place of land, i.e. stocks, shares in industrial companies which either were not in shape to produce or had no possible market anywhere within dreamable range of the selling price of stocks in New York.

Hume's reasons for wanting what he calls a prosperous state were manifestly despicable, consisting mainly in the idea that if a state were prosperous some disgusting louse like Louis XIV would be able to pay the dregs of the population (his own or some one else's) to go kill or rob some one else. But that is no reason for not observing Hume's intelligence. He already saw through money, saw through coined money at that.

Some of his propositions are still valid, and possibly unsupercedable.

You will probably find nothing more valid inside its own scope than the statement that prosperity depends not on the quantity of money in a country but on its *constantly increasing*.

This was before the term inflation was in daily use.

DISSOCIATE. Inflation, first used as a derogative term and now (1932) advised as policy 'all over the place'.

DISSOCIATE inflation from steady increase. The term inflation might be limited to mean disproportionate and faked augmentation of the amount of paper currency, an augmentation having no relation to fact, or having a faked relation to fact.

INCREASE or proper augmentation.

As certificate of an increasing productivity, increase of product, increase of means of production there SHOULD be an increase in the printed certificates of value (circulatable certificates).

But here again one must distinguish, and here in particular one can learn from history and in particular the American history of the 1830's. At that time there was a land boom. Fools bought land and boosted the sale price regardless of the fact that the merchandise (land) wasn't producing, wasn't being worked, couldn't be worked at once or for a considerable time, and there were crises and panics, etc.

'Worthless' land was just as worthless then as worthless machinery and factories are now.

To need certificates of value the product (of land or of factory) must be wanted by someone, and there must be means of getting it to them.

There are four elements; and it is useless trying to function with three:

1. The product.
2. The want.
3. The means of transport.
4. AND the certificates of value, preferably legal tender and 'general', in the sense that they should be good for wheat, iron, lumber, dress goods, or whatever the heart and stomach desire.

And (repeating an earlier proposition), everybody must be able to get a certain number of these certificates on what might be called decent conditions, i.e. without torture and without excessive worry.

Preferably on 'fair-terms', namely that the conditions for getting them must not be violently different in the cases of A, B and C.

For the *n*th time, I repeat that the straightest road to such a desirable condition is *via* the formula: a small amount of work for everyone, with a certificate of work done as the consequence.

The brains of the nation or group to be used in discerning WHAT work is most needful, what work is less necessary and what is desirable even though not strictly necessary.

Such work should be paid. It would not fill up any man's day.

The rest of his day he could employ in expressing his difference of opinion with the majority, and in such 'work' or activity as he (as distinct from the brains of the country officially organized) might consider proper, necessary or desirable.

Ultimately your credit board or your bank scoundrels or whoever is the financial and economic executive would have one main function and would be judged intelligent or imbecile according as this was performed with competence. They are there to determine, and so far as possible to keep steady, the rate of increase in the printed certificates of value.

And their motivation should be the *bonum publicum*, the commonweal and not the shifting and shaking the sieve for the benefit of a few highly-placed crooks, scoundrels and exploiters.

The most opportune citation is from a Spaniard whose name is not, in my source, printed, debating the new constitution, he observed that where the financial influences had been too strong and uncontrolled, freedom had suffered.

THE BASES OF ECONOMICS are so simple as to render the subject almost wholly uninteresting.

The complication of the subject is hardly a complication, it arises

A. from the extreme difficulty of foreseeing what will be wanted;

B. from the rascally nature of certain men, from selfishness of exploiters and those in 'favoured positions' who fear to lose an 'advantage'.

The best system of government, economically speaking, is that which best balances the four elements listed above, be it republic, monarchy, or soviet or dictatorship. In future it will probably be a republic save in special cases, but republic or soviet, the government which best manages this balance, which manages it with the least bunk and blah and the greatest honesty, will and should probably prevail 'as a system of government'.

Dictatorship as a Sign of Intelligence

Popular fancy and Ludwigian cheap-jackery show the dictator as man of the hour, force of will, favoured of fortune.

The phase 'intelligence' is more interesting. Mussolini as intelligent man is more interesting than Mussolini as the Big Stick. The Duce's aphorisms and perceptions can be studied apart from his means of getting them into action.

'We are tired of a government in which there is no responsible person having a hind name, a front name and an address.'

231

'Production is done by machines but consumption is still performed by human beings.'

Also his Perception of the Dimension Quality
It is something, it was indeed a bright day when some ruler perceived that there was a limit to the dimension quantity in the nation's productivity, I mean a limit to quantity of production that could be advantageous either to a given nation or to the world, but that there is no limit to the dimension quality. There have been attained maxima, *vide* my criticism of art and letters for cited examples, but these attained maxima are not ineluctable limits. Nothing forbids us to desire a better art than that of the Quattrocento. We may be or may not be damned unlikely to get it, but there is no harm in trying. At any rate, in the dimension QUALITY there is ample field for all human energy, no one need feel cramped at having only four hours a day for paid work.

After that, the problem of civilisation is pretty well outside the domain of the economist. Neither the billionaire nor the whole howling populace can bribe, coax or bully the artist into surpassing his own qualifications.

Five hundred people can get any kind of civilisation they like, *up to* the capacity of their best inventor and maker. But all they can do for him is to feed, clothe, and give him leisure and space to work in.

Finale
Within twenty-four hours of writing the above I find that R. H. C. (in *New English Weekly* for 16 June 1932) has at last found an expression simple enough to be understood by almost anyone, save possibly Maynard Keynes or some paid mouthpiece of British Liberalism.

'Would you call it inflation to issue tickets for every seat in a hall, despite the fact that the hall had never before been filled, or more than a fourth of the seats sold, because of there not being enough tickets available?
'Inflation would consist in issuing more tickets than there are seats.'

That is the foundation stone of the New (Douglas) economics.
Keynes may have found it out by now; he was incapable of understanding it in 1920, and until he makes definite public acknowledgment of the value of C. H. Douglas, I shall be compelled either to regard him as a saphead or to believe that his writings arise from motives lying deeper in the hinterland of his consciousness than courtesy can permit me to penetrate.

A B C OF ECONOMICS

Conclusions: Or a Postscript in the Spring

'. . . and they adopt a hundred contrivances, which serve no purpose but to check industry, and to rob ourselves and our neighbours of the common benefits of art and nature.'

DAVID HUME: *The Balance of Trade*.

An economic system in which it is more profitable to make guns to blow men to pieces than to grow grain or make useful machinery, is an outrage, and its supporters are enemies of the race.

2. The immediate problem is distribution.

3. National dividends are possible.

4. The moment you conceive money as certificate of work done, taxes are an anomaly, for it would be perfectly simple to issue such certificates of work *done for the* state, without wasting effort in re-collecting certificates already in circulation.

This doesn't mean that the state should buy just anything it fancies. There would be a rush of 'gold-diggers' the moment such a concept began to function, but there should also be an aroused sense of proportion in values TO the state.

There would be no miserliness in regard to sanitation, healthy houses, medical and dental services. England now wastes three million lives in peace time for every million lives spent in the war.

5. The popular instinct against taxation is sound. I repeat that national dividends are possible, but I doubt their immediate necessity, and in any case the first step toward them, whether you regard it as proved right or as experiment, could (? should) be made by this direct payment in newly conceived money for work publicly needed. This might very possibly provide the just proportion of increase in circulating medium needed to keep exchange healthy.

'Prosperity comes of exchange' (meaning exchange of different goods, regardless of the steps, book-keeping, etc., which may intervene).

6. A lot of rot is talked because of failure to dissociate different meanings in the term 'gold standard'.

Gold could serve *as measure* even with the new and newest fancy brands of economics, so long as the issuance of money (needed for exchange) isn't ham-strung or exploited by people who happen to have the gold at a given moment.

It is perfectly easy to increase the volume of money in circulation without debasing its value.

7. If any of the author's opinions are wrong he will be only too glad to change 'em on proof being adduced to their contraries, but he will not alter them merely to please gunmakers' touts or subsidised economists who for twenty or more years have done nothing save their utmost to wrap up the subject in tissue paper, and to involve it in

mystery. Their opinions are suspect because of probable motives, and they never meet open statement by open statement but solely by avoidance or by running off at a bias.

I personally heard one of the chief and most despicable fakers describe himself as an 'orthodox economist'. 'Orthodox' and subsidised physicists condemned Galileo.

Political bearing
Both in England and in America the new party should be a MATERIAL PARTY with three parts to its platform:

1. When enough exists, means should be found to distribute it to the people who need it.

2. It is the business of the nation to see that its own citizens get their share, before worrying about the rest of the world.

(If not, what is the sense of being 'united' or organised as a state? What is the meaning of 'citizen'?)

3. When the potential production (the possible production) of anything is sufficient to meet everyone's needs, it is the business of the government to see that both production *and* distribution are achieved.

John Buchan's 'Cromwell'[1]

A NOTE

By great wisdom sodomy and usury were seen coupled together. If there comes ever a rebirth or resurrection of Christian Church, one and Catholic, a recognition of divinity as

La somma sapienza e il primo amore

it will come with a recognition and an abjuration of the great sin *contra naturam*, of the prime sin against natural abundance.

Art registers the state of man's soul (or whatever you want to call the compendium of his faculties). The silly prejudice against Leo Frobenius should fall before his indubitably great contemporary service to enlightenment in hammering on this fundamental.

The non-theological can take it as 'the swift perception of relations', and leave out supernatural connotations. The manifest are from light to black festering darkness can be measured in the material facts:

I. The church of St. Hilaire in Poitiers.

II. The bomb-proof, gas-proof cellar beneath the Rothschild private palace in Paris, whereto the works of art (as having commercial VALUE, monetary worth) are transported when the great chief usurer leaves that fatal and mentally foetid city.

The latter is the objective and material register of progressive human degradation, as result of moral obtuseness.

Dr. Hackett found two kinds of mosquito. No difference under the strongest microscope; but they lay different kinds of eggs, one virulent with malaria, the other innocuous. *Usury* and the *increment of association* under unobservant eye were confused one with the other. The brutal and savage mythology of the Hebrews was revived with the fall of mediaeval civilisation and the festering mind of Calvin, haeresiarchus, perditissimus, distilled a moral syphilis throughout the whole body of society. The grossening and fattening of European architecture was the contemporary imprint of his diseased condition.

John Buchan, although professing no very clear economic ideas, has been fairly clear on pages 8–9 of his 'Cromwell'[2] as to the decline of English mentality, from Bucer and Latimer toward the decadence.

It shows in England's versification. These things move parallel. Spectamur agendo. From all the beauty that was full of light, from all the mediaeval respect for intelligence, the sanity that could see the

[1] *The New English Weekly*, 6 June 1935.   [2] *Oliver Cromwell*, by J. Buchan. Houghton Mifflin.

theologian as athlete of the spirit, this curve descends in ratio with the rise of old-testament-olatry, with the commodity theory of money, and the elevation of usury to pre-eminence, with the cant about parity, the kow-tow to sterility.

Given the degree of economic sensibility in the more lively contemporary historians, one is impatient of a good deal of Buchan's detail. We can, however, isolate the facts that fall inside our field of interest. Thomas Cromwell, born about 1485, travelled and learnt international banking, settled in London as merchant and moneylender. Zealous for publication of Bible in England, 'cared nothing for religion'. Page 56, 'the difficulty was money': 444 pages, not a history for social creditors, a history for arm-chair retrospectors with a hobby. I wonder if this is too severe a judgment on a book that must have cost a good deal of labour to its compiler?

I wonder whether we can't get to the root by saying that Governor-General Buchan has a little mislaid the real reason for writing and reading history, namely that the past should be a light for the future. That the purpose of history is instruction, that is to make people think and to guide their thought toward what will elucidate today and tomorrow.

In any case a certain tedium is bound to inhere, increasingly, in all histories that do not aim chiefly to focus their knowledge upon the most vital issues of today (or, conjecturally, of tomorrow).

The human interest in Cromwell is of secondary order. The seventeenth century is not, relatively, a very interesting epoch – by comparison, that is, with periods in which there was more crucial struggle over issues more intimately bound up with our own.

This mustn't be taken extremely. But we should distinguish between historic study having purposeful focus on life as we know it, and a sort of extension of books of reference, 'mines' as they are called, for those who want to collect matter which can be so focused.

'Purposeful focus' does not mean distortion. An air of impartiality may give grace to narrative, but it may also cause history to fall short of greatness. John Buchan's historic curiosity is not of the most biting kind, it is not an insatiable curiosity determined to understand *all* the facts of Cromwell's career. A man could conceivably write with this high burning curiosity and keep it directed strictly on to the PAST, thus making it serve, even more effectively, as an escape mechanism. Even that would have produced a livelier book than the present, a book no more purposeful than Ludwig's popular cheap-jackery.

Over and above these exercises, whether commercial speculation, juggling for notoriety, or in Buchan's case the gentlemanly exercise of wide leisure, there could be a more eminent kind of history, that which would do its utmost to use past ascertainable fact as enlightenment to present, all too oppressive, problems.

History and Ignorance[1]

Istory that omits economics will not eternally be accepted as anything but a farce or a fake. The gross cloacal ignorance of professors, of reporters who offer chronicles with no economic analysis, can not forever pass as enlightenment.

It, as a matter of fact, has not always passed as enlightenment. The real foci of power have never swallowed this sort of tosh. *Vide*, let us say, the Venetian ambassador, Barton Morosini's report on John Law, to the Venetian Senate 28 January 1723.

Somewhere or other, perhaps in Barney Baruch's private files, there is or has been some history. Zaharoff once knew some history. An intelligentsia that accepts anything less is merely an ignorantsia with an Ersatz lion's skin draped over its ass ears.

> 'Because no one
>   can sell the moon
>   to the moon.'

The *Manchester Guardian* howl that poetry should be a lavender sachet bag, and omit all the major content of the Divina Commedia comes well from fake pacifist quarters.

Pacifists who refuse to investigate the economic causes of war make common cause with the gun sellers.

I sincerely hope Congressman Tinkham will keep on with his agitation for the investigation of endowments, in particular re the use of funds by the Carnegie Endowment for Peace.

As an historian I have a legitimate curiosity as to why so little attention has been given to economics as a factor in incitement to war (direct or indirect) or why so little curiosity has been shown as to economic determinism as a factor in cause of hostilities; or why American education so tamely accepts titular heads whose cause of being is wrapped in so many veils.

Should a National Academy have or not have intellectual curiosity, should it stimulate inquisitive minds? Should the education of the élite be focussed solely or predominantly on the manufacture of robots and tame rabbits?

Should a national academy DESIRE a correlation of active knowledge? Should it take any ACTION to promote it? Has the American Academy ever shown the faintest interest in living thought? And if so who hides the documents that would prove it?

[1] *The New English Weekly*, 25 July 1935.

What percentage of American college presidents owe their advancement to complacency? Is the Harding-Hoover era the ideal summit of American intellection? Are the left overs of this era the ideal guides for the next generation?

Harvard, I hear, is still afflicted with Sprague. I was deceived by a catalogue of one section of their beanery, whereas Sprague has been put back of the smoke screen in another. This kind of professor trained our solons. In the stratosphere on a pink cloud we observe the era when someone will look into American education and find it vapid; into American 'Foundations' and find them putrid.

Are men who were perfectly adjusted to this era, who 'rose to prominence' during those murky days, the best eyes for the people? And so forth.... The best of us can not avoid contagion. Major Douglas himself, can resist strictly economic lies, but somewhere comes the moment of fatigue or inattention. I have known it and I know no man who has not. By sheer dint of repetition we have all of us imbibed, absorbed prejudice, if not about the matters we were specifically intent on, certainly on periphery matter: e.g., even I was misled re Italian censorship simply by foreign lies.

I have already cited both Tour du Pin and Marx as IGNORING money, as being unconscious of the problem IN MONEY. It is less the matters we think about, than the things 'we never think OF' that lead us into error.

The teaching of literature was so inefficient in my young days (and probably still is), that I have had to find out at 49 what I might perfectly well have been told at 17. Dr. Rouse's correspondence during the past months, shows that he has not escaped similar experience.

Jefferson, forgotten, Van Buren simply kept under cover, the simplest possible equations, such as those recently cited by Congressman Goldsborough, are KEPT OUT of the mind not only of the man in the street, but of the men who should specifically be not only vaguely aware of them, but specifically and acutely ALERT to them.

Omissions such as those Reckitt found in Somervell, should and probably will be found comic in some decently informed future era.

The intelligentsia do not get ideas, they merely get the spare parts of ideas. Put it another way: cranks and doctrinaires try to propagate specific details of a system often without understanding the system to which these details belong, let alone the relation of that system to any other.

A work of art, any serious work vivifies a man's total perception of relations.

It makes no difference whether the work is a Bach fugue or a drawing by Dürer or the movement of words in the Odyssey.

Les arts decoratifs, are mere relaxation, slumber stuff, escape mechanisms.

The hat trick is possible because this escape does in a way resemble

238

the great breath, the refreshment and reinvigoration that comes with emergence from immediate fuss over some personal impasse. This is found in great art WHEN the beholder isn't too dulled or fatigued to deal with the great or real art at all.

Naturally the bastards who do not want truth, who do not want a democratization of the perception of relations, howl and weep whenever poetry emerges from the lavender sachet and bric-à-brac category.

There are even in England, and they have to my disgust penetrated even to the purlews of Chancery Lane, mangy mice so low that they want to eliminate the whole major domain of writing–let us say, the major domain of the Divina Commedia–from the scope of the poets.

This is in part due to stinking snobism, part to craven and bootlicking cowardice, and part to sheer gross and utter ignorance of the tradition of writing, and of the great works of literature.

The maintainers of mass murder and mass malnutrition have in these people very useful, if unconscious, allies.

Banks[1]

Two kinds of banks have existed: The MONTE DEI PASCHI and the devils.

Banks built for beneficence, for reconstruction; and banks created to prey on the people.

Three centuries of Medici wisdom went into the Monte dei Paschi, the *only* bank that has stood from 1600 till our time.

Siena was flat on her back, without money after the Florentine conquest.

Cosimo, first duke of Tuscany, had all the Medici banking experience behind him. He guaranteed the capital of the Monte, taking as security the one living property of Siena, and a certain amount of somewhat unhandy collateral.

That is to say, Siena had grazing lands down toward Grosseto, and the grazing rights worth 10,000 ducats a year. On this basis taking it for his main security, Cosimo underwrote a capital of 200,000 ducats, to pay 5 per cent to the shareholders, and to be lent at $5\frac{1}{2}$ per cent; overhead kept down to a minimum; salaries at the minimum and all excess of profit over that to go to hospitals and works for the benefit of the people of Siena. That was in the first years of the seventeenth century, and that bank is open today. It outlasted Napoleon. You can open an account there tomorrow.

And the lesson is the very basis of solid banking. The CREDIT rests *in ultimate* on the ABUNDANCE OF NATURE, on the growing grass that can nourish the living sheep.

And the moral is in the INTENTION. It was not for the conquerors immediate short-sighted profit, but to restart the life and productivity of Siena, that this bank was contrived.

The hell banks have, from as far as the record takes us, started as gangs of creditors, associated to strangle the last ounce of profit out of their debtors. This they have done with splendour, boasts and parade. They have stood for exactitude in accounting. Once the dice have been loaded, they have counted up every point, every decimal. Chief and most glorified was the Banca S. Giorgio, the pitiless company of Genoese creditors, the model bank among bankers, against which I am, for all I know, the first to utter detraction.

'About the year 1200 there existed in Genoa, divers societies . . .

[1] From *Social Credit: An Impact* (1935). See Cantos XLII–LI. Ed.

'In 1252 they united. . . .

'In 1451, 9th April. The commune of Genoa vested in perpetuity its dogana (that is the collection of all import tax), in the Banca S. Giorgio.'

That means the bank got all the proceeds.

'1539. The Doge, governors and procurators confirmed and anew conceded and assigned to the protectors of S. Giorgio all the proceeds of the salt tax . . . approving the addition of the taxes on oil and grain, meat, wine, etc. . . . with the right to sell the same if they chose.

'1749 the bank got the right to tax church property also, but at a fourth less than secular.

'The revolution of 1797 disorganised its collection of taxes, the provisional government leaving the bank of (S. Giorgio) provisionally its internal administration and the collection of customs, took from its directors their *absolute civil and criminal jurisdiction* as incompatible with unity of the republic, and the sovereignty of the people.' *Memorie sulla banca di S. Giorgio*, Genoa, 1832. Compiled by their keeper of archives, Antonio Lobero.

Lobero seems rather indignant at this infringement of bankers' omnipotence, his spirit appears reincarnate in our day in Paul Einzig.

This shows what bankers will placidly do if you let 'em. The great company of St. George could be both plaintiff and judge in a civil or criminal suit against its interests.

The arts did not flourish in Genoa, she took almost no part in the intellectual activity of the renaissance. Cities a tenth her size have left more durable treasure.

The Individual in his Milieu[1]

A STUDY OF RELATIONS AND GESELL[2]

Twenty years ago little magazines served to break a monopoly, to release communication, mainly about letters, from an oppressive control, and they now wither on the stalk because they refuse to go on from where the late Henry James was interrupted

H. J. perceived the *Anagke* of the modern world to be money; he thought he ought to 'go down town', and found that he couldn't He left, for posthumous publication, an unfinished meditation on the money-acquiring faculty. Proust was, by comparison, an insignificant snob, with no deep curiosity as to the working of modern society, apart from his own career in it (a boot-licking sycophantic crawl in wake of a few contemptible remnants).

The diseased periphery of letters is now howling that literature and poetry in especial, should keep within bounds. I find this limitation entitled 'respect itself', which phrase is perverted to mean that literature should eschew the major field by omitting and leaving untackled a great deal of the subject matter that interested such diverse writers a Propertius, Dante and Lope de Vega.

The *Anagke* of our time is money. Cf. Colombus' rhapsody in Lope de Vega's *Nuevo Mundo*. Curiosity sank very low during the nineteenth century. Marx and La Tour du Pin were equally deaf, dumb and blind to money. La Tour du Pin managed to write a whole chapter in denunciation of usury without looking into its substance.

Economics in our time is where medicine was when professor studied the subject in Aristotle and refused to look at dissecting tables The history of money is yet to be written. Even the scattered fragment are comprehensible only to men who start clean, that is with observation of present day facts, and refuse to lie down until they have studied the relations and causes of actual present phenomena.

Literature that tries to avoid the consideration of causes remain silly bric-à-brac.

The archaeologist and serendipidist can wander back through Claudius Salmasius and find the known beginnings of usury entangled with those of marine insurance, sea lawyers, the law of Rhodes, the disputed text of Antoninus Pius on the limits of his jurisdiction. Even

[1] *The Criterion*, October 1935.
[2] Silvio Gesell: *The Natural Economic* *Order*. Published by Hugo Fack, 30 Madison Street, San Antonio, Texas

then the dealers in metal appeared to be privileged over other merchants, and the insurance risk mainly paid by the takers of greater risk. Vast mines of anecdote lie still unexploited.

Apart from the eminent Claudius Salmasius; we offer the retrospector and serendipidist, the labours by and of Gabriele Biel, doctissimo viro or vir doctissimus, Francisco Curtio, Albert Bruni, Antonii Solae, if not as enlightenments at least to show that human curiosity does not set sail for the first time into these regions.

The revivers of Hebrew mythology lose interest when they come to Leviticus. The Roman Empire may have risen via the substitution of land usury for sea usury. The 'Church' declined and fell on this issue. Historians have left the politics of Luther and of Calvin in the blurr of great ignorance.

Gesell was right in thanking his destiny that he had begun his study of money unclogged by university training. But as focus in 1935? What other possible subject could bring together the Pope of Rome, a Scotch engineer in the orient, the English Church Assembly, a German business man in the Argentine, a physicist, a biologist, a medical journalist, an orthologist and historian of philosophy, and the present practitioner of versification?

Voila l'estat divers d'entre eulx!

The only class excluded being blind journalists, second-rate writers, literary hangers-on and their ambience.

The little magazine rose with the need for cleansing our language, in the domain of logic and philosophy, this meant the elimination of false dilemmas and indefinite middles, in the domain of morals it was basic and essential. Until a man can speak of one thing or one category of actions as distinct from another it is useless for him to try to define right and wrong.

The Church slumped into a toleration of usury. Protestantism as factive and organised, may have sprung from nothing but pro-usury politics. And the amazing history of the nineteenth century is summed up in: 'Marx found nothing to criticise in money.' That phrase applied to all the latter half of one nineteenth century. It applied down to 1915 when Gesell opened fire.

We have yet to improve on Gesell's criteria:

> 'He would judge money not by its chemical analysis, but by the number of unemployed and by the unsold inventories. These he regarded as the real tests of monetary efficiency. With regard to the compilation of an index number, he would have the relative importance of each commodity determined according to the number of men employed in its production.'[1]

---

[1] (*Stabilised Money.* I. Fisher, assisted by H. R. L. Cohrssen, Allen and Unwin, 1935.)

I attempted in my *ABC* to proceed in more or less Euclidean fashion to list the essential elements of the whole problem, i.e., those few elements without which no economic system can be.

The question for our time is: 'What is money?' After reading and writing and before arithmetic, or even before reading and writing the first human instruction, in our time, should lie in this query. We have seen an American administration tricked because it did *not* observe a transition (*videlicet* hat trick) from pure mathematics, the pure science of arithmetic (numbers) to numeration in terms of money (i.e., to the numeration of something unstable).

Gesell entered history with this question, and with the perception of nineteenth-century blindness (specifically Marx's).

He entered the ranks of great men by a detection of injustice coupled with a passion for justice. The merchants of money, the makers and dealers in money had privilege above all other citizens. This privilege was enormous, secret, unacknowledged.

On his passion a sect arose, and demonstrated his justice. And on this sole base he stands established in contemporary thought, wherever that thought is deep and alive.

No one man corrals all thought, and no one man ends all invention. No man carries on the world's thought without concurrent thinking by others.

Gesell *invented* counter-usury. He did this straight off his own bat. He had, almost certainly never heard of ecclesiastical bracteates. Even the obscure chapter of history wherein they are recorded can hardly dim his claim to invention.

I doubt if anyone will make a satisfactory summary of *The Natural Economic Order*, and I doubt if the printing costs would be as wisely spent on such summary as on an attempt to show the relation of that book to its decade and to the few years therafter. The appalling and nauseous decadence of architecture, stone cutting, art forms after 1500 etc., the loss of moral and terminological clarity, the reduction of philosophy to mere lackeyship toward material sciences all of them run contemporary with each other, and in that barocco was lost the distinction between usury and partaggio.[1]

Whatever Gesell saw, he did not make clear or emphasise Marx's failure to focus the source of value and he, Gesell, did *not* proclaim the distinction between usury and the increment of association.

No economic system can neglect these fundamental dissociations, and no monetary system can rise above the status of gadget if it be not in concord with some *order of thought*, with some system of moral criteria.

Mildness may lead a man to very clear perception, and the phrase 'burning for justice' may lie outside the scope of present discussion.

---

[1] Cf. Canto XLVI. Ed.

There will be, *ad infinitum*, a series of professors who have lecture hours to fill and who can go into Gesell retrospectively. My problem is the utility and vitality of Gesell in the year 1935 and in the months there immediate following.

Gesell questioned the privilege of money over and above all other products of human ingenuity, and he declared against its being the sole fabrication free of tax in a world wherein the good life was being, with increasing acrimony, taxed and stifled out of existence. He, thereupon, devised a tax on money, which requires no bureaucracy to levy it, and which falls with utter impartial justice on every hoarder or delayer of money.

That there should remain any single free trader, any inheritor of that imperfect sect, too dull to glorify Gesell is almost beyond the bounds of imagination, and can be set down only to crass and very black ignorance.

The present state of economic sectarian fugg could be paralleled only by an ignorance which refused to believe in a Westinghouse brake, because it had just heard of a turbine.

Gesell was so right that ignorant men, and/or men ignorant of his writing, are now (after 20 years' interval) moving toward him without knowing it.

But lying outside its scope and apart from Gesell's love of freedom, and his concept of *Freiwirtschaft*, yet serving to establish its locus, stands the declaration: value in our time arises mainly from the cultural heritage.

Economically speaking that heritage is the whole aggregate of human inventions, ameliorations of seed, of agricultural and mechanical process belonging to no one man, and to no group, escaping the possibilities of any definition of patents under any possible system of patent rights, and all this was forerun and fore-paralleled by ancient moderations, by ancient justices in regard to the increment of association, and in the establishment of common land, held simultaneous with fief and with freehold.

The overplus of what a group of men can do acting together, over and above the sum of what they can do each acting alone, is a reality, and no system either of thought or action can be perfect or even reasonably just or complete if it refuse to take count of this reality.

Between Douglas and Gesell there is a contest of justice with justice, neither, of a right, excluding the other's justice.

Take it at the surface and wrangle over detail and you will get nowhere, or merely into a tangle. Carry it down to its root *in justice* and you find no needful contradiction.

There is no more reason for refusing either justice than for refusing to drink because you have eaten.

So long as Douglasites refuse to consider (if they any of them really do so refuse) the unjust privileges of money above any other product, so long as Gesellites refuse to consider the cultural heritage (the increment of association, and the possibilities inherent in a right proportion in the issue of fixed money and Schwundgeld, monnaie fondante, stamp scrip) for just so long will both groups sabotage each other and delay economic light.

A membership ticket in neither party exempts its holder from the natural human frailty of being bored at the thought of changing a painfully acquired set of ideas.

No Douglasite can improve on Gesell's criteria for money.

No Gesellite will get deeper than Douglas's fountain of values.

The peripheries of both sects are adumbrated by superstition, the Gesellites haven't (at date of writing 1935) got rid of the work complex (clarified months ago by the Church of England Assembly).

Neither side shows adequate readiness to define their lines of agreement with the other.

II

As there may be, even at this late date, occasional readers who have no very clear idea of Gesell's chief monetary invention it might be well to describe it, at the same time stating one's system for assessing it in relation to the only other two systems of our time worth serious attention.

Philosophically one will estimate these systems on a basis of justice.

Gesell protested against the unjust privileges of money over all other human products and inventions. He invented (roughly speaking) counter-usury. And his mechanism is comprehensible to the simplest. He proposed and his disciples have issued paper money which requires (in its best mode) the affixation of a monthly stamp to maintain its par value. This stamp in Woërgl was for 1 per cent of face value of the notes. Thus taxation was fixed on the money itself, and accelerated the circulation of this money, whereas all other forms of taxation weigh on, cramp, sabotage exchange.

It must, however, be confessed that stamp scrip has never yet functioned in an hermetically sealed area. It has functioned in concurrence with and been measurable by, a fixed or old-fashioned money.

If the present writer has been of any use, it may be found (bar competitors unknown to him) that he at least tried to summarise, lay out the essential elements in *any* economic system, as you would find the elements and primary machines in the opening chapters of a text book on physics, and that the great mass of economic literature is either special pleading, special description beginning haphazard, talking of a state of things, or moving in vaguely chronological order.

In a more or less Euclidean treatment or frame-work we find goods of different durabilities–from quickly perishable fruit and vegetables to the art works of Chaldae.

Gesell, as merchant and agricultural thinker, was oppressed by the hideously unjust privilege of durable money over and above farm produce and merchandise.

He did not greatly consider works of art, though he was acquainted with hoardable goods.

He did, with absolute and incontrovertible justice, consider the evils of usury, the injustice of supposing that money 'grows' (*vide* Shylock, etc.), while goods perish. I won't say that the 'rise in value' of rarities concerned him sufficiently. But at any rate I offer the proposition that with a just *proportion* between Schwundgeld, res moneta, monnaie fondante, stamp scrip *and* a fixed money not needing a monthly stamp, you would have the simplest possible system for maintaining a mone-tary *representation* of extant goods, i.e., A 'money picture' of extant goods.

The various degrees of durability, fruit, grain, clothing, houses, wood, stone and machinery, art works, could conceivably (but very cumbrously) be *each* represented by money that should melt at parallel rate. No man in his senses would propose such a system for practical use. *But* a just proportion between a fixed and a diminishing money *would* equate the value of all goods to the value of available money.

For what it may be worth my *ABC*, written in ignorance of Gesell, left a place for Schwundgeld. This ought to have a confirmative value, just as a table of known chemical elements, with certain lacunae, serves to validate the existence, or be ready to welcome a newly discovered chemical element.

Once discovered I don't see how Gesell's idea can disappear. It will not crawl back again into its box. We find honest economists sporadi-cally coming on it independently as soon as they begin to *think* of modern conditions.

Gesell's limitation in regard to the corporate state, lay perhaps only in space, time and energy. He was born long before Mussolini, he had not the Duce's organising capacity or his knowledge of men.

In respect to C. H. Douglas, Gesell as business man, having discovered a most marvellous mechanism for unshackling commerce, for liberating all trade and consumption from the manacles of the money monopoly, having invented an unhoardable money, a money that cries to be spent within a given period of time, went on only toward consideration of land.

A concrete mind. The solidity of his good sense indisputably demon-strated at Woërgl and Lillienthal, where the continuity of his mechan-ism in practice, a working (therefore workable) system was only interrupted by brute force, the Austrian government playing catspaw to the international thieves' and murderers' association, by no right, by no justice, by brute stupidity and malevolence, with force on the spot and the power of preventing very wide publicity of their infamy from spreading outside their own tyrannised borders.

Germany under the heel of Dr. Schacht (no better than William or Von Papen) has suppressed all her *Freiwirtschaft* organisations and deserves whatever she gets. This is her own crime against herself and goes to augment the long list of high commercial treasons committed by Germans since 1919 against their own fatherland.

No country can suppress truth and live well. No people that permits the suppression of science either deserves to or can maintain its internal freedom. Germany is less the waiting brigand than the betrayer of herself from within. This self-betrayal she has committed by vending inventions to enemies, by keeping her people in ignorance of their potential deliverers. Nevertheless, faced with Douglas, Gesell neither saw nor demanded to know more about the generation of value.

He saw (to his eternal glory) that Marx did not question money.

Douglas saw the limitation of Marx's value theory. He saw that if value arises from *work*, a vast deal of that work has already been done by men who can no longer eat its fruit, namely by the dead, by Edison, Carleton, and ten thousand others, who have rendered it needless to get up water from wells with buckets, to put oil into individual lamps, to dig and burn coal in order to cook and run railway trains, etc., etc., etc., *ad infinitum*.

When Dr. Fack and the noble Gesellites consider this perfectly justifiable extension of justice which in no way invalidates Silvio Gesell, they will be ready for a scientific economy, as distinct from a sectarian.

Gesell, fighting usury, did not specifically *confuse* it with the increment of association.

But if he consciously noted their difference, he failed to spend any great verbal energy in sorting out one from the other.

If we are to regard economics as part of a gentleman's education, we must distinguish between workable a-moral mechanisms, and 'la più alta giustizia sociale'. We must even distinguish, at least in our studies and drawing rooms, between a partially just and workable system, and further developments of justice which are equally subject to 'natural dimostramento', to sanction by praxis (alias their being able to deliver the goods).

Rabid doctrinaires, the extremely non-perceptive red left, attack Douglas because he leaves a bit of our civilisation standing. Why philosophic communists haven't flocked to Douglas, and why all the slabsided canting levellers haven't flocked to Gesell is a mystery or would be if one failed to allow for the non-existence of *philosophic* communists, or for the lack of any real reasoning or intelligence among levellers (dominated by hate and envy and deficient in the greater part of the sensitive and perceptive gamut).

The Corporate State existing in space and time, has employed itself settling and building a mechanism for fair trading *with* foreign countries.

This lies largely outside the domains of both Gesell and Douglas, but in no way obstructs them, or could by them be obstructed. You promote the peace of the world by the good *internal* government of your country.

Douglas and Gesell both aim at enabling the whole people *in any one* country, to use their own product, and both release the entire people from dependence on export. That is to say make it possible for them to *buy* what they have, instead of placing them under the murderous necessity of throwing it overboard at the command of ghouls and tyrants in order to get purchasing power to buy steadily decreasing amounts of steadily worsening food, cloths, etc.

This possibility to eat, sleep and keep warm at home without invading foreign markets, conduces to that sanity which Mussolini has obtained largely by force of character, aided by control of his banking system, the checking of foreign devils who wanted to sink the value of the lira, etc.

Many of his measures would be considered emergency measures by either Douglas or Gesell. They are none the less valid.

All the candied fruit companies save two have gone bankrupt and so forth. (23 April 1935.) Yet it is possible that by the time this essay reaches the printing room the Italian people will be able to buy a higher percentage of their *Home* produce than at present.

At the date of revising this article, 3 June 1935, the official Italian publications contain more honesty and intelligence than all the other government publications in Europe and America put together. A will toward truth, toward the good of the people, must, if enlightened, take count of possibility *in* space and time, that is in a particular time and in a particular area, amid given material circumstance. At the present moment no other major government has any such will whatsoever.

Germany is most enslaved, France most befuddled, and neither England or America inspire a hog's worth of respect outside their own publics hypnotised by news control and perverted publicity. (23 April 1935, anno XIII, tredici.)

It is impossible in our time to discuss economic *thought* save with regard to time and orthology. The 'place' of any man in the history of economics, the vitality of any idea is measurable by its consequence, I mean its consequence *in ideas*, not only in reference to ideas emerging specifically from it, as fruit and flower, but in ideas and dissociations of ideas caused in the attempt to combat or to rectify it.

Thus you can measure both Douglas and Gesell by events, as for example by the English Church Assembly's dissociation of work from employment, which latter is the *Sale* of work usually under economic pressure. You can see the double stream moving past Congressman Goldsborough's statement regarding the infamy of national borrowing.

In considering historic *Periods* you will note that Gesell and Douglas focus attention on the nature of money, whereas both Marx and La Tour du Pin were equally blind to the nature of money.

In contrast to the idiotic accumulation of debt by Roosevelt, observe that *if* such government expenditure be necessary or advisable, the direct payment of workers, etc., in stamp scrip would in eight years consume itself, and leave the next decade *free* of all debt. The Roosevelt system is either a fraud or a selling of the nation's children into slavery without the ghost of excuse.

Fifteen years ago the idea of governments distributing great masses of purchasing power, would have seemed hazardous. England taxed to the bone, swilling out millions in doles and in subsidies is in no position to ridicule either Gesell or Major Douglas. Were the public perceptive in any degree, they would by now be beginning to consider at least some of the things Douglas, back in 1919, was predicting.

The demonstration (you can't call it an experiment) in Woërgl should satisfy any sane man as to Gesell's workability. No ones denies or denied what happened. All the murderers could do against the Mayor of Woërgl was to damp down the news transmission. Senator Bankhead rose to very considerable greatness in the debate on his Bill, February 1932. After which 'they' must have 'turned on the heat'.

The second most prominent American professor wrote me: 'I don't think anyone here will touch it, but we are very glad you are going on with it.' That was before Dr. Hugo Fack started publishing Gesell in San Antonio, Texas, with (naturally) *no* financial support and no cooperation from established publishers or the American publishing system.

The truth about economics has had no warmer welcome than had a few simple and known facts about the tradition in metric and poetry during a couple of preceding decades. The parallel would be comic were it not freighted with tragedy, death, malnutrition, degradation of the national health in a dozen countries. No intelligent man will be content to treat economics merely as economics, and probably no writer could write anything of interest in so doing. The stupidities taught in our universities up till very recently amounted to little more than treatises *De Modo*, that is to say they were confined mainly to the topic of marketing, the habits of traders, as commented by Adam Smith, 'conspiring against the general public'.

Official philosophy had sunk equally low. If *oikos* was bastardised to mean merely *agora*, the love of wisdom had been degraded to mean merely the discussion of generalities. The nature of cliché or generality is to use a loose categorical label to cover a group or mass of *ignota*, of unknown particulars, the attempt being to cover the speaker's incompetence, laziness, ignorance or half-masted parroting.

Nothing breaks cliché or will break any writer's use of it, save first-hand knowledge of individual phenomena. (And in another dimension: rien ne pousse à la concision comme l'abondance d'idées.)

In another eighty years a few people may begin to see that the present author's insistence on *Ideogrammic* method has not been mere picking daisies. Fenollosa saw the possibilities of a *method*. The effects of his vision were sabotaged right and left, and the small group of men comprising 'the learned world' will some day feel a disgust for Paul Carus in particular.

You can study economics almost entirely as dissociation of ideas. It has not until now been so studied. For ten thousand bigots who quote the Bible on work, there is scarcely one who will, or can, quote it on usury. A mild old country priest said to me: 'I suppose it must have been along in the eighteenth century, they had to admit it.' The Church of England has not to date found me a parson to say when usury became Episcopal and respectable. Somewhere in the time of Medici tropism the distinction between *partaggio* and *usura* was muddled.

The increment of association is not usury. It exists. The English Church dissociated work from employment, which latter implies the sale of human energy usually under pressure.

E. S. Woodward in his *Canada Reconstructed* is still bubbling about work. The facts giving rise to technocracy and substantiated in the H. Loeb Chart of Plenty, haven't yet pulled E. S. W. out of that inherited mental habit.

You would think Gesellites would be more fully alive to the energy in new money; since that is the main plank in their rectitude. You would think they would see that land is progressively less important, meaning less important *now* than before we had farm machinery or the results of Mark Carleton's research.

We cannot (let us grant it for all the grandsons who learned their Henry George at mama's knee) dispense with land, and we are unlikely to become orchids, even with the most active aeronautic and aerostatic inventions.

The earth has been under our feet for some ages, and into it we return dead, bar cremation and deep sea drowning. Nothing is deader than the reiteration of Henry George's opinions, or his data on land values and land speculation.

Given a tractless wilderness to begin on, and no intellectual needs above those of a rural robot, there might be something left to be said for or about it. Grain, trees and vegetables must have earth wherein to grow. We do not live by bread and synthetic products alone.

But on the whole the agriculturalist is a *Producer* and the world's problems today do not lie in production. As W. E. Woodward (not to be confused with E. S. Woodward) has remarked: 'Of course financing should start with the consumer not with the producer. He (the producer) doesn't need any financing if there is a demand for his goods.' (Demand here meaning *if* people who want 'em have the power to buy 'em.)

Marx's thought did not stop during his lifetime. Disciples are more trouble than they're worth when they start anchoring and petrifying their mahatmas. No man's *thought* petrifies. His own mind may decompose, but if there is real thought, it continues. The Gesellites are loaded up (like all groups) with a lot of dead baggage. It is not in group nature to distinguish very clearly between the live and the dead part of their equipment. The basket is, metaphorically, easier to handle than the cat inside the basket. Hence the fugg of universities and of academic abominations.

The land part of Gesellism may be all right, but it is right as a part of the chronicles, of the history of where economics had, at a certain date, got to.

E. S. Woodward's analysis of the present and infamous situation is almost verbatim Douglas. Any unprejudiced observer with enough patience will come out at the same place. The conspiracy of two and two to make four, is bound to be in the long run, successful. The most gross anomaly, and best illustration of sectarian muddle I know, was offered by a Gesellist denying Douglas's 'time lag', whereas the whole of Gesell's monetary system is aimed at eliminating this specific defect of the present system. Al. Einstein was nearly as funny, quoting Gesell unconsciously under the impression that he was refuting him.

It is inconceivable that Gesell could have lived another decade without seeing that a great deal of the work wherefrom values rise, has already been done, by our predecessors.

The quality of his mind was such that, once mentioned, this state of things would have been self-evident to him; ditto the increment of association.

It is impossible to imagine oneself making these statements to a committee of Gesell, Marx and Lenin without their accepting them almost instantly.

It is equally impossible to imagine Aquinas, Scotus Erigena not doing likewise.

You can not make good economics out of bad ethics.

Values[1]

I would put up a dozen brass tablets to one phrase of Constantin Brancusi's:

ONE OF THOSE DAYS WHEN I WOULD NOT HAVE GIVEN FIFTEEN MINUTES OF MY TIME FOR ANYTHING UNDER HEAVEN.[2]

There speaks the supreme sense of human values. There speaks WORK unbartered. That is the voice of humanity in its highest possible manifestation.

[1] From *Demarcations, British Union Quarterly*, January–April 1937.   [2] Quoted in Canto LXXXV. Ed.

For a New Paideuma[1]

T he term Paideuma has been resurrected in our time because of a need. The term Zeitgeist or Time Spirit might be taken to include passive attitudes and aptitudes of an era. The term Paideuma as used in a dozen German volumes has been given the sense of the active element in the era, the complex of ideas which is in a given time germinal, reaching into the next epoch, but conditioning actively all the thought and action of its own time.

Frobenius has left the term with major implications in the unconscious (if I understand him rightly). I don't assert that he would necessarily limit it to the unconscious or claim that the conscious *individual* can have no effect in shaping the paideuma, or at least the next paideuma.

I take it that the 'indifferent have never made history', and that the paideuma makes history. There are in our time certain demands, demands, that is, of the awakened intellect, and these demands are specific. It is useless to discuss them 'at large' and in the vague if one can't bring them down to particulars.

As a minimum for a decent education in our time, that is from July 1937 onward, the following reforms must be made in all curricula, if those curricula are to be considered henceforth as anything but dead fish and red herring.

1. Economics can no longer be taught as a jumble of heteroclite empiric statements. And no sane student will permit himself henceforth to be taught it in that manner, and no fond father will pay tuition to have his son's mind muddled by the present asinine relics of confusion. A student of the sciences is not prey to sectarians who suppose that a discovery in physics, or a new mechanical device, cancels out, or is in opposition to, the combination of a new chemical.

In Economics one demands that text-books start with a clear definition of the terms, especially of the basic terms used (such as money, credit, interest, usury).

One demands that the total problem of economy be defined, not merely assumed. And this definition of the total problem must follow the definition of the particular terms.

2. In Palaeography, whether literary, historic or musical, one demands a sane use of photographic technique, which has now gone on to using the cinema film, and reading from this film, or print of it, by an en-

[1] *The Criterion*, January 1938.

larging machine, thus cutting the costs of adequate photographic documentation from that of 8 by 10 inch or 6 by 4 plates, to that of the normal film (or even the midget film), and bringing said costs within range not only of 'foundations' but of commerce.

3. One demands, in the study of letters, a complete revision of contrasts. It is sheer squalor to remain content with the worn down remnants of renaissance culture.

If Greek awoke Europe in the fifteenth century, we have to a great extent utilised and worn out that stimulus.

With no disrespect to the best Greek culture, but indeed with proper respect, we should take stock of it. We should examine it in relation to other cultures now known and available.

One can, without even learning the language, make an approximate guess at its (the Greek) contents from the Loeb library. Given an acquaintance with the language, even a meagre acquaintance, no man should imagine the Greek heritage as something to be thrown overboard at the whim of any pragmatic vulgarian.

That however is no reason for not weighing it against other cultures. As human contact a means of communication with 400,000,000 living men, might seem to have certain advantages, balanced by the relative worth of the two cultures. No Sinologue has admitted that the Chinese donation is less than the Greek. It has in our day a lure for the explorative mind.

The man who doesn't now *want* to learn ideogram is a man half-awake. No one in Europe is in position to say whether Japan or China contains, at the moment of writing, the greater cultural energy. Evidence of Japanese awakeness I have on my desk as I write this. I know of no group of poets in Europe or America as alert as Mr. Kitasono's Tokio friends. I mean to say as conscious of the day that we live in. And this proves nothing whatever.

I am sick of the pretences of clerics (in the university sense) who continue to act as if the next generation should be content to know no more than we do, or have their approach to full human culture as inefficient and obstructed as ours was.

Homer was as Mediterranean as Greek, and the Greek authors went down hill mostly after Homer.

Virgil is his inferior, but Latin gives us or has preserved a great deal that is not in Greek.

The two donations can be weighed one against other. Since the desuetude of Latin as an university language, I mean as a language wherein instruction was given in classroom not used merely in the study of 'classic' Latin authors, Europe has greatly forgotten all the culture embodied in Latin writers who are not 'classics', meaning who aren't studied for their style or as part of 'Latin literature courses'.

We can't swallow this lacuna. It needs looking into.

It is my firm belief that no study of Greek authors offers a fully satisfactory alternative to reading of Tacitus, Catullus, Ovid, Propertius. And also that a great deal of specific study of history and economics suffers from sheer ignorance of Latin predecessors in those specific fields.

Looking eastward even my own scant knowledge of ideogram has been enough to teach me that a few hours' work on it is more enlivening, goes further to jog a man out of fixations than a month's work on a great Greek author. I don't know how long such enlivenment would endure. At the moment I see no end to it, but I assert that for Europe and for occidental man there is here an admirable means of getting out of his ruts and his stupidities.

The Sinologues have been either too uninterested in the subject or too lacking in civil imagination to see what this treasure can mean to total Europe.

A man of fifty has a right to stop picking daisies and think what he would like to teach the next generation, he has a right to take stock of what he doesn't know and would like to.

A sane university curriculum will put Chinese where Greek was, or at least put it in the smaller position whereto Greek has now fallen, that is as a luxury study.

An alert University (speaking of the possible and non-existent) would set its cultural faculty to examining *ex novo* the merits of the authors taught in its (usually uncorrelated) courses in letters and language.

For thirty or more years an occasional pedagogue, usually German, has murmured a few words about comparative literature, but the study has not been enlivened.

France has so recently ceased being the whole hog and centre of European culture that one can't probably offer any suggestions to the Sorbonne, one can only marvel at the laxity and lack of serious criteria that crop up, or that have on occasion cropped up, in particular Sorbonne courses, and publications.

In Italy where they go about organising, and taking education *sui serio* there will or will not (as the case may be) occur a revision. Either Italian authors and pedagogues will renovate their curriculum of Italian authors, or they will drop out of, or remain far in the rear of, an era they have never yet joined.

Mediaeval poetry rose in Provence, Italy was at the top for an epoch (of Cavalcanti and Dante). Nobody outside Italy has ever supposed that Italian drama or Italian novels were serious concurrents for total primacy. Italy has, on the other hand, a vast amount of secondary, solid and meritorious work on special topics, which has scarcely been recognised, or at any rate, never at its full value, and I think never used as corrective acid on French pretensions.

FOR A NEW PAIDEUMA

'What needs my Shakespeare? etc.'

People who are determined to know only one language must be content to know that their estimate of books applies to books in that language, with a penumbra of books translated, which latter can be weighed only as books in the language whereinto.

As attempt to locate the foregoing, it might be inexact to say that the war was the end of French culture. Phases end. The few people who are willing to consider symptoms even though they appear on the surface irrelevant to, say, the strength of a nation, might be persuaded to reflect on the fact that when Rémy de Gourmont died there remained no one in Paris whom I could trust for a monthly letter to the *Little Review*. I mean there was no French writer with critical apparatus and a general awareness both of land of origin and country whereto, which fitted him to send *us* the news of French thought and French publication.

When the Dial readers later wanted 'something from an actual Frenchman' they succeeded in getting journalism and infantile reminiscence of Sarah Bernhardt. Yet the mind of Paris was far from dead.

The *Trial of Barrès* was a definite intellectual act. Picabia's tremendous phrase, 'Europe exhausted by the conquest of Alsace-Lorraine' ought to have enlightened more men than it did. All war in Europe is civil war from henceforth, it is a man tearing at his own viscera.

It is in perspective four centuries since Milan declined to make war on Venice, on ground that war between buyer and seller could profit neither. Ideas do not go into mass action the day they are born.

All of which thoughts are driven into me yet again by the chicken-headedness of red propaganda. Mr. Tzara was dada, Gide was born Gide and will die Gide, Mr. Aragon did not in the old days keep up with Picabia.

He has been *told* that economics exist; that economic forces enter into the social problem, but this notion does not, apparently enter the red mind at all. *Vide* Russia, etc. We are, I suppose all of us, bombarded by red, pink, orange manifestos. And we might go back to the Trial of Barrès for a perspective. Perhaps 'Paris' (Paris of books and young men, and of now a new set of still more immature adolescents) has forgotten it, and it needs in any case exposition for the English and American reader.

It was a show, as I remember it, in a smallish hall near the Boulevard Mich'. M. Aragon in legal robes as prosecutor, Barrès a wax barber's dummy, and Aragon talked too long. He wore out the audience. That isn't essential. The drama existed when, I think it was, Eluard (it may have been Crevel) came on in a gas mask. That was the antithesis, the dead rhetoric *vs.* the cannon fodder. A system of clichés had broken down. A bit of stale gas had been left in the mask and the protagonist at a certain point nearly suffocated, could stand it no longer, and tore off the mask. One very red faced real youth sputtering in the stage set.

It ought to have made people think *more*. At any rate I take it no one actually in the hall has forgotten it. Mme. Rachilde was indignant. All this was seventeen years ago.

France has built nothing whatever on it. (Unless we count 'young' Rostand's *Marchands de Canons*.) Any man who thinks in our time and who reads any respectable part of serious controversy and of the all too sincere ranting put out by a dozen parties, ought to start sorting out the confusions. Against which sea there is no dyke save a clear terminology.

The ranting, be it about Spain, Russia, France or economy, shows utter failure to dissociate:

1. credit from money (corollary: social credit from social money which is not the same thing);
2. social credit from anti-social credit.

The divers empiric sects have not been diligent in correlating their notions, ideas, discoveries with known history, knowable history or the sound thought in other camps.

You have two (I think only two) main groups of actors: you have those who keep murmuring 'It isn't wholly a money problem.'

You have those (at diametric opposite) who keep murmuring what amounts to an assertion that 'You can cure it without any sort of guild organisation'.

The magnanimous observer ought to ask himself whether at least some attention ought not to be given both to possible organisations and to money. Recognising that organisation will be part of historic process growing out of places and customs, and not merely put on like a top hat or a pair of braces.

The guild idea seems incompatible with the English or American temperament. Neither country can even set up an academy, foregoing attempts have been travesty. Our social dilemma is: can monetary reform be instituted without some form or at least adumbration of guild organisations correlated to a centre?

An intelligentsia unable to organise *itself* will be able to organise others?

Can one even introduce the discussion of literary organisation in good company without being thought daft? Can one even indicate errors in immature attempts? Such as the something or other in America which treats writing as production of a trade commodity instead of as a communications service?

Starting with the idea that writing is communication I see but one valid and viable form of literary guild. The natural nuclei are groups, hitherto utterly informal. If the nuclei be formed merely on geographic basis they will remain as ineffective as they have hitherto been, and as powerless to defend or foster the members of 'our craft', let alone powerless of participation in a general social order.

If on the other hand it were possible for writers of different tendencies to organise on their own bases, say, writers desiring a parochial criterion gathered about their 'leaders', and writers desiring an international or metropolitan about theirs, there would be at least some articulation. A guild nucleus could conceivably start with five or six men who might associate without feeling ridiculous, it could admit applicants according to its own criteria, and such centred groups might conceivably after considerable interval be correlated into a *sindicato* which would have some vitality. 'Our' hope being that the mutual disagreements between the silly, the stupid, the trashy guilds would more or less cross out and that the valid would have some sort of chance when things (if ever) came to a vote.

Vast American endowments remain a hangover of an earlier era, ineffective because their choice of candidates is entrusted to unfit persons. A new appeal on my desk suggests a group of twelve to pass on six appointments. This would be no better than the present foundations. The only chance for a real writer would occur if the twelve were divided into six groups, each pair selecting a candidate.

The attempt to organise letters along the lines of a system started in the plumbing trade a century ago, seems to me inept. I can't see that old style trade unionism offers us a solution. I can see a slim chance of slight amelioration if the organisers attended a little to the nature of the writer as such, allowing for considerable variety and not trying to jam all the divers endocrine species of 'writers' into one straitjacket.

The question for writers in the Anglo-American idioms may be for our time a mere exotic, dragged in by analogy from more highly organised states.

What can not be dismissed as merely exotic is the state of our terminology. This is part of our job as writers. Our gross (in general) insensitivity to the personality of men in 'high official' status in whatever formal intellectual organisations who have for our sorrow been 'wished on us' by wool-headed forebears, or the general lack of mental discipline in high civic places, cannot be dismissed as exotic.

What is money for?[1]

W e will never see an end of ructions, we will never have a sane and steady administration until we gain an absolutely clear conception of money. I mean an absolutely not an approximately clear conception.

I can, if you like, go back to paper money issued in China in or about A.D. 840, but we are concerned with the vagaries of the Western World.

FIRST, Paterson, the founder of the 'Bank of England', told his shareholders that they would profit because 'the bank hath profit on the interest of all the moneys which it creates out of nothing'.

What then is this 'money' the banker can create 'out of nothing'?

(1) MEASURE OF PRICE

Let us be quite clear.

MONEY IS A 'MEASURED' TITLE OR CLAIM.

That is its basic difference from unmeasured claims, such as a man's right to take all you've got, under war-time requisition or as an invader or thief just taking it all.

Money is a measure which the taker hands over when he acquires the goods he takes. And no further formality need occur during the transfer, though sometimes a receipt is given.

The idea of justice inheres in ideas of measure, and *money is a measure of price*.

(2) MEANS OF EXCHANGE

Money is valid when people recognise it as a claim and hand over goods or do work up to the amount printed on the face of the 'ticket', whether it is made of metal or paper.

Money is a general sort of ticket, which is its only difference from a railway or theatre ticket. If this statement seems childish let the reader think for a moment about different kinds of tickets.

A railway ticket is a measured ticket. A ticket from London to Brighton differs from one for London to Edinburgh. Both are measured, but in miles that always stay the same length. A money ticket, under a corrupt system, wobbles. For a long time the 'public' has trusted people whose measure was shifty.

[1] 1939.

WHAT IS MONEY FOR?

Another angle. Theatre tickets are timed. You would probably not accept a ticket for Row H, Seat 27, if it were not dated. When six people are entitled to the same seat *at the same time* the tickets are not particularly good. (Orage asked: 'Would you call it inflation, if there were a ticket for every seat in the house?')

You will hear money called a 'medium of exchange', which means that it can circulate freely, as a measure of goods and services against one another, from hand to hand.

(3) GUARANTEE OF FUTURE EXCHANGE

We will have defined money properly when we have stated what it is in words that can NOT be applied to anything else and when there is nothing about the essential nature of money that is omitted from our definition.

When Aristotle calls money 'a guarantee of future exchange' that merely means that it is an undated ticket, that will be good when we want to use it.

Tickets have sometimes stayed good for a century.

When we do not hand over money at once for goods or services received we are said to have 'credit'. The 'credit' is the other man's belief that we can and will some time hand over the money OR something measured by money.

PURPOSE OF MONEY

Most men have been so intent on the individual piece of money, as a measure, that they have forgotten its PURPOSE, and they have got into inextricable muddles and confusions regarding the TOTAL amount of money in a country.

A perfectly good hammer is useless to pick your teeth with. If you don't know what money is FOR, you will get into a muddle when using it, and still more will a government get into a mess in its 'monetary policy'.

Statally speaking, that is from the point of view of a man or party that wants to govern justly, a piece of money is a ticket, the country's money is a mass of tickets for getting the country's food and goods justly distributed.

The job for a man today who is trying to write a pamphlet on money is not to say something new, it is SIMPLY to make a clear statement about things that have been known for 200, and often for 2,000 years.

You have got to know what money is FOR.

If you think that it is a man-trap or a means of bleeding the public

261

you will admire the banking system as run by the Rothschilds and international bankers. If you think it is a means of sweating profits out of the public, you will admire the stock exchange.

Hence ultimately for the sake of keeping your ideas in order you will need a few principles.

THE AIM of a sane and decent economic system is to fix things so that decent people can eat, have clothes and houses up to the limit of available goods.

THE VALUE OF MONEY

Take money IN SUCH A SYSTEM as a means of exchange, and then realise that to be a JUST means of exchange it must be MEASURED.

What are you going to USE to measure the value of anything? An egg is an egg. You can eat it (until it goes bad). Eggs are not all the same size, but they might serve among primitive people as an approximate measure.

Unterguggenberger, the Austrian monetary reformer, used WORK as a measure, 'Arbeitswert', 10 schillings' worth of work. That was O.K. in a mountain valley where everyone could do pretty much the same kind of work in the fields.

Charlemagne had a grain measure, so many pecks of barley, wheat or rye worth a DENAR, or put it the other way on. The just price of barley was so much the peck.

In A.D. 796 it was 2 denars.

And in A.D. 808 it was 3 denars.

That means that the farmer got MORE denars for the same quantity of barley. And let us hope that he could buy more other goods with those denars.

Unfortunately the worth of all things depends on whether there is a real scarcity, enough or more than can be used at a given time.

A few eggs are worth a great deal to a hungry man on a raft.

Wheat is worth MORE in terms of serge in some seasons than in others. So is gold, so is platinum.

A single commodity (EVEN GOLD) base for money is not satisfactory.

STATE AUTHORITY behind the printed note is the best means of establishing a JUST and HONEST currency.

The Chinese grasped that over 1,000 years ago, as we can see from the Tang STATE (not Bank) NOTE.

SOVEREIGNTY inheres in the right to ISSUE money (tickets) and to determine the value thereof.

American interests HIDE the most vital clause in our constitution.

The American government hasn't, they say, the right to fix prices. BUT IT HAS THE RIGHT TO DETERMINE THE VALUE OF MONEY and this right is vested in Congress.

WHAT IS MONEY FOR?

This is a mere difference in legal formalities and verbal arrangements.

The U.S. Government has the right to say 'a dollar is one wheat-bushel thick, it is one serge-foot long, it is ten gallons of petrol wide.'

Hence the U.S. Government could establish the JUST PRICE, and a just price system.

THE JUST PRICE

Out of barter grew the canonist doctrine of the just price, and a thousand years' thought from St. Ambrose to St. Antonio of Florence, as to HOW to determine the just price.

Both the Douglas Social Crediters and modern Catholics POSTULATE the JUST PRICE as a necessary part of their systems. The valid complaint against Douglas is that he didn't invent and set up machinery for ENFORCING the just price. A priest recently reported to me that the English distributists had about got round to realising that they had no mechanism for instituting and enforcing just price.

Only the STATE can effectively fix the JUST PRICE of any commodity by means of state-controlled pools of raw products and the restoration of guild organisation in industry.

THE QUANTITY OF MONEY

Having determined the size of your dollar, or half-crown or shilling, your Government's next job is to see that TICKETS are properly printed and that they get to the right people.

The right people are all the people who are not engaged in CRIME, and crime for the duration of this pamphlet means among other things CHEATING the rest of the citizens through the money racket.

In the United States and England there is NOT enough money. There are not enough tickets moving about among the WHOLE people to BUY what they need—EVEN when the goods are there on the counter or going to rot on the wharves.

When the total nation hasn't or cannot obtain enough food for its people, that nation is poor. When enough food exists and people cannot get it by honest labour, the state is rotten, and no effort of language will say how rotten it is.

But for a banker or professor to tell you that the country cannot do this, that or the other because it lacks money is as black and foetid a lie, as grovelling and imbecile, as it would be to say it cannot build roads because it has no kilometres! (I didn't invent that phrase, but it is too good to leave idle.)

Roosevelt and his professors were on the right line with their commodity dollar. BUT they hooeyed and smoke-screened and dodged the problem of having ENOUGH TICKETS to serve the whole people, and of keeping those tickets MOVING.

It is the business of the STATE to see that there is enough money in the hands of the WHOLE people, and in adequately rapid EXCHANGE, to effect distribution of all wealth produced and produceable.

Until every member of the nation eats three times a day and has shelter and clothing, a nation is either lazy or unhealthy. If this occurs in a rich state the state's riches are 'not fully employed'.

SOCIAL CREDIT

All value comes from labour and nature. Wheat from ploughing, chestnuts from being picked up.

BUT a lot of WORK has been done by men (mostly inventors, well-diggers, constructors of factory plant, etc.) now DEAD, and who therefore can NOT eat and wear clothes.

In respect of this legacy of mechanical efficiency and scientific advance we have at our disposal a large volume of SOCIAL CREDIT, which can be distributed to the people as a bonus over and above their wage packet.

Douglas proposed to bring up the TOTAL purchasing power of the whole people by a *per capita* issue of tickets PROPORTIONAL to available goods. In England and U.S. today available and desired goods remain unbought because the total purchasing power (i.e. total sum of tickets) is inadequate.[1]

Mussolini and Hitler wasted very little time PROPOSING. They started and DO distribute BOTH tickets and actual goods on various graduated scales according to the virtues and activities of Italians and Germans.

Douglas may object that this is not 'democratic' (that is egalitarian) BUT for the monetary scientist or economist the result is the same. The goods are getting distributed.

There is a slightly different angle in the way these different men look on justice. They all agree that deficiency in a nation's total purchasing power must be made up. Ten or more years ago I said that Mussolini had achieved more than Douglas, because Douglas has presented his ideas as a greed system, not as a will system.

Both systems, Fascist and Douglasite, differ as the day from night from the degradation of the DOLE, from the infamy of the British system wherein men who are out of jobs are paid money taken from men who do work, and where the out-of-works are rendered progressively UNFIT to work or to enjoy the sensations of living.

[1] 1939.

Not only are they a drag on workers, but they are made a drag on all people who are trying to maintain a decent standard of living. The whole scale of values is defiled. Every year sees less sense of SOCIAL VALUE; less sense of having people lead lives which do not harm others; of lives in which some measure and prudence is observed.

There is nothing new in creating money to distribute wealth.

If you don't believe the Emperor Tching Tang issued the first national dividend in 1766 B.C. you can call it something else. It may have been an emergency dole, but the story will at least clear up one muddle. The emperor opened a copper mine and issued round coins with square holes and gave them to the poor 'and this money enabled them to buy grain from the rich', but it had no effect on the general shortage of grain.

That story is 3,000 years old, but it helps one to understand what money is and what it can do. For the purpose of good government it is a ticket for the orderly distribution of WHAT IS AVAILABLE. It may even be an incentive to grow or fabricate more grain or goods that is, to attain abundance. But it is NOT in itself abundance.

INFLATION

The term 'inflation' is used as a bogey to scare people away from any expansion of money at all.

Real INFLATION only begins when you issue MONEY (measured claims) against goods or services that are undeliverable (assignats of the French Revolution issued against the state lands) or issue them in excess of those WANTED.

That amounts to saying: two or more tickets for the same seat at the same time, or tickets in London for a theatre performance tonight in Bombay, or for a dud show.

MONEY can be expended as long as each measured claim can be honoured by the producers and distributors of the nation in goods and services required by the public, when and where they want them.

GESELL'S STAMP SCRIP

INFLATION is one danger: STAGNATION is another.

Gesell, the South American monetary reformer, saw the danger of money being hoarded and proposed to deal with it by the issue of 'stamp scrip'. This should be a government note requiring the bearer to affix a stamp worth up to 1 per cent of its face value on the first day of every month. Unless the note carries its proper complement of monthly stamps it is not valid.

This is a form of TAX on money and in the case of British currency might take the form of ½d. or 1d. per month on a ten shilling note, and 1d. or 2d. on a pound. There are any number of possible taxes, but Gesell's kind of tax can only fall on a man who has, in his pocket, *at the moment* the tax falls due, 100 times, at least, the amount of the tax.

Gesell's kind of money provides a medium and measure of exchange which cannot be hoarded with impunity. It will always keep moving. Bankers could NOT lock it up in their cellars and charge the public for letting it out. It has also the additional benefit of placing the sellers of perishable goods at less of a disadvantage in negotiating with owners of theoretically imperishable money.

I am particularly keen on Gesell, because once people have used stamp scrip they HAVE a clear idea about money. They understand tickets better than men who haven't used stamp scrip. I am no more anxious than anyone else to use a new kind of stamp, but I maintain that the public is NOT too stupid to use postage stamps and that there is no gain in pretending that they are too stupid to understand money.

I don't say you *have* to use Gesell's method. But once you understand WHY he wanted it you will not be fleeced by bank sharks and 'monetary authorities' WITHOUT KNOWING HOW you are being fleeced. That is WHY Gesell is so useful as a school teacher. He proposed a very simple means of keeping his tickets moving.

STATAL MONEY

In 1816 Thomas Jefferson made a basic statement that has NOT been properly digested, let alone brought into perspective with various 'modern proposals' for special improvements of the present damned and destructive 'system' or money racket.

The reader had better FRAME Jefferson's statement:

'... And if the national bills issued be bottomed (as is indispensable) on pledges of specific taxes for their redemption within certain and moderate epochs, and be of *proper denominations* for *circulation*, no interest on them would be necessary or just, because they would answer to every one of the purposes of metallic money withdrawn and replaced by them.'

Jefferson to Crawford, 1816.

Jefferson's formula is SOLID. IF the state emits ENOUGH money for valid and justifiable expenses and keeps it moving, circulating, going out the front door and coming in the tax window, the nation will not suffer stagnation.

The issue of HONEST MONEY is a service, and when the state performs this service the state has a right to a just recompense, which differs from nearly all known forms of tax.

I say 'when the state issues it,' because when states are weak or incompetent or their issue inadequate, individuals and congeries of men or localities HAVE quite properly taken over this activity (or have retained it from pre-statal eras), and it is better, it is in fact necessary, that the function of the measure of exchange should be carried on than that it stop or break down altogether.

On the other hand a nation whose measure of exchange is at the mercy of forces OUTSIDE the nation, is a nation in peril, it is a nation without national sovereignty. It is a nation of incompetent idiots drifting to ruin.

Let us repeat.

Sovereignty inheres in the right to ISSUE measured claims to wealth, that is MONEY.

No part or function of government should be under closer surveillance, and in no part or cranny of government should higher moral criteria be ASSURED.

STATAL MONEY based upon national wealth must replace GOLD manipulated by international usurers.

NECESSARY SAFEGUARDS

The sane order in founding a dynasty or reorganising a government is
FIRST to get the results, that is to see that the people are fed and housed.

THEN so to regulate the mechanism of distribution (monetary system or whatever) that it will not fall into decay and be pilfered.

For example J. Q. Adams, one of the American founders, had some nice socialist or statal ideas about reserving the national wealth for educational and 'higher purposes'. His proposals were UNTIMELY. Jackson opened the land: settlers could go and take quite a bit each, free and gratis. It was timely and useful. But no provision was made to prevent the settlers transferring this land WHEN THEY HAD NO FURTHER USE FOR IT and didn't want to work it themselves. Hence the U.S. land has fallen into great ownership.

The same danger applies to monetary systems as to land settlement.

Set up a perfect and just money system and in three days rascals, the bastards with mercantilist and monopolist mentality, will start thinking up some wheeze to cheat the people. The concession hunter will sprout in some new form as long as dung stinks and humanity produces mental abortions.

John Adams early saw that stock jobbers would replace fat country small squire tyrants.

In the 1860's one of the Rothschilds was kind enough to admit that the banking system was contrary to public interest, and that was before the shadow of Hitler's jails had fallen ACROSS the family fortunes.

It is this generation's job to do what was left undone by the early democrats. The guild system, endowing the people by occupation and vocation with corporate powers, gives them means to protect themselves for all time from the money power.

If you don't like the guild idea, go get results with some other, but don't lose your head and forget what clean men are driving at.

And don't lie to yourselves and mistake a plough for a mortgage and vice versa.

AN ECONOMIC SYSTEM

It is useless to talk of economics or to listen to talk about economics or to read books on the subject until both reader and writer know what they mean by the half-dozen simplest and most necessary terms most frequently used.

The first thing for a man to think of when proposing an economic system is: WHAT IS IT FOR?

And the answer is: to make sure that the whole people shall be able to eat (in a healthy manner), to be housed (decently) and be clothed (in a way adequate to the climate).

Another form of that statement is Mussolini's:

DISCIPLINE THE ECONOMIC FORCES AND EQUATE THEM TO THE NEEDS OF THE NATION.

USURY

The Left claim that private ownership has destroyed this true purpose of an economic system. Let us see how OWNERSHIP was defined at the beginning of a capitalist era during the French Revolution.

OWNERSHIP 'is the right which every citizen has to enjoy and dispose of the portion of goods guaranteed him by the law. The right of ownership is limited, as are all other rights, by the obligation to respect the rights of others. It cannot be prejudicial to the safety, nor to the liberty, nor to the existence, nor to the ownership of other men like ourselves. Every possession, *every traffic*, which violates this principle is illicit and immoral.'—Robespierre.

The perspective of the damned nineteenth century shows little else than the violation of these principles by demoliberal usurocracy. The doctrine of Capital, in short, has shown itself as little else than the idea that unprincipled thieves and anti-social groups should be allowed to gnaw into the rights of ownership.

This tendency 'to gnaw into' has been recognised and stigmatised from the time of the laws of Moses and he called it *neschek*.

And nothing differs more from this gnawing or corrosive than the right to share out the fruits of a common co-operative labour.

Indeed USURY has become the dominant force in the modern world.

'Moreover, imperialism is an immense accumulation of money capital in a few countries, which as we have seen, amounts to 4 or 5 thousand million pounds sterling in securities. Hence the extraordinary growth of a class, or rather a stratum, of *rentiers*, i.e. persons who live by 'clipping coupons', who take absolutely no part in any enterprise, and whose profession is idleness. The exportation of capital, one of the most essential economic bases of imperialism, still further isolates this *rentier* stratum from production, and sets the seal of parasitism on the whole country living on the exploitation of labour of several overseas countries and colonies.'

> V. I. Lenin, quoting Hobson, in
> 'Imperialism, the highest stage of Capitalism'.

Very well! That is from Lenin. But you could quote the same substance from Hitler, who is a Nazi (note the paragraph from 'Mein Kampf' magnificently isolated by Wyndham Lewis in his 'Hitler':

'The struggle against international finance and loan capital has become the most important point in the National Socialist programme: the struggle of the German nation for its independence and freedom.'

You could quote it from Mussolini, a fascist, from C. H. Douglas, who calls himself a democrat and his followers the only true democrats. You could quote it from McNair Wilson, who is a Christian Monarchy man. You could quote it from a dozen camps which have no suspicion that they are quoting Lenin.

The only people who do NOT seem to have read and digested this essay of his are the British Labour Party and various groups of professing communists throughout the Occident.

Some facts are now known above parties, some perceptions are the common heritage of all men of good will, and only the Jewspapers and worse than Jewspapers, try now to obscure them. Among the worse than Jewspapers we must list the hired professors who misteach new generations of young, who lie for hire and who continue to lie from sheer sloth and inertia and from dog-like contempt for the well-being of all mankind.

At this point, and to prevent the dragging of red-herrings, I wish to distinguish between prejudice against the Jew as such and the suggestion that the Jew should face his own problem.[1]

---

[1] Pound has defined his attitude to the Jews and usury elsewhere. In *The Guide to Kulchur* (1938) he wrote:

'The red herring is scoundrel's device and usurer's stand-by.... Race prejudice is red herring. The tool of the man defeated intellectually, and of the cheap politician ... It is nonsense for the anglo-saxon to revile the Jew for beating him at his own game.'

Some sentences Pound wrote in *The New English Weekly* should also be read in this context:

'Tour du Pin curses usury. He baptises the XIXth century the "Age of Usury". He says several good things in so doing.

269

DOES he in his individual case wish to observe the law of Moses?

Does he propose to continue to rob other men by usury mechanism while wishing to be considered a 'neighbour'?

This is the sort of double-standard which a befouled English delegation tried to enforce via the corrupt League of Nations (frontage and face wash for the worst international corruption at Basel.)

USURY is the cancer of the world, which only the surgeon's knife of Fascism can cut out of the life of nations.

APPENDIX

(Some quotes and observations.)

1. 'The banking business is declared a state monopoly,'

Lenin, Krylenko, Podvolsky, Gorbunov.

Which, of course, means 'all power' the state.

2. 'Discipline the economic forces and equate them to the needs of the nation,'

Mussolini, Consegna for the year XII.

3. 'Problems of production solved, economists prodded on by the state should next solve the problem of distribution.'

Ibid.

4. Rossoni, Italian Minister, indicates the policy of *ammassi*, or assemblages of grain with possibilities of a totally different tax system in kind.

NOTE that extortion has often consisted in forcing men to pay in a substance or via a medium (money) which they have not and which they are forced to obtain at an unjust price.

5. Bankhead proposed Stamp Scrip in the U.S. Senate, possibly the

He then without documents or much detail, blames the Jews for Aryan inability to think clearly. This runs back into retrospect, the Templars, etc. He blames the Jews equally for Calvin and for Voltaire. Taking it impartially as a transpontine Confucian I fail to see why the Jews should commit race suicide merely because Aryans can't think clearly. And I still more emphatically fail to see why any Jew should be expected to think so.'

American Notes, 18 April 1935.

'Usurers have no race. How long the whole Jewish people is to be sacrificial goat for the usurer, I know not. . . .

It cannot be too clearly known that no man can take usury and observe the law of the Hebrews. No orthodox Jew can take usury without sin, as defined in his own scriptures.

The Jew usurer being an outlaw runs against his own people, and uses them as his whipping boy. . . .

But the Jew is the usurer's goat. Whenever a usurer is spotted he scuttles down under the ghetto and leaves the plain man Jew to take the bullets and beatings.

All hostilities are grist to the usurer, all racial hates wear down sales resistance on cannon.'

American Notes, 21 November 1935.

Ed.

only 100 per cent honest monetary proposal made in U.S. legislature since American civilisation was destroyed by and after the Civil War (1861–5).

6. Daladier, whatever his errors, proposed Stamp Scrip in a French Radical Party assembly, possibly the only 100 per cent honest monetary proposal made in that worm-eaten and miserable country since Necker brought in his vermin, and since the Banque de France was riveted on the back of the people.

These statements should be faced and either verified or disproved.

A very great and slimy ignorance persists. American concerns hire the lowest grade of journalists to obscure the public mind. Are we to suppose that neither employer nor writer know that wages are paid in money; that dividends are paid in money; that raw materials and finished products are bought with money?

As for prize lies there is no ascertainable limit from the 'Saturday Evening Post's' 'Kreuger is more than a financial titan' to the daily and hourly pronouncements of the British 'statesmen' and press.

ON ENGLAND

So far as I know no 100 per cent honest monetary policy has been officially proposed in the British Parliament since the Bank of England was founded. Nor has any of the larger religious bodies in England come out for common monetary honesty.

Your tax system is an infamy. The farm hand does not eat more because the paintings by Raeburn or Constable are taken out of the Manor House and put in the dealer's cellar under a black and iniquitous inheritance tax.

The obscuring of the sense of the NATURE of money has destroyed all these fine things USELESSLY. The dismantled Manor House, that could be and ought to show a model of how to live, is made a skeleton for NO PURPOSE.

If any hedger, or ditcher got a half-ounce more beefsteak BECAUSE the Manor House library was sold off and its pictures put up to auction, there might be some justification in taxes. But there is NO justification in taxes as now suffered in Britain.

FOR ARKANSAS

'In Mississippi the average cotton farmer makes four bales of cotton a year worth, at the present market, 42.50 dollars a bale. This is 170 dollars for a year's work. A daughter of this family averaging 12 dollars a week in a nearby industrial plant earns 624 dollars for a year's work, over three times the income from the farm'.

–Thus the 'Commonwealth College Fortnightly'
of Mena, Arkansas. 1 March 1938.

Hence the claims that 'money isn't all' and that 'it is not exclusively a monetary problem.'

You could have a just and stable coinage; measured by eggs, by work or by a logarithmic price-index, and that FARMER could STILL get only 42.50 dollars per bale and be unable to grow more cotton per acre.

Will this statement content my bolshevik friends in Arkansas and the gents who think I am concerned SOLELY with money?

Freedom de Facto[1]

[Free speech without freedom of radio is a mere goldfish in a bowl.

E.P. in *The Townsman*, June 1940]

The incapacity of abstract statement to retain meaning or utility is perhaps nowhere more apparent than in the declaration of the rights of man. The definition of liberty therein contained seems at first sight perfect: Liberty is the right to do anything that does not injure others (*qui ne nuit pas aux autres*).

It is among the best formulations of principle that mankind has produced and it has led to unending quibble and distortion and sophistry as to what does actually injure others.

Mankind's muddle is not merely a muddle in his ideas but a muddle as to the very nature of ideas. The possession of ideas even of the 'right ideas' is no indication that a man understands anything or at any rate it is a very imperfect indication. A man with the 'wrong ideas' or a man whose verbal manifestations appear inexact may often understand things quite well.

For example Levy-Bruhl has a number of excellent ideas about savages and primitive language, but he leaves no conviction that he understands savages. In fact he spends a good deal of space definitely stating that these things are pretty much incomprehensible to civilised man.

He may do this from excess of scruple or because he is writing for logic-chopping Frenchmen or because he is really intelligent and wants at any price or at a great price to keep the reader from thinking he understands the matter *before* he has got to the gist of it.

On the other hand one never doubts Frobenius' understanding, even though academic persons may have found his ideas, or the verbal manifestation of such ideas, wild or 'poetic'.

The understanding of things implies a quick and ready perception of when the given case fits the general formula. The major part of all work in the civil courts consists in the endeavour to determine when the 'given case' fits the general principle or its legal formulation.

Talk of Liberty usually begins in great ignorance of what we have of it and what we should have, and of what we could, under abnormal circumstances, exercise for a limited time.

[1] Written *c*. 1940–1. First published *Agenda*, 1971.

Michelet's name is not, I believe, fashionable in current discussions but parts of his method might still serve in determining the actual state of society. At any rate functioning society consists of, first, a 'small number of people' who make the future; whose opinion passes ultimately as indicative of the time (e.g. the encyclopaedists, Bayle or Rabelais) or at any rate it is registered as 'the best thought of the time'.

In our time no one knows what properly belongs to the state and what to the individual. There are monolinear doctrinaires with one remedy for everything and there is a great mass of people who think that there is a known answer to this problem. But the answer is not known and the hardest thinking of everyone capable of thinking at all will not manage to find the answer in a hurry.

It is quite possible that we have already attained the maximum liberty compatible with civilisation. It has also been stated that 'all our liberties are surreptitious'.

It appears to me that 'the small number of people' recognise neither church nor state when it comes to a matter of their own personal conduct.

This fact is neither trivial nor insignificant. It does not mean that the 'small number of people' is either frivolous or irresponsible.

The 'small number' that I am considering is usually very thoughtful. They have formulated or accepted a fixed or an experimental individual code and govern themselves accordingly. They do not interfere with the actions of others and if they pass judgment on others they do not express it. They assume that our knowledge of other people's actions is of necessity incomplete.

Most of these people have paid 'the price' or a price usually fairly heavy. I have seldom heard them uttering ululations. Neither have I heard them preaching doctrines or suggesting that their line of conduct should be followed by everyone else.

Even when unformulated or unanalyzed this silence is logical and rises from perception of the difference between Greek law and Roman. Roman law being in intention right for the majority of cases and Greek law being supposedly adapted to fit the individual case however fantastic.

Sane man does not try to erect a principle out of an exceptional circumstance. The doctrinaire has, historically speaking, usually failed to differentiate the exceptional case, but the fault of nearly all social and economic thought has been deeper down than that.

Human theorising has proceeded from an Euclidian stasis, from statecraft to music the theoreticians have dealt with a still world, and received derision, quite properly.

Opportunist politics has dealt with a flowing world and succeeded. The low proportion of opportunist failure as compared to theoretic failure gives us our measure for the value of the single element i.e., movement or flow in the functioning of society.

The proportion of opportunist failure gives us our measure for the value of the lump of *all* the other elements put together, and these elements have been fairly well in the grasp of the theoreticians.

What we have needed is not less theory but more theory. Machiavelli's democracy was theoretic, even his idea of movement is a circle and did not attain any conception whatever of the flow, his point was revolving in a fixed orbit. Herbert of Cherbury corrected him by indicating the opportunist (the strictly opportunist) value of having a just cause. You can take it that Cherbury's justifying justice on an opportunist basis is indicative of his time-spirit.

Liberty is not defendable on a static theory. Certain measures of liberty are *de facto* possessed first by the 'small number of people', secondly by the official aristocracy, who assume habitual exemptions and do not discuss anything, thirdly by bohemia and the intelligentsia who feel little or no responsibility but who discuss everything. Fourthly in a clumsier manner by those who have easy money.

Outside these groups the word probably indicates nothing more than a week-end holiday. The populace does not greatly care for liberty and no people will make any effort to maintain any group of rights that has been handed to it on a platter i.e. they defend only recent acquisitions of liberty.

One has only to consider the enormous and hardly conscious sacrifices of long held immunities made during and since the war, the depredations of bureaucracies, passport idiocies etc. When constitutions are not violated by legislature they are quietly subverted by departmental orders and the only defence against such pervasive tyranny lies in the education and discrimination of the individual. To be free he must know his law, that is his own law, the law of his country or countries, he must know his history, the supposed principles underlying it and he must fight every encroachment with every legal and ethical means his knowledge provides.

A Visiting Card[1]

FASCIO

A thousand candles together blaze with intense brightness. No one candle's light damages another's. So is the liberty of the individual in the ideal and fascist state.

THE STATE

In August, 1942, the following elucidatory statement was heard on the Berlin radio: the power of the state, whether it be Nazi, Fascist, or Democratic, is always the same, that is—absolute; the different forms of administration are merely a matter of the different activities which one agrees not to allow.

The revolution, or the revolutions of the nineteenth century, defined the idea of liberty as the right to do anything that does not injure others. But with the decadence of the democratic—or republican—state this definition has been betrayed in the interests of usurers and speculators.

In the beginning was the word, and the word has been betrayed.

The introduction to any ordered discourse is composed of conscious or unconscious quotations. For 2,500 years Europe has been quoting Aristotle, wittingly or unwittingly. In China every dynasty that lasted as long as three centuries was based on the *Ta Hsüeh* or 'Great Learning'[2] of Confucius and had a group of Confucians behind it. The Master Kung collected the Odes and the historical documents of the ancient kings, which he considered instruments worthy of preservation.

We find two forces in history: one that divides, shatters, and kills, and one that contemplates the unity of the mystery.

'The arrow hath not two points.'

There is the force that falsifies, the force that destroys every clearly delineated symbol, dragging man into a maze of abstract arguments, destroying not one but every religion.

---

[1] Written in Italian and first published in Rome, 1942. Translation by John Drummond, first published by Peter Russell, 1952.
[2] '*Studio Integrale*' in the text. *Tr.*

But the images of the gods, or Byzantine mosaics, move the soul to contemplation and preserve the tradition of the undivided light.

BROOKS ADAMS

This member of the Adams family, son of C. F. Adams, grandson of J. Q. Adams, and great-grandson of J. Adams, Father of the Nation, was, as far as I know, the first to formulate the idea of *Kulturmorphologie* in America. His cyclic vision of the West shows us a consecutive struggle against four great rackets, namely the exploitation of the fear of the unknown (black magic, etc.), the exploitation of violence, the exploitation or the monopolisation of cultivable land, and the exploitation of money.

But not even Adams himself seems to have realised that he fell for the nineteenth-century metaphysic with regard to this last. He distinguishes between the swindle of the usurers and that of the monopolists, but he slides into the concept, shared by Mill and Marx, of money as an accumulator of energy.

Mill defined capital 'as the accumulated stock of human labour'.[1]

And Marx, or his Italian translator (U.T.-E.T. edition): 'commodities, in so far as they are values, are *materialised* labour,'[2]

so denying both God and nature.

With the falsification of the word everything else is betrayed.

Commodities (considered as values, surplus values, food, clothes, or whatever) are manufactured raw materials.

Only spoken poetry and unwritten music are composed without any material basis, nor do they become 'materialised'.

The usurers, in their obscene and pitch-dark century, created this satanic transubstantiation, their Black Mass of money, and in so doing deceived Brooks Adams himself, who was fighting for the peasant and humanity against the monopolists.

'... money alone is capable of being transmuted immediately into any form of activity.'[3]–This is the idiom of the black myth!

One sees well enough what he was trying to say, as one understands what Mill and Marx were trying to say. But the betrayal of the word begins with the use of words that do not fit the truth, that do not say what the author wants them to say.

Money does not contain energy. The half-lira piece cannot *create* the

---

[1] Quoted by Brooks Adams, *The Law of Civilization and Decay*, new edition, Knopf, New York, 1943, p. 297. *Tr.*

[2] In the text: 'le merci, in quanto son valori, sono lavoro *materializzato*';

in the original: '... alle Waaren als Werthe vergegenständlichte menschliche Arbeit' (*Das Kapital*, III, i). *Tr.*

[3] Brooks Adams, *loc. cit. Tr.*

platform ticket, the cigarettes, or piece of chocolate that issues from the slot-machine.

But it is by this piece of legerdemain that humanity has been thoroughly trussed up, and it has not yet got free.

Without history one is lost in the dark, and the essential data of modern history cannot enlighten us unless they are traced back at least to the foundation of the Sienese bank, the Monte dei Paschi; in other words, to the perception of the true basis of credit, viz., 'the abundance of nature and the responsibility of the whole people'.

MONEY

The difference between money and credit is one of time. Credit is the future tense of money. Without the definition of words knowledge cannot be transmitted from one man to another.

One can base one's discourse on definitions, or on the recounting of historical events (the philosophical method, or the literary or historical method, respectively).

Without a narrative prelude, perhaps, no one would have the patience to consider so-called 'dry' definitions.

The war in which brave men are being killed and wounded our own war here and now, began–or rather the phase we are now fighting began–in 1694, with the foundation of the Bank of England.

Said Paterson in his manifesto addressed to prospective shareholders, 'the bank hath benefit of the interest on all moneys which it creates out of nothing'.[1]

This swindle, calculated to yield interest at the usurious rate of sixty per cent was impartial. It hit friends and enemies alike.

In the past, the quantity of money in circulation was regulated, as Lord Overstone (Samuel Loyd) has said, 'to meet the real wants of commerce, and to discount all commercial bills arising out of legitimate transactions'.[2]

But after Waterloo Brooks Adams saw that 'nature herself was favouring the usurers'.[3]

For more than a century after Waterloo, no force stood up to the monopoly of money.[4] The relevant passage from Brooks Adams is as follows:

[1] Quoted by Christopher Hollis, *The Two Nations*, Chapter III. See also Pound's Canto XLVI. *Tr.*

[2] Quoted by Brooks Adams, *op. cit.*, pp. 307–8. *Tr.*

[3] *Ibid.*, p. 306. *Tr.*

[4] *Ibid.*, pp. 310, 326–7, and Chapter XI generally. *Tr.*

A VISITING CARD

Perhaps no financier has ever lived abler than Samuel Loyd. Certainly he understood as few men, even of later generations, have understood, the mighty engine of the single standard. He comprehended that, with expanding trade, an inelastic currency must rise in value; he saw that, with sufficient resources at command, his class might be able to establish such a rise, almost at pleasure; certainly that they could manipulate it when it came, by taking advantage of foreign exchange. He perceived moreover that, once established, a contraction of the currency might be forced to an extreme, and that when money rose beyond price, as in 1825, debtors would have to surrender their property on such terms as creditors might dictate.[1]

I'm sorry if this passage should seem obscure to the average man of letters, but one cannot understand history in twenty minutes. Our culture lies shattered in fragments, and with the monetology of usurocracy our economic culture has become a closed book to the aesthetes.

Your revolution is our revolution; and ours was, and is, yours: against a common, putrescent enemy. The peasant feeds us and the gombeen-man strangles us – if he cannot suck our blood by degrees.

The dates of American history are as follows:

1694-6 – Foundation of the stinking Bank, a private company, styled 'of England'.

1750 – Sanctions against Pennsylvania, forbidding the colony to issue its own paper money.

(A number of different, secondary events are mentioned in the obscurantist text-books administered to the victims in the schools and universities of the U.S.A.)

1776 – Beginning of the American Revolution.

Various frauds and betrayals follow on the part of Hamilton, of speculating Congressmen, and of those who hoarded up depreciated veterans' certificates, their face value being restored after their purchase by Congressmen, etc.

1791 and 1816 – Foundation of the first and second Banks 'of the United States'.

1830-40 – The war of the people against the Bank, won by the people under the leadership of Jackson and Van Buren.

The most interesting decade in American history: a decade that has practically disappeared from the school-books.

1861-5 – The Civil War, between debtors and creditors, on the moral pretext that the debtors possessed negro slaves.

Right in the middle of this war the Government was betrayed and

---

[1] *Ibid.*, p. 315. *Tr.*

279

the people were sold into the hands of the Rothschilds, through the intermediaries John Sherman, Ikleheimer, and Van der Gould.

1865–Assassination of Lincoln, followed by eighty years of decadence.

But one can understand nothing of American history unless one understands the great betrayal.

OVERHOLSER

A small country lawyer, 'not trained in research', which means he was not in the pay of usurocratic capital and the monopolists, not dominated by the trusted functionaries of some 'university'–Overholser gives us, in his *History of Money in the United States*, the essential documents.

> The great debt that (our friends the) capitalists (of Europe) will see to it is made out of the war must be used to control the volume of money. . . . It will not do to allow the greenback, as it is called, to circulate . . . for we cannot control them. ('Hazard Circular', 1862).[1]

Lincoln, assassinated soon after, had said '. . . and gave the people of this Republic the greatest blessing they ever had–their own paper to pay their own debts.'[2]

Without understanding these facts, and their bearing on each other, one cannot understand history.

History is written with a knowledge of the despatches of the ambassador Barbon Morosini (particularly one dated from Paris, 28 January 1723 (Venetian style), describing the Law affair), together with a knowledge of the documents leading up to the foundation of the Monte dei Paschi, and the scandalous pages of Antonio Lobero, archivist of the Banco di San Giorgio of Genoa.

We are still in the same darkness which John Adams, Father of the Nation, described as 'downright ignorance of the nature of coin, credit, and circulation'.[3]

MONEY

Money is a title, quantitatively determined, exchangeable at will against any kind of commodities offered on the market. In this respect

[1] Quoted by Willis A. Overholser, *op. cit.*, Chapter IV. See also H. Jerry Voorhis, Extension of Remarks in the House of Representatives, 6 June 1938, *Congressional Record*, Appendix, Vol. 83, Part 11, p. 2363. *Tr.*

[2] From a letter to Colonel E. Taylor,

1864, about the origin of the greenback, see *Writings of Abraham Lincoln*, Constitutional Edition, Vol. VII, p. 270. *Tr.*

[3] Quoted by H. Jerry Voorhis, *loc. cit. Tr.*

it differs from a railway ticket, which is a specific title without any general application.

It is not enough to say of the new money that it is a 'symbol of work'.

It is a symbol of collaboration. It is a certificate of work done within a system, estimated, or 'consecrated', by the state.

State or imperial money has always been an assertion of sovereignty. Sovereignty carries with it the right to coin or print money.

'Within a system' means that the money must be a certificate of work done useful to the nation, the value to the nation of the work in question being estimated by the state.

Misunderstandings about money have been, and continue to be, intentional. They derive neither from the nature of money nor from any natural stupidity of the public.

It was a Rothschild who wrote: 'Those few who can understand the (ursurocratic) system will be ... busy getting profits, ... while the general public ... will probably never suspect that the system is absolutely against their interests.' (From a letter of Rothschild Bros., quoting John Sherman, addressed to the firm of Ikleheimer, Morton and Van der Gould, dated 25 June 1863.)

The cultural tradition with regard to money, which should never have become separated from the main stream of literary culture, may be traced from Demosthenes to Dante; from Salmasius to M. Butchart's *Money* (an anthology of opinions of three centuries); from the indignation of Antoninus Pius, that people should attempt to exploit other people's misfortunes (e.g., shipwrecks), to

> ... il duol che sopra Senna
> induce, falseggiando la moneta.   (*Par.* XIX, 118–19).

After the statements of the Ministers Riccardi and Funk it would probably be pointless to recapitulate the whole controversy, now passed into history, over the campaign for 'work-money', and in any case one could not cover it adequately in a 'Visiting Card'.

Credit is a social product. It does not depend on the individual alone. The confidence you have that I will pay you 100 lire in ten years' time depends on the social order, the degree of civilisation, the probabilities and possibilities of the human congeries.

To say that the state cannot take action or create something because it 'lacks the money' is as ridiculous as saying that it 'can't build roads because it's got no kilometres.'

Statements that were thought crazy seven or twenty years ago seem quite clear to the reader of today; they are no longer considered the mischievous tales of some crack-brained traveller or pilgrim.

It is nature, the actual existence of goods, or the possibility of producing them, that really determines the capacity of the state. Yet it resides above all in the will and the physical force of the people. And the will becomes concentrated in the few.

Said Machiavelli, 'gli uomini vivono in pochi'.

It is within my power to think when I want to think. I will not go into the mystery of the transformation, or transit, from thought to the mobilisation of other people's activities.

As a Cavourian I long neglected the writings of Mazzini. The economists of the last thirty years did not read Mazzini. Their propaganda has not, therefore, been based on the following passage from the last chapter of the *Duties of Man*.

> The establishment of public storehouses or depots from which, the approximate value of the commodities deposited having been ascertained, the Associations would issue a document or *bond*, similar to a banknote, capable of circulating and being discounted, so that the Association would be able to continue its work without being thwarted by the need of quick sales, etc.

He speaks, moreover, of a 'fund for the distribution of *credit*', thus anticipating the theories of the Scotsman, C. H. Douglas, inventor of Social Credit, a monetary system already tried out in Alberta, but hamstrung by the English.

'The distribution of this *credit*', Mazzini continues, 'should not be undertaken by the Government, nor by a National Central Bank; but, with a vigilant eye on the National Power, *by local Banks administered by elective Local Councils*.'

And at this point he enters into questions of administration which do not concern me.

What counts is the direction of the will.

The nineteenth century: the century of usury! Mazzini wrote, '. . . the history of the last half-century, and the name of this half-century is *Materialism*.'

The name of the Fascist era is *Voluntas*.

AUTOBIOGRAPHICAL

I am not going back to Mazzini, and I am not going back to Social Credit. The latter was the doorway through which I came to economic curiosity, and for this reason, among others, your 'Continuous Revolution' interests me perhaps more than it does you. Having seen and experienced so-called reforms and revolutions which have not, in fact, taken place, the mystery of the Fascist and Nazi Revolutions interests me for reasons that would never occur to you, for you have lived through these revolutions instinctively and have experienced their results without worrying about the mystery.

I insist on the identity of our American Revolution of 1776 with your Fascist Revolution. Two chapters in the same war against the usurers, the same who crushed Napoleon.

Let them erect a commemorative urinal to Mond, whose brother said in the year of Sanctions:

> '*Napoleon wath a goodth man, it took uth*
> *20 yearth to crwuth him;*
> *it will not take uth 20 years to crwuth Mussolini*'

adding as an afterthought

> '*and the economic war has begun.*'[1]

I know that drawing-room; that sofa where sat the brother of Imperial Chemicals. I know it. It is not something I read in some newspaper or other; I know it by direct account. Fortunately these messes have no sense of proportion, or the world would already be entirely under their racial domination.

C'EST TOUJOURS LE BEAU MONDE QUI GOUVERNE

Or the best society, meaning the society that, among other things, reads the best books, possesses a certain ration of good manners and, especially, of sincerity and frankness, modulated by silence.

The Counsellor Tchou said to me 'These peoples (the Chinese and Japanese) should be like brothers. They read the same books.'

Le beau monde governs because it has the most rapid means of communication. It does not need to read blocks of three columns of printed matter. It communicates by the detached phrase, variable in length, but timely.

Said the Comte de Vergennes, 'Mr. Adams, the newspapers govern the world.'[2]

And Adams in his old age:

> *Every bank of discount is downright corruption*
> *taxing the public for private individuals' gain.*
> *and if I say this in my will*
> *the American people wd/ pronounce I died crazy.*[3]

[1] See Canto LXXVIII (The *Cantos*, p. 508, or p. 477, U.S. edition). *Tr.*

[2] Recounted in a letter to Samuel Perley, 19 June 1809, see the *Works of John Adams* (Boston, 1850–6), Vol. IX, p. 622, and the author's Canto LXXI. *Tr.*

[3] From a letter to Benjamin Rush, 28 August 1811, see *Works*, Vol. IX, p. 638. The Italian text, however, follows the author's own paraphrase in Canto LXXI, which is therefore used here. *Tr.*

CIVILISATION, MONEY AND HISTORY

The democratic system was betrayed. According to Adams, Jefferson, Madison, and Washington, it rested on two main principles of administration, local and organic. The basis was roughly geographical, but it also represented different ways of life, different interests, agrarian, fisheries, etc. The delegates of the thirteen colonies formed, more or less, a chamber of corporations.

And the nation controlled the nation's money—in theory at least until 1863, and occasionally even in fact. This essential basis of the republican system of the U.S.A. is today a dead letter, though it can still be seen printed in the text of the U.S. Constitution:

'The Congress shall have Power ... To coin Money (and) regulate the Value thereof.'

WÖRGL

At about the beginning of the second decade of the Fascist Era, the small Tyrolean town of Wörgl sent shivers down the backs of all the lice of Europe, Rothschildian and others, by issuing its own Gesellist money (or rather the Gesellist variety of Mazzinian money). Each month every note of this money had to have a revenue stamp affixed to it of a value equal to one per cent of the face-value of the note. Thus the municipality derived an income of twelve per cent per annum on the new money put into circulation.

The town had been bankrupt: the citizens had not been able to pay their rates, the municipality had not been able to pay the schoolteachers, etc. But in less than two years everything had been put right, and the townspeople had built a new stone bridge for themselves etc. All went well until an ill-starred Wörgl note was presented at the counter of an Innsbruck bank. It was noticed, all right—no doubt about that! The judaic-plutocratic monopoly had been infringed. Threats, fulminations, anathema! The burgomaster was deprived of his office, but the ideological war had been won.

Senator Bankhead proposed an emission of dollar-bills up to a limit of a milliard dollars (Bankhead-Pettengill Bill, 17 February 1933), but the stamps were to be affixed at the insane rate of two cents per week, equal to an interest of 104 per cent per annum. Incomprehension of the principle of the just price could not have been carried to absurder lengths. And the Social Creditors in Alberta committed equally gross stupidities: the prescribed stamp was impractiably small and provided with a very unadhesive gum.

A PRINCIPLE

The state can lend. The fleet that was victorious at Salamis was built with money advanced to the shipbuilders by the State of Athens.

A VISITING CARD

The abuse of this state prerogative was demonstrated during the decadence of the Roman Empire. The state loaned money to unworthy borrowers who did not repay it. With stamp scrip the reimbursement is automatic. Anyone who does not want to pay up watches his purchasing-power being gradually annulled.

The Colony of Pennsylvania lent its colonial paper money to the farmers, to be repaid in annual instalments of ten per cent, and the prosperity that resulted was renowned throughout the western world. Equally renowned was the system of the Jesuits in Paraguay.

STAMP SCRIP

Gesell aimed at an increased velocity of circulation, and argued that money should not enjoy privileges not vouchsafed to commodities. A form of money that is subject to tax if it has not been spent within the month does not stagnate. This is how the mercantilist sees it.

From the point of view of the government, the administration, or the state, on the other hand, stamp scrip offers a means not only of taxing the public but of dispensing with other taxes up to the total value of the stamps to be affixed.

The advantages of this form of taxation are that it costs little to collect and that the accounting is practically automatic. One knows that for every million spent by the state there will be an income of 120,000 per annum. And this tax will never fall on anyone who does not have in his pocket, *at the very moment* it falls due, one hundred times the sum demanded.

CANCELLATION

Among all the so-called mysteries of economics none is so little understood as that of the cancellation of superfluous money or credit.

Under the Gesellist system this becomes so simple as to be practically understandable by a child.

Every given sum of money emitted cancels itself in 100 months (eight years and four months), and therefore acts, to a certain extent, as a safeguard against inflation.

Note that inflation occurs when commodities get consumed quicker than money, or when there is too much money about. It seems to me stupid that in order to furnish the state its purchasing-power, money should be collected as it is by the regular taxation system, in accordance with the superstitions of the mercantilist and usurocratic epochs. As ridiculous as it would be for someone who possessed a tin mine to go about collecting old tin cans.

The moral effect of certain regulations, and of institutions such as the *ammassi* (grain pools), should not be underestimated, but a point

285

comes when it might be more convenient to control the harvesting by means of taxable government drafts, which instead of creating an additional burden of interest-bearing debt would function as a source of income to the state.

To sum up: The Gesellist systems means an advantage of 17 per cent per annum to the state compared with the system of government loans. For loans cost the government approximately 5 per cent per annum, which has to be collected from the public in the form of additional taxation. Stamp scrip, on the other hand, if issued by the state for any kind of service *useful* to the state, would lessen pre-existing taxation to an amount equal to 12 per cent of the quantity of Gesellist money spent by the state.

SAVING

We need a medium for saving and a medium for buying and selling, but there is no eternal law that forces us to use the same medium for these two different functions.

Stamp scrip might be adopted as an auxiliary currency, and not as the sole form of money.

The proportion of normal money to stamp scrip, if judiciously and accurately estimated, could be used to maintain a just and almost unvarying ratio between the amount of available and wanted commodities and the total quantity of the nation's money, or at least to bring its fluctuations within tolerable limits.

Bacon wrote: 'money is like muck, no good except it be spread.'

Jackson: 'The safest place for deposits is in the pants of the people.'

Age-old economic wisdom does not hide itself behind university faculties. And we have proof of it now in the recent war-time campaigns to give up your 'gold for the Country', your 'wool for the troops'.

The Roman Empire was ruined by the dumping of cheap grain from Egypt, which sold at an unjustly low price. And usury corrodes.

From the day when the T'ang Emperors began to issue their state notes, (in about A.D. 656 it is thought) the use of gold in the manufacture of money was no longer necessary and became a matter of ignorance or a means of usury. These notes kept their original form from the year 656 down to 841–7, and the inscription is substantially the same as that to be seen on an Italian ten-lire note.

All these facts fit into the system. We may write or read explanations, or we may reflect and understand by ourselves, without wasting optical energy deciphering printed pages.

THE ICONOCLASTS

The power of putrefaction aims at the obfuscation of history; it seeks to destroy not one but every religion, by destroying the symbols, by leading off into theoretical argument. Theological disputes take the place of contemplation. Disputation destroys faith, and interest in theology eventually goes out of fashion: not even the theologians themselves take any more interest in it.

The power of putrefaction would destroy all intrinsic beauty. Whether this power is borne by certain carriers, or by certain others, remains to be determined. It is spread like the bacilli of typhus or bubonic plague, carried by rats wholly unconscious of their role.

Suspect anyone who destroys an image, or wants to suppress a page of history.

Latin is sacred, grain is sacred. Who destroyed the mystery of fecundity, bringing in the cult of sterility? Who set the Church against the Empire? Who destroyed the unity of the Catholic Church with this mud-wallow that serves the Protestants in the place of contemplation? Who decided to destroy the mysteries within the Church so as to be able to destroy the Church itself by schism? Who has wiped the consciousness of the greatest mystery out of the mind of Europe—to arrive at an atheism proclaimed by Bolshevism, in Russia but not of Russia?

Who has received honours by putting argumentation where before there had been faith?

COMMUNICATIONS

Who, what is more, attacks, continuously, the nerve centres, the centres of communication between nation and nation? How is it that you know only a chance selection of the books by your foreign contemporaries, but almost never any of their principle or key works? Who controls and impedes the commerce of perception, of intuition, between one people and another?

I demand, and I shall never cease to demand, a greater degree of communication. It is already too late for you to know eighty per cent of the English and American books that I could have suggested to you in 1927, for translation or for reading in the original.

Joyce is familiar to you, but not Wyndham Lewis or E. E. Cummings. You were introduced to Eliot without too serious a time-lag, but you do not know Ford Madox Ford, nor W. H. Hudson. The copying of the France of 1920 continues, but you do not know Crevel. And so on. The crap has been delivered in abundance–in superabundance. The form of critical activity known as '*saggistica*' is like that of the street-sweeper: a lump of dung from *every* horse, to be analysed by chemists or 'specialists'.

Nicholas V, on the other hand, considered every book translated from the Greek as a conquest. The better the book, then, the greater the conquest?

The conquest of a Wodehouse is not as great as that of a Hardy or, say, of Trollope's *The Warden*. To conquer a chance work by a good writer means less than to conquer a masterpiece by the same author or by another equally great.

The enemy has been at work during these very twenty years of Fascism that you have lost to him through procrastination. Twenty years at five per cent in which he has doubled his capital while he goes on drawing interest. This sum that he pockets is your loss.

THE CRITIC

The worth of the critic is known not by his arguments but by the quality of his choice. Confucius has given us the best anthology in the world, which has already lasted 2,400 years. He collected the documents of a history already ancient in his own time, as were the *Songs of the Kingdoms*.

Criticism may be written by a string of names: Confucius, Ovid, and Homer. Villon, Corbiere, Gautier.

One does not discuss painting with a man who is ignorant of Leonardo, Velasquez, Manet, or Pier della Francesca. In my efforts to establish the distinction between the first and second degree of poetic intensity, it's no good my arguing; one cannot condense a score of volumes into a pamphlet. I have edited several anthologies. I do not believe they have yet been digested here in Italy. Even my small anthology of nineteenth-century French poets contains observations that I cannot state more concisely. But with a score of books I could give you a basis for fruitful discussion–at least I believe so.

I included one or two poems by E. E. Cummings in the anthology *Profile*, published in 1932 by G. Scheiwiller at Milan. Eliot you already know.

I have translated *Moscardino* by Pea: the only time in my life that I have ever wanted to translate a novel. And now, at last, in the Year XXI of the Fascist Era, it seems to me that the Fascist style may be beginning to take root. Controversy is valuable only insofar as it influences action, and the *Book of Mencius* is the most modern book in the world.

A VISITING CARD

Peanuts could bring self-sufficiency in food to Italy or, rather to the empire, for these 'monkey nuts' would grow better in Cyrenaica. The pedlar brings you plenty of stuff in his pack. *News is what one hasn't heard.*[1]

Wealth comes from exchange, but judgment comes from comparison.

We think because we do not know.

THE HISTORY OF LITERATURE

Yeats said: 'They don't like poetry; they like something else, but they like to think they like poetry.'

There are at least three kinds of people who practise the art of writing: the instinctives, almost unconsciously; the inventors; and the exploiters. They ought to be organised in separate divisions of the Fascist Syndicate, or given separate Syndicates in the Corporation.

When the group succeeds in organising itself into a component of a corporation, then we shall have arrived at the state of Utopia.

Philologists, writers of theses, etc., frequently mistake the clamour of exploitation for inventive work. Eliot would recognise, I imagine, a greater influence of Lanman and Woods, his professors of Sanskrit, than the superficial influence of the French poets. And I consider the hours spent with Layamon's *Brut*, or copying a prose translation of Catullus by W. MacDaniel; Ibbotson's instruction in Anglo-Saxon, or W. P. Shepard's on Dante and the troubadours of Provence – more important than any contemporary influences. One who really understood the question of clear expression was Ford Madox Ford.

Literary criticism gets bogged-up in useless arguments if the following categories are not accepted:

(1) what is read by the young serious writer for the purpose of learning his profession, i.e., to learn to know a masterpiece and to form his own critical standards;

(2) what is read as a narcotic, easy reading for the lazy, for the illiterate and dilettante public;

(3) what may be usefully introduced from one country into another in order to nourish the intellectual life of the latter.

The first and third of these categories may overlap, but they do not necessarily have the same boundaries.

[1] Also in English in the text. *Tr.*

289

PAIDEUMA

A culture is an organism made up of:
(1) a direction of the will;
(2) certain ethical bases, or a general agreement on the relative importance of the various moral, intellectual, and material values;
(3) details understood by specialists and members of the same profession.

To replace the marble goddess on her pedestal at Terracina is worth more than any metaphysical argument.

And the mosaics in Santa Maria in Trastevere recall a wisdom lost by scholasticism, an understanding denied to Aquinas. A great many images were destroyed for what they had in them.

> Ma dicon, ch'è idolatra, i Fra' Minori,
> per invidia, che non è lor vicina.[1]

In his *After Strange Gods* Eliot loses all the threads of Arachne[2], and a new edition of Gabriele Rossetti's *Mistero dell'Amor Platonico* (1840) would be useful.

Eliot, in this book, has not come through uncontaminated by the Jewish poison.

Until a man purges himself of this poison he will never achieve understanding. It is a poison that lost no time in seeping into European thought. Already by the time of Scotus Erigena it had begun to make a bog of things. Grosseteste thinks straight when his thought derives from European sources. And the best poets before Dante were Ghibelline.

To want to settle ethical relationships, i.e., to settle the ethical problem without confusing it with the metaphysical, is quite a different matter. In these essays Eliot falls into too many *non sequitors*. Until he succeeds in detaching the Jewish from the European elements of his peculiar variety of Christianity he will never find the right formula. Not a jot or tittle of the hebraic alphabet can pass into the text without danger of contaminating it.

Cabbala, black magic, and the whole caboodle. Church against Empire, Protestantism against the unity of the Mother Church, always destroying the true religion, destroying its mnemonic and commemorative symbols.

---

[1] A popular image of the Madonna then in Orsanmichele renowned as a miracle worker

'But the Friars Minor say that it's idolatry,

For envy, as it's not in their back yard.'

(Cavalcanti, Sonnet XXXV). *Tr.*

[2] See footnote on page 91. Ed.

A VISITING CARD

OF WANDERERS

It is amusing, after so many years, to find that my disagreement with Eliot is a religious disagreement, each of us accusing the other of Protestantism. Theophile Gautier and Swinburne are members of my church. But what Eliot says about Confucius is nonsense, or nearly so. He has renounced America ever since the time of his first departure, but if he would consider the dynasty of the Adamses he would see that it was precisely because it lacked the Confucian law that this family lost the Celestial Decree.

In five generations we have had a president, another president, an ambassador, and two writers; and now one or two almost anonymous officials, absolutely outside public life – with the nation in the hands of the enemy.

STYLE

In one's youth one discusses style – or one should. The poetical reform between 1910 and 1920 coincided with the scrutiny of the word, the cleaning-up of syntax. This should be tackled in addition to, almost apart from, the question of content: one should seek to define the image, to discover the truth, or a part of the truth, even before one has learned that it may not be the whole truth.

For those without access to my criticism in English, I repeat: the art of poetry is divisible into *phanopœia*, *melopœia*, and *logopœia*. Verbal composition, that is to say, is formed of words which evoke or define visual phenomena, of words which register or suggest auditory phenomena (i.e., which register the various conventional sounds of the alphabet and produce, or suggest, a raising or lowering of the tone which can sometimes be registered more accurately by musical notation), and, thirdly, of a play or 'dance' among the concomitant meanings, customs, usages, and implied contexts of the words themselves.

In this last category Eliot surpasses me; in the second I surpass him. Part of his *logopœia* is incompatible with my main purpose.

We have collaborated in *literary* criticism, we have made decisions and taken measures against certain diseases of writing. The problem of the word cannot be exhausted in a single lifetime. It consists of at least two parts:

(1) the word of literary art which presents, defines, suggests the visual image: the word which must rise afresh in each work of art and come down with renewed light;

(2) the legal or scientific word which must, at the outset, be defined with the greatest possible precision, and never change its meaning.

As for ethics, I refer the reader to the *Studio Integrale* of Confucius in my bilingual edition produced in collaboration with Alberto Luchini.[1]

Of religion it will be enough for me to say, in the style of a literary friend, 'ogni ravennate che si rispetta, viene procreato, o almeno riceve spirito o alito di vita, nel mausoleo di Galla Placidia' (G.B.V.)– 'every self-respecting Ravennese is procreated, or at least receives spirit or breath of life, in the Mausoleum of Galla Placidia'.

Dante perhaps said too much in the *Paradiso* without saying enough. In any case the theologians who put reason (logic) in the place of faith began the slithering process which has ended up with theologians who take no interest in theology whatsoever.

Tradition *inheres* ('*inerisce*'[2]) in the images of the gods, and gets lost in dogmatic definitions. History is recorded in monuments, and *that* is why they get destroyed.

SYSTEM

Russia the arsenal of judæocracy from 1919 to the present; the United States the proposed arsenal of tomorrow, or until another is established in South America. Once the barbarians are aroused a usurers' headquarters moves on, betraying one nation, one race, after another.

'It took us twenty years to crush Bonaparte.'

One should distinguish between the fraud of enjoying interest on money created out of nothing, and the swindle of raising the value of the monetary unit through the manipulation of some monopoly, so forcing debtors to pay double in terms of the commodities or property they got at the time of the loan.

Whence one descends, or returns, to another ancient fraud, that of forcing a nation to purchase commodities (often useless) for twice as much as they are worth.

I would say that every book of value contains a bibliography declared or implied. The *De Vulgari Eloquio* refers us to Richard of St. Victor, Sordello, Bertran de Born, and Arnaut Daniel. Dante was my Baedeker

---

[1] This edition, published at Rapallo in 1942, consists of the Chinese text with an Italian translation. The author's latest rendering of the *Ta Hsüeh* in English is *The Great Learning* (Stone Classics Text, 1951), *Tr.*

[2] A blockhead of a lexicographer informs me that two Latin verbs have disappeared forcing one to use the copula and a participle simply because another blockhead who died in the seventeenth century lost the tradition.

Inhaereo, inhaeresco! If the latter is wanting in certain forms in Latin, it is certainly not wanting in the present indicative. Abandoning the active forms of verbs makes the whole language weak and flabby. *Inere*, or *inhaere*, might perhaps be a better form.

in Provence. Here I may mention *Il Giusto prezzo nel Medio Aevo* by the Sac. L. P. Cairoli, apart from the other books of Brooks Adams and Overholser already referred to.

Terminology is not science, but every science advances by defining its terminology with ever greater precision.

With a clear and exact definition of money, a clear understanding of the nature of money, years of economic bewilderment and stupidity will be avoided. Add definitions of credit and circulation, and you will practically arrive at an economic erudition that can be recorded in a few pages and really understood in a few months of study.

Without understanding economics one cannot understand history. John Adams was amazed that very few men had studied systems of government. Between his time and that of Aristotle political literature is scarce enough. And Salmasius? *De Modo Usurarum* appears not to have been reprinted since 1639 or 40.

The emphasis given to economics by Shakespeare, Bacon, Hume, and Berkeley does not seem to have been enough to have kept it prominent in the Anglo-Saxon public conscience. After the arch-heretic Calvin, it seems, discussion of usury has gone out of fashion. A pity! As long as the Mother Church concerned herself with this matter one continued to build cathedrals. Religious art flourished.

KULTURMORPHOLOGIE

To repeat: an expert, looking at a painting (by Memmi, Goya, or any other), should be able to determine the degree of the tolerance of usury in the society in which it was painted.

Art is a means of communication. It is subject to the will of the artist, yet goes beyond it.

'The character of the man is revealed in every brush-stroke (and this does not apply only to ideograms).

TEXT-BOOKS

The text-book for anyone who wants to study the art of metric, the art of making verses, remains the *De Vulgari Eloquio*, but no one can become an expert without knowing Bion ('Death of Adonis'), the troubadours mentioned by Dante, and the technical development in France during the nineteenth century, including a score of poets without great importance for the matter they had to communicate (see *Make it New*).

We can already understand Chinese *phanopœia* up to a point, both in the original and in good translations, but their art of sound and metric must remain a closed book to the West until the advent of a really impassioned sinologue.

To learn what poetry is one cannot dispense with a score of authors who did not write in the language of Petramala:

'Quoniam permultis ac diversis idiomatibus negotium exercitatur humanum, . . .' (*D.V.E.*, I, vi).

Unless you know Homer, Sappho, Ovid, Catullus, Propertius, Dante, Cavalcanti, a few songs of the troubadours together with a few of von der Vogelweide or Hans Sachs, Villon, and Gautier, you won't know European poetry. And your understanding will not be complete unless you take a look at Anglo-Saxon metric.

The appellation 'anseres naturali' is not mine (see *D.V.E.*, II, iv).

No one who is unprepared to train himself in his art by comparative study of the culture today accessible, in the spirit of the author of the *De Vulgari Eloquio*, can expect to be taken seriously. The matter to be examined is more extensive–that is all.

Confucius was an anthologist–the greatest.

Dante was content to cite the first lines of certain *canzoni*.

The convenience of printing allows us to make things easier by giving an entire poem.

In the latter half of the nineteenth century technical and metrical development was centred in France. After 1917 it was continued in the English language. It was my intention that there should have been two classes of Imagists: Hellenists and modernists. Mercantilism intervened. The development continued. Practically no one has succeeded in producing satisfactory English translations from the Greek: only a few fragments have come through successfully. Perhaps the most beautiful books of poetry in the English language are Arthur Golding's translation of Ovid's *Metamorphoses*, printed in 1567, and Gavin Douglas's *Eneados*, done half a century earlier, in a Scots dialect that no one can read today without a glossary. No one has succeeded in translating Catullus into English, yet technical development has made progress since Eliot, and E. E. Cummings achieves a Catullian ferocity in his untranslatable:

DIRGE

flotsam and jetsam
are gentleman poeds
useappeal netsam
our spinsters and coeds)

A VISITING CARD

thoroughly bretish
they scout the inhuman
itarian fetish
that man isn't woman

vive the millenni
um three cheers for labor
give all things to enni
one buggar thy nabor

(neck and senektie
are gentleman ppoyds
even whose recta
are covered by lloyds

In his *tour de force* L. Zukofsky gives a phonetic representation of an American chewing chewing-gum. We must distinguish between the masterpieces of world poetry and a certain few poems which are necessary to keep us informed of what our contemporaries are doing elsewhere.

Twenty years ago Guy Charles Cros and Vlaminck wrote a few verses; ten years ago Basil Bunting wrote some too. Of these, and of the novel *Les Pieds dans le Plat* by the late René Crevel, it may be said that they are better than the foreign crap currently displayed on the book-stalls.

EN FAMILLE

No one, perhaps, has ever built a larger tract of railway, with nothing but his own credit and 5,000 dollars cash, than that laid down by my grandfather. The credit came from the lumbermen (and in face of the opposition of the big U.S. and foreign steel monopolists) by printing with his brother the paper money of the Union Lumbering Co. of Chippewa Falls, bearing the promise to 'pay the bearer on demand . . . in merchandize or lumber'.

It was only when my father brought some old newspaper clippings to Rapallo in 1937 that I discovered that T.C.P. had already in 1878 been writing about, or urging among his fellow Congressmen, the same essentials of monetary and statal economics that I am writing about today.

SOCIAL

Credit is a social phenomenon. The credit of the nation belongs to the nation, and there is not the slightest reason why the nation should have to pay rent for its own credit. There is nothing to force it to hire

295

credit from private interests. Thus Jefferson wrote to Crawford as long ago as 1816:

> . . . and if the national bills issued be bottomed (as is indispensable) on pledges of specific taxes for their redemption within certain and moderate epochs, and be of proper denominations for circulation, no interest on them would be necessary or just, because they would answer to every one of the purposes of the metallic money withdrawn and replaced by them.

This quotation[1] forms the second chapter of my *Introductory Text-book* (which teaches the economic history of the United States in four chapters). The first chapter consists of an observation of John Adams already referred to:

> All the perplexities, confusion, and distress in America arise, not from defects in their Constitution or confederation, not from want of honor or virtue, so much as from downright ignorance of the nature of coin, credit, and circulation.[2]

The third chapter is Lincoln's

> . . . and gave the people of this Republic the greatest blessing they ever had–their own paper to pay their own debts.[3]

And the last is from the Constitution of the United States, Article I, Section 8, clause 5:

> The Congress shall have Power . . .
> To coin Money, regulate the Value thereof, and of foreign Coin, and fix the Standard of Weights and Measures;
> > [signed] George Washington– President
> > and deputy from Virginia

The 'Book' consists of only one page, followed by half a page of bibliographical data mentioning, in addition to the authors already cited in this pamphlet, Christopher Hollis, R. McNair Wilson, and P. J. Larranaga.

Anyone who has mastered these four short chapters will be well advanced in the understanding of monetary and political economy.

Money is a title and a measure. If it is metallic it is subject to assay to ensure that the coin is of specified fineness and weight. The use of such money still falls under the classification of barter. When people begin to understand the function of money as a title, the desire to barter disappears. When the state understands its duties and powers it does

---

[1] See the *Writings of Thomas Jefferson*, Memorial Edition, Vol. XV, p. 31. *Tr.*

[2] See p. 280 above, note 3. *Tr.*

[3] See p. 280 above, note 2. *Tr.*

not leave its sovereignty in the hands of private interests that are irresponsible or arrogate to themselves unwarranted responsibilities. It is not right to say that 'work-money' is a 'symbol of work'. More exactly it is a symbol of a collaboration between nature, the state, and an industrious population.

The beauty of the designs on ancient coins rightly symbolizes the dignity of sovereignty inherent in royal or imperial responsibility. The disappearance of numismatic art coincides with the corruption of the governments concerned.

The Rothschilds financed the Austrian armies against Venice and Romagna. Naturally.

The Rothschilds financed the armies against the Roman Republic. Naturally. They tried to buy over Cavour. Naturally. Cavour accomplished the first stage towards Italian unity, allowing himself to be exploited according to the custom of his times, but he refused to be dominated by the exploiters.

```
R O M A
O     M
M     O
A M O R
```

Above all this, the substantiality of the soul, and the substantiality of the gods.

DICHTEN=CONDENSARE

The German word *Dichtung* means 'poetry'. The verb *dichten–condensare*.

In our intellectual life–or 'struggle', if you prefer it–we need facts that illuminate like a flash of lightning, and authors who set their subjects in a steady light.

The writings of Frobenius contain flashes of illumination. From nineteenth-century philology, relegating everything to separate compartments, creating specialists capable of writing monographs or articles for encyclopaedias without the least understanding of their import or relation to the total problem, Frobenius advanced to Kulturmorphologie. He brought the living fact to bear on the study of dead documents. It began–*incipit vita nova sua*–with his hearing that certain railway contractors were in conflict with some local tradition. A king and a girl had driven into the ground where there was a certain hillock: they ought not to make a cutting through the sacred place. The materialist contractors took no notice and went ahead–and unearthed a bronze car with effigies of Dis and Persephone.

Later he wrote, 'Where we found these rock drawings there was always water within six feet of the surface.'

The oral tradition, surviving rites, and also the practical import of archaeological findings are all part of his total perception. He saw nothing ridiculous in a child's wanting to know if the last letter of the word *Katz* stood for the cat's tail, and the first one for its head. But to the school teacher, who cared little for intelligence or lively curiosity, the child just seemed stupid.

To be worthy of the heroes who penetrated into the harbour of Gibraltar ... but!–but they are not even up to Davis Cup players. To live we need facts, and opportunities for comparison. We want no foreign dumping, neither of material goods nor of psuedo-literary produce. But samples for comparison, certainly. To know the best model, and to improve on it. To know the masterpieces, and then achieve self-sufficiency. Conquests in the manner of Nicholas V.

A comparison between Confucius and Aristotle would hurt no one's 'Italianity'. A reform of the universities could be effected, in my opinion, by the infusion of certain known facts condensable into a few pages. Confucius, Mencius, the anthology compiled by Confucius of poems already ancient in his time. A dozen Chinese poets, and a general idea, at least, of the nature of the ideogram as a means of verbal and visual expression. This vitalizes.

A proper sense of the maxima of poetry. Homer not to be neglected. The study of metre will require an odd half-hour or so with Bion, the troubadours, and French poetry between 1880 and 1910. A certain snobbery, dating back to the Renaissance, has perhaps unduly boosted the Greek authors at the expense of Ovid, Propertius, and Catullus.

Do not overburden the student, but do as one would in taking him to a picture-gallery containing a few paintings by the greatest masters. Quality, not quantity.

In teaching history: a synthesis not inferior to that of Brooks Adams and, with reference to the last two centuries, some indication of the continuity, or identity, of the revolutions of 1776 and today, viz., the American and your own.

Together with the chronology already given near the beginning of this pamplet.

Our friend T. E. Hulme truly said: 'All a man ever *thought* would go onto a half sheet of notepaper. The rest is application and elaboration.'
Without strong tastes one does not love, nor, therefore, exist.

DE MODO USURARUM

Getting into debt is one way of having a career in politics. The Mandarin Wu Yung tells us that when he was appointed Governor the bankers pressed him to borrow money from them. He insisted that he

298

would never have been able to repay them out of his salary. That was a mere detail that didn't worry them in the least.

This anecdote has its bearing on the life of an usher I knew at a library in Venice, who hanged himself after forty years of faithful service. The note of hand

> ... rompe i muri e l'armi.[1]

and a policy of unjustly low salaries can favour the usurers' game.

The emphasis is on the adverb 'unjustly'. Such a policy derives from an imperfect understanding of the nature of money, and of the power of the state. The state monetary authorities can supply the needs of the people and provide for all work useful to the state, up to a limit imposed by the availabilities of raw materials and the people's brain-power and muscle-power, without having to ask permission of the Rothschilds or to have recourse to the Cavourian alternative.

MONEY A WARNING

It is not yet sufficiently understood that every sound economic system, every economic procedure, depends on justice. Money is a measure. It is a warning or notification of the amount the public owes to the bearer of the coin or note. 'Not by nature, but by custom, whence the name NOMISMA.'

The state can lend. There is more justice in the state being paid for work done or administered by itself than for the work, or some of the work, done by non-state employees.

In producing these metallic discs, or pieces of paper, which serve as a means and a measure of exchange, the state is doing work; and it would be perfectly just that the employees and officials of the state were remunerated for doing this work rather than that the state should collect taxes on the products of other people's work. The ethical and intellectual work that goes to determining the measure of the just price deserves its due reward. This is the ethical basis of the Gesellist idea, though Gesell may not have said so himself.

There is no reason why an inventor should understand all the implications of his invention. Gesell saw his system from the point of view of the merchant who wants a rapid, and always more rapid, exchange of goods. 'Wealth is exchange.' Rossoni[2] saw at once the advantage it would bring to the state: 'Then the state will get something out of it too,' he said.

It would be fair gain, not filthy lucre. The state income is as important as the acceleration of trade. It is perfectly just that the state be

---

[1] 'breaks through walls and weapons' (*Inf.*, XVII, 2). *Tr.*

[2] Italian Minister of Agriculture, 1935–9. *Tr.*

remunerated for the work it does. It is unjust that money should enjoy privileges denied to goods. It would be better, too, if money perished at the same rate as goods perish, instead of being of lasting durability while goods get consumed and food gets eaten.

Monetary theory is worthy of study because it leads us to the contemplation of justice.

CIRCUIT

Should the circulation of capital be automatic? We must distinguish between capital and purchasing-power. Striving for a clear terminology one might limit the term capital to the sense of 'productive undertaking', or the securities of such an undertaking, i.e., securities that presuppose a material basis which yields a produce that can be divided periodically, paying interest (share interest in monetary form) without creating inflation, which is a superfluity of paper money in relation to available goods.

Stamp scrip creates an automatic purchasing-power circuit. Each new issue of this money cancels itself in 100 months. In other words: an automatic circuit that returns to the starting-point in eight years and four months. It cannot be hoarded. Anyone who thinks to keep it put by in a stocking will find it slowly melting away. Anyone who needs it to live by, or who uses it to stimulate and increase the well-being of the nation, will profit by it.

This money, as it cancels itself, is a source of income to the treasury. Government loans do not cancel themselves; they become a permanent liability. It seems to me that stamp scrip is the sole means of increasing the state's monetary income by spending. No one denies that the state should derive an advantage from the operation of electric power stations, etc., but the usual systems of taxing these new industries are more than necessarily complicated.

The government loan creates a liability of five per cent. Stamp scrip creates a source of income. The loan serves to distribute purchasing-power among those who subscribe to it. This may be useful to the state up to a point–up to an income, let us say, of 50,000 lire per annum in the case of any person who merits it. We might even say up to 100,000 lire, but not *ad infinitum*.[1]

UNIVERSITY

The modern university was founded at Frankfurt by Leo Frobenius, or at least it was the first approach to the modern university. If I had

---

[1] This range would have been roughly equivalent to £500–£1,000 or $2,500–$5,000 at the time of writing. *Tr.*

been thirty-five years younger I would have wanted to enrol myself as a student. If I wish to know, for example, if J. S. Mill is right in saying that certain African tribes have a money of account—a money which, according to him, was a concept of value, having a name that meant nothing other than this indication of the value of a means of exchange—I write to Frankfurt. In this particular case I received, within ten days, a list of all the tribes that used, or had used, the 'makute'. It had become an abstract measure, though it had originally meant one of the mats or circles of plaited straw that the natives carry slung behind them as a protection against damp, thorns, etc., when they sit down.

It was an article of commerce that served to calculate the prices of other goods, such as salt, or knives—until the Portugese began to coin metal 'makutes', and to counterfeit them.

When I wanted to know how the primitive telegraph, tapped out on wooden drums, worked, I wrote to Frankfurt. I believe that Frobenius has marked the transition from the stage of 'comparative philology' to that of 'Kulturmorphologie', but in any case one cannot fully understand modern thought without some awareness of Frobenius's work. *Gli uomini vivono in pochi*. The books that change our understanding are few. Several Germans tell me that they make no distinction between 'der Kundiger' and 'der Kenner'.

The foreigner is liable to acquire some queer ideas about other people's languages, but I'm not sure that he's always wrong. At any event you have no translation of *Erlebte Erdteile*, and I would say that you could do with ten or fifteen volumes of Leo Frobenius. I'm not going to condense so rich a work, nor to explain more of it than I know.

The syndicate of scholars is still waiting to be organised on fascist and corporative lines. The communications systems is slow and imperfect. I want a printer who, at least once a month, will print what I want him to print, *pro bono publico* and not for immediate gain.

As long as all the really interesting books are in the hands of only a hundred—even a dozen—individuals, how is one to find keen and competent translators? A young friend wanted to read Galdos, but we couldn't find any editions. Eventually I had to send to London, but I received only secondary works, not the principal masterpieces.

Two years ago or more, I drew attention to the enterprise of the Barcelona publishers Yunque, who brought out a series of bilingual texts.

The amount of matter to be introduced from abroad is quantitatively small. It is the quality that counts in this commerce, not the bulk. We need to import every year say twenty, perhaps even fifty, books that are not crap and filth. Moral filth is perhaps less poisonous than intellectual filth, when it comes to considering the printed page. Moral filth, in print, poisons the reader; intellectual filth can be toxic to a whole race. The means a nation chooses (or lets be chosen) for the distribution of books and printed matter are of importance. For the last hundred years few have worried about them. Flaubert published his *sottisier*. But half a century later the study of what was actually printed and offered for sale on the bookstalls was considered eccentric on the part of the present writer. I made an analysis in eighteen numbers of the *New Age*, but no publisher has wanted to reprint the series, which was, in any case, cut short by the protests of the readers of the said journal. Yet a whole system is collapsing, and for want of having paid attention to the symptoms of its own defilement.

The pathology of the printed page is pathology. The pathology of art is pathology. Getting some idiotic idea believed is preparing for the crackup. Yeats knew a 'founder of a religion' who managed to get a score of victims to believe that the world was a hollow sphere and that we lived inside it.

We must get rid of the stooges and straw men. We must distinguish between the intellectual construction of Europe, and poison. Perhaps in re-reading the *Divina Commedia* we may find this dissociation of ideas. I cannot say. Geryon is biform. He takes you lower down. And after the eighth canto of the *Paradiso*, who understands the meaning?

It seems that only a few persons occupied about the temples, at least at Rome, were enough to keep alive the cult of the old gods. The preservation of verities, the process of history, the rise and fall of a dogma, whether or not affected by contingent events, is a great deal more interesting than is commonly supposed.

Italy has lived more fully than other nations because she has kept up the habit of placing statues in gardens. The grove calls for the column. *Nemus aram vult.*

GOOD GOVERNMENT

I believe that the most useful service that I could do for Italy would be to put before you, every year, a few lines of Confucius, so that they might sink into the brain. One reads a phrase of Confucius, and it seems nothing. Twenty years later one returns to think over its meaning. When I was thirty I read a French translation, then an English one, and then gradually I have profited from Fenollosa's notes. One cannot get the full meaning without analysing the ideograms. Legge translates a certain ideogram[1] with the word 'beclouding', but the basic idea it conveys is one of wild vegetation which encroaches

upon and grows over everything, creating a dense and tangled confusion, which would imply 'overgrowing' in English. This ideogram-
matic component of wild vegetation with broken water, meaning
'swamp', is frequently encountered in ideogram lexicons.

I will leave it to some great Italian stylist to find a single word to
render this complex of graphic suggestions, and give you instead a
piece of dialogue.

Tseu Lou. If the Prince of Wei appointed you head of the government,
to what would you first set your mind?
Kung-fu-tseu. To call people and things by their true and proper names.

Tseu Lou. You really mean that? Aren't you dodging the question?
What's the use of that?
Kung. You're a fat-head [a blank—a page with nothing written on it].
An intelligent man hesitates to talk of what he don't understand.
He feels embarrassment.

If the terminology be not exact, if it fit not the thing, the governmental instructions will not be explicit; if the instructions aren't
clear and the names don't fit, you can not conduct business properly.[1]

It all seems too easy? The more responsibilities you have the more
you will understand the meaning.

And I have to thank Dante for having drawn our attention to a
treatise of Richard of St. Victor *De Contemplatione* in which the three
words *cogitatio meditatio* and *contemplatio* are defined.

Writing in the *Lavoro Fascista* of the 11 January 1942, Corrado Caja, in
an article on the cult of the 'verbo vero' made a contribution to clear
thinking, citing a poem beginning:

> L'apparenza e il profumo
> si dilagano.[2]

Towards order in the state: the definition of the word. But if I have
made any contribution to criticism I have done so by introducing
the ideogrammic system. True criticism will insist on the accumulation of these concrete examples, these facts, possibly small, but gristly

[1] The wording of this passage from
the *Analects*, XIII, iii, follows the
author's version in the *Guide to Kulchur*,
p. 16, except for one or two minor
instances where the Italian does not
correspond. *Tr.*

[2] 'Appearance and perfume inun-
date.' *Tr.*

and resilient, that can't be squashed, that insist on being taken into consideration, before the critic can claim to hold any opinion whatsoever.

Let us get together and consider certain facts of literature; let us mark out the categories whenever it may be convenient or possible, but *not* before knowing the facts (i.e., the masterpieces, either of the highest intensity or superior in particular aspects). When we know them we can discuss them–but not painting without a knowledge of Mantegna or Manet, not poetry if we dare not make comparisons.

Italian songs include 'Ahi ritorna l'eta dell'oro' and the stornelli of Romagna. Good, so-called 'popular' songs, often have this value: the music renders the words without deforming them. There is no snobbery that the critics won't lick from the boots of an established reputation.

After ten days' struggle, Gino Saviotti was reduced to 'there are days when one feels the need of a peppermint cream' (*Difesa della Poesia di Francesco Petrarca*, last chapter).

After Cavalcanti and Dante the Italian writers are those who have had something precise to relate. The stylists declined from the moment they wanted to write in Latin instead of Italian.[1]

And anyone who wrote in Latin then went and imitated his own watered-down style in the so-called vulgar tongue (cf. *De Vulgari Eloquio*).

France began to become tongue-tied with the *Pleiade*. She recovered again after Stendhal, who wrote badly. Gautier did not write badly–when he wrote verse.

Thought is organic. It needs these 'gristly facts'.

The idea is not achieved until it goes into action. The idea is completed by the word. It is completed by its going into action. The idea that does not go into action is a truncated idea. It lacks an essential part. This does not mean, of course, that it has to go into action half an hour after it's born.

We think because we do not know.

ROMA
O   M
M   O
AMOR

I don't know what evil plague has come to rage over Italy for four centuries that people should want to destroy the vocabulary, the

---

[1] I mean the Italians who wrote in Latin during the Renaissance. What I say here doesn't contradict what I say further on about Italian usage and syntax.

304

language of Dante, and set about speaking a language of shopkeepers and hairdressers – and not even the language of real hairdressers: a language no hairdresser would use.

If Dante has used a word that word belongs to your language. The same goes for 'l'amico suo', Cavalcanti.

'VOI'

The banning of the 'Lei'[1] marks the beginning of the great task of salvaging the Latin strength that underlies the decadence of the Italian language. May this revolution continue, until we have regained the full force of the Latin language and the Ghibelline poets!

Dammit all! one might at least consider Dante's own terminology in his classification of words: "pexa", "hirsuta." Sleek words and shaggy words, he calls them.[2]

When Caesar conquered Britain he didn't have to say 'la sua' every time for 'sua', or 'il vostro' for 'vostro'. The article 'il' is sometimes superfluous.

Who denies his great-grandfather would deny his race.

It seems to me that many departures from Latin usage and syntax, not to mention the insertion of useless words, might well be dispensed with. They are born of ignorance, mediaeval or other. I don't mean that we should create a latinising snobbery, but that when a writer, faced with a problem of style, falls into Latin syntax he should not correct it simply because some louse of a pedagogue has decreed a 'rule'. The Latinist, on the other hand, should not interfere by correcting whomever writes his mother tongue as he has learnt it from a speech, whose forms have perhaps arisen from Latin as it was spoken.

It is ridiculous that when I write English I can use Latin words and forms that you don't dare to adopt (*mal franxese*); and that you are afraid to adopt the verbal force and syntactical freedom of the Ghibelline poets. The damnable Della Crusca: chaff but no grain!

Amo ergo sum.

[1] 'Polite' form of address, discouraged latterly under Fascism in favour of 'voi' (= Fr. 'vous'). *Tr.*

[2] *De Vulgari Eloquio*, II, vii. *Tr..*

Gold and Work[1]

1944

THE WAY OF UTOPIA

On the 10th of September last, I walked down the Via Salaria and into the Republic of Utopia, a quiet country lying eighty years east of Fara Sabina. Noticing the cheerful disposition of the inhabitants, I enquired the cause of their contentment, and I was told that it was due both to their laws and to the teaching they received from their earliest school days.

They maintain (and in this they are in agreement with Aristotle and other ancient sages of East and West) that our knowledge of universals derives from our knowledge of particulars, and that thought hinges on the definitions of words.

In order to teach small children to observe particulars they practise a kind of game, in which a number of small objects, e.g., three grains of barley, a small coin, a blue button, a coffee bean, or, say, one grain of barley, three different kinds of buttons, etc., are concealed in the hand. The hand is opened for an instant, then quickly closed again, and the child is asked to say what it has seen. For older children the game is gradually made more elaborate, until finally they all know how their hats and shoes are made. I was also informed that by learning how to define words these people have succeeded in defining their economic terms, with the result that various iniquities of the stock market and financial world have entirely disappeared from their country, for no one allows himself to be fooled any longer.

And they attribute their prosperity to a simple method they have of collecting taxes or, rather, their one tax, which falls on the currency itself. For on every note of 100 monetary units they are obliged, on the first of every month, to affix a stamp worth one unit. And as the government pays its expenses by the issue of new currency, it never needs to impose other taxes. And no one can hoard this currency because after 100 months it would have lost all its value. And this solves the problem of circulation. And because the currency is no more durable than commodities such as potatoes, crops, or fabrics,

---

[1] Title of original work, is *Oro e Lavoro*, in Memory of Aurelio Baisi, Rapallo. It was first published in Rapallo, 1944. This translation, by John Drummond was first published by Peter Russell in 1951.

the people have acquired a much healthier sense of values. They do not worship money as a god, they do not lick the boots of bloated financiers or syphilitics of the market-place. And of, course, they are not menaced by inflation, and they are not compelled to make wars to please the usurers. In fact, this profession–or criminal activity–is extinct in the country of Utopia, where no one is obliged to work more than five hours a day, because their mode of life makes a great deal of bureaucratic activity unnecessary. Trade has few restraints. They exchange their woollen and silk fabrics against coffee and groundnuts from their African possessions, while their cattle are so numerous that the fertiliser problem almost solves itself. But they have a very strict law which excludes every kind of surrogate from the whole of their republic.

Education for these people is almost a joy, and there are no redundant professors. They say that it is impossible to eliminate idiotic books, but that it is easy to distribute the antidote, and they do this by means of a very simple system. Every bookseller is obliged to stock the best books; some of outstanding merit must be displayed in his window for a certain number of months each year. As they become familiar with the best books, the disgusting messes served up periodically by *The Times* or the *Nouvelle Revue Française* gradually disappear from the drawing-rooms of the more empty-headed young ladies–of both sexes.

They attach the importance to skill in agricultural tasks that I attached in my youth to skill at tennis or football. In fact, they have ploughing contests to see who can drive the straightest furrow. As for myself, I felt I was too old for such activities, and recalled the case of a young friend who had also been seized by this archaic passion: he wrote that his first acre 'looked as if a pig had been rooting about all over it'.

After I had heard these very simple explanations of the happiness of these people, I went to sleep under the Sabine stars, pondering over the astonishing effects of these reforms, apparently so trifling, and marvelling at the great distance separating the twentieth-century world from the world of contentment.

Inscribed over the entrance to their Capitol are the words:

THE TREASURE OF A NATION IS ITS HONESTY.

PARTICULARS OF THE CRIME

It is no use assembling a machine if a part is missing or defective. One must have all the essential parts. Fully to understand the origins of the present war it will be useful to know that:

The Bank of England, a felonious combination or, more precisely, a gang of usurers taking sixty per cent interest, was founded in 1694.

Paterson, the founder of the bank, clearly stated the advantages of his scheme: 'the bank hath benefit of the interest on all moneys which it creates out of nothing'.[1] In 1750 the paper currency of the Colony of Pennsylvania was suppressed. This meant that this confederacy of gombeen-men, not content with their sixty per cent, namely, the interest on the moneys they created out of nothing, had, in the fifty-six intervening years, become powerful enough to induce the British Government to suppress, *illegally*, a form of competition which had, through a sane monetary system, brought prosperity to the colony.

Twenty-six years later, in 1776, the American colonies rebelled against England. They were thirteen independent organs, divided among themselves, but favoured by geographical factors and European discords. They conquered their perennial enemy, England, but their revolution was betrayed by internal enemies among them. Their difficulties might serve to stimulate Italians today, and the problems of that time might suggest solutions in Italy now.

The imperfections of the American electoral system were at once demonstrated by the scandal of the Congressmen who speculated in the 'certificates of owed pay' that had been issued by the various Colonies to the soldiers of the Revolution.

It was an old trick, and a simple one: a question of altering the value of the monetary unit. Twenty-nine Congressmen conspired with their associates and bought up the certificates from veterans and others at twenty per cent of their face value. The nation, having now established itself as an administrative unit, then *'assumed'* responsibility for redeeming the certificates at their full face value.

The struggle between the financial interests and the people was continued in the battle between Jefferson and Hamilton, and still more openly when the people were led by Jackson and Van Buren. The decade between 1830 and 1840 has practically disappeared from the school-books. The economic facts behind the American 'Civil' War are extremely interesting. After the Napoleonic wars, after the 'Civil' one, after Versailles, the same phenomena may be observed.

Usurocracy makes wars in succession. It makes them according to a pre-established plan for the purpose of creating debts.

For every debt incurred when a bushel of grain is worth a certain sum of money, repayment is demanded when it requires five bushels or more to raise the same sum. This is accompanied by much talk of devaluation, inflation, revaluation, deflation, and a return to gold. By returning to gold, Mr. Churchill forced the Indian peasant to pay two bushels of grain in taxes and interest which a short time before he had been able to pay with one only.

---

[1] Quoted by Christopher Hollis: *The Two Nations*, Chapter III. See also Pound's Canto XLVI. *Tr.*

C. H. Douglas, Arthur Kitson, Sir Montagu Webb give the details. The United States were sold to the Rothschilds in 1863. The Americans have taken eighty years to discover the facts that are still unknown in Europe. Some of them were made known in Congress by Charles A. Lindbergh, the aviator's father, and later included by Willis A. Overholser in his *History of Money in the United States*.

A letter from the London banking firm of Rothschild Bros., dated 25 June 1863, addressed to the New York bank of Ikleheimer, Morton & Van der Gould, contains the following words of fire:

> '*Very few people*
> '*will understand this. Those who do will be occupied*
> '*getting profits. The general public will probably not*
> '*see it's against their interest.*'[1]

The favourite tricks of the usurocracy are simple, and the word 'money' is not defined in the clerks' manual issued by the Rothschilds, nor in the official vocabulary 'Synonyms and Homonyms of Banking Terminology'. The tricks are simple: taking usury at sixty per cent and upwards, and altering the value of the integer of account at moments advantageous to themselves.

IGNORANCE

Ignorance of these tricks is not a natural phenomenon; it is brought about artificially. It has been fostered by the silence of the press, in Italy as much as anywhere else. What is more, it has been patiently and carefully built up. The true basis of credit was already known to the founders of the Monte dei Paschi of Siena at the beginning of the seventeenth century.

This basis was, and is, the abundance, or productivity, of nature together with the responsibility of the whole people.

There are useful and potentially honest functions for banks and bankers. One who provides a measure of prices in the market and at the same time a means of exchange is useful to the nation. But one who falsifies this measure and this means is a criminal.

A sound banking policy aims, and in the past has aimed, as Lord Overstone (Samuel Loyd) has said, 'to meet the real wants of

[1] The Italian text follows the author's own paraphrase in Canto XLVI, which is therefore used here. These particular words are quoted (enthusiastically) from a letter received by the Rothschild firm from 'a certain Mr John Sherman', presumably to be identified with the American statesman who was then Senator for Ohio and later Secretary of the Treasury. Overholser gives the full text in the fourth chapter of his book. *Tr.*

commerce, and to discount all commercial bills arising out of legitimate transactions'.[1]

Nevertheless, at a certain moment at about the beginning of the century, Brooks Adams was moved to write:

> Perhaps no financier has ever lived abler than Samuel Loyd. Certainly he understood as few men, even of later generations, have understood, the mighty engine of the single standard. He comprehended that, with expanding trade, an inelastic currency must rise in value; he saw that, with sufficient resources at command, his class might be able to establish such a rise, almost at pleasure; certainly that they could manipulate it when it came, by taking advantage of foreign exchange. He perceived moreover that, once established, a contraction of the currency might be forced to an extreme, and that when money rose beyond price, as in 1825, debtors would have to surrender their property on such terms as creditors might dictate.[2]

So now you understand why the B.B.C., proclaiming the liberation of Europe, and of Italy in particular, never replies to the question: *And the liberty of not getting into debt—how about that?*

And you will understand why Brooks Adams wrote that after Waterloo no power had been able to resist the force of the usurers.[3]

And you will understand why Mussolini was condemned twenty years ago by the central committee of the usurocracy. And why wars are made, i.e., in order to create debts which must be paid in appreciated money, or not paid at all, according to circumstances.

War is the highest form of sabotage, the most atrocious form of sabotage. Usurers provoke wars to impose monopolies in their own interests, so that they can get the world by the throat. Usurers provoke wars to create debts, so that they can extort the interest and rake in the profits resulting from changes in the values of monetary units.

If this is not clear to the novice, let him read and meditate the following sentences from the Hazard Circular of the year 1862:

> The great debt that (our friends the) capitalists (of Europe) will see to it is made out of the war must be used to control the volume of money. . . . It will not do to allow the greenback, as it is called, to circulate . . . for we cannot control them (i.e., their issue, etc.).[4]

---

[1] Quoted by Brooks Adams: *The Law of Civilization and Decay* (new edition), Knopf, New York, 1943, pp. 307–8. *Tr.*

[2] Brooks Adams, *op. cit.*, p. 315. *Tr.*

[3] *Ibid.*, pp. 306, 310, 326–7, and Chapter XI generally. *Tr.*

[4] Quoted by Overholser, *op. cit.*, Chapter IV. Also by H. Jerry Voorhis: Extension of Remarks in the House of Representatives, 6 June 1938, *Congressional Record*, Appendix, Vol. 83, Part II, p. 2363. *Tr.*

In fact, after the assassination of President Lincoln no serious measures against the usurocracy were attempted until the formation of the Rome-Berlin Axis. Italy's ambition to achieve economic liberty –the liberty of not getting into debt–provoked the unleashing of the ever-accursed sanctions.

But the great Italian publishing houses, more or less open accomplices of the perfidious Italian press, have not published the works of Brooks Adams and Arthur Kitson in which these facts are given. The press has been perfidious and the great publishing houses have been more or less conscious accomplices according to their capacity. One cannot hope to prevail against bad faith by making known the facts, but one might against ignorance. The publishers have received their information through certain channels; they have taken their tone from *The Times Literary Supplement* and from books distributed through Hachette and W. H. Smith & Son, or approved by the *Nouvelle Revue Française*.

Nothing, or practically nothing, has arrived in Italy that has not been picked over by the international usurers and their blind or shifty-eyed servitors. And the result is to be seen in an artificially created ignorance and snobbery. Neomalthusianism needs looking into. In Italy, as elsewhere, crime fiction has served to distract attention from the great underlying crime, the crime of the usurocratic system itself. If this may seem of no importance to politicians and men of action, it has nonetheless created a vast blockage of passive inertia in the very so-called 'literary' or 'cultured' circles which set the tone of printed matter. They read, they write, and the public gets the sweepings. And from this dishwashing process derives the CREDULITY that has contaminated a great part of the public with the 'English disease', namely, a pathological disposition to believe the fantastic tales put out from London and disseminated gratis by indigenous simpletons.

Of the liberals (who are not always usurers) we would ask, Why are usurers always liberals?

Of those who demand the dictatorship of the proletariat we would ask, Must the proletariat of one country impose dictatorship on the proletariat of another?

To those who inveigh against the concept of autarchy, saying it costs too much; that grain should be bought in the cheapest market–we would recall that it was precisely the importing of cheap grain from Egypt that ruined Italian agriculture under the Roman Empire. And if this fact appears too remote from our own times, it may be noted that those who speak of this kind of free trade usually end up by talking about the export of *labour*, that is, the export of workers, the export of human beings, in exchange for commodities

Many are beginning to understand that England, in her sadistic attempt to destroy Italy, is destroying herself, though the public still fails to understand the origin of this mania for destruction. Deny, if you like, that the purely and exclusively economic man exists, yet the analysis of economic motives is useful for an understanding of avarice. The greed for monopoly is a fundamental evil. It may be seen in the transgression of the unjust price, condemned by the economic doctrine of the Church throughout the period of its greatest splendour.

It must be understood that the whole of the current taste in literature and the entire journalistic system are controlled by the international usurocracy, which aims at preserving intact the public's ignorance of the usurocratic system and its workings. The details of the military betrayal are known, but the intellectual betrayal has not yet been understood. Ignorance of this system and these mechanisms is not a natural phenomenon; it has been created.

Liberalism and Bolshevism are in intimate agreement in their fundamental contempt for the human personality. Stalin 'disposes' of forty truckloads of human 'material' for work on a canal. We find the liberals talking about the export of 'labour'.

Liberalism conceals its baneful economics under two pretexts: the freedom of the spoken and written word, and the freedom of the individual, protected, in theory, by trial in open court, guaranteed by the formula of *habeas corpus*. Enquire in India, or in England, to what extent these pretexts are respected. Ask any American journalist what freedom of expression is left him by the big advertisers.

Some further items of useful knowledge:

(1) We need a means of exchange and a means of saving, but it does not follow that the means must be the same in each case.

(2) The state can LEND. The fleet that was victorious at Salamis was built with money lent to the shipbuilders by the Athenian state.

(3) To simplify both government and private management, a system which can operate at the counter, whether of a government or private office, is preferable.

A NATION THAT WILL NOT GET ITSELF INTO DEBT
DRIVES THE USURERS TO FURY

THE PIVOT

All trade hinges on money. All industry hinges on money. Money is the pivot. It is the middle term. It stands midway between industry and workers. The pure economic man may not exist, but the economic factor, in the problem of living, exists. If you live on clichés and lose your respect for words, you will lose your 'ben dell' intelletto'.[1]

[1] Dante, *Inf.* III, 18. 'Homely english wd. get that down to 'USE OF YOUR WITS' but I reckon Dante meant something nearer to Mencius meaning:... sense of EQUITY.' E.P. in a radio speech, see *If This be Treason*, p. 32. *Tr.*

GOLD AND WORK

Trade brought prosperity to Liguria; usury lost it Corsica. But in losing the ability to distinguish between trade and usury one loses all sense of the historical process. There has been some vague talk in recent months about an international power, described as financial, but it would be better to call it 'usurocracy', or the rule of the big usurers combined in conspiracy. Not the gun merchants, but the traffickers in money itself have made this war; they have made wars in succession, for centuries, at their own pleasure, to create debts so that they can enjoy the interest on them, to create debts when money is cheap in order to demand repayment when money is dear.

But as long as the word 'money' is not clearly defined and as long as its definition is not known to all the peoples of the world, they will go blindly to war with each other, never knowing the reason why.

This war was no whim of Mussolini's, nor of Hitler's. This war is a chapter in the long and bloody tragedy which began with the foundation of the Bank of England in far-away 1694, with the openly declared intention of Paterson's now famous prospectus, which contains the words already quoted: 'the bank hath benefit of the interest on all moneys which it creates out of nothing'.

To understand what this means it is necessary to understand what money *is*. Money is not a simple instrument like a spade. It is made up of two elements: one which measures the prices on the market, one which bestows the power to purchase the goods. It is this twofold aspect that the usurers have taken advantage of. You know well enough that a watch contains two principles, a mainspring and a hairspring, with a train of wheels between the two. But if someone asks you what money is, you don't know what the ten-lire notes and the twenty-centesimi pieces, which you have in your pockets, are.

Until the seventh century after Christ, when an Emperor of the T'ang Dynasty issued state notes (*state* notes, not bank notes, mind you), the world was practically compelled to use as money a determined quantity of some commonly used commodity, such as salt or gold according to the degree of local sophistication. But since A.D. 654, at least, this metal has no longer been necessary for trading between civilised people. The state note of the T'ang Dynasty, of the year 856, which is still in existence, has an inscription almost identical with the one you read on your ten-lire notes.

The note measures the price, not the value; or in other words, prices are calculated in monetary units. But who supplies these notes? And, before the present war, who controlled the issue of international money? If you want to discover the causes of the present war, try and find out who controlled *international* money, and how it came under such control.

For the moment I will give you only one hint from the history of the United States of America:

> The great debt that (our friends the) capitalists (of Europe) will
> see to it is made out of the war must be used to control the volume
> of money. . . . It will not do to allow the greenback, as it is called, to
> circulate . . . for we cannot control them.[1]

This is from the Hazard Circular of the year 1862. It seems to me that
a similar situation existed in 1939. I would say that Italy, not wanting to
get herself into debt, drove the great usurers to fury. Think it over!
And think of the nature of money itself, and of the economists'
invariable irresponsibility when we ask them to define such words as
money, credit, interest, and usury.

If we are going to talk about monetary policy, monetary reform, or
a monetary revolution, we must know first of all exactly what money
is.

THE ENEMY

The enemy is ignorance (our own). At the beginning of the nineteenth
century John Adams (Pater Patriae) saw that the defects and errors of
the American government derived not so much from the corruption
of government officials as from ignorance of coin, credit, and circulation.

The situation is the same today. The subject is considered too dry
by those who do not understand its significance. For example, at
about the end of last December a banker boasted to me that at a
certain period he could remember Italian paper money was worth
more than gold. One concludes that in that particular 'golden age'
the Rothschilds were wanting to purchase gold cheap, in order to
send its price rocketing later.

In the same way the Sassoons and their accomplices profited from
the slump in silver. At one period, in fact, silver fell to 23 cents per
ounce, and was later bought by certain American idiots at 75 cents per
ounce, in order to please their masters and to '*save India*', where, with
the return to gold, Mr. Churchill, as we have remarked, forced the
peasants to pay two bushels of grain in taxes and interest which a short
time before could have been paid with only one.

To combat this rigging of the gold and silver markets we must know
what money is. Today money is a disk of metal or a slip of paper which
serves to measure prices and which confers, on its possessor, the right
to receive in exchange any goods on sale in the market up to a price
equal to the figure indicated on the disk or slip of paper, without any
formality other than the transfer of the money from hand to hand.
Thus money differs from a special coupon, such as a railway or theatre
ticket.

[1] See note 4 p. 310, above. *Tr.*

314

This universal quality confers special privileges on money which the special coupon does not possess. Of these I will speak another time.

Besides this tangible money, there is also intangible money, called 'money on account', which is used in accounting and banking transactions. This intangibility belongs to a discussion of credit rather than a treatise on money.

Our immediate need is to clarify current conceptions with regard to the so-called 'work-money', and to make clear that money cannot be a 'symbol of work' without any other qualification. It could be a *certificate of work done* on condition that the work is done within a system. The validity of the certificate would depend on the honesty of the system, and on the authority of the certifier. And the certificate would have to refer to some work useful–or at least pleasurable–to the community.

An item of work not yet completed would serve as an element of credit rather than as a basis for money properly understood. Speaking metaphorically, one might call credit the 'future tense of money'.

The elaborate assay procedure of mints has been developed to guarantee the quality and quantity of the metal in coined money; no less elaborate precautions would be necessary to guarantee the quality, quantity, and appropriateness of the work which will serve as the basis for what is to be called 'work-money' (meaning 'certificate-of-work-done-money').

The same frauds of *accounting* practised by the gombeen-men of the past in order to swindle the public under a metallic monetary system will, of course, be attempted by the gombeen-men of the future in their attacks on social justice, irrespective of the kind of monetary system that may be established. And they will be just as likely to succeed unless the nature and workings of these practices have been fully understood by the public–or at least by an alert and efficient minority.

It is only one plague-spot that the creation of work-money would eliminate. I mean that the advantages of the gold-standard system lauded by the bankers are advantages for the bankers only–for *some* bankers only, in fact. Social justice demands equal advantages for all.

The advantage of work-money mainly derives from one fact alone: work cannot be monopolised. And this is the very reason for the bitter opposition, for the uproar of protest, natural and artificial, which issues from the ranks of the gombeen-men, whether they be exotic or indigenous.

The idea that work might serve as a *measure* of prices was already current in the eighteenth century, and was clearly expounded by Benjamin Franklin.

As for monopolisability: no one is such a fool as to let someone else have the run of his own private bank account; yet nations,

315

individuals, industrialists, and businessmen have all been quite pre-pared–almost eager–to leave the control of their national currencies, and of international money, in the hands of the most stinking dregs of humanity.

Work cannot be monopolised. The function of work *as a measure* is beginning to be understood. The principle has been clearly put before the Italian public as, for example, when the *Regime Fascista* reports that the Russian worker must pay 380 working hours for an overcoat which a German worker can procure with only 80.

An article by Fernando Ritter in the *Fascio* of Milan, 7 January 1944, refers to money not in generic words and abstract terms such as 'capital' and 'finance', but in terms of grain and fertilisers.

As for the validity of primitive forms of money such as a promissory note written on leather, we have C. H. Douglas's memorable comment that it was valid enough as long as the man who promised to pay an ox *had* an ox.

In the same way the certificates of work done will be valid provided that the utility of the work done is honestly estimated by some proper authority.

It should be remembered that the soil does not require monetary compensation for the wealth extracted from it. With her wonderful efficiency nature sees to it that the circulation of material capital and its fruits is maintained, and that what comes out of the soil goes back into the soil with majestic rhythm, despite human interference.

THE TOXICOLOGY OF MONEY

Money is not a product of nature but an invention of man. And man has made it into a pernicious instrument through lack of foresight. The nations have forgotten the differences between animal, vegetable, and mineral; or rather, finance has chosen to represent all three of the natural categories by a single means of exchange, and failed to take account of the consequences. Metal is durable, but it does not reproduce itself. If you sow gold you will not be able to reap a harvest many times greater than the gold you sowed. The vegetable leads a more or less autonomous existence, but its natural reproductiveness can be increased by cultivation. The animal gives to and takes from the vegetable world: manure in exchange for food.

Fascinated by the lustre of a metal, man made it into chains. Then he invented something against nature, a false representation in the mineral world of laws which apply only to animals and vegetables.

The nineteenth century, the infamous century of usury, went even further, creating a species of monetary Black Mass. Marx and Mill, in spite of their superficial differences, agreed in endowing money with properties of a quasi-religious nature. There was even the concept of energy being 'concentrated in money', as if one were speaking of the divine quality of consecrated bread. But a half-lira piece has never created the cigarette or the piece of chocolate that used, in pre-war days, to issue from the slot-machine.

The durability of metal gives it certain advantages not possessed by potatoes or tomatoes. Anyone who has a stock of metal can keep it until conditions are most favourable for exchanging it against less durable goods. Hence the earliest forms of speculation on the part of those in possession of metals – especially those metals which are comparatively rare and do not rust.

But in addition to this potentiality for unjust manipulation inherent in metallic money by virtue of its being metallic, man has invented a document provided with coupons to serve as a more visible representation of usury. And usury is a vice, or a crime, condemned by all religions and by every ancient moralist. For example, in Cato's *De Re Rustica* we find the following piece of dialogue:

'And what do you think of usury?'

'What do *you* think of murder?'

And Shakespeare: 'Or is your gold . . . ewes and rams?'

No! it is not money that is the root of the evil. The root is greed, the lust for monopoly. 'CAPTANS ANNONAM, MALEDICTUS IN PLEBE SIT!' thundered St. Ambrose – 'Hoggers of harvest, cursed among the people!'

The opportunity of dishonest dealing was already offered to the possessors of gold at the dawn of history. But what man has made he can unmake. All that is needed is to devise a kind of money that cannot be kept waiting in the safe until such time as it may be most advantageous for its owner to bring it out. The power to swindle the people by means of coined or printed money would thus disappear almost automatically.

The idea is not new. Bishops in the Middle Ages were already issuing money that was recalled to the mint for recoining after a definite period. The German, Gesell, and the Italian, Avigliano, almost contemporaneously, devised a still more interesting means of achieving a greater economic justice. They proposed a paper-money system by which everyone was obliged, on the first of the month, to affix a stamp on every note he possessed equal to one per cent of the note's face value.

This system has given such praiseworthy results in certain restricted areas where it has been put into operation, that it is the duty of any far-sighted nation to give it serious consideration. The means is simple. It is not beyond the mental capacity of a peasant. Anyone is capable of sticking a stamp on an envelope, or on a receipted hotel bill.

From the humanitarian point of view, the advantage of this form of taxation over all others is that it can only fall on persons who have, at the moment the tax falls due, money in their pockets worth 100 times the tax itself.

Another advantage is that it doesn't interfere with trade or discourage building activity; it falls only on superfluous money, namely on the money that the holder has not been obliged to spend in the course of the preceding month.

As a remedy for inflation its advantages will be seen immediately. *Inflation* consists in a superfluity of money. Under Gesell's system each issue of notes consumes itself in 100 months–eight years and four months–thus bringing to the treasury a sum equal to the original issue.

(To make this still clearer, imagine a note left in the safe for 100 months. It will be a note on strike which, for 100 months, fails to function as a means of exchange and does not serve its purpose. Well then, the tax on this laziness will equal its face value. On the other hand, a note that passes from hand to hand can play its part in hundreds of transactions each month before it has to be taxed at all.)

The expense of numerous departments whose present function is to squeeze taxes out of the public would be reduced to a minimum and practically vanish. Office workers don't go to the office to amuse themselves. They could be given the chance of spending their time as they liked, or of raising the cultural level of their social circle, while still receiving their present salaries, without the need of diminishing the material wealth of Italy by a single bushel of grain, or by a litre of wine. Those who are not studiously inclined would have time to produce something useful.

A cardinal error of so-called liberal economics has been to forget the difference between food and stuff you can neither eat nor clothe yourself with. A republican[1] realism should call the public's attention to certain fundamental realities.

Philip Gibbs, writing of Italy for Anglo-American readers, cannot see that anything can be done with a product except sell it. The idea of *using* it does not penetrate the Bolshevik-Liberal psychology.

THE ERROR

The error has been *pecuniolatry*, or the making of money into a god. This was due to a process of denaturalisation, by which our money has been given false attributes and powers that it should never have possessed.

Gold is durable, but does not reproduce itself–not even if you put two bits of it together, one shaped like a cock, the other like a hen.

[1] At the time of writing the Fascist Social Republic was established in northern Italy, while 'liberated' Italy was still a monarchy. *Tr.*

GOLD AND WORK

It is absurd to speak of it as bearing fruit or yielding interest. Gold does not germinate like grain. To represent gold as doing this is to represent it falsely. It is a falsification. And the term *'falsificazione della moneta'* (counterfeiting or false-coining) may perhaps be derived from this.

To repeat: we need a means of exchange and a means of saving, but it does not follow that the means must be the same in each case. We are not forced to use a hammer for an awl.

The stamp affixed to the note acts as the hair-spring in the watch. Under the usurocratic system the world has suffered from alternate waves of inflation and deflation, of too much money and too little. Everyone can understand the function of a pendulum or hair-spring. A similar mental grasp should be brought to bear in the field of money.

A sound economic system will be attained when money has neither too much nor too little potential. The distinction between trade and usury has been lost. The distinction between debt and interest-bearing debt has been lost. As long ago as 1878 the idea of non-interest-bearing debt was current—even of non-interest-bearing *national* debt. The interest that you have received in the past has been largely an illusion: it has functioned on a short-term basis leaving you with a sum of money arithmetically somewhat greater than that which you had 'saved', but expressed in a currency whose units have lost a part of their value in the meantime.

Dexter Kimball collected statistics of American rail bonds issued over a period of half a century, and made interesting discoveries as to the proportion of these obligations that had simply been annulled for one reason or another. If my memory doesn't betray me, the figure was as high as seventy per cent.

That industrial concerns and plants should pay interest on their borrowed capital is just, because they serve to increase production. But the world has lost the distinction between production and corrosion. Unpardonable imbecility! for this distinction was known in the earliest years of recorded history. To represent something corrosive as something productive is a falsification—a forgery. Only fools believe in false representations. Give money its correct potential; make it last as long as things last in the material world; give it, above all, its due advantage (i.e., that of being exchangeable for any goods at any moment, provided the goods in question exist)—but do not give money, beyond this advantage, powers that correspond neither to justice nor to the nature of the goods it is issued against or used to purchase. This is the way that leads to social justice and economic sanity.

MILITARY VALOUR

There can be no military valour in a climate of intellectual cowardice.

No individual should get angry if the community refuses to accept his proposals, but it is intellectual cowardice if one is afraid to formulate one's own concept of society. This is all the more so at a time full of possibilities, at a time when the formulation of a new system of government is announced. Everyone who has some competence as an historian, and is in possession of certain historical facts, should formulate his concepts in relation to that part of the social organism in which his studies have given him authority to act as a judge.

To cultivate this competence in future generations one must begin, in the schools, with the observation of particular objects, as an introduction to the apprehension of particular facts in history. The individual does not need to know everything on an encyclopaedic scale, but everyone with any kind of public responsibility must have knowledge of the essential facts of the problem he has to deal with. It begins with the game of the objects shown to the child for an instant in the hand that is then quickly closed again.

Thought hinges on the definition of words. Aristotle and Confucius bear witness. I would conclude the compulsory studies of every university student with a comparison–even a brief one–between the two major works of Aristotle (the *Nichomachean Ethics* and the *Politics*), on the one hand, and, on the other, the Four Books of China (i.e., the three classics of the Confucian tradition–the *Ta Hsüeh* or 'Great Learning',[1] *The Unwobbling Axis*,[2] and the *Analects*–together with the *Works of Mencius*).

Extra-university education and that of the public in general could be taken care of by means of a simple ordinance relating to bookshops: every bookseller should be obliged to stock and, in the case of certain more important works, display in the window for a determined number of weeks per year certain books of capital importance.

Anyone who is familiar with the masterpieces, especially those of Aristotle, Confucius, Demosthenes, together with Davanzati's[3] 'Tacitus', will not be taken in by the nasty messes now offered to the public. As for money, it will be enough if everyone thinks for himself of the principle of the hair-spring, of the national and social effects, in other words, that would result from the mere application of a stamp in the most appropriate place. Better on the currency note than on the receipted hotel bill.

One used to speak of 'Cavalieri di San Giorgio',[4] never identifying them with due precision. Money can cause injury, and economic

---

[1] 'Studio Maturo' in the text. *Tr.*

[2] i.e., the *Chung Yung*, or 'Doctrine of the Just Mean', rendered in the text as 'L'Asse che non Vacilla'. The author's latest rendering of this title is 'The Unwobbling Pivot'. *Tr.*

[3] Bernardo Davanzati (1529–1606), celebrated translator of Tacitus. *Tr*

[4] Italian nickname for gold sovereigns. *Tr.*

knowledge is today about as crude as was medical science when it was realised that a broken leg was damaging but when the effects of germs were unknown. It is not so much the money that buys a Badoglio, but the hidden work of interest that is everywhere gnawing away, corroding. This is not the interest paid to the private individual on his bank account, but interest on money that does not exist, on a mirage of money; interest equivalent to sixty per cent and over as opposed to money that represents honest work or goods useful to mankind.

To repeat: the distinction between production and corrosion has been lost; and so has the distinction between the sharing-out of the fruits of work done in collaboration (a true and just dividend, called *partaggio* in the Middle Ages) and the corrosive interest that represents no increase in useful and material production of any sort.

It is, of course, useless to indulge in antisemitism, leaving intact the Hebraic monetary system which is a most tremendous instrument of usury.

And we would ask the Mazzinians why they never read those pages of the *Duties of Man* which deal with banks.

BULLETIN OF CIVIC DISCIPLINE

Arguments are caused by the ignorance of ALL the disputants.

Until you have clarified your own thought within yourself you cannot communicate it to others.

Until you have brought order within yourself you cannot become an element of order in the party.

The fortune of war depends on the honesty of the régime.

Sovereignty[1]

Sovereignty inheres in the power to issue money. The sovereign who does not possess this power is a mere rex sacrificulus, non regnans.

If this power be handed over to a group of irresponsible crooks and/or idiots, the country will not be well governed. In a republic, where the citizen has rights and responsibilities, the citizen who will not inspect the problem of monetary issue is simply not exercising his functions as citizen.

To be distracted by questions of administrative forms, race hatreds, man hunts, or socialisation of everything but the national debt, is merely swallowing sucker-bait.

[1] *The European* 1, March 1953.

Del Mar[1]

The imbecility of striking for higher wages while leaving the control of the purchasing power of those wages in the hands of extortioners is not monopolised by the labour Parties. Del Mar struggled in vain to inculcate the notion that a coin is not a unit but the fraction of a larger unit, still called the 'volume of money'.

[1] *Agenda* 1, January 1959.

Feasible Justice[1]

A sane and decent tax system should, and if you grant the possibility of the electors having even a small particle of good sense, could have the following characteristics.

1. Aiming at feasible justice it could, as Mencius said it should, consist in a share of the available products.[2] Mencius used very considerable lucidity in demanding a share, not a fixed charge, which latter might not be available in a poor farm year, or produce in a rich year a reserve against famine or future contingency.

2. The system should aim at minimum cost of collection. Mr. Jefferson had some pithy remarks on the price of tobacco in France, in relation to what the producer got, what the government got as profit, and the cost of gouging out of consumers.

3. The convenience of the collection should be considered, though this might be considered as component in the cost of same.

4. It should encourage production, not sabotage it. I have a letter of decades back suggesting that I specialise in examining taxation as highway robbery. The *Secolo* of Genoa recently managed to print a line referring to the current tax system as 'un furto organizzato che punisce ogni atto produttivo'. The mills grind slowly. It takes time to get simple ideas past a copy desk.

5. It should not create crime, i.e. it should not penalize simple and often useful activities, by making them crimes by statute. The bootlegger in the A.H. of the army understood perfectly well that his profession could only function when there was a tax on, or prohibition of booze (1959).

---

[1] *Impact* (1960).
[2] Taxes for public utility,
    a share of a product', (Canto XCIX). Ed.

Gists[1]

BOURGEOIS

What the working man becomes the moment he has the least opportunity.

SPENDING

The value of a nation's money depends, in the long run, on what the nation (which includes its inhabitants) spends its money FOR.

A SLAVE

A slave is one who waits for someone else to free him.

THIERS

Thiers borrowed from the bank at 3 per cent when they were charging individuals 5 or 6 per cent. He then got money for 1 per cent. When he proposed to follow Andrew Jackson, the whole set of 'em, Orleanists, Bourbons, Bonapartists ganged up against him. Hence the lack of interest in Thiers on the part of professorial historians.

CRITICS

To be judged far more by their selections than by their palaver.

CERTAIN CIRCLES

Any proposal for reduction of government personnel causes a curious uneasiness in certain circles.

BOURGEOIS

A term of abuse applied by young writers to writers seven years older than themselves when the latter can afford seven francs more per day for hotel bills.

NATIONAL WELL BEING

No country can suppress truth and live well.

[1] *Impact*, 1960.

324

GISTS

POISON

It is not arsenic in bottle and labelled that is dangerous, but arsenic in good soup.

LAW

The right aim of law is to prevent coercion, either by force or by fraud.

UTOPIA

Where every man has the right to be born free of debt and to be judged, in case of disagreement, by a jury capable of understanding the nature and implications of the charges against him.

ONE AT A TIME

Every man has the right to have his ideas examined one at a time.

USURY

Usury, a charge for the use of purchasing power, levied without regard to production, sometimes without regard even to the possibilities of production.

SOVEREIGNTY

Sovereignty inheres in the power to issue money, or to distribute the power to buy (credit or money) whether you have the right to do so or not.

CIVILISATION

Civilisation depends on local control of purchasing power needed for local purposes.

PART SEVEN
The Art of Poetry

PART SEVEN

The Wisdom of Poetry[1]

A book which was causing some clatter about a year ago, and which has been mercifully forgotten, a book displaying considerable vigorous, inaccurate thought, fathomless ignorance, and no taste whatever, claimed, among other things less probable, that it presented the first 'scientific and satisfactory definition of poetry'. The definition ran as follows: 'Poetry is the expression of insensuous thought in sensuous terms by means of artistic trope, and the dignification of thought by analogically articulated imagery.' The word 'artistic' remains undefined and we have, therefore, one unknown thing defined in terms of another unknown thing of similar nature; a mode of definition neither 'scientific' nor 'satisfactory'–even though one should agree with the dogma of trope.

There follows this 'more extended definition': 'Poetry is the expression of imaginative thought by means only of the essentials to thought, conserving energy for thought perception–to which end all animate, inanimate and intangible things may assume the properties and attributes of tangible, living, thinking and speaking things, possessing the power of becoming what they seem, or of transfiguration into what they suggest.'

This is applicable in part to the equations of analytics, *in toto* to painting, sculpture and certain other arts; for it is nonsense to consider words as the only 'essentials to thought'; some people think in terms of objects themselves, some in pictures, diagrams, or in musical sounds, and perception by symbolic vision is swifter and more complex than that by ratiocination.

Throughout the volume our scientist shows himself incapable of distinguishing between poetry and a sort of florid rhetorical bombast, but the definitions quoted do not suffice to prove his ignorance of his subject. They betray rather his confused mode of thought and his nescience of the very nature of definition. I shall assume that any definition to be 'scientific' or 'satisfactory' should have at least four parts; it should define with regard to: purpose or function; to relation; to substance; to properties.

Poetry, as regards its function or purpose, has the common purpose

[1] *Forum*, New York, April 1912.

of the arts, which purpose Dante most clearly indicates in the line
where he speaks of:

> 'That melody which most doth draw
> The soul unto itself.'

Borrowing a terminology from Spinoza, we might say: The function
of an art is to free the intellect from the tyranny of the affects, or,
leaning on terms, neither technical nor metaphysical: the function
of an art is to strengthen the perceptive faculties and free them from
encumbrance, such encumbrances, for instance, as set moods, set
ideas, conventions; from the results of experience which is common
but unnecessary, experience induced by the stupidity of the experi-
encer and not by inevitable laws of nature. Thus Greek sculpture
freed men's minds from the habit of considering the human body
merely with regard to its imperfections. The Japanese grotesque frees
the mind from the conception of things merely as they *have been* seen.
With the art of Beardsley we enter the realm of pure intellect; the
beauty of the work is wholly independent of the appearance of the
things portrayed. With Rembrandt we are brought to consider the
exact nature of things seen, to consider the individual face, not the
conventional or type face which we may have learned to expect on
canvas.

Poetry is identical with the other arts in this main purpose, that
is, of liberation; it differs from them in its media, to wit, words
as distinct from pigment, pure sound, clay and the like. It shares
its media with music in so far as words are composed of inarticulate
sounds.

Our scientist reaching toward a truth speaks of 'the essentials to
thought'; these are not poetry, but a constituent substance of poetry.

The Art of Poetry consists in combining these 'essential to thought',
these dynamic particles, *si licet*, this radium, with that melody of
words which shall most draw the emotions of the hearer toward
accord with their import, and with that 'form' which shall most
delight the intellect.

By 'melody' I mean variation of sound quality, mingling with a
variation of stress. By 'form' I mean the arrangement of the verse [*sic*],
into ballades, canzoni, and the like symmetrical forms, or into blank
verse or into free verse, where presumably, the nature of the thing
expressed or of the person supposed to be expressing it, is antagonistic
to external symmetry. Form may delight by its symmetry or by its
aptness.

The methods of this fusing, tempering and shaping concern the
artist; the results alone are of import to the public.

Poets in former ages were of certain uses to the community; i.e., as historians, genealogists, religious functionaries. In Provence the *gai savoir* was both theatre and opera. The troubadour and jongleur were author, dramatist, composer, actor and popular tenor. In Tuscany the canzone and the sonnet held somewhat the place of the essay and the short story. Elizabethan drama appeared at a time when it was a society fad to speak beautifully. Has the poet, apart from these obsolete and accidental uses, any permanent function in society? I attempt the following scientific answers:

Thought is perhaps important to the race, and language, the medium of thought's preservation, is constantly wearing out. It has been the function of poets to new-mint the speech, to supply the vigorous terms for prose. Thus Tacitus is full of Vergilian half lines; and poets may be 'kept on' as conservators of the public speech, or prose, perhaps, becoming more and more an art, may become, or may have become already, self-sustaining.

As the poet was, in ages of faith, the founder and emendor of all religions, so, in ages of doubt, is he the final agnostic; that which the philosopher presents as truth, the poet presents as that which appears as truth to a certain sort of mind under certain conditions.

'To thine own self be true. . . .' were nothing were it not spoken by Polonius, who has never called his soul his own.

The poet is consistently agnostic in this; that he does not postulate his ignorance as a positive thing. Thus his observations rest as the enduring data of philosophy. He grinds an axe for no dogma. Now that mechanical science has realised his ancient dreams of flight and sejunct communication, he is the advance guard of the psychologist on the watch for new emotions, new vibrations sensible to faculties as yet ill understood. As Dante writes of the sunlight coming through the clouds from a hidden source and illuminating part of a field, long before the painters had depicted such effects of light and shade, so are later watchers on the alert for colour perceptions of a subtler sort, neither affirming them to be 'astral' or 'spiritual' nor denying the formulae of theosophy. The traditional methods are not antiquated, nor are poets necessarily the atavisms which they seem. Thus poets may be retained as friends of this religion of doubt, but the poet's true and lasting relation to literature and life is that of the abstract mathematician to science and life. As the little world of abstract mathematicians is set a-quiver by some young Frenchman's deductions on the functions of imaginary values—worthless to applied science of the day—so is the smaller world of serious poets set a-quiver by some new subtlety of cadence. Why?

A certain man named Plarr and another man whose name I have forgotten, some years since, developed the functions of a certain obscure sort of equation, for no cause save their own pleasure in the work. The applied science of their day had no use for the deductions, a few sheets of paper covered with arbitrary symbols—without which we should have no wireless telegraph.

What the analytical geometer does for space and form, the poet does for the states of consciousness. Let us therefore consider the nature of the formulae of analytics.

By the signs $a^2+b^2 = c^2$, I imply the circle. By $(a-r)^2 + (b-r)^2 = (c-r)^2$, I imply the circle and its mode of birth. I am led from the consideration of the particular circles formed by my ink-well and my table-rim, to the contemplation of the circle absolute, its law; the circle free in all space, unbounded, loosed from the accidents of time and place. Is the formula nothing, or is it cabala and the sign of unintelligible magic? The engineer, understanding and translating to the many, builds for the uninitiated bridges and devices. He speaks their language. For the initiated the signs are a door into eternity and into the boundless ether.

As the abstract mathematician is to science so is the poet to the world's consciousness. Neither has direct contact with the many, neither of them is superhuman or arrives at his utility through occult and inexplicable ways. Both are scientifically demonstrable.

The Approach to Paris

VILDRAC[1]

It is a silly thing to give people labels, and I am, I dare say, no more
fortunate in conferring the title of Unanimist on M. Vildrac than
was Georges Duhamel in calling his chapters 'Jules Romains et les
dieux', and 'Charles Vildrac et les hommes'. No one who has read
'Un Etre en Marche' would say that M. Romains is less interested in
humanity than is his friend. I do not know whether M. Vildrac sub-
scribes to the unanimist 'religion'. Or perhaps no cult has ever more
than one member. Vildrac's 'Gloire' might, at first sight, seem a sort
of counterblast to the 'Ode à la foule qui est ici'. M. Romains flows
into his crowd, or at least he would have us believe so. The subject of
M. Vildrac's poem is of the Nietzschean, pre-unanimist type. He tries
to impress his personality on the crowd and is disillusioned.

The poems are in contrast, not in contradiction, and they make
interesting comparison.

The 'Ode to the crowd here present' begins roughly as follows:

> O crowd, you are here in the hollow of the theatre
> Docile to the walls, moulding your flesh to the shell,
> And your black ranks go from me as a reflux.
> You exist.
> This light where I am, is yours.

> The city is outside, quite near, but you no longer hear it;
> In vain will she make large the rumour of her streets
> To beat against your walls and to wish your death;
> You will not hear it, you will be full
> Of your own peculiar silence and of my voice.

He feels the warmth of the crowd, he feels the focus of eyes.

> Je ne vois pas si sa prunelle est noire ou bleue;
> Mais je sens qu'il me touche;

He becomes the 'crater' or vortex.

> Ecoute; Little by little the voice issues from my flesh—
> And seeks you—and trembles—and you tremble.

[1] From 'The Approach to Paris' IV,
The New Age, 25 September 1913.

The voice is within the crowd 'invasion and victory' the crowd must think his words:

> Ils pénètrent en rangs dans les tetês penchées,
> Ils s'installent brutalement, ils sont les maîtres;
> Ils poussent, ils bousculent, ils jettent dehors
> L'âme qui s'y logeait comme une vieille en pleurs.

> All the meditations of these people here,
> The pain they have carried for years,
> The sorrow born yesterday, still increasing, and the grief
> That they do not speak of, of which they will not speak.
> That sorrow that gives them tears to drink in the evening,
> And even that desire which dries their lips,
> Is over. Is needless. I do not will it. I drive it out.
> Crowd, your whole soul is upright in my flesh.
> A force of steel, whereof I hold the two ends
> Pierces your mass, and bends it.

> Ta forme est moi. Tes gradins et tes galeries,
> C'est moi qui les empoigne ensemble et qui les plie,
> Comme un paquet de souples joncs, sur mon genou.

> Do not defend yourself crowd-woman,

> Soon you will die, beneath the feet of your hours,
> Men, unbound, will flow away through the doors,
> The nails of darkness will tear you apart.
> What of it.
> You are mine before death.
> As for the bodies here,
>   let the city take them!
> They will keep upon their foreheads the ashen cross,
> Your sign, god that you are for the moment.

Such, in rough outline, is the 'Ode à la foule qui est ici'. I have naturally lost all semblance of the original sweep and of the original sound, partly because the translation rights are reserved and there is not time to write for permission to break them, partly because I do not wish to interpose a pretentious translation between the reader and the easily obtainable original.

M. Vildrac's poem begins almost as if in antistrophe.

GLOIRE

He had been able to gain to him
Many men together
With a cry that they all loved to hear
With a high deed whereof they spoke together.

There was a scrap of the world
Where they knew his life
His acts and his face.

He stood up before the crowd
And knew the drunkenness
Of feeling them submissive to his speech
As wheat-blades are to the wind.

        *   *   *

And his happiness was to believe
That, when he left the crowd,
Each one of these men loved him
And that his presence lasted
Innumerable and strong among them
As, in brands dispersed,
The gift and mark of the fire.

Or un jour il en suivit un
Qui retournait s'chez soi, tout seul;
Et il vit son regard s'éteindre
Dès qu'il fut un peu loin des autres.

Then he meets a man who remembers him, 'mais n'avait rien gardé
de lui dans son esprit ni dans son coeur', and then he sees a crowd
under the influence of a charlatan.

Then he knew that he had conquered too much
And too little.

That to make a crowd-soul
Each man lends for an instant
But the surface of his own.

He had reigned over a people—
As a reflection on water;
As a flame of alcohol
Which takes no grip,
Which burns what it strokes
Without warming.

Then he begins to take men one at a time.

En demeurant et devisant avec chacun
Quand ils étaient bien eux, quand ils étaient bien seuls.

However far these compositions may be from 'poetry' it cannot be denied that they contain poetical lines, and the latter poem is convenient to quote as it gives us, I think, a fair clue to M. Vildrac's attitude.

M. Vildrac is, I dare say, over prone to imaginative reason, still it is not my intention to discuss the shortcomings of contemporary French authors, but to tell what virtues and what matters of interest I have found in their works. If M. Vildrac were merely a writer with a philosophy of life slightly different from that of M. Romains I would not trouble to read him, but M. Vildrac is an artist. He is at his best, I think, in short narrative sketches such as 'Visite' and 'Une Auberge' (both in 'Livre d'Amour', published by E. Figuière, 7, Rue Corneille). 'Visite' has been often quoted and, I believe, translated, but as I have not the translation by me, I give a rough prose version of my own, printing, where convenient, line for line of the original.

VIS TE

He was seated before his table,
His dreams indolently marked out
Within the domain of his lamp
And he heard against his window
The fragile attacks of the snow.

And suddenly he thought
Of a man whom he knew
And whom he had not seen for a long time.
And he felt an oppression in his throat,
Part sadness and part chagrin.

He knew that this man was without pride
Either in heart or in word
And that he was without charm
Living like the trees
Isolated, on a barren plain;

He knew that for months
He had been promising this man
To visit him,
And that the other
Had thanked him gently for each one of these promises
And had pretended to believe it.

He goes out through the snow to pay the long-deferred visit. After the first words, when he had come into the light and sat down, between this man and his companion, both surprised and 'empressés' –however you want to translate it. Eager.

Il s'aperçut qu'on lui ménageait.

(Another untranslatable word, I suppose we might say, 'He felt that
they were beating about the bush.')

> These silences full of questions
> Like the white that one leaves
> In a design of writing—
> He noted upon their faces
> A furtive inquietude
> He thought, and then understood it.
>
> These people did not believe
> That he had come without forethought
> So late, from such distance, through the snow
> Merely for his pleasure and theirs,
> Merely to keep his promise:
> And both of them were waiting
> Until he should disclose, of a sudden,
> The real cause of his visit.
> They were anxious to know
> What fortune he brought
> Or what service he wished of them.
>
> He wished to speak all at once.
>
> He wished to undeceive them but
>> He was thus separated from them
>> Until the long delayed moment
>> When he rose to go.

Then there was a 'detente' (literally a discharge as of a pistol).

> Then they ventured to understand
> He had come for them!
> Someone had wanted to see them,
> Just that, to see them, to be in their house,
> To talk with them and to listen,
> And this desire had been
> Stranger than the cold and than the snow!
> In short, someone had come.
>
> Their eyes were gay now,
> And tender
> They spoke very quickly
> And both together
> Trying to keep him.
> They stood up before him
> Betraying a childish need
> Of skipping and clapping their hands . . .

He promised to come again.
But before reaching the door
He set clearly in his memory
The place that bordered their lives,
He looked carefully at each object
Then at the man and woman also,
Such fear did he have at the bottom of his heart
That he would never come back.

I have been told that this is sentiment and therefore damned. I am
not concerned with that argument. I dare say the poem makes a poor
showing in this rough and hurried translation; the point is that
M. Vildrac has told a short story in verse with about one fifth of the
words that a good writer of short stories would have needed for the
narrative. He has conveyed his atmosphere, and his people, and the
event. He has brought narrative verse into competition with narrative
prose without giving us long stanzas of bombast.

You may make whatever objection you like to genre painting. My
only question is: would it be possible to improve on M. Vildrac's
treatment of the given situation?

M. Vildrac had given us a more serious story in 'Une Auberge', I
think he has written two lines too many; I mean the last two lines of
the poem; but he has achieved here some of his finest effects, in such
lines as:

Mais comme il avait l'air cependant d'être des nôtres!

The poem begins:

C'est une auberge qu'il y a
Au carrefour des Chétives-Maisons,
Dans le pays où il fait toujours froid.

There are three houses there:

Et la troisième est cette auberge au coeur si triste
. . .
C'est seulement parce qu'on a soif qu'on entre y boire,
. . .
Et l'on n'est pas forcé d'y raconter son histoire.

A work-wrecked man drifts in, leans heavily on the table.

Il mange lentement son pain
Parce que ses dents sont usées,

Quand il a fini
Il hésite, puis timide
Va s'asseoir un peu
A côté du feu.

338

He sits there all in a heap, until a child comes in

> Et voilà qu'elle approche tout doucement
> Et vient appuyer sur la main de l'homme
> La chair enfantine de sa bouche;
> Et puis lève vers lui ses yeux pleins d'eau
> Et lui tend de tout son frêle corps
> Une pauvre petite fleur d'hiver qu'elle a.
>
> Et voilà que l'homme sanglote . . .

Then the drab woman at the counter begins her narrative:

> Il est venu un homme ici qui n'était pas des nôtres.
> Il n'était pas vieux comme nous, de misère et de peine,
> Il était comme sont sans doute les fils des reines.
> Mais comme il avait l'air cependant d'être des notres!
>
> Et quand il s'est levé, a fallu que je pleure
> Tellement il ressemblait à celui de mes seize ans . . .
>
> Il ouvrait déjà la porte
> Pour retourner dans le vent
> Mais quand il apprit pourquoi
> Me venaient des larmes.
> Il la renferma, la porte.
>
> . . . malgré sa jeunesse et malgré mon lit si froid,
> Malgré mes seins vidés et mes épaules si creuses,

To some these very simple tales of M. Vildrac will mean a great deal, and to others they will mean very little. If a person of this latter sort dislikes the choice of subject he may do worse than to consider the method of narration. Mr. D. H. Lawrence can do, I dare say, as well, but M. Vildrac's stories are different; they are, I think, quite his own.

As to the method of verse, if the reader's ear be so constituted that he derives no satisfaction from the sound of

> Et il vit son regard s'éteindre
> Dès qu'il fut un peu loin des autres.

One cannot teach him by theory to derive satisfaction from this passage, or from the assonance of ensemble and entendre, drawn at the end of their lines, or from half a hundred finer and less obvious matters of sound.

I do not think that the public is under any moral obligation to take interest in such affairs.

> If the gentle reader wishes to
> Crush the something drops of pleasure
> From the something grapes of pain.

It is certainly no concern of mine. I, personally, happen to be tired of verses which are left full of blank spaces for interchangeable adjectives. In the more or less related systems of versification which have been adopted by Romains, Chennevière, Vildrac, Duhamel, and their friends, I do not find such an excessive allowance of blank spaces, and this seems to me a healthy tendency.

If the gentle reader still enjoys reading or writing such 'amorous twins' as mountain and fountain, mother and brother, him and forests dim, God forbid that I should interfere with *his* delights.

If a man wants his jokes in 'Punch' and his rhymes where he expects them it is no affair of mine. God forbid that I should exhort any man to satisfactions of the senses finer than those for which nature has designed him.

I am aware that there are resolutions of sound less obvious than rhyme. It requires more pains and intelligence both to make and to hear them. To demand rhyme is almost like saying that only one note out of ten need be in melody, it is not quite the same. No one would deny that the final sound of the line is important. No intelligent person would deny that all the accented sounds are important. I cannot bring myself to believe that even the unstressed syllables should be wholly neglected.

I cannot believe that one can test the musical qualities of a passage of verse merely by counting the number of syllables, or even of stressed syllables, in each line, and by thereafter examining the terminal sounds.

God, or nature, or the Unanim, or whoever or whatever is responsible or irresponsible for the existence of the race has given to some men a sense of absolute pitch, and to some a sense of rhythms, and to some a sense of verbal consonance, and some are colour-blind, and some are tone-deaf, and some are almost void of intelligence, hence we are lead to believe that it would be foolish to expect to move the hearts of all men simultaneously either by perfection of musical sounds, either articulate or inarticulate, or by an arrangement of colours or by a sane and sober exposition in wholly logical prose.

Those who are interested in ritual and in the history of invocation may have been interested in M. De Gourmont's litanies, those who are interested in a certain purging of the poetic idiom may be interested in the work of such men as Vildrac and P. J. Jouve.

CORBIERE[1]

But all France is not Paris, and if anything were needed to refute these generalities it could be found in the work of Corbière. Tristan Corbière is dead, but his work is scarcely known in England, and for all his having been a contemporary of Verlaine his work can hardly be said to have been 'published' until the 'nineties. He has left only one book and this alone would set him apart from 'the French poets' and place him in that very narrow category which contains Villon and Rimbaud. He was in fact Breton and had about as much affiliation with his Parisian contemporaries as had J. M. Synge with the London aesthetes.

Because his versification is more English than French, because he was apparently careless of all versification, I think that his one volume will lie half open on the tables of all those who open it once. They said he was careless of style, etcetera! He was as careless of style as a man of swift mordant speech can afford to be. For the quintessence of style is precisely that it should be swift and mordant. It is precisely that a man should not speak at all until he has something (it matters very little what) to say.

> Je voudrais être alors chien de fille publique
> Lécher un peu d'amour qui ne soit pas payé;

Or earlier in the same poem:

> Ah si j'étais un peu compris! Si par pitié
> Une femme pouvait me sourire à moitié,
> Je lui dirais: oh viens, ange qui me consoles!...
> ... Et je la conduirais à l'hospice des folles.

The dots are in the original.

> Damne-toi, pure idole! et ris! et chante! et pleure,
> Amante! et meurs d'amour!... à nos moments perdus.

Or again by way of encouragement.

> Couronne tes genoux!...
>   Mais ... nous avons la police,
> Et quelque chose en nous d'eunuque et de recors.

These scraps are from his Parisian gasconadings, but even in Paris he looked the thing in the eye and was no more minded to be a 'stand-pat-er' or to sooth the world or the world-of-letters with flattery than he would have been to deceive himself about the state of the Channel

[1] From 'The Approach to Paris', V,
The New Age, 2 October 1913.

off his native village, the fishing town where his personal appearance had earned him the nickname 'an Ankou' (the corpse).

He 'stands', as the phrase is, by his songs of the Briton coast, and the proper introduction to him is 'La Rapsode Foraine', or the song in it, to St. Anne.

Mère taillée à coups de hache.

Bâton des aveugles! Béquille
Des vieilles! Bras des nouveau-nés!
Mère de madame ta fille!
Parente des abandonnés!

Des croix profondes sont tes rides,
Tes cheveux sont blancs comme fils . . .

Fais venir et conserve en joie
Ceux à naitre et ceux qui sont nés.
Et verse, sans que Dieu te voie,
L'eau de tes yeux sur les damnés!

One garbles it so in quotation and it is much too long to give in full. The note of the sea is in the sound of his

AU VIEUX ROSCOFF
Trou de filibustiers, vieux nid
A corsaire! . . .

Dors: tu peux fermer ton Oeil borgne
Ouvert sur le large, et qui lorgne
Les Anglais, depuis trois cent ans. . . .

One has got a long way from that mélange of satin and talcum powder which we are apt to believe to be French verse. And Corbière himself is most capable of defining those qualities of the national literature which least attract one.

Ne m'offrez pas un trône!
A moi tout seul je fris,
Drole, en ma sauce jaune
De *chic* et de mepris.

Que les bottes vernies
Pleuvent du paradis. . . .

It was he who called Hugo 'Garde national épique' and Lamartine

Inventeur de la *larme écrite*,
Lacrymatoire d'abonnés!

He is more real than the 'realists' because he still recognises that force of romance which is a quite real and apparently ineradicable part of our life, he preceded and thereby escaped that spirit or that school which was to sentimentalise over ugliness with a more silly sentimentality than the early romanticists had shown toward 'the beauties of nature'.

In short, I go on reading him even though I have finished my article.

I feel at present as if I had found another poet to put on the little rack with Villon and Heine, with the poets whom one actually reads. This is, I dare say, an enthusiasm of the moment, a thing of no critical value. I tell it for what it is worth.

Affirmations[1]

AS FOR IMAGISME

The term 'Imagisme' has given rise to a certain amount of discussion. It has been taken by some to mean Hellenism; by others the word is used most carelessly, to designate any sort of poem in *vers libre*. Having omitted to copyright the word at its birth I cannot prevent its misuse. I can only say what I meant by the word when I made it. Moreover, I cannot guarantee that my thoughts about it will remain absolutely stationary. I spend the greater part of my time meditating the arts, and I should find this very dull if it were not possible for me occasionally to solve some corner of the mystery, or, at least to formulate more clearly my own thoughts as to the nature of some mystery or equation.

In the second article of this series I pointed out that energy creates pattern. I gave examples. I would say further that emotional force gives the image. By this I do not mean that it gives an 'explanatory metaphor'; though it might be hard to draw an exact border line between the two. We have left false metaphor, ornamental metaphor to the rhetorician. That lies outside this discussion.

Intense emotion causes pattern to arise in the mind–if the mind is strong enough. Perhaps I should say, not pattern, but pattern-units, or units of design. (I do not say that intense emotion is the sole possible cause of such units. I say simply that they can result from it. They may also result from other sorts of energy.) I am using this term 'pattern-unit', because I want to get away from the confusion between 'pattern' and 'applied decoration'. By applied decoration I mean something like the 'wall of Troy pattern'. The invention was merely the first curley-cue, or the first pair of them. The rest is repetition, is copying.

By pattern-unit or vorticist picture I mean the single jet. The difference between the pattern-unit and the picture is one of complexity. The pattern-unit is so simple that one can bear having it repeated several or many times. When it becomes so complex that repetition would be useless, then it is a picture, an 'arrangement of forms'.

Not only does emotion create the 'pattern-unit' and the 'arrangement of forms', it creates also the Image. The Image can be of two sorts. It can arise within the mind. It is then 'subjective'. External

[1] *The New Age*, 28 January 1915.

causes play upon the mind, perhaps; if so, they are drawn into the mind, fused, transmitted, and emerge in an Image unlike themselves. Secondly, the Image can be objective. Emotion seizing up some external scene or action carries it intact to the mind; and that vortex purges it of all save the essential or dominant or dramatic qualities, and it emerges like the external original.

In either case the Image is more than an idea. It is a vortex or cluster of fused ideas and is endowed with energy. If it does not fulfil these specifications, it is not what I mean by an Image. It may be a sketch, a vignette, a criticism, an epigram or anything else you like. It may be impressionism, it may even be very good prose. By 'direct treatment', one means simply that having got the Image one refrains from hanging it with festoons.

From the Image to Imagisme: Our second contention was that poetry to be good poetry should be at least as well written as good prose. This statement would seem almost too self-evident to need any defence whatsoever. Obviously, if a man has anything to say, the interest will depend on what he has to say, and not on a faculty for saying 'exiguous' when he means 'narrow', or for putting his words hindside before. Even if his thought be very slight it will not gain by being swathed in sham lace.

Thirdly, one believes that emotion is an organiser of form, not merely of visible forms and colours, but also of audible forms. This basis of music is so familiar that it would seem to need no support. Poetry is a composition or an 'organisation' of words set to 'music'. By 'music' here we can scarcely mean much more than rhythm and timbre. The rhythm form is false unless it belong to the particular creative emotion or energy which it purports to represent. Obviously one does not discard 'regular metres' because they are a 'difficulty'.

Any ass can say:

'John Jones stood on the floor. He saw the ceiling' or decasyllabicly,
'John Jones who rang the bell at number eight.'

There is no form of platitude which cannot be turned into iambic pentameter without labour. It is not difficult, if one have learned to count up to ten, to begin a new line on each eleventh syllable or to whack each alternate syllable with an ictus.

Emotion also creates patterns of timbre. But one 'discards rhyme', not because one is incapable of rhyming neat, fleet, sweet, meet, treat, eat, feet, but because there are certain emotions or energies which are not to be represented by the over-familiar devices or patterns; just as there are certain 'arrangements of form' that cannot be worked into dados.

Granted, of course, that there is great freedom in pentameter and that there are a great number of regular and beautifully regular metres fit for a number of things, and quite capable of expressing a wide range of energies or emotions.

The discovery that bad *vers libre* can be quite as bad as any other sort of bad verse is by no means modern. Over eleven centuries ago Rihaku (Li Po) complained that imitators of Kutsugen (Ch'u Yuan) couldn't get any underlying rhythm into their *vers libre*, that they got 'bubbles not waves'.

Yo ba geki tai ha Kai riu to mu giu.

'Yoyu and Shojo stirred up decayed (enervated) waves. Open current flows about in bubbles, does not move in wave lengths.' If a man has no emotional energy, no impulse, it is of course much easier to make something which looks like 'verse' by reason of having a given number of syllables, or even of accents, per line, than for him to invent a music or rhythm-structure. Hence the prevalence of 'regular' metric. Hence also bad *vers libre*. The only advantage of bad *vers libre* is that it is, possibly, more easy to see how bad it is . . . but even this advantage is doubtful.

By bad verse, whether 'regular' or 'free', I mean verse which pretends to some emotion which did not assist at its parturition. I mean also verse made by those who have not sufficient skill to make the words move in rhythm of the creative emotion. Where the voltage is so high that it fuses the machinery, one has merely the 'emotional man' not the artist. The best artist is the man whose machinery can stand the highest voltage. The better the machinery, the more precise, the stronger, the more exact will be the record of the voltage and of the various currents which have passed through it.

These are bad expressions if they lead you to think of the artist as wholly passive, as a mere receiver of impressions. The good artist is perhaps a good seismograph, but the difference between man and a machine is that man can in some degree 'start his machinery going'. He can, within limits, not only record but create. At least he can move as a force; he can produce 'order-giving vibrations'; by which one may mean merely, he can departmentalise such part of the life-force as flows through him.

To recapitulate, then, the vorticist position; or at least my position at the moment is this:

Energy, or emotion, expresses itself in form. Energy, whose primary manifestation is in pure form, i.e., form as distinct from likeness or association can only be expressed in painting or sculpture. Its expression can vary from a 'wall of Troy pattern' to Wyndham Lewis's 'Timon of Athens', or a Wadsworth woodblock. Energy expressing itself in pure sound, i.e., sound as distinct from articulate speech, can only be expressed in music. When an energy or emotion 'presents an image', this may find adequate expression in words. It is very probably a waste of energy to express it in any more tangible medium. The verbal expression of the image may be reinforced by a suitable or cognate rhythm-form and by timbre-form. By rhythm-form and timbre-form I do not mean something which must of necessity have a 'repeat' in it. It is certain that a too obvious 'repeat' may be detrimental.

The test of invention lies in the primary figment, that is to say, in that part of any art which is peculiarly of that art as distinct from 'the other arts'. The vorticist maintains that the 'organising' or creative-inventive faculty is the thing that matters; and that the artist having this faculty is a being infinitely separate from the other type of artist who merely goes on weaving arabesques out of other men's 'units of form'.

Superficial capability needs no invention whatsoever, but a great energy has, of necessity, its many attendant inventions.

Beddoes and Chronology[1]

Keats, born in 1795, died in 1821; Shelley, three years his senior, died the year after; Byron's life extended from 1788 to 1824. Beddoes is said to have begun 'Death's Jest Book, or the Fool's Tragedy', at Oxford in 1825. This and the rest of Beddoes' writings were almost inaccessible to the public until 1890, when Edmund Gosse edited Beddoes' 'Poetical Works'. For which edition, however many friendly and unfriendly differences one may have with Mr. Gosse, one must give due thanks and credit.

Out of Beddoes' life, work and 'literary position' there arise at least two riddles of interest. One might and does ask why so good a poet should have remained so long in obscurity; was it due to a quality of his style; or should a poet choose his birth date with great care: should a young poet begin just after the death of three men of recognised genius, and more or less great popularity? One might say with Keats, Byron and Shelley all dead there was surely plenty of room for a new poet. Or one might say, 'No, the public absorbed in the three romantic deaths of three fascinating young men, and giving to their poetry that added attention which demise ever demands, would certainly not pay attention to any new writer. Besides Wordsworth was still alive.'

Perhaps 'alive' is scarcely the word one would apply to the 'luminary' of the Lake District. Wordsworth drew his first orderly and deliberate breath in 1770, and continued the alternate processes of inhalation and exhalation until 1850. Coleridge and Lamb survived until 1834. Landor lived from 1775 until 1864. But he was too unpopular to have obscured any young man's chance with the public. Blake died in 1827. So on the whole we must say that Beddoes' 'position' can not be very well explained by chronology. People say, 'There was a time when there *was only* Beddoes.' But it seems difficult to place this exact period. Beddoes was born in 1803, and Tennyson six years later, Browning in 1812; if Browning waited for recognition, it is equally certain that Tennyson did not wait very long. So that chronologically Beddoes had neither especially good nor bad luck, and bare dates will not explain him one way or the other.

He is perhaps more 'Elizabethan' than any so modern poet, that is, if by being 'Elizabethan' we mean using an extensive and Elizabethan vocabulary full of odd and spectacular phrases: very often quite fine ones. Lamb had rediscovered old plays, Keats and Shelley had imitated

[1] *The Future*, September 1913.

348

the period. There was nothing unusual or original in picking this sort of speech as a model. But Beddoes did the thing very well:

> '*Athulf*: A fair and bright assembly: never strode
> Old arched Grussau over such a tide
> Of helmed chivalry, as when to-day
> Our tourney swept, leaping billow-like,
> Its palace-banked streets. Knights shut in steel,
> Whose shields, like water, glassed the soul-eyed maidens,
> That softly did attend their armed tread,
> Flower-cinctured on the temples, whence gushed down
> A full libation of star-numbered tresses,
> Hallowing the neck unto love's silent kiss,
> Veiling its innocent white: and then came squires,
> And those who bore war's silken tapestries,
> And chequered heralds: 'twas a human river,
> Brimful and beating as if the great god,
> Who lay beneath it, would arise. So sways
> Time's sea, which Age snows into and makes deep,
> When, from the rocky side of the dim future,
> Leaps into it a mighty destiny,
> Whose being to endow great souls have been
> Centuries hoarded, and the world meanwhile
> Sate like a beggar upon Heaven's threshold,
> Muttering its wrongs.'

It is quite possible to carp at this passage. Its opening is possibly too 'descriptive'. Current taste may call the end rhetoric. Still it is magnificent rhetoric, and it is only of recent years that people have taken exception to this paraphernalia of Romanticism. Certainly neither Hugo nor Swinburne would have thought this a fault of our author. If he is 'tapestry rather than painting', surely the pre-Raphaelites loaded with their own mediaevalism, would not have minded this.

But can these charges be made against the following passage:

> 'No more of friendship here: the world is open:
> I wish you life and merriment enough
> From wealth and wine, and all the dingy glory
> Fame doth reward those with, whose love-spurned hearts
> Hunger for goblin immortality.
> Live long, grow old, and honour crown thy hairs,
> When they are pale and frosty as thy heart.
> Away. I have no better blessing for thee.'

Very well, says the opponent in my head, but this is 'Romanticism', there is nothing Elizabethan about it.

'The swallow leaves her nest,
The soul my weary breast;
But therefore let the rain
    On my grave
Fall pure; for why complain?
Since both will come again
    O'er the wave.'

At any rate this strophe is lyric. Prose comes into the play.

'*Isbrand*: Dead and gone! a scurvey burthen to this ballad of life.
There lies he, Siegfried; my brother, mark you; and I weep not, nor
gnash the teeth, nor curse: and why not, Siegfried? Do you see this?
So should every honest man be: cold, dead, and leaden-coffined.
This was one who would be constant in friendship, and the pole
wanders: one who would be immortal, and the light that shines upon
his pale forehead now, through yonder gewgaw window, undulated
from its star hundreds of years ago. That is constancy, that is life. O
moral nature!'

This passage foregoing is not out of key with Leopardi. And it were
perhaps academic to carp at the few unneeded words in the following:

'I do begin to feel
As if I were a ghost among the men,
As all, whom I loved, are; for their affections
Hung on things new, young, and unknown to me,
And that I am is but the obstinate will
Of this my hostile body.'

I try to set out his beauties without much comment, leaving the
reader to judge, for I write of a poet who greatly moved me at eighteen, and for whom my admiration has diminished without disappearing. I have a perfectly definite theory as to why my admiration
has waned, but I would rather the reader came to his own conclusion.
The critic should never be wholly governed by his stylistic beliefs, nor
should the layman always think the critic is calling a substance brass,
when he, the critic, is only attempting to define gold that is not quite
24 carat. This next speech is simpler syntactically:

'Tremble not, fear me not
The dead are ever good and innocent,
And love the living. They are cheerful creatures,
And quiet as the sunbeams, and most like
In grace and patient love and spotless beauty,
The new-born of mankind. 'Tis better too
To die, as thou art, young, in the first grace
And full of beauty, and so be remembered

As one chosen from the earth to be an angel;
Not left to droop and wither, and be borne
Down by the breath of time.'

The pomps of poetry are at his disposal, but a phrase like—

'the sea's wide leafless wind'

is perhaps too fine to be dismissed as one of them.

The patter of his fools is certainly the best *tour de force* of its kind since the Elizabethan patter it imitates:

'The dry rot of prudence hath eaten the ship of fools to dust; she is no more seaworthy. The world will see its ears in a glass no longer; so we are laid aside and shall soon be forgotten; for why should the feast of asses come but once a year, when all days are foaled of one mother? O world, world! The gods and fairies left thee, for thou wert too wise, and now, thou Socratic star, thy demon, the Great Pan, Folly, is parting from thee. The oracles still talked in their sleep, shall our grand-children say, till Master Merriman's kingdom was broken up: now is every man his own fool, and the world's sign is taken down.'

'Farewell thou great-eared mind.'

'My jests are cracked, my coxcomb fallen, my bauble confiscated, my cap decapitated. Toll the bell; for oh, for oh! Jack Pudding is no more.'

'I will yield Death the crown of folly. He hath no hair, and in this weather might catch cold and die.'

For all this briskness, and for all the pageantry of his speech, and number of decorations in which he might seem to have forestalled the pre-Raphaelites, one speech of the play may well be turned into self-criticism:

'an I utter
Shadows of words, like to an ancient ghost,
Arisen out of hoary centuries
Where none can speak his language.'

These lines are as beautiful as anything he has written, but they bring us directly to the question: Can a man write poetry in a purely archaic dialect? Presumably he can, and Beddoes has done so; but would not this poetry, his poetry be more effective, would not its effectiveness be much more lasting if he had used a real speech instead of a language which may have been used on the early Victorian stage, but certainly had no existence in the life of his era?

Making all due allowance; granting that he may be as easy to read as Webster and some of the late Elizabethans, is not this the secret of his comparative unpopularity? Even grant that he is too macabre to

351

suit the 'wider' audience which will take nothing but sugary optim-ism? Grant that he suffers from the samples given in anthologies, which are always the slight lyrics. His best work is in the plays and dramatic fragments. The song, 'Old Adam, the Carrion Crow', quoted in the Oxford Book, loses a deal of its force if one have not the introductory lines:

> 'Thus, as I heard the snaky mermaids sing
> In Phlegethon, that hydrophobic river,
> One May-morning in Hell.'

Or even the whole speech:

> '*Wolfram:* Good melody! If this be a good melody,
> I have at home, fattening in my stye,
> A sow that grunts above the nightingale.
> Why this will serve for those who feed their veins
> With crust, and cheese of dandelion's milk,
> And the pure Rhine. When I am sick o' mornings,
> With a horn spoon tinkling in my porridge-pot,
> 'Tis a brave ballad: but in Bacchanal night,
> O'er wine, red, black, or purple-bubbling wine,
> That takes a man by the brain and whirls him round,
> By Bacchus' lip! I like a full-voiced fellow,
> A craggy-throated, fat-cheeked trumpeter,
> A barker, a moon-howler, who could sing
> Thus, as I heard, etc. . . . '

Still the tragedy and the beauty, for he has both, are in the main lost in the gaudiness of the words. His plot in 'The Fool's Tragedy' is based on the stabbing of a Duke of Munsterberg by his court jester. Despite the magical element in the play, the passions are great enough to carry the improbabilities. But they will not quite lift the vocabulary. On the other hand, so many people who call themselves lovers of poetry are in reality only lovers of high-sounding words and imposing verbosity, and to them Beddoes should give very great pleasure, for he carries these things in poetry, whereas many others who try to display them do not come anywhere near the seats of the Muses.

Where in Francis Thompson, for example, will you find a page worth the following?–

> 'To trust in story,
> In the old times Death was a feverish sleep,
> In which men walked. The other world was cold
> And thinly-peopled, so life's emigrants
> Came back to mingle with the crowds of earth:
> But now great cities are transplanted thither,

Memphis, and Babylon, and either Thebes
And Priam's towery town with its one beech,
The dead are most and merriest: so be sure
There will be no more haunting, till their towns
Are full to the garret; then they'll shut their gates,
To keep the living out, and perhaps leave
A dead or two between both kingdoms.'

Landor (1775-1864)[1]

Our poetry and our prose have suffered incalculably whenever we have cut ourselves off from the French. All that we most hate in the Victorian era is due to an interruption of the current; the Napoleonic wars occurring just when French eighteenth-century culture should, by rights, have been infiltering through the English; and this loss has scarce been made good. Such losses are perhaps never made good.

Our prose is only just taking count of the existence of Stendhal and Flaubert. On the other hand, one must not exaggerate. The exchange between the two countries is not wholly uneven. England, to her glory, was not always dowdy Victorian, Voltaire was indebted to English philosophers, and if we reach back to Fielding we find a prose author worthy of any continental tradition; or, receding further, Burton of the 'Anatomy' can perhaps hold his own against the robust phrasing of Brantome.

The Eighteen Nineties in England were doing very much what Gautier had been doing in France in the Eighteen Thirties, and there is a fineness in Gautier's later work for which one will seek in vain among the English poets succeeding. They might indeed have learned it from Gautier; or they might have learned it from Landor, but this latter study would have been almost as heretical as the former. The Victorian cult of the innocuous so distressingly interposed itself. One is tired of hearing depreciation of Tennyson, but he is a very convenient example. The 'Spectatorial' mind, whether in press or in school-room, has recommended 'safe' poets. Mr. Wordsworth, a stupid man, with a decided gift for portraying nature in vignettes, never yet ruined anyone's morals, unless, perhaps, he has driven some susceptible persons to crime in a very fury of boredom. Milton, because at a convenient time he utilised a then popular phase of religion, has long enjoyed a reputation based only in small part on his actual poetic value.

Landor, a republican, at a time when such politics were more suspect than syndicalism is at present, was carefully edged out of the way. In his dialogue on the Chinese Emperor, the little children of the palace oppose their simple arithmetic to the western doctrine of the Trinity. Landor has not been a popular author.

His collected works are nevertheless the best substitute for a Univer-

[1] *The Future*, November 1917.

sity education that can be offered to any man in a hurry. His fame is by
no means the 'faultless fame' of Swinburne's poem in memorial of
him. He is a very uneven author; but there is no difficulty in knowing
what Swinburne had in mind when he, in his first youth, wrote those
verses, for Gautier himself has never given to the world a more
chiselled marmorean quatrain than Landor's:

> *Past ruin'd Ilion Helen lives,*
> *Alcestis rises from the shades;*
> *Verse calls them forth; 'tis verse that gives*
> *Immortal youth to mortal maids.*

It was typical that Landor should have inserted an address 'To
General Andrew Jackson, President of the United States,' at the beginning of the second volume of 'Pericles and Aspasia' (edition of 1842).
The poem, almost needless to say, has nothing whatever to do with
'Pericles and Aspasia'. There are those who have no middle ground in
the mind, Landor was conceivably of them, now writing the perfect
and incomparable sentence, and now tumbling into most utter
incongruity.

We have had so many translations marked only by a clumsy approximation to certain Greek and Latin grammatic idioms that one may
perhaps open with prejudice even the classical dialogues in the
'Imaginary Conversations'. The vocative case, and second person
singular of the pronoun, intrude even in the almost *vers libre* of the
Peleus and Thetis (spoken in 'Epicurus, Leontion and Ternissa'):

PELEUS: 'Goddess! to me, to thy Peleus, Oh how far more than goddess! why then this sudden silence? why these tears? The last we
shed were when the Fates divided us, saying the earth was not
thine, and the brother of Zeus, he the ruler of waters, had called
thee. Those that fall between the beloved at parting are bitter, and
ought to be: woe to him who wishes they were not! but these that
flow again at the returning light of the blessed feet should be
refreshing and divine as morn.

TERNISSA (as THETIS): 'Support me, support me in thine arms, once
more, once only. Lower not thy shoulder from my cheek, to gaze at
those features that (in times past) so pleased thee. The sky is serene;
the heavens frown not on us: do they prepare for us fresh sorrow?
Prepare for us! ah me! the word of Zeus is spoken: our Achilles is
discovered; he is borne away in the black hollow ships of Aulis, and
would have flown faster than they sail, to Troy.

'Surely there are those among the gods, or among the goddesses,
who might have forwarned me: and they did not! Were there no
omens, no auguries, no dreams, to shake thee from thy security?
no priest to prophesy? And what pastures are more beautiful than

Larissa's? what victims more stately? Could the soothsayers turn aside their eyes from these?

PELEUS: 'Approach with me and touch the altar, O my beloved! Doth not thy finger now impress the soft embers of incense? how often hath it burned, for him, for thee! And the lowings of the herds are audible for their leaders, from the sources of Apidanus and Enipeus to the sea-beach. They may yet prevail.'

THETIS: 'Alas! alas! Priests can foretell but not avert the future; and all they can give us are vain promises and abiding fears.'

I do not know whether Landor first wrote the dialogue in this curious mixture of broken verses turning now and again into prose, and then later put it into regular metre, without improving it; or whether being unsatisfied with his 'regular' verse he re-wrote the passages in this rhythmically interesting agglomerate. In it Peleus mentions old age, as if it might also befall the immortal Thetis, and then breaks off:

'Had I forgotten thy divinity? forgotten it in thy beauty? Other mortals think their beloved partake of it then mostly when they are gazing on their charms; but thy tenderness is more than godlike; and never have I known, never have I wished to know, whether aught in our inferior nature may resemble it.

THETIS: 'A mortal so immutable! the Powers above are less.

PELEUS: 'Time without grief would not have greatly changed me.

THETIS: 'There is a loveliness which youth may be without, and which the gods want. To the voice of compassion not a shell in all the ocean is attuned; and no tear ever dropped from Olympus. . . .'

'Classicism' in English, or shall we say 'Greekism and Latinism' have moved by clearly marked stages. There is perhaps a good deal of Ovid in Chaucer. Gavin Douglas improved perhaps upon Virgil whenever the text touches the sea or the elements. He is perhaps never Virgilian. Chapman retained a great deal of the 'surge and thunder', but it is extremely difficult to read more than a few pages of him at a sitting. It is possible that certain lines and passages in Marlowe's Ovidian Elegies are the first which successfully render in English the exact tone of the original. The eighteenth and late seventeenth centuries put the classics into silk stockings.

I find in a rather rare book of criticism, published in 1885, some remarks on the poet's 'power of looking out of his own age, and of reaching the standpoint of another'. The author of this book says that Shelley seemed to have had a foretaste of it. He then states that with Tennyson, Browning and Arnold, English poetry entered a new phase: 'We could not say of the English poets, before these, that they had been interpreters of any age but their own.'

Surely all this glory is Landor's. Surely no man has ever interpreted more different eras with sureness and thoroughness, whether it be in 'Pericles and Aspasia', or his dialogues between Chaucer, Petrarch and Boccaccio, or in the Normanby dialogue, which is contemporary and almost a novel.

Surely also this statement in 1885 is typical of the way Landor is overlooked; he is not even mentioned in the essay.

The critic, an admirer of Mathew Arnold's, may defend the letter of his statement by saying that Landor, though a poet, did most of his 'interpretation' in prose. But it is almost incredible that Landor should not even be mentioned. There is no need of opening the quibble over the 'border line'. Indubitably Landor never gave so complete a verse interpretation as 'The Ring and the Book'. There are, indeed, too many absolutely unanswerable questions aroused by any attempt to compare these two writers. Browning in verse is presumably the better poet; largely perhaps because Landor never learned to write a long passage of verse without in some way clogging and blocking the reader's attention. Yet Browning must constantly have envied him his perfect lines, his perfect commencements:

> *Tanagra! think not I forget*
> *Thy beautifully-storied streets;*
> *Be sure my memory bathes yet*
> *In clear Thermodon, and yet greets*
> *The blythe and liberal shepherd-boy,*
> *Whose sunny bosom swells with joy*
> *When we accept his matted rushes*
> *Upheav'd with sylvan fruit; away he bounds, and blushes.*

How incomparable if it had stopped at 'Thermodon'; how fine we should think him if we had found the three and a half opening lines cut in a fragment of stone! How utterly it goes to pieces when we come upon 'The blythe and liberal shepherd-boy'! And how 'Browningesque' it turns with the 'matted rushes'!

Landor's second strophe continues:

> *I promise to bring back with me*
> *What thou with transport wilt receive,*
> *The only proper gift for thee,*
> *Of which no mortal shall bereave*
> *In later times thy mouldering walls,*
> *Until the last old turret falls;*
> *A crown, a crown from Athens won,*
> *A crown no God can wear, beside Latona's son.*

Questions crop up as fast as one transcribes the quotation: Why is there so much more to be said for 'Latona's son' than for 'Apollo' in just this particular line; why is the effect of finish so given, by this utterly useless bit of mythical genealogy? And the 'Browningism' in the former strophe, the particularisation which makes Landor's later work so much better than his early poems: does it come from the elder man or from the younger?

And Landor himself, the first useful critic, or the first analytical critic in English; the first man to go through an English poem line by line marking what was good, what was poor, what was excessive; the first person seriously to consider and write down this, almost the only, sort of criticism that can profit a later writer: can we put down any satisfactory comment on his ten volumes without taking at least two volumes to do it in?

Prefatio Aut Cimicium Tumulus[1]

M<sup>r. F. V. Morley, with a misplaced sense of humour, has suggested that I write a fifty page preface to two hundred pages of contemporary poesy. This to me, who have for a quarter of a century contended that critics should know more and write less. No two hundred pages of contemporary poetry would sustain the demands I could make in half such a preface. I am moreover confining my selection to poems Britain has not accepted and in the main that the British literary bureaucracy does NOT want to have printed in England.

I shall therefore write a preface mainly about something else.

Mr. Eliot and I are in agreement, or 'belong to the same school of critics', in so far as we both believe that existing works form a complete order which is changed by the introduction of the 'really new' work.

His contempt for his readers has always been much greater than mine, by which I would indicate that I quite often write as if I expected my reader to use his intelligence, and count on its being fairly strong, whereas Mr. Eliot after enduring decennial fogs in Britain practically always writes as if for very very feeble and brittle mentalities, from whom he can expect neither resilience nor any faculty for seeing the import instead of the details or surfaces.

When he talks of 'commentation and elucidation' and of the 'correction of taste', I go into opposition, or rather, having been there first, I note that if I was in any sense the revolution I have been followed by the counter-revolution. Damn your taste, I would like if possible to sharpen your perceptions, after which your taste can take care of itself.

'Commentation' be damned. 'Elucidation' can stand if it means 'turn a searchlight on' something or preferably some work or author lying in shadow.

Mr. Eliot's flattering obeisance to 'exponents of criticism', wherein he says that he supposes they have not assumed that criticism is an 'autotelic activity', seems to me so much apple-sauce. In so far as the bureaucracy of letters has considered their writing as anything more than a short cut to the feeding trough or a means of puffing up their personal importances, they have done little else for the past thirty years than boost the production of writing about writing, not only as

[1] From *Active Anthology* (1933).

autotelic, but as something which ought to receive more attention from the reading victim than the great books themselves.

Granted that nobody ought to be such a presumptuous imbecile as to hold up the autotelic false horizon, Mr. Eliot describes a terrestrial paradise and not the *de facto* world, in which more immediate locus we observe a perpetual exchange of civilities between pulex, cimex, vermiformis, etc., each holding up his candle before the shrines of his similars.

A process having no conceivable final limit and illustratable by my present activity: I mean on this very page, engaging your attention while I talk about Mr. Eliot's essay about other essayists' essays. In the course of his eminently professorial volume he must have mentioned at least forty-five essayists whom tomorrow's readers will be most happy not to hear mentioned, but mention of whom must have contributed enormously to Mr. Eliot's rise to his deserved position as arbiter of British opinion.

KRINO

'Existing monuments form an ideal order among themselves.' It would be healthier to use a zoological term rather than the word monument. It is much easier to think of the *Odyssey* or *Le Testament* or Catullus' *Epithalamium* as something living than as a series of cenotaphs. After all, Homer, Villon, Propertius, speak of the world as I know it, whereas Mr. Tennyson and Dr. Bridges did not. Even Dante and Guido with their so highly specialised culture speak of a part of life as I know it. ATHANATOS.

However, accepting for the moment Mr. Eliot's monumental or architectural simile: the KRINO, 'to pick out for oneself, choose, prefer' (page 381 my edition of Liddell and Scott) which seems to me the major job, is to determine, first, the main form and main proportions of that order of extant letters, to locate, first the greater pyramids and then, possibly, and with a decently proportioned emphasis, to consider the exact measurements of the stone-courses, layers, etc.

Dryden gives T. S. E. a good club wherewith to smack Milton. But with a modicum of familiarity or even a passing acquaintance with Dante, the club would hardly be needed.

A volume of quite sound statistical essays on poesy may quite easily drive a man to the movies, it may express nothing save the most perfect judgements and the utmost refinements of descriptivity and whet, nevertheless, no appetite for the unknown best, or for the best still unread by the neophyte.

A book 66 per cent concerned with manipulating and with re-handling the errors of seventy contemporary pestilential describers

and rehashers of opinion, and only 34 per cent concerned with focus-
ing the reader's attention on the *virtu* of books worth reading is, at least
to the present victim, more an annoyance than a source of jocundity.

And if I am to put myself vicariously in the place of the younger
reader or if I am to exercise parental protectiveness over some imagined offspring, I can find myself too angry for those mincing polite-
nesses demanded by secondary editorial orders.

My opinion of critics is that:
The best are those who actually cause an amelioration in the art
which they criticise.
The next best are those who most focus attention on the best that is
written (or painted or composed or cut in stone).
And the pestilential vermin are those who distract attention *from* the
best, either to the second rate, or to hokum, or to their own critical
writings.

Mr. Eliot probably ranks very high in the first of these three groups,
and deserves badly of us for his entrance into the last.

He uses Dryden legitimately in reducing exaggerated adulation of
Milton, but the fact of his resurrecting Dryden poisons Professor
Taupin, and so on *and* so on, thence further proceeding.

I don't at this point mean to criticise Taupin's *Quatres Essais*, but they
offer me a fine chance to make an addendum.

Taupin is interesting while writing of Frobenius and Dante. In the
latter case I suspect a Flamand ancestry has saved him from the n.r.f.
dither and wish-wash. There is (naturally?) a let down in the pages
following. I suppose this is due to Taupin's respect for his elders.
Professor Eliot in a fit of misanthropy dug up Dryden and Taupin
was lured into reading him. The citation from Dryden may have been
cleverly inserted by Taupin, at any rate it acts as a foil for his own
somewhat contorted style to which one returns with relief from
Dryden's platitude and verbosity. I am unable to determine whether
Taupin is being superlatively astute and counting on the reader 'seeing
for himself ', or whether he was simply in a hurry, but 30 pages furnish
a magnificent *basis* for deduction. Which he refrains from making.
He may have expected the reader to see it for himself.

I know from longer experience than Dr. René's that there is no use
in expecting the reader to do anything of the sort. (No one has, for
example, ever noticed the ground-plan of my *Instigations*.)

On page 161 Taupin quotes Condillac: 'Il y a deux espèces: le talent
et le génie. Celui-là continue les idées d'un art ou d'une science
connue, d'une manière propre à produire les effets qu'on en doit

naturellement attendre . . . Celui-ci ajoute au talent l'idée d'esprit, en quelque sorte créateur.'

Talent 'continues the ideas of a known art or science to produce naturally expectable results'.

On page 164 he quotes Milton: 'and twilight gray had in her sober livery all things clad'.

No one can be so ignorant as to suppose this manner of expression is anything save that of an art *known* and applied by several dozen dramatists. The Shakespearian original or model will instantly spring to the mind of almost any literate reader.

But the known process is vilely used. It is disgustingly used.

The Shakespearian line contains, I admit, one word not absolutely essential to the meaning. It is a monosyllable and three of its four letters serve to concentrate and fulfil the double alliteration preceding.

Anybody but a botcher would have omitted the two useless words from the Milton. He not only derives but dilutes.

However, Taupin continues (still without heaving rocks at the victim) on the next page we find:

'the setting sun. . . .'

Gentlemen, ah wubb-wubb, what did the setting sun do?

'the setting sun. . . .

                    DESCENDED.'

The abject and utter nullity of British criticism in general for over two centuries is nowhere so squalid and naked as in the fact that generations of Britons and humble Americans have gone on swallowing this kind of rubbish. (Despite what Landor had shown them in his notes on Catullus.)

The only camouflage used to put over this idiocy is a gross and uninteresting rhythm.

The clodhoppers needed only one adverb between the subject and predicate to hide the underlying stupidity.

Chateaubriand, in a passage subsequently cited, was not, as Taupin seems to imply, supinely imitating the passage, but possibly trying to correct it, everything in his description is in place. His paragraph, like most so called prose poetry, lacks adequate rhythmic vitality and has, consequently, the dullness germane to its category.

MR. ELIOT'S GRIEF

Mr. Eliot's misfortune was to find himself surrounded by a horrible and microcephalous bureaucracy which disliked poetry, it might be too much to say 'loathed' it. But the emotion was as strong as any in the bureaucratic bosom. Bureaucracy has no loves and is composed mainly of varied minor dislikes. The members of this bureaucracy, sick with inferiority complex, had just enough wits to perceive that Eliot was their superior, but no means of detecting his limits or measuring him from the outside, and no experience that would enable them to know the poisons wherewith he had been injected. For that diagnosis perhaps only a fellow American is qualified, one having suffered an American University. The American University is or was aware of the existence of both German and English institutions, being younger and in a barbarous country, *its* inferiority complex impelled it to comparison and to a wish to equal and surpass, but gave it no immunity from the academical bacilli, inferiority complex directed against creative activity in the arts.

That there is a percentage of bunk in the *Selected Essays* Mr. Eliot will possibly be the last to deny, but that he had performed a self-analysis is still doubtful.

This kind of essay assumes the existence of a culture that no longer subsists and does nothing to prepare a better culture that must or ought to come into being. I say 'better', for the new paideuma will at least be a live paideuma not a dead one.

Such essays are prepared NOT for editors who care about a living literature or a live tradition, or who even want the best of Eliot's perception applied to an author of second or third or fourth category (per ex. Seneca), they want to maintain a system wherein it is possible to receive fifteen guineas for an article of approximately 3,000–4,000 words, in a series to which Mr. Eliot's sensitivity and patience will give lustre and wherein his occasional eminence will shed respectability on a great mass of inferior writing.

Their mentality is not far from that of a publisher of cheap editions who occasionally puts in a good book, so that the serious German will think that the miscellany is intellectual (*ipse dicebat*). Given the two or three real books in his series he believes the German highbrow will buy the rest thinking it the right thing to do.

IN HAPPIER ERA

The study of Latin authors was alive a century and a quarter, perhaps hardly more than a century ago.

Young men are now lured into colleges and universities largely on false pretences.

We live in a vile age when it is impossible to get reprints of the few dozen books that are practically essential to a competent knowledge of poetry. When Alexander Moring and Doctor Rouse set out to republish the books that had been good enough for Shakespeare, the enterprise went on the rocks. You can't get a current edition of Golding's *Metamorphoses*, or of Gavin Douglas, or of Salel; the British grocer will break a contract for printing Cavalcanti when he would not dream of breaking a contract for prunes.

In the matter of education, if the young are not to profit by our sweats, if they are not to pluck the fruits of our experience in the form of better curricula, it might be well to give it up altogether. At any rate the critic not aiming at a better curriculum for the serious study of literature is a critic half-baked, swinging in a vacuum. It would be hypocrisy to pretend that Eliot's essays are not aimed at professors and students.

The student is best aided by being able to read and to own conveniently the best that has been created.

Yeats, who has always been against the gang and the bureaucracy, now muddled, now profound, now merely Celtic or erroneously believing that a free Ireland, or at least a more Oirish Ireland, would help the matter, long ago prayed for a new sacred book.

Every age has tried to compound such a volume. Every great culture has had such a major anthology. Pisistratus, Li Po, the Japanese Emperor who reduced the number of Noh dramas to about 450; the hackneyed Hebrew example; in less degree the Middle Ages, with the matter of Britain, of France, and of Rome le Grant.

The time to be interested in Seneca may possibly have been before Mr. Shakespeare had written his plays. But assuming that Mr. Eliot's plenum exists, the relations of its different components have been changed in our time; there are most distinctly the movies which bear on all dramatic construction, and there are Max Ernst's few volumes of engravings which have distinctly said their word about the Freudian novel.

If the past 30 years have a meaning, that meaning is not very apparent in Mr. Eliot's condescensions to the demands of British serial publication. If it means anything it means a distinct reduction in the BULK of past literature that the future will carry.

I should have no right to attack England's most accurate critic were it not in the hope of something better, if not in England, at least somewhere in space and time.

There is a habit or practice of attacking the lists in *How to Read*. Young academes who have not read the works listed say my choice is capricious, most of them do not stop to see what my lists are lists OF.

I have catalogued the towns in Dorset without mentioning Durham. I have listed the cities in England and Scotland and omitted Berwick-on-Tweed. Therefore the assistant professor or the weekly reviewer is educated, superlatively educated, and I am still *impetuus iuventus*, sipping with the bally bee and wholly unscientific in my methods.

Mr Aldington was perhaps the most vociferous, he vociferised about forty contradictions of things that I hadn't said, perhaps out of kindness, thinking it the only way his paper would give the booklet two columns, perhaps because he fawncied himself as the fine olde northern rough-haired St. Bernard defending the kittens of Alexandria. He has always tended to lose his shirt and breeches if one made any restrictive remarks about Greeks, even though it were only to suggest that some Greeks wrote better than others.

Ut moveat, ut doceat, ut delectet.

There are at least three kinds of inaccurate statement which might with advantage be dissociated.

1. The somewhat violent statement conveying a perception (quia perception it is something perceived by the writer), the inaccuracy of such statement is often more apparent than real, and as every reader resists an opinion diverse from his own, such statement is often, one might say is usually, corrected or more than corrected in transit.

2. There is the apparently careful statement containing all the possible, or at least so many, modifications of the main proposition that the main meaning is either lost in transit or so dampened down that it has no effect on the reader.

Both these kinds of statement can be justified in various ways depending on where and why they are used.

3. There is the inaccurate statement that is just simply vague, either because the writer doesn't KNOW or because he is incompetent in expression.

Such ignorance in successful vendors of their wares to current publications very often disguises itself as verity No. 2.

Camouflage might be further subdivided:

A. 'Sound opinion', i.e. restating accepted opinion without any direct or personal knowledge.

B. Covering this ignorance either with restrictive clauses, or scintillating with paradox.

There is gongorism in critical writing as well as in bad poetry. You might say that discussion of books ceases to be critical writing and becomes just the functioning of bureaucracy when the MAIN END (telos) is forgotten.

As we cannot educate our grandfathers, one supposes that critical writing is committed for the purpose of educating our offspring, our contemporaries, or ourselves, and that the least a critic can do is to be aware of the present even if he be too swinish to consider the future.

The critic is either a parasite or he is concerned with the growth of the next paideuma.

Marinetti is thoroughly *simpatico*. Writing and orating *ut moveat*, he has made demands that no one considers in their strict literal sense, but which have, and have had, a definite scope.

'An early play of no merit whatever', 'the brain of a fourth-rate playwright' as matters of an highly specialised clinic may conceivably have something to do with critical standards. The impression is that their importance must be limited to some very minor philological field. Their import for tomorrow's paideuma is probably slight.

As specialist and practising writer one might want to know whether Seneca wrote any other lines as effective as

> Per alta vada spatia sublimi aethere
> testare nullos esse, qua veheris, deos.

Mr. Eliot can think of no other play which reserves such a shock for the last word. (Ref. or cf. O. Henry's stories, bell in the last pages.)

The only trouble with the citation is that it is a bit ambiguous: Mr. Eliot and Professor Miller disagreeing as to its theological import, Mr. Eliot inclining to the Christian interpretation, or what Seneca ought to have meant. No, I mustn't exaggerate. Seneca is not being Christian. Mr. Eliot votes against a sweeping atheistical meaning. I can't personally see that the old half-bore goes further than asserting that the gods are not in that particular district of the aether. If there is anything about justice, it must be in the context, not in the two lines quoted.

In the present decomposition and under the yoke of the present bureaucracy it would probably be too much to demand that before discussing an author a reviewer answer the following questions:

1. Have you read the original text of the author under discussion? or how much of it have you read?

2. Is it worth reading? or how much of it is worth reading? and by whom?

As for Elizabethan dramedy, Lamb and Hazlitt are supposed to have set the fad, but Lamb at any rate did pick out a volume of selections; showing what he thought might be the basis of an interest.

The proportion between discussion and the exhibits the discusser dares show his reader is possibly a good, and probably a necessary, test of his purpose. In a matter of degree, I am for say 80 per cent exhibit and 20 per cent yatter.

Mr. Eliot and Miss Moore are definitely fighting against an impoverishment of culture, against a paucity of reading programme. Neither they nor anyone else is likely to claim that they have as much interest in life as I have, or that I have their patience in reading.

That does not make it any less necessary to distinguish between Eliot registering his belief *re* a value, and Eliot ceding to the bad, not to say putrid habits of the bureaucracy which has surrounded him.

As alarmist, as capricious, perverse, etc., I repeat that you cannot get the whole cargo of a sinking paideuma on to the lifeboat. If you propose to have any live literature of the past kept in circulation, available (flat materialism) in print at prices the eager reader can pay, there has got to be more attention to the best and to the basic. Once that is established you can divagate into marginalia, but the challenge will be more incisive and the criteria will be more rigorous.

In citing the Miltonic burble I am merely on my way towards a further assertion.

The critical sense shows more in composition than in a critical essay.

The unwelcome and disparate authors whom I have gathered in this volume have mostly accepted certain criteria which duller wits have avoided.

They have mostly, if not accepted, at any rate faced the demands, and considered the works, made and noted in my *How to Read*. That in itself is not a certificate of creative ability, but it does imply a freedom from certain forms of gross error and from certain kinds of bungling which will indubitably consign many other contemporary writings to the ash-bin, with more than expected celerity.

Mr. Bunting probably seems reactionary to most of the other contributors. I think the apparent reaction is a definite endeavour to emphasise certain necessary elements which the less considering American experimentors tend to omit. At any rate Mr. Bunting asserted that ambition some years ago, but was driven still further into the American ambience the moment he looked back upon British composition of, let us say, 1927-8.

I believe that Britain, in rejecting certain facts (facts, not opinions) in 1912-15 entered a sterile decade.

Willingness to experiment is not enough, but unwillingness to experiment is mere death.

If ten pages out of its two hundred and fifty go into a Corpus Poetarum of A.D. 2033, the present volume will amply be justified. (Yes, I know I have split the future of that verb. Var. will, and amply.)

I have not attempted to represent all the new poets, I am leaving the youngest, possibly some of the brightest, to someone else or to future effort, not so much from malice or objection to perfect justice, as from inability to do everything all at once.

There are probably fifty very bright poems that are not here assembled. I suspect Mr. S. Putnam has written two or three. Mr. Bridson is champing on the bit. Someone more in touch with the younger Americans ought to issue an anthology or a special number of some periodical, selected with *criteria*, either his or mine.

The assertion implicit in this volume is that after ten or twenty years of serious effort you can consider a writer uninteresting, but the charges of flightiness and dilettantism are less likely to be valid. In fact they are unlikely to be valid if a consistent direction can be discovered.

Other things being equal, the results of processes, even of secondary processes, application, patience, etc., are more pertinent from living writers than from dead ones, or are more pertinent when demonstrably IN RELATION with the living present than with the classified past.

Classic in current publishers' advertisements seems to have attained its meaning via classé, rangé.

The history of literature as taught in many institutions (? all) is nothing more (hardly more) than a stratified record of snobisms in which chronology sometimes counts for more than the causal relation and is also often wholly ignored, I mean ignored usually when it conflicts with prejudice and when chronological fact destroys a supposed causal relation.

I have resisted several temptations to reply to attacks on *How to Read*, because on examination the stricture was usually answered in my own text, and the attacker, had he been serious, could have found the correction where he assumed the fault. Several objectors (*ut ante*) simply have not taken the trouble to consider what my lists are lists of.

Others ignorant of the nature of some of the texts cited have assumed that they are not what they are.

Others have assumed that where, for sake of brevity, I have not given reasons for the inclusion of certain items, no reasons exist or can possibly.

Madox Ford made a serious charge, but not against what is on the pages of the booklet. He indicated that a section of what would be a more nearly complete treatise on the whole art of composition was not included. You can't get everything into 45 pages. Nor did the author of *How to Read* claim universal knowledge and competence. Neither in the title nor anywhere in the text did the booklet claim to be a treatise on the major structure of novels and epics, nor even a guide to creative composition.

As for experiment: the claim is that without constant experiment literature dies. Experiment is ONE of the elements necessary to its life. Experiment aims at writing that will have a relation to the present analogous to the relation which past masterwork had to the life of its time.

Eliot applying what he has learned from
   Morire.
        Cupio.
            Profugo.
                Paenitiunt fugae.
  Medea.
     Fiam.
        Mater es.
           Cui sim vides.
applying what he has learned by being bored with as much of the rest
of Seneca as he has bothered to read, is a vastly more vital Eliot, and a
much more intensively critical Eliot than when complying with the
exigencies of the present and verminous system for the excernment of
book-reviews.

I might also assert that Eliot going back to the original has derived a
vastly more vivid power than was possible to the century and more of
Elizafiers who were content to lap the cream off Lamb and Hazlitt or to
assume a smattering of Elizabethan bumbast from Elizabethan derivers. *Quod erat demonstrandum. Quod erat indicatum,* even by the present
disturber of repose anno 1917 and thereabouts. And herein lies also the
confutation of that horrible *turba parasitorum paedagogorumque volgus* which
Mr. Eliot tolerates in his vicinage.

'ACTIVE ANTHOLOGY'
(Retrospect twenty months later)

A dislike of Bunting's poetry and Zukofsky's is possibly due to haste.
Their verse is more thoughtful than toffee-lickers require. At intervals,
months apart, I remember a passage, or I re-open my volume of
excerpts and find something solid. It did not incinerate any Hudson
river. Neither did Marianne Moore's when it first (20 years since) came
to London. You have to read such verse slowly.

Apart from Bunting and Zukofsky, Miss Moore's is the solidest stuff
in the Anthology. Williams' is simple by comparison—not so thoughtful. It has a larger audience because of its apparent simplicity. It is the
lyric of an aptitude. Aptitude, not attitude. Anschauung, that Dr.
Williams has stuck in and to for half a century. The workmanship is
not so much cared for. And yet Williams has become the first prose
writer in America, the best prose writer who now gets into print,
McAlmon having disappeared from circulation, and being a different
case altogether, panoramic Velasquez, where Williams is just solid.

What goes into his case note is THERE. If there is any more solid
solidity outside Papa Gustave, I don't know where to find it.

Joyce was not more substantial in the *Portrait of the Artist*. I am not sure that the cutting hasn't lightened his block.

In his verse Williams' integrity passes for simplicity. Unadulterated non-elaboration in the phrase, a 'simple substance', simple has an analogous meaning; whereas Zukofsky, Bunting and Miss Moore are all thoughtful, much more so than the public desires.

'Man is not an end product', is much too condensed a phrase to tickle the gobbler.

The case of Cumming's 'eimi' and the bearing of Cocteau's sensibility on this discussion will have to wait further, and more thorough, treatment than I have given them. Mr. Wyndham Lewis' *Apes* looms somewhere in the domain of Gulliver and Tristram Shandy.

PART EIGHT
Contemporaries

PART EIGHT

*The Divine Mystery** [1]

'I was sitting like Abraham in my tent door in the heat of the day, outside a Pagan city of Africa, when the lord of the thunder appeared before me, going on his way into the town to call down thunder from heaven upon it.

'He had on his wizard's robe, hung round with magical shells that rattled as he moved; and there walked behind him a young man carrying a lute. I gave the musician a piece of silver, and he danced before me the dance that draws down the thunder. After which he went his way into the town; and the people were gathered together in the courtyard of the king's house; and he danced before them all. Then it thundered for the first time in many days; and the king gave the thunder-maker a black goat—the immemorial reward of the performing god.

'So begins the history of the Divine Man, and such is his rude nativity. The secret of genius is sensitiveness. The Genius of the Thunder who revealed himself to me could not call the thunder, but he could be called by it. He was more quick than other men to feel the changes of the atmosphere; perhaps he had rendered his nervous system more sensitive still by fasting or mental abstraction; and he had learned to read his own symptoms as we read a barometer. So, when he felt the storm gathering round his head, he put on his symbolical vestment, and marched forth to be its Word, the archetype of all Heroes in all Mysteries.'

So begins the most fascinating book on folk-lore that I have ever opened. I can scarcely call it a book on 'folk-lore', it is a consummation. It is a history of the development of human intelligence. It is not a mass of theories, it is this history told in a series of vivid and precise illustrations, like the one I have chosen for quotation. It is not a philosophy, yet it manages to be an almost complete expression of philosophy. Mr. Upward has been 'resident' in Nigeria; he has had much at first hand, and in all his interpretation of documents he has never for an instant forgotten that documents are but the shadow of the fact. He has never forgotten the very real man inside the event or

---

* *The Divine Mystery*, by Allen Upward. (Garden City Press.)

[1] *The New Freewoman* (*The Egoist*), 15 November (1913).

373

the history. It is this which distinguishes him from all the encyclopaedists who have written endlessly upon corn gods, etc.

Moreover, he thinks.

He thinks, *il pense*. He is intelligent. Good God! is it not a marvel that
in the age of Cadbury and Northcliffe, and the 'Atlantic Monthly' and
the present 'English Review', etc., etc., *ad nauseam*, is it not an overwhelming wonder that a thinking sentient being should still inhabit
this planet and be allowed to publish a book!

Very well then. Mr. Upward is intelligent. He is cognizant of the
forces of intelligence and has traced, in some measure, their influence.
He has traced the growth of religion and superstition from the primitive type of the thunder-maker to the idea of the messiah. He has
traced many of the detestable customs of modern life to their roots in
superstition.

The first half of the book is planned, if it can be called so, on the slow
recognition of the sun. That is to say, primitive man turns from his
worship of the dead, and of the earth and of various fears, to a worship
of the life-giving Helios. The solar missionary says it is unnecessary to
bury a man in the cornfield in order that crops shall rise by virtue
of his spirit. The Aten disc is explained. The 'Dies Irae' turns out to be
a relic of fire worship. The 'Divine Mystery' necessitates a new translation of the bible. And if the ecclesiastical mind were not ossified beyond
all hope of revivification we should see the introductory notes
above the chapters abandoned in favour of something related to
truth.

Mr. Upward has left the charming pastoral figure of Jesus in a more
acceptable light than have the advocates of 'That religion which the
Nazarene has been accused of having founded.'

He has derived the word God from the word Goat, which will be a
satisfaction to many. He has related prophecy to astrology, and has
shown the new eras to be related to the ascent of the successive signs
of the zodiac in which the sun appears, changing his mansion about
once in each eight centuries.

The book itself is a summary, a leisured summary, that does not cut
corners, or leave one with insufficient information. Still it contains so
much and so much of vivid interest that it is very nearly impossible to
review it.

It is a book full of suggestion for half a dozen sorts of specialist, at the
same time it is legible and so clearly written that one has no need of
specialised knowledge to read it.

I, personally, find in it clues and suggestions for the Provençal love
customs of the Middle Ages–in the chapter on early marriage laws.
Modern marriage is, apparently, derived from the laws of slave con-
cubinage, not from the more honourable forms of primitive European
marriage. So much for the upholders of 'Sacrament'.

It is great satisfaction to find a nice, logical book, where all the canting fools who have plagued one are–no, not 'abused', but where an author, writing in a gentle and reasonable tone, presenting simple fact after simple fact, undermines their position, and shows them naked in all their detestability, in all their unutterable silliness.

The lovely belief in a durable hot hell dates back to the Parsee who squatted over a naphtha volcano. And various other stupidities still prevalent are shown to be as little inspired by either divine or human intelligence. It is a great book for liberations.

Someday, when the circulationists are nearly forgotten, people will take note of Mr. Upward's work in fundamentals. His 'The New Word' will be recognised, instead of being ranted about by a few enthusiasts.

He is wholly careless of certain matters; he is apparently quite willing that his work should be immortal in general belief, instead of being 'preserved' in specific works.

This author is a focus, that is to say he has a sense of major relations. The enlightenments of our era have come to him. He has seen how the things 'put together'.

It is pleasing to know that the ordinary native's hunt in Africa sets out with an ark of the covenant every whit as sacred as the junk box which the Israelites carried before them.

Especially if one has been 'reared in the Christian faith' and been forced to eat at the same table with ministers and members of the Y.M.C.A., it is pleasant to know for certain just what part of their conversation is pure buncomb.

I do not wish to lead anyone into the belief that this is an impious book. I believe Allen Upward to be one of the devoutest men of the age. He insists that the real God is neither a cad nor an imbecile, and that is, to my mind, a fairly good ground for religion.

'All that has been was right, and will be wrong.' He shows that even the crusades of the earlier and now detestable religions came in their own time as liberations.

It is a very difficult work to review. How Mr. Upward has managed to tell so many interesting facts in three hundred pages, is somewhat beyond me. It is, I must repeat, a clarifying book, it is not a set of facts very rigorously chosen in proportion to their interest. The idea of the goddess, the mother goddess, is analysed; queenship and kingship and the priesthood are treated. Mr. Upward is not only perspicacious, but his mind is balanced by nature and by a knowledge of the Chinese classics. He is nowhere content with a sham.

Speaking in moderation, I suppose one might call 'The Divine Mystery' a book indispensable to clergymen, legislators, students of folk-lore, and the more intelligent public.

I do not write this as a specialist; but judging by those points where Mr. Upward's *specialité* coincides with my own, I should say that he was led by a scholarship not only wide but precise. He shows remarkable powers of synthesis.

However correct or incorrect I may be in my estimate, of this at least I am certain: no sane man will be bored during the hours he gives to the reading of this book.

Allen Upward Serious[1]

'It is a curious thing about England'???? No, it is not a 'curious thing' about England or about anywhere else, it is a natural habit of il mal seme d' Adamo that they neglect the clear thinker in his own day. And if a man have done valuable work of one sort, and have, at the same time, done vendible work of another, the vendible work will kill him among the little clique who decide whether or no one is to be 'taken seriously'. So Mr. Upward is known for short stories of a sort, and not for two books, as interesting philosophically as any that have been written in our time.

Of course, any man who thinks is a bore. He will either make you think or he will despise, irritate and insult you if you don't, and all this is very distressing.

What for instance could be more distressing to a wooden-headed imbecile, fat with his own scholastic conceit, than such a clearly-written paragraph as that which follows?

'That old talk about the Gods, which is called mythology, is confused in many ways, partly because all language is confused, partly because it is a layer of many languages. When the talkers no longer used the beast as an idol they used it as a symbol, in short a word; when they no longer slew the real Christ at Easter they named the sun at Easter, Christ. Their language is tangled and twisted beyond our power wholly to unravel because it was beyond their power; because it began as a tangle when man's mind was still a blur, and he saw men as trees walking, and trees as men standing still. How hard the old cloistered scholarship to which the Nobels of a bygone age gave their endowments has toiled to understand the word glaukopis given to the goddess Athene. Did it mean blue-eyed or grey-eyed, or–by the aid of Sanskrit–merely glare-eyed? And all the time they had not only the word glaux staring them in the face, but they had the owl itself cut at the foot of every statue of Athene and stamped on every coin of Athens, to tell them that she was the owl-eyed goddess, the lightning that blinks like an owl. For what is characteristic of the owl's eyes is not that they glare, but that they suddenly leave off glaring like lighthouses whose light is shut off. We may see the shutter of the lightning in that mask that overhangs Athene's brow and hear its click in the word glaukos. And the leaf-age of the olive whose writhen trunk bears, as it were, the lightning's

[1] *The New Age*, 23 April 1914.

brand, does not glare but glitters, the pale under face of the leaves alternating with the dark upper face, and so the olive is Athene's tree and is called glaukos.[1] Why need we carry owls to Oxford?'

That is the sort of clarity and hard writing that one finds all through 'The New Word'. Of course, it is very irritating: if you suggest to Mr. Upward that his mind is as clear as Bacon's, he will agree with you. If you suggest to Mr. Upward that his middles are less indefinite than Plato's, he will agree with you. If you suggest to him that one man who thinks is worth a dozen ambulating works of reference, he will agree with you; and all this is very annoying to the supporters of things at large, for our ambulating works of reference are far more numerous than our thinkers.

The writer of this present essay has suffered from a modern education; he has met a number of ambulating works of reference; his respect for the mnemonic mind has been lessened by contact, and by the presence in the modern world of the cinematograph and the gramophone.

Mr. Upward has taken up the cause of intelligence, of the perceptive man; it is the height of quixotism on his part. If you refer to him as a thinker, if you say his mind is less messy than Bergson's, they tell you he writes detective stories. Yet if 'The New Word' and 'The Divine Mystery' had been written by a civil servant or a clerk in a dry goods shop, or by a broken-down parson, they would have been acclaimed as great works. They would have been patted on their covers by 'The Edinburgh', etc.

But there is something so degrading—at least, one would think that there were something so degrading in the practice of writing as a trade—that anyone who has once earned a livelihood, or part of it, obviously and openly, by popular writing, can never be seriously regarded by any great number of people. And then, of course, 'he does too much'. The populace, the reading populace, is like the fat critic in 'Fanny's First Play', it cannot conceive the same man doing two kinds of work, or at least it won't. It is perfectly logical. It is insanely logical.

On the other hand, one clear, hard paragraph like the one quoted is enough to queer a man's chances. 'How,' say the professors, 'is this man a classicist? Why does he not stick to his trade? Why does he expose our patent error? To hell with him!'

'How!' says the windy logomachist, who believes that if a thing is worth doing it is worth doing badly. 'Clear, hard, serious, specialised writing from a journalist. Damn him.'

And then of course, there's the church; nearly everybody has an uncle or a cousin who gets paid for believing, officially, in the estab-

[1] See Canto LXXIV, p. 466, Faber   CX. Ed.
edition, U.S. Edition p. 438, and Canto

lished church. It won't do to think about religion too seriously or else
we'll have to scrap the lot: all the established salaries. We must not
treat this gentleman too gravely. Let us label him a brilliant superficial
writer. So it goes.

Mr. Upward has taken up the cause of the sensitive; and the sensi-
tives are too few and too indolent to support him, save in their slow
and ultimately victorious manner.

Of course, what Mr. Upward says will be believed in another twenty
of fifty or a hundred years, just as a lot of Voltaire's quiet thrusts are
now a part of our gospel. Mr. Upward will be nicely buried and no
living curate will be out of a job, so that will be all right.

Mr. Upward takes on the lot of 'em. If he were content to poke fun
at one science . . . ah! But he says most scientists are stupid, or something of that sort: most of the rank and file–but what is the use of
talking about mosts?

Let us search for Mr. Upward's dangerous and heretical doctrines.
Most mild is their aspect. Thus:

'When, instead of thinking of men one by one you think of them
all at once and call your thought humanity, you have merely
added a new word to the dictionary and not a new thing to the
contents of the universe.'

That ought to be fairly obvious.

'Altruism is the principle that mankind ought to serve those who
are serving it, but not those who are not serving it.'

Ah!

'It used to be written . . . "All men are liars." . . . "It repented the
Lord that he had made man." No one would dare to say such things
about Humanity."

'The religion of Humanity is not the worship of the best man nor
of the best in man. It is the worship of the middling man.'

This begins to look ugly.

And still he goes on. He draws an invidious comparison between
science and 'scientology'. He propounds riddles. He asks: 'When is the
good not good?' and answers, 'When it is an abstract noun.' Perplex-
ing!

'In the beginning the Goat created heaven and earth.'

It is the astrological goat, but it gets the churchman's.

'The religion which that Idealist (i.e., Christ) has been accused of
founding.'

'The ultimate nature of Materialism is the worship of fixity under
a hundred names.'

'I think that no two men have ever had wholly the same religion, and I am sure no two men ought to.'

'Whatever is has been right and will be wrong.'

'The Churchmen had no doubt that Aquinas was a saint. They applied a simple test and found that, however impartial might be the summing up, the verdict was always in their favour.'

'Today this book (Aquinas), the greatest book of Catholic Theology, ranks as a curiosity rather than as literature. And that is not because, like the book of Copernicus it has done its work, but because no one any longer hopes that it can do any work.'

'The bloodiest iconoclasts the world has ever seen ought not to whine so miserably when their own idol is being washed.'

Of course, Mr. Upward should not assail the scientists, the philologists and the churchmen all in one book. What faction will come to his aid? What formed party will support him?

The clear-headed logician has lost sight of psychology, of crowd psychology. One should always compromise with fools, one should always be sure to please a majority of the dullards, if one desire immediate results.

What! Not desire immediate results? Do I suggest that any man is content to await the verdict of the future, or at least of the next generation?

Supposing I do?

Of course, I am not an impartial judge. I think all established churches an outrage, save in so far as they teach medicine and courage to the more obfuscated heathen, and they don't do such a lot of that.

But on the whole they are nearly as great a pest as were the 'fat bellies of the monks toward the end of the Middle Ages'; they sit in fat livings; they lead lives of intellectual sloth supported by subsidies originally intended, at least in part, for 'clerks', for clerics who were supposed to need a certain shelter wherein to conduct the intellectual life of the race. One demands purely and simply that people oust the parson from his feathered eyrie, and put in it some constructive person, some thinker, or artist, or scientific experimenter, or some teacher of something or other, which he can himself take seriously and which might conceivably be of some use to the race. They might take to reading Confucius . . . if it amused them. Or they might even talk seriously about their professed religion instead of playing the barrister. But this is a matter aside. It is one of the minute corollaries of Mr. Upward's work as I understand it. It is a part of what he calls 'Altruism'.

I recognise the danger of leaving Mr. Upward at large. Not an immediate peril! I recognise also the need of some sort of delayed book reviewing. I mean that the present advertising system provides that all books of whatever merit shall be praised by a certain number of people the instant they appear; that certain kinds of books, or certain particular books, shall be largely circulated; and that certain, practically all, books, save books of verse, go into desuetude within a year or so.

There should be a new sort of semi-critic, semi-reviewer, to go over the mess of books that are a few years old and pick out the few worth saving, the few that he still remembers. It is something of that sort that I am trying.

We all recognise the type of writer produced by present conditions, who keeps in the public eye by a continuous output of inferior work. He is known for his persistent ubiquity. Damn him! I want some more efficient machinery for the preservation of the sort of writer who only writes when he has something to say, who produces odd sorts of books in uncommercial sizes.

I think also that we should try to discriminate between the real man and his secondary emanations. Does it matter the least whether Mr. Upward plays golf or writes detective stories in the intervals between his serious work?

I present Mr. Upward's dicta rather jerkily, partly because I think the readers of *The New Age* are heartily sick of my writing, and partly because I believe they do not want their pabulum diluted, and that they are able to build up the intellectual consequences of a given theme. However, I cannot quote Mr. Upward entire, and I cannot adequately represent his trend in scattered quotations, so I must needs make a partial summary of certain things that he stands for, or that he appears to me to stand for; certain conclusions which I draw more or less from his books.

1. That a nation is civilised in so far as it recognises the special faculties of the individual, and makes use thereof. You do not weigh coals with the assayer's balance.

1a. Corollary. Syndicalism. A social order is well balanced when the community recognises the special aptitudes of groups of men and applies them.

2. That Mr. Upward's propaganda is for a syndicat of intelligence; of thinkers and authors and artists.

2a. That such a guild is perfectly in accord with Syndicalist doctrines. That it would take its place with the guilds of more highly skilled craftsmen.

3. That Mr. Upward 'sees further into a mile-stone, etc.', I mean that his propaganda is for the recognition of the man who can see the meaning of data, not necessarily as opposed to, but as supplementary to, the man who is only capable of assembling or memorising such data. NOTE.–This latter sort of man is the only sort now provided

for by the American University system. I cannot speak for the English.

Aristotle said something about 'the swift perception of relations'. He said it was the hall mark of genius.

The *Century Magazine* wants to bring its fiction 'as near to truth, and make it as interpretive of life, as conditions allow' (*Century Magazine* for September, 1913, page 791, col. 2, lines 29 and 30). Mr. Upward has nothing to do with this spirit. 'As conditions allow' ! ! ! ! ! ! 'Let the bridge come as near to bearing the strain of traffic "as conditions allow". '

4. That since Christ's notable success—in gaining a reputation, I mean—a number of people have desired to 'save the world' without undergoing the inconvenience of crucifixion.

5. That Mr. Upward is a very capable thinker, and that he deserves more attention than he now gets.

Remy de Gourmont[1]

I

It is foolish, perhaps, to say that a man 'stands for all that is best in such and such a country'. It is a vague phrase, and the use of vague phrases is foolish, and yet Remy de Gourmont had in some way made himself into a symbol of so much that is finest in France that one is tempted to apply some such phrase to him.

I think no man in France could have died leaving so personal a sense of loss among scattered groups of intelligent young men who had never laid eyes on him. I do not mean to say that he was the 'greatest writer in France'. That method of assessing authors by size is unfortunate and Victorian. There were in France a few pre-eminently good writers: Anatole France, Remy de Gourmont, Henri de Regnier, Francis Jammes, Laurent Tailhade. There are popular figures and crazes like Maeterlinck, Claudel, and Paul Fort. I am not an examining board trying to determine which of these gentlemen is to receive the highest award. I am not determining a percentage of bay leaves. The writings of the five first-mentioned men are all of them indispensable to one's comfort.

Yet before the war Anatole France was so old that communication between him and the active part of our world had almost ceased. And Henri de Regnier was set apart, as it were, amid 'The Spoils of Poynton', or behind some such metaphorical barrier. And Jammes, after four beautiful books to his credit, had gone *gaga* over catholicism, and from Remy de Gourmont alone there proceeded a personal, living force. 'Force' is almost a misnomer; let us call it a personal light.

The man was infused through his work. If you 'hold a pistol to my head' and say: 'Produce the masterpiece on which you base these preposterous claims for De Gourmont!' I might not be able to lay out an array of books to equal those of his elder friend, Anatole France, or of De Regnier, or to find three volumes of poems to compare with the first books by Francis Jammes, or, indeed, to uphold that test against various men whose names I have not mentioned. You, on the other hand, would be in very much the same fix if you were commanded suddenly to produce the basis of your respect for De Quincey or Coleridge.

[1] The *Fortnightly Review*, 1915.

It is, I think, Coleridge who says that the test of a great poet is not to be found in individual passages, but in a mysterious pervasive essence, 'everywhere present and nowhere a distinct excitement'.

As you read De Gourmont's work it is not any particular phrase, poem, or essay that holds you, so much as a continuing sense of intelligence, of a limpid, active intelligence in the mind of the writer.

I express, perhaps, a personal and an unpopular emotion when I say that this constant sense of the intelligence of the man behind the writing is a great comfort. I even hope that intelligence, in writers, is coming back, if not into fashion, at least into favour with a public large enough to make certain kinds of books once more printable. We have suffered a period in which the glorification of stupidity and the worship of unintelligent, 'messy' energy have been too much encouraged. (With the appearance of James Joyce and T. S. Eliot, and the more 'normal' part of Mr. Wyndham Lewis's narrative writings, one may even hope that intelligence shall once more have its innings, even in our own stalwart tongue.)

The qualities of Remy de Gourmont's intelligence? Limpidity and fairness and graciousness, and irony, and a sensuous charm in his decoration when he chose to make his keen thought flash out against a richly-coloured background; these things were all in his writing. The peculiarity of his narrative work may have been just this method of resting the mind as it were by an 'aroma'. What shall I call it?

He stirs the 'senses of the imagination', the reader is pervaded by luxurious rest, and then when the mind is most open, De Gourmont darts in with his acumen, a thrust, an incisive or revolutionary idea, spoken so softly.

His 'Diomèdes' searches for truth in the Rue Bonaparte and environs. As Turgenev builds up a whole novel to enforce two or three Russian proverbs; to make you know that he, the author, has understood some very simple phrase in all its profundity; as in the 'Nichée de Gentilshommes' he has put first, 'The heart of another is a dark forest,' and then in the middle of the book, man, his hero, opposed to the old trees of his dismantled garden, and then finally old Maria Timofevna's 'Nothing but death is irrevocable,' so, in a very different manner Remy de Gourmont has embedded his philosophy in a luxurious mist of the senses. But this particularity of method would in itself amount to very little.

De Gourmont wrote twice a month, a little 'Epilogue' in the *Mercure de France*. Early in his career he had written a large and beautiful book *Le Latin Mystique du Moyen Age*, and in this book he laid before his few readers a great amount of forgotten beauty, the beauty of a period slighted by philological scholars. These were causes contributory to his position, but no one of them would have accounted for it.

His work had what very little work ever has, despite continuous advertisements to the contrary. It had a personal charm, and this charm was that of intelligence.

Ideas came to him as a series of fine wines to a delicate palate, and he was never inebriated. He never ran *amok*. And this is the whole difference between the French and Tedescan systems: a German never knows when a thought is 'only to be thought'–to be thought out in all its complexity and its beauty–and when it is to be made a basis of action.

I believe England guards against such mistakes by mistrusting thought altogether. At least I once saw a very amusing encounter, as follows: A Russian, who had taken degrees at Leipzig on prehistoric Greek philosophers, came to England. He believed that 'The Germans are the only Greeks of today.' He was going, at least he said he was going, 'to convert England to philosophy'. It was a noble adventure.

He propounded his crusade in a company consisting of two foreigners, myself, and one Englishman. All the Englishman said was, 'I don't believe in ideas.'

It was a very sincere personal statement. The Russian shortly afterwards retired to Paris, to start a peripatetic school in the 'Jardins du Luxembourg', but he finally went to America, and was at once made a professor.[1]

England has been very safe with her 'Don't believe in ideas.' Germany has got decidedly and disgustingly drunk. But Paris is the laboratory of ideas; it is there that poisons can be tested, and new modes of sanity be discovered. It is there that the antiseptic conditions of the laboratory exist. That is the function of Paris.

It was peculiarly the function of De Gourmont.

For years he has written 'controversially', if I may use a word with such strong connotations. I believe he has never once made an overstatement, or, for that matter, an under-statement of his thought. I don't say that he has always been right. But he had this absolute fairness, the fairness of a man watching his own experiment in laboratory. And this absolute fairness, this absolute openness to all thought, is precisely the most difficult thing to attain.

We are all touched with the blight of Tertullian. Whatever our aims and ambitions and our firm conviction to the contrary, we have our moments off guard when we become unfair, and partisan, and personal in our spite, and intolerant.

De Gourmont carried his lucidity to the point of genius. All ideas, all works of art, all writing came to him, and he received them all graciously, and he praised graciously, or he ignored graciously.

---

[1] This tale is not a figment of my imagination; it is not allegory, but fact.

And he wrote beautifully and graciously from himself. He was the friend of intelligence. He had not lost touch with '*les jeunes*'.

And that last is more important and more difficult than one might think. If a man has 'come in' with one generation and taken part in the development of and triumph of one 'new' set of ideas, it is especially and peculiarly difficult for him to adapt himself to the next set, which comes in some twenty years later. No man can lead two movements, and it is very hard for him to understand two movements. A movement degenerates into over-emphasis. It begins with the recognition of a neglect. When youth is divided into acrimonious parties it is perhaps difficult for age to tell which side has the intelligence, but you could trust Remy de Gourmont to discover intelligence in whatever form it might appear.

It is a slight thing that I am going to tell now, but it is not without its minute significance. When I was in Paris some years ago I happened, by merest accident, to be plunged into a meeting, a vortex of twenty men, and among them five or six of the most intelligent young men in Paris. I should say that Paris is a place like another; in 'literature' the French are cursed with amorphous thought, rhetoric, bombast, Claudel, etc., stale Hugo, stale Corneille, etc., just as we are cursed here with stale Victoriana, stale Miltoniana, etc. The young party of intelligence in Paris, a party now just verging on the threshold of middle-age, is the group that centred about 'L'Effort Libre'. It contains Jules Romains, Vildrac, Duhamel, Chennevière, Jouve, and their friends. These men were plotting a gigantic blague. A 'blague' when it is a fine blague is a satire upon stupidity, an attack. It is the weapon of intelligence at bay; of intelligence fighting against an alignment of odds. These men were thorough. They had exposed a deal of ignorance and stupidity in places where there should have been the reverse. They were serious, and they were 'keeping it up'. And the one man they mentioned with sympathy, the one older man to whom they could look for comprehension, and even for discreet assistance, was Remy de Gourmont. Remy would send them a brief telegram to be read at their public meeting.

That is, at first sight, a very trifling matter, but, if examined closely, it shows a number of things: first, that de Gourmont was absolutely independent, that he was not tied to any institution, that his position was based on his intelligence alone and not on his 'connections' (as I believe they are called in our 'literary world').

'Franchement d'écrire ce qu'on pense, seul plaisir d'un écrivain.' 'To put down one's thought frankly, a writer's one pleasure.' That phrase was the centre of Gourmont's position. It was not a phrase understood superficially. It is as much the basis of a clean literature, of all literature worth the name, as is an antiseptic method, the basis of sound surgical treatment.

'Franchement', 'Frankly', is 'Frenchly', if one may drag in philology. If, in ten lines or in a hundred pages, I can get the reader to comprehend what that one adjective *means* in literature, what it means to all civilisation, I shall have led him part of the way toward an understanding of de Gourmont's importance.

'Frankly' does not mean 'grossly'. It does not mean the overemphasis of neo-realism, of red-bloodism, of slums dragged into light, of men writing while drugged with two or three notions, or with the lust for an epigram. It means simply that a man writes his thought, that is to say, his doubts, his inconclusions as well as his 'convictions', which last are so often borrowed affairs.

There is no lasting shelter between an intelligent man and his own perception of truth, but nine-tenths of all writing displays an author trying, by force of will, to erect such shelter for others. De Gourmont was one of the rare authors who did not make this stupid endeavour; who wholly eschewed malingering.

It was not a puritanical privation for him, it was his nature to move in this way. The mind, the imagination is the proper domain of freedom. The body, the outer world, is the proper domain of fraternal deference.

The tedium and the habit of the great ruck of writers is that they are either incoherent and amorphous, or else they write in conformity to, or in defence of, a set of fixed, rigid notions, instead of disclosing their thought... which might, in rare cases, be interesting. It is to be noted that de Gourmont is never tedious. That is the magic of clarity.

'A very few only, and without gain or joy to themselves, can transform directly the acts of others into their own personal thoughts, the multitude of men thinks only thoughts already emitted, feels but feelings used up, and has but sensations as faded as old gloves. When a new word arrives at its destination, it arrives like a post-card that has gone round the world and on which the handwriting is blurred and obliterated with blots and stains.' I open the 'Chevaux de Diomèdes' at random and come upon that passage of Gourmont's thought.

> 'Non è mai tarde per tentar l'ignoto,[1]
> Non è mai tarde per andar più oltre,'

but it was never with the over-orchestration of the romantic period, nor with the acrid and stupid crudity of societies for the propagation of this, that, and the other, that de Gourmont's mind went placidly out into new fields.

He never abandoned beauty. The mountain stream may be as

---

[1] Quoted in Canto XCIII. Ed.   See note on page 25. Ed.

antiseptic as the sterilised dressing. There was the quality and the completeness of life in de Gourmont's mode of procedure. Just as there is more wisdom, perhaps more 'revolution', in Whistler's portrait of young Miss Alexander than in all the Judaic drawings of the 'prophetic' Blake, so there is more life in Remy than in all the reformers.

Voltaire called in a certain glitter to assist him. De Gourmont's ultimate significance may not be less than Voltaire's. He walked gently through the field of his mind. His reach, his ultimate efficiency are just this; he thought things which other men cannot, for an indefinitely prolonged period of time, be prevented from thinking. His thoughts were not merely the fixed mental habits of the animal *homo*.

And I call the reader to witness that he, de Gourmont, differed from Fabians, Webbists, Shavians (all of whom, along with all dealers in abstractions, are ultimately futile). He differed from them in that his thoughts had the property of life. They, the thoughts, were all related to life, they were immersed in the manifest universe while he thought them, they were not cut out, put on shelves and in bottles.

Anyone who has read him will know what I mean. Perhaps it is quite impossible to explain it to one who has not.

In poetry as in prose de Gourmont has built up his own particular form. I am not sure that he was successful, in fact I am rather convinced that he was not successful in the 'Simone', where he stays nearer the poetic forms invented by others. His *own* mode began, I think, with the translation of the very beautiful 'sequaire' of Goddeschalk in *Le Latin Mystique*. This he made, very possibly, the basis of his 'Livre de Litanies', at least this curious evocational form, the curious repetitions, the personal sweeping rhythm, are made wholly his own, and he used them later in 'Les Saints de Paradis', and last of all in the prose sonnets.

These 'sonnets' are among the few successful endeavours to write poetry *of our own time*. I know there is much superficial modernity, but in these prose sonnets Remy de Gourmont has solved the two thorniest questions. The first difficulty in a modern poem is to give a feeling of the reality of the speaker, the second, given the reality of the speaker, to gain any degree of poignancy in one's utterance.

That is to say, you must begin in a normal, natural tone of voice, and you must, somewhere, express or cause a deep feeling. I am, let us say, in an omnibus with Miscio Itow. He has just seen some Japanese armour and says it is like his grandfather's, and then simply running on in his own memory he says: 'When I first put on my grandfather's helmet, my grandmother cried ... because I was so like what my grandfather was at eighteen.'

You may say that Itow is himself an exotic, but still, there is material for an hokku, and poetry does touch modern life, or at least pass over it swiftly, though it does not much appear in modern verses.

De Gourmont has not been driven even to an exotic speaker. His sonnets begin in the metropolis. The speaker is past middle age. It is a discussion of what he calls in the course of the sequence of poems 'la géométrie subordonnée du corps humain'.

I shall give a dozen or more phrases from the sequence (which consists, if I remember rightly, of about two dozen poems). By this means I shall try to give, not a continuous meaning, but simply the tone, the conversational, ironic, natural tone of the writing, the scientific dryness, even, as follows:

'Mes déductions sont certains. . . .
'Mais le blanc est fondamental. . . .
'J'ai plus aimé les yeux que toutes les autres manifestations corporelles de la beauté. . . .
'Les yeux sont le manomètre de la machine animale. . . .
'Et leurs paroles signifient le désir de l'etre, ou la placidité de sa volonté. . . .
'Mais on pense aussi avec les mains, avec les genoux, avec les yeux, avec la bouche et avec le coeur. On pense avec tous les organes, . . .
'Et à vrai dire, nous ne sommes peut-être que pensée. . . .
'Je parlerais des yeux, je chanterais les yeux toute ma vie. Je sais toutes leurs couleurs et toutes leurs volontés, leur destinée. . . .
'Dont je n'ignore pas les correspondances. . . .
'C'est une belle chose qu'une tête de femme, librement inscrite dans le cercle esthétique. . . .'

Or even more solidly:

'Je sculpte une hypothèse dans le marbre de la logique éternelle. . . .
'Les épaules sont des sources d'où descend la fluidité des bras. . . .'

And then, when one is intent and wholly off guard, comes, out of this 'unpoetic', unemotional *constatation*, the passage:

'Les yeux se font des discours entre eux.
Près de se ternir . . . les miens te parleront encore, mais ils n'emporteront pas bien loin ta réponse,
Car on n'emporte rien, on meurt. Laisse-moi donc regarder les yeux que j'ai decouverts,
        Les yeux qui me survivront.'

He has worn off the trivialities of the day, he has conquered the fret of contemporaneousness by exhausting it in his pages of dry discussion, and we come on the feeling, the poignancy, as directly as we do in the old poet's–

Λέγουσιν αἱ γυναῖκες
Ἀνακρέων γέρων εἶ

'Dicunt mihi puellae
Anacreon senex es.'

It is the triumph of skill and reality, though it is barbarous of me to try to represent the force of the original poems by such a handful of phrases taken at random, and I am not trying to convince anyone who will not read the 'Sonnets in Prose' for himself.

II[1]

Remy de Gourmont is dead and the world's light is darkened. This is another of the crimes of the war, for de Gourmont was only fifty-seven, and if he had not been worried to death, if he had not been grieved to death by the cessation of all that has been 'life' as he understood it, there was no reason why we should not have had more of his work and his company.

He is as much 'dead of the war' as if he had died in the trenches, and he left with almost the same words on his lips. 'Nothing is being done in Paris, nothing can be done, *faute de combattants*.' There was an elegy on current writing by him in the *Mercure*. It was almost the same tone in which Gaudier-Brzeska wrote to me a few days before he was shot at Neuville St. Vaast: 'Is anything of importance or even of interest going on in the world – I mean the "artistic London"?'

Remy de Gourmont is irreplaceable. I think I do not write for myself alone when I say no other Frenchman could have died leaving so personal a sense of loss in the minds of many young men who had never laid eyes on him. Some fames and reputations are like that; Mallarmé is almost a mantram, a word for conjuring. A critique of de Gourmont's poetry would be by no means a critique of his influence. For, again, I think that every young man in London whose work is worth considering at all, has felt that in Paris existed this gracious presence, this final and kindly tribunal where all work would stand on its merits. One had this sense of absolute fairness–no prestige, no over-emphasis, could work upon it.

'*Permettre à ceux qui en valent la peine d'écrire franchement ce qu'il pense–seul plaisir d'un écrivain*': these were almost the last words he wrote to me, save a postscript on the outside of the envelope; and they are almost his 'whole law and gospel'. And indeed a right understanding of them means the whole civilisation of letters.

[1] *Poetry*, January 1916.

Outside a small circle in Paris and a few scattered groups elsewhere, this civilisation does not exist. Yet the phrase is so plain and simple: 'to permit those who are worth it to write frankly what they think.'

That is the destruction of all rhetoric and all journalism. I mean that when a nation, or a group of men, or an editor, arrives at the state of mind where he really understands that phrase, rhetoric and journalism are done with. The true aristocracy is founded, permanent and indestructible. It is also the end of log-rolling, the end of the British school of criticism for the preservation of orderly and innocuous persons. It is the end of that 'gravity' to which Sterne alludes as 'a mysterious carriage of the body to cover the defects of the mind'.

De Gourmont did not make over-statements. His Diomedes is a hero because he is facing life, he is facing it quite sincerely, with no protection whatever. Ibsen with his smoky lightning had rumbled out, 'There is no intermediator between God and man.' De Gourmont, with his perfect and gracious placidity, had implied—yes, implied, made apparent rather than stated—that no formula can stand between man and life; or rather that no creed, no dogma, can protect the thinking man from looking at life directly, forming his own thought from his own sensuous contact and from his contact with thoughts.

Nietzsche has done no harm in France because France has understood that thought can exist apart from action; that it is perfectly fitting and expedient clearly to think certain things which it is neither fitting nor expedient to 'spoil by action'.

'Spoil by action' is perhaps a bad memory of the phrase; but just as Dante was able to consider two thoughts as blending and giving off music, so Diomedes in De Gourmont's story is able to think things which translation into action would spoil. As for Diomedes' career, I am perfectly willing to accept Robert Frost's statement that 'there is nothing like it in New England'. What there is in all provincial places is an attempt to suppress part of the evidence, to present life out of proportion with itself, squared to fit some local formula of respectability.

Remy de Gourmont had written throughout his life in absolute single-blessedness; it was to express his thought, his delicate, subtle, quiet and absolutely untrammelled revery, with no regard whatsoever for existing belief, with no after-thought or beside-thought either to conform or to avoid conforming. That is the sainthood of literature.

I think I can show what I mean almost by a single sentence. In the midst of the present whirlwind of abuse he said quietly: 'By Kultur, the Germans mean what we mean by "state education".'

It had been so all his life; on whatever matter, however slight the matter or however strong his own passion, there had been that same quiet precision, that same ultimate justness.

The rest of us are caught in the flurry of controversy. Remy de

Gourmont had found–it might not be incorrect to say that Paris had given him–a place where all things could be said quietly and openly, where one would not think of circumlocution and prejudice, where circumlocution and prejudice would have seemed un-natural.

En tous les pays il y a un noyau de bons esprits, d'esprits libres. Il faut leur donner quelque chose qui les change de la fadeur des magazines, quelque chose qui leur donne confiance en eux-mêmes, et leur soit un point d'appui.

That is good news, but for years M. de Gourmont had believed it and written accordingly. He had written selflessly, and was glad when other men could write well. He dared to write for the few, for the few who are not a clique or a faction, but who are united by the ability to think clearly, and who do not attempt to warp or to smother this faculty; who do not suppress part of the evidence.

The significance of Remy de Gourmont and the significance of his poetry are two things apart. He has written for the most part beautiful prose, much controversy, a book on *Le Latin Mystique du Moyen Age*, etc. He has written a *poème champêtre* and some *Litanies*.

I have praised these litanies elsewhere, and a man's obituary notice is not, perhaps, the best place for analysing his metric. Suffice it to say that the litanies are a marvel of rhythm, that they have not been followed or repeated, that de Gourmont was not of 'the young French school'. If he is 'grouped' anywhere he must be grouped, as poet, among *les symbolistes*. The litanies are evocation, not statement.

De Gourmont was indubitably 'of the young' in the sense that his mind had not lost its vigour, that he was alive to contemporary impressions, that he had not gone gaga over catholicism like poor Francis Jammes, nor wallowed in metrical journalism like the ill-starred Paul Fort. He had never lost touch with the men born ten or twenty years after he was; for a man of fifty-seven that is a very considerable achievement. Or rather it is not an achievement, for it can not be done by effort; it can only come from a natural freshness and aliveness of the mind, and is a matter of temperament.

I had forgotten the French Academy until an article in *L'Humanité* reminded me that de Gourmont was not a member thereof; that the ancient association which contains Auguste Swallou, Thibaudet de Mimmil, and so many other 'immortals' had not seen fit to elect him.

It is evident that the 'Académie Françoise' has outlived its usefulness, and if France does not set an example what *can* be expected of other academies? In de Gourmont's case the academy had no excuse. He had not only written supremely, but he had given back to the world a lost beauty–in *Le Latin Mystique*, in the *Sequaire* of Goddeschalk with its *Amas ut facias pulchram*.[1]

---

[1] Quoted Cantos XCIII and XCVIII. Ed.

But perhaps, as a friend of mine wrote when Swinburne was refused sepulture in Westminster Abbey (they said there was no room and buried the canon's wife the week after), perhaps, as my friend wrote at the time, 'perhaps it is just as well–he suffered fools badly'.

I have known also that the really distinguished member, at a meeting of another 'great body', encouraged one of his more serious colleagues, who was showing signs of tedium, with 'Come, come, we are not here to enjoy ourselves.'

De Gourmont has gone–

Blandula, tenulla, vagula–

almost with a jest on his lips, for his satire on *M. Croquant et la Guerre* continues in the current *Mercure*.

Marianne Moore and Mina Loy[1]

In the verse of Marianne Moore I detect traces of emotion; in that of Mina Loy I detect no emotion whatever. Both of these women are, possibly in unconsciousness, among the followers of Jules Laforgue (whose work shows a great deal of emotion). It is possible, as I have written, or intended to write elsewhere, to divide poetry into three sorts; (1.) melopoeia, to wit, poetry which moves by its music, whether it be a music in the words or an aptitude for, or suggestion of, accompanying music; (2.) imagism, or poetry wherein the feelings of painting and sculpture are predominant (certain men move in phantasmagoria; the images of their gods, whole countrysides, stretches of hill land and forest, travel with them); and there is, thirdly, logopoeia or poetry that is akin to nothing but language, which is a dance of the intelligence among words and ideas and modification of ideas and characters. Pope and the eighteenth-century writers had in this medium a certain limited range. The intelligence of Laforgue ran through the whole gamut of his time. T. S. Eliot has gone on with it. Browning wrote a condensed form of drama, full of things of the senses, scarcely ever pure logopoeia.

One wonders what the devil anyone will make of this sort of thing who has not in their wit all the clues. It has none of the stupidity beloved of the 'lyric' enthusiast and the writer and reader who take refuge in scenery description of nature, because they are unable to cope with the human. These two contributors to the 'Others' Anthology write logopoeia. It is, in their case, the utterance of clever people in despair, or hovering upon the brink of that precipice. It is of those who have acceded with Renan 'La bêtise humaine est la seule chose qui donne une idée de l'infini.' It is a mind cry, more than a heart cry. 'Take the world if thou wilt but leave me an asylum for my affection' is not their lamentation, but rather 'In the midst of this desolation, give me at least one intelligence to converse with.'

The arid clarity, not without its own beauty, of le tempérament de l'Americaine, is in the poems of these, I think, graduates or postgraduates. If they have not received B.A.'s or M.A.'s or B.Sc-s they do not need them.

The point of my praise, for I intend this as praise, even if I do not burst into the phrases of Victor Hugo, is that without any pretences and without clamours about nationality, these girls have written a

[1] From a review of 'Others', [Anthology for 1917], part of *A List of Books*, *The Little Review*, March 1918.

distinctly national product, they have written something which would not have come out of any other country, and (while I have before now seen a deal of rubbish by both of them) they are, as selected by Mr. Kreymborg, interesting and readable (by me, that is. I am aware that even the poems before me would drive numerous not wholly unintelligent readers into a fury of rage-out-of-puzzlement.)

Wyndham Lewis at the Goupil[1]

M̲r. Lewis' picture of the Gun Pit is one of the few outstanding works at the Canadian War Records exhibit, but his drawings now at the Goupil Gallery are an advance on the painting, or else the painting is a retrogression from the drawings, one of which appears to be a more personal study for the left lower corner of the big picture.

As Mr. Lewis implies in his preface to the catalogue, there are two ways of regarding 'war paintings'; first, as paintings (*vide* Mr. Lewis' remarks about Uccello); secondly, as illustrations of war (*vide* Mr. Lewis' remarks about Goya); as 'paintings' Mr. Lewis' drawings are about the most successful war show we have had. There are fragmentary drawings like the detail of mechanism of the camouflaged gun, a mere study; there are intermediary states, and there are fully finished works like the drawings of gun-pits; works which can be submitted to all the criteria. These works are signally free from the violence which characterised Mr. Lewis' pre-war productions. The artist is the antidote for the multitude. At least, there is antidotal art, whether one approves it or no. There is also art which needs antidotes. Mr. Lewis' art does not. The drawings in this exhibit could, most of them, hang in one's study without palling. This means that they are well composed, well constructed, and harmonious in their colour schemes.

What are called the tactile, but should be called the lift-ile values are excellent. I mean there is definite proof of anatomic skill in the degrees of tenseness of the various figures: the men, particularly the centre man, lifting the short balks preparatory to building the gun-pit; the men hauling the gun; the larger figures pulling on the rope (40) all display the different, the quite different mechanical or physical strain of their attitudes; and this expression or exposure of bodily capability is shown by the artist with the fine graduation of a master. The layman will be hard put to tell you just why each figure expresses such a strain: the per-kilo, per-foot pressure in each instance. That is to say, the strain is exposed with great economy of means. So also is the devitalisation of the wounded as they return over their duck-boards.

By subtle gradations we come out of the technical problems of composition into the problems of 'drawing', and thence into the illustrational qualities: man the alert animal peeping dog-like out of his protective burrow, nosing danger.

[1] *The New Age*, 20 February 1919.

Another property of Mr. Lewis' work is its 'partialness'. I mean that every series of the three series of Lewis' drawings I have seen appears to be the beginning of some exposition which might go on indefinitely for the rest of the artist's life. (In two cases it has been continued by imitators.)

There seems no reason why Mr. Lewis should not go on for years unrolling the panorama of artillery labour, phase by phase of the operations; there is a complete world of the matter; just as there was a complete possible world of violent or impassive forms suggested by his 'Timon'; or by drawings at the old Doré Gallery in 1914. The present show is manifestly only one corner of Mr. Lewis. But it is no function of mine to speculate about potentialities. I am here merely to find the good in each show as it opens regardless of 'school', whether it be Mr. Nicholson's conscientious still life; or Mr. Geo. Belcher's gratuitous labour in refining his tones for drawings that will be made mediocre in weekly reproductions. Mr. Lewis' show is of no particular school; it touches his vorticist work at one corner, and Uccello or Signorelli, or perhaps Kunisada at another. One should perhaps run over to the National Gallery to discover just which primitive it should 'recall' to one's memory. There is, or was, the little Judas in or near the front hall; and various other scenes of the crucifixion. Before the renaissance there were simplifications and eliminations quite as 'revolutionary' as any we shall find at the Goupil. But I cannot see that these early Italians were more satisfactory.

It also appears to me a sign of resource that a man known chiefly as a revolutionary inventor of forms, and what his adherents termed 'forms in combination', should now appear as a narrative painter with an apparently unlimited subject-matter, a capacity for suggesting unlimited subject-matter. I think the readers of *The New Age* have by now become reconciled to Matisse, Brancusi, Picasso, or, at least, to Van Gogh, Gaudier, Cézanne. I do not think the majority will find the present work of Wyndham Lewis 'too advanced'. There is, from the purely aesthetic point of view, a calm pleasure to be derived from clear tones, the cold air, the desolation of the Ypres Salient, with the pyramidal arrangement of three men in the wilderness. The sketches in the entrance room lose nothing by comparison with Turner's water-colours. Those who ragged Mr. Lewis five years ago for his cubism, futurism, vorticism, and so forth, will vainly seek for the old points of attack in these drawings. My own preference is for the rough, spirited oil painting, 'To Wipe Out'; here the purely optical effects of shell-burst and of battle are fused with emotional expression. The figures in the lower right-hand corner are, I think, more satisfactory than even the pink-shirted nigger in the Canadian War Records picture. I would draw attention to the forms in 11, to the 'Walking Wounded' (No. 17), to the treatment of combined figures in 29, to the concentration of force, to the gun-mouth in 19, to the detail of 52: and my aim in this article has been to suggest that Nos. 11, 17, 32, 36, 39, 40, 41, 43, 45, 47, 53, are the best art that has 'come out of the war'; but they have come a good deal more out of art; out of art's resistance to war, than out of war's much-vaunted 'effect upon art'. Indeed, Mr. Lewis would seem to suggest that art is a cut above war; that art might even outlast it.

Hudson: Poet Strayed into Science[1]

udson's art begins where any man's art is felicitous in beginning: in an enthusiasm for his subject matter. If we begin with *The Naturalist in La Plata* we may find almost no 'art' whatever; there are impassioned passages, naïve literary homages, and much unevenness and a trace of rhetoric in the writing. *The Shepherd's Life* must, at the other end of the scale, be art of a very high order; how otherwise would one come completely under the spell of a chapter with no more startling subject matter than the cat at a rural station of an undistinguished British provincial railway.

Hudson is an excellent example of Coleridge's theorem 'the miracle that can be wrought' simply by one man's feeling something more keenly, or knowing it more intimately than it has been, before, known.

The poet's eye and comprehension are evident in the first pages of *The Naturalist*: the living effigies in bronze rising out of the white sea of the pampas. Then the uneven eloquence:

> 'And with the rhea go the flamingo, antique and splendid; and the swans in their bridal plumage; and the rufous tinamou–sweet and mournful melodist of the eventide; and the noble crested screamer.... These, and the other large avians, together with the finest of its mammalians, will shortly be lost to the pampas utterly.' ...

> ... 'What a wail there would be in the world if a sudden destruction were to fall on the accumulated art-treasures of the National Gallery, and the marbles in the British Museum, and the contents of the King's Library–the old prints and mediaeval illuminations! And these are only the work of human hands and brains–impressions of individual genius on perishable material, immortal only in the sense that the silken cocoon of the dead moth is so, because they continue to exist and shine when the artist's hands and brain are dust: and man has the long day of life before him in which to do again things like these, and better than these, if there is any truth in evolution. But the forms of life in the two higher vertebrate classes are Nature's most perfect work; and the life of even a single species is of incalculably greater value to mankind, for what it teaches and would continue to teach, than all the chiselled marbles and painted canvases the world contains; though doubtless there are many

[1] *The Little Review*, May–June 1920.

persons who are devoted to art, but blind to some things greater than art, who will set me down as a Philistine for saying so.

'And, above all others, we should protect and hold sacred those types, Nature's masterpieces, which are first singled out for destruction on account of their size, or splendour, or rarity, and that false detestable glory which is accorded to their successful slayers. In ancient times the spirit of life shone brightest in these; and when others that shared the earth with them were taken by death, they were left, being more worthy of perpetuation.'

One may put aside quibbles of precedence, whatever the value of evidence of man's fineness, and in an age of pestilence like our own there is little but the great art of the past to convince one that the human species deserves to continue; there can be no quarrel between the archaeologist who wishes to hear the 'music of the lost dynasty', or the gracious tunes of the Albigeois, and the man who is so filled with a passion of the splendour of wild things, of wild birds which:

'Like immortal flowers have drifted down to us on the ocean of time . . . and their strangeness and beauty bring to our imaginations a dream and a picture of that unknown world, immeasurably far removed, where man was not; and when they perish, something of gladness goes out from nature, and the sunshine loses something of its brightness.'

The voice is authentic. It is the priesthood of nature. Yet if an anthropologist may speak out of his pages to the 'naturalist', it is not only the bird and furred beast that suffer. A bloated usury, a cowardly and snivelling politics, a disgusting financial system, the sadistic curse of Christianity work together, not only that an hundred species of wild fowl and beast shall give way before the advance of industry, i.e., that the plains be covered with uniform and verminous sheep, bleating in perfect social monotony; but in our alleged 'society' the same tendencies and the same urge that the bright plumed and the fine voiced species of the genus anthropos, the favoured of the gods, the only part of humanity worth saving, is attacked. The milkable human cows, the shearable human sheep are invited by the exploiters, and all other regarded as *caput lupinum*, dangerous: lest the truth *should* shine out in art, which ceases to be art and degenerates into religion and cant and superstition as soon as it has tax-gathering priests; lest works comparable to the Cretan vases and Assyrian lions *should* be reproduced and superseded.

There is no quarrel between the artist and Mr. Hudson, and he is right in saying that there would be more 'wail' over the destruction of the British Museum than over the destruction of wild species. Yet how little the 'public' cares for either. And how can it be expected to care so long as so much of it is 'at starvation level', so long as men are taught that work is a virtue rather than enjoyment and so long as men render lip service to a foul institution which has perpetuated the writing of Tertullien and of men who taught that the human body is evil.

As long as 'Christendom' is permeated with the superstition that the human body is tainted and that the senses are not noble avenues of 'illumination', where is the basis of a glory in the colour-sense without which the birds-wings are unapprehended, or of audition without which the bell-cry of the crested screamers is only a noise in the desert.

'Their strangeness and their beauty' may well go unheeded into desuetude if there be nothing to preserve them but usurers and the slaves of usury and an alleged religion which has taught the supreme lie that the splendour of the world is not a true splendour, that it is not the garment of the gods; and which has glorified the vilest of human imaginations, the pit of the seven great stenches, and which still teaches the existence of this hell as a verity for the sake of scaring little children and stupid women and of collecting dues and maintaining its prestige.

My anger has perhaps carried me away from Hudson who should have been my subject; yet his anger is germane to it. Mediaeval Christianity had one merit, it taught that usury was an evil. But in our day Rockefeller and the churches eat from the one manger, and the church has so far fallen into vacuity that it does not oppose 'finance', which is nothing but a concatenation of usuries, hardly subtle, but subtle enough to gull the sheep and cow humans.

And for the same system man is degraded, and the wild beasts destroyed. So I have perhaps not lost my subject after all, but only extended my author's exordium.

The foregoing paragraphs can hardly be taken as introduction to Mr. Hudson's quiet charm. He would lead us to South America; despite the gnats and mosquitoes we would all perform the voyage for the sake of meeting a puma, Chimbicá, friend of man, the most loyal of wildcats. And, as I am writing this presumably for an audience, more or less familiar with my predilections, familiar with my loathing of sheep, my continual search for signs of intelligence in the human race, it should be some indication of Hudson's style that it has carried even me through a volume entitled *A Shepherd's Life*, a title which has no metaphorical bearing, but deals literally with the subject indicated.

'Caleb's shepherding period in Doveton came to a somewhat sudden conclusion. It was nearing the end of August and he was beginning to think about the sheep which would have to be taken to the "Castle" sheep-fair on 5th October, and it appeared strange to him,' etc.

John B. Yeats has written somewhere: 'I found that I was interested in the talk, not of those who told me interesting things, so much as of those who were by natural gift truthful tellers'; a phrase which is as good a qualification of Hudson's work as I can find. Hudson's books are indeed full of interesting things, of interesting 'information', yet it is all information which could, like all information whatsoever, have been made dull in the telling. But the charm is in Hudson's sobriety. I doubt if, apart from the *Mayor of Casterbridge*, and *The Noble Dames*, and the best of Hardy, there is anything so true to the English countryside as Hudson's picture. F. M. Hueffer must not be forgotten; there is his *Heart of the Country*, and passages in other of his books to maintain the level; and Hueffer is perhaps at his best when he approaches most closely to Hudson's subject matter; when he is least clever, when he is most sober in his recording of country life.

This is not however an arranging of hierarchies and an awarding of medals for merit. Hudson touches Hueffer when dealing with England and Cunninghame Graham in dealing with La Plata. And it is very foolish to wail over the decadence of English letters merely because some of the best work of these three men is possibly ten years old.

It is perhaps faddism and habit that causes people still to gossip of Poe, when 'El Ombú' has been written, not as a grotesque but as tragic elegy, as the ordered telling of life as it must have happened. And then Poe's prose? Poe's prose is as good as Hudson's in places, and Hudson is indubitably uneven; relieved if not by *hokkus* at least by the sense of the 'special moment' which makes the hokku: thus his trees like images of trees in black stone.

This image-sense is an enrichment, perhaps 'dangerous' to the unity of his style, but very welcome to the lover of revelation. And to balance it there is the latent and never absent humour as in 'Marta Riquelme'.

'What is, is; and if you talk until tomorrow you can not make it different, although you may prove yourself a very learned person.'

Jean Cocteau Sociologist[1]

The livest thing in Paris 1933 was Jean Cocteau. A dark inner room, no clatter of outside Paris. He talked, I should say almost without interruption for two hours and over, with never a word that wouldn't have been good reading. I mean with never a bit of gossip, never a triviality, nothing but thought about matters of interest to more than the two people present.

By contrast Louis Aragon was simply distressed that the Surrealist movement was being blown to bits by mere *personal* squabbles in no way connected with thought, in no way connected with art, writing or politics.

The post-war boys in France were a set of orphans in the worst sense of the term. After the death of Gourmont there was no elder writer whom they could respect. War blew up a lot of clichés. Patriotism in the service of a set of escrocs does not conduce to respect for one's elders, for tradition, for sanctified verbal formulations.

Among the mature French writers there was no one to stand by. France was worse off than England. It might be pointed out that the Shaw-Wells-Bennett line have NOT founded a group for the same reasons that Barrès and the rest of 'em have not done so. They haven't had any cause wherewith young men could form an alliance. And on that ground Orage was immeasurably their superior though, as I have said before, it will take the public some time to discover it.

A man's writing is his own. But his principles are shareable treasure.

Cocteau is so essentially a writer–so probably the FIRST continental writer, apart from a few late lapidary and practically unknown prose paragraphs of D'Annunzio, that no one has yet mentioned his contents.

The *eterna freschezza* that we would all like to attain, seems so weightless that no one considers its strength.

With no disrespect to the distinction of 'M. Teste', a writer can't live thirty years on the reputation of one prose sketch, and apart from 'M. Teste' and a few professorial studies, better done than those of the average American fresh water professor, because France is a more civilised country, and neat finishing more habitual in Paris than in Peoria, one wonders what, in the last balance and weighing, Paul Valéry has to set against the sheer bulk of Cocteau's writing. There is

---

[1] *The New English Weekly*, 10 January 1935.

some very pretty verse in the very much manner of Mallarmé, but why all this spate of critical jabber, in every half-baked English or American magazine, about the French academician, in contrast to the extreme difficulty of getting Cocteau published in translation?[1]

True, we had the same difficulty about Rémy de Gourmont, and Cocteau is a better writer than Gourmont.

Possibly a feminine reader hit the mark with: 'But it is MUCH too fine, of course they will never get it.'

Nevertheless in asking a proportionate estimate of Cocteau against a number of writers who recently received high consideration, it might be well to consider both the bulk of his writing, and its nobility. I am aware that the public's Cocteau is the Cocteau of Marie Laurencin's portrait, the exquisite, the wing of the rarest possible moth. But are we expected to stop at the Cocteau of yesterday, Cocteau of 'Le Mot'?

Among writers, may we be permitted the privilege of weighing a writer who WRITES, while other bookmakers are 'joining', 'adopting', preaching pacifism, without inspecting economics, 'turning', communist, bolshevik, or this, that and the other AFTER the battles–oh yes, usually, in fact almost always, AFTER the victories.

Cocteau's writings include: Poésie (a good, full volume), Opéra, Heurtebise, Le Potomac, Le Grand Ecart, Thomas l'Imposteur, Les Enfants Terribles, six volumes of criticism that no one else could have written, Antigone, Œdipe Roi, Orphée, La Voix Humaine, La Machine Infernale, and various works with musicians.

That is to say as writer, and nothing else but writer, apart from being a unique perceptive intelligence (as shown in his criticism) we have three novels that are not any other man's novels. We have an unique contribution to drama that has but one living competitor, the author of *Six Characters in Search of an Author*, and we have perhaps the one living dramatist whom Pirandello READS with respect.

Pirandello was *concerned*, while Cocteau was writing Œdipe, for Cocteau's danger of tackling that subject without a plop into Freud, or it may have been only a passing thought that floated up over the luncheon table, in brief conversation, but it ended with the Italian's shrug: 'NO, on the whole no, he won't fall into Freudian mess. Il est trop bon poète.'

Which is emphatically true. Cocteau is the one man who can do, and has done things in the theatre which are beyond Pirandello's capacity. There is a rigour in Cocteau that has not been in Pirandello,

---

[1] *Le Mystère Laïc*, translated by Olga Rudge, appeared in *New Directions I* in 1936. E. P.
Alan Neame's translation of *Léone* appeared in *Agenda* (Volume 2, Nos. 2–3, December–January 1960–61). Ed.

at least not since the Six Characters, and Cocteau's force is so different that there is no profit in comparison. Thank God for both authors in an otherwise rather desolate stage-scape.

Cocteau has the freest mind, and the purest, in Europe; I mean if you can carry up your thought to the *nous*, to the mind of the world AS MIND, and not a secretion of tissues.

Living writers attain nobility? Indeed! and how many. Yeats has a sort of nobility in his somewhat clouded way, in his language that is the speech of no man. But neither Yeats nor Pirandello could attain the: 'T'as inventé la justice.' in Cocteau's *Antigone*.

I am *stufo* and *arcistufo*, *j'en ai diablement marre*, *archimarre*, I call on Jarry to express me with an extra 'r' in his favourite expletive. I am fed *u p* (up) with young idiots who can't see that history does not exist without economics; who do not know that Bithinian mortgages at 12 per cent are a matter of history; who think that any man can understand history in the book, without economics, or that 'l'histoire morale' can get on without economics any more than any other department of history, or that literature keeps its head in a bag.

A writer's awareness to relations is vastly other than an impulse to write treatises. I write treatises because I am a species of pachyderm, I am a porter of teak, I am a beast of burden because the circumjacent literati are weaklings, they are piffling idiots that can't get on with the job, they can not even write text books. It is necessary to start in the grammar schools, and I can type for eight hours a day.

It is necessary for me to dig the ore, melt it, smelt it, to cut the wood and the stone, because I am surrounded by ten thousand nincompoops and nothing fit to call an American civilisation or a British civilisation; but that is no reason for Cocteau's writing treatises.

There is every reason for his providing something for ME to read.

The more a man knows, oh well, no use my trying to write that, Gourmont has done it. 'Rien ne pousse à la concision comme l'abondance des idées.'

Nothing conduces to limpidity so much as does perfect acquaintance. Nothing has been more use to Cocteau than domesticity with the Greek language.

If it hadn't been the Greek drama something else would have served him, but the Greek LANGUAGE need not be confused with Greek drama. No man has ever been less likely to get spattered with the kind of mud I have had for 25 years slung at my head. Cocteau knows enough Greek, so that it passes unnoticed. At least I suppose so. As to Greek drama, before Cocteau had published any, Eliot and I looked over the ground. This is no place to say what we thought of it. But it is, permissably, a place to register the fact that we DID nothing about it, except possibly form a few critical opinions that we wouldn't have had, if we hadn't prodded and poked at father Æschylus.[1]

Cocteau has brought not a resuscitated old corpse, but an ephèbe out of the sepulchre, with a young step and a living language.

'Alors, si l'idée de fantôme te fait sauter en l'air, c'est que tout le monde, riche ou pauvre à Thebes, sauf quelques gros légumes[2] qui profitent de tout . . .'

That is language full charged with meaning. It has in it indeed the *whole political wisdom* of the past two decades and it has NOT penetrated the skulls of ten dozen people. Orage has written it time and again, I have written it less often than he did, and I have been quoted by brother Munson as having enlightened his darkness, and I have, without any false modesty, enlightened several coagulations of darkness, but I have not done half so well as Jean Cocteau. There IS a French civilisation. Flaubert is a good deal OF French civilisation. Flaubert's books are considered, by half-wits, too heavy. For example, Père Rouault's letter has a whole life on a page.

Compare that texture with Cocteau's. It will take a decade's teaching to make people, once they have understood why Flaubert's weight is of tremendous importance, understand that you can have a great lightness. Cf. Henry Ford on the idiocy of making railway trains extra heavy. The bottom of p. 22 in *La Machine Infernale*, has a condensation equal to Flaubert's.

'Guerre c'est déjà pas drôle, mais crois-tu que c'est un sport que de se battre contre un ennemi qu'on ne connait pas. On commence à en avoir soupé des oracles, des joyeuses victimes et des mères admirables.'

A writer's greatness can, in certain dimensions, be measured by the amount of his time he contains.

It is time we stopped tolerating discussion of Cocteau as a mere society writer, and, if we have any respect for our own critical estimates, it is time we placed him where he belongs, certainly above all living French academicians, certainly in the rank with his peers, however few of them be still living.

---

[1] Pound translated Sophokles' *Woman of Trachis* in 1954 (Faber paper-covered editions, 1970). Ed.

[2] Quoted in Canto LXXXVII. Ed.

Obituary: A. R. Orage[1]

HE PULLED HIS WEIGHT

The sudden death of Orage at this time, on the day after his broadcast, is a graver loss to England than to his oldest friends. For a forty years' war on evil no man stood his equal in Britain. During two longish stretches of that fight there were probably a dozen other men who each thought he stood nearest to him. I can only say that for one period we seemed almost to get out the old *New Age* between us, and that the small dissident minority who profess to get some profit from my writings owe debt, above whatever they realise, to the man whose weekly guinea fed me when no one else was ready to do so, and that for at least two years running.

The public's loss will be more apparent to them in ten years' time than today.

The actual battle with ignorance, in the acute phase wherein I shared, began with Douglas's arrival in Cursitor Street. The earlier Guild Socialism, and all other political or social theory had lain outside my view. (This statement is neither boast nor apology.) I take it I was present at some of the earliest talks between the two leaders. At any rate my economic study dates from their union, and their fight for its place in public knowledge.

A selfless fight. A fight that should have brought them international recognition far sooner. The resistance to Douglas's ideas was the greatest incentive. I think I could say, it was so to all of us.

Orage's impersonality was his greatness, and the breadth of his mind was apparent in the speed with which he threw over a cumbrous lot of superstitions, and a certain number of fairly good ideas, for a new set of better ones.

But it was the gag that aroused one. Why, if Douglas was right, should people be afraid of discussing him or his formulations?

I take it that in 30 years of journalism Orage never printed a line he didn't believe. This is not the year nor the decade when England can spare that sort of honesty.

During 21 years, I think that Orage never admired a single author whom I admired, and that, in my own work, he liked only that part which differentiates me from the living writers whom I have respected

---

[1] *The New English Weekly*, 15 November 1934.

or eulogised. The sole exception was, during the last year or so, Carlos Williams. I mean that our 23 years' friendship was a friendship of literary differences and never one difference concealed.

In economics we had but one divergence, namely re. the *expediency of* Gesselite demurrage money or stamp scrip. As to the corporate state, I believe differences were more a matter of time and location than of any root disagreement. He died exactly one month after the speech to the Milan workers. It was natural that he should not see this in the same light that I do, or rather that he should have estimated it differently, as a victory, certainly, but perhaps not yet fully as the great and final collapse of Scarcity Economics. Monday night his voice came over the radio, curiously gentle and patient, without the fire I had known or the sharp snap and crack of the sentences, but very clear, as the transmission was mostly good, though the last sentence went with a crackle (thunder probably in the Alps).

He had written to me during the last year when his hand was weary from physical labour of writing. A dozen others must have known the same thing, and known that he had a specific sense of his mission. That both he and I were fatigued should be apparent from an egregious typing error in the last issue, that I should have written it, from fatigue, and, as I had no proofs in Rapallo, that he should have passed it, warned me that I needed rest, but he, apparently, did not take similar warning.

On Oct. 24. Three opponents 'had reconsidered'.
On Oct. 10, writing to me of the Duce's Milan speech he was:

'Not satisfied that he (Mussolini) sees any alternative to *Employment* as the only legitimate title to purchasing power.'
That letter ends 'perhaps I write not for men but for God!
'Yours ever, A. R. ORAGE.'

With the full signature, as valediction, where he signed normally with initials.

Orage's superiority over the men of his decade and over the prominent or protuberant public figures and writers a decade or so older than himself was that he pulled his weight. In an age of funking abuleia, of passing the buck, he never waited for cats to jump, he never shirked the *responsibility of forming an opinion*. Shirking of that kind is fundamentally the technique of certain gross forms of worldly success. It is so easy to profess ignorance, it is so cravenly easy to keep ignorance real.

That is why I say that the public, which never knew Orage at his full size, will take another ten years to discover what is now missing. The present government of the United States will have lost its most faithful foreign critic.

Its domestic critics can be divided mainly into corrupt reactionaries, the slime of the Hoover, Mellon, McCormick, Patterson contingent, howling for usury, and the sloppy half-baked liberalistic ballyhoo of the semi-ignorant backers of the Administration, trying to apply the *Saturday Evening Post* methods to not very sage aspiration.

Precisely the focus of thought, and the focus of information that was in the weekly notes of this paper, will have disappeared.

However much one may have protested against the rigidity of Orage's viewpoint, the function of that rigidity, of its inestimable utility became clear whenever one, over a period of weeks or months, compared it with the waftier and less stable editorial policies of more 'tolerant' advanced papers.

In thought as in warfare, you must have both scouts, and fixed positions and bases. Orage's very obstinacy constituted a value.

Douglasites grouped in England may know what they mean to do next, or Douglasites gathered into groups anywhere may have a definite line of project, but the scattered social creditors who kept in touch with the movement via *The New English Weekly* will be, at least temporarily, 'taken aback', not knowing whether the captain is dead in the moment of victory assured, or if an aggregate of individuals, with more or less common belief, but with no cohering organisation, and no capacity for concerted action is left scattered, and drifting.

This is no time for a burial service. It is a time to rally and to get on with the work: A concentration and reprint of the pith of Orage's economic writings, as soon as possible.

And for the training of a later generation, a biography. For a man who writes 'books', biography matters nothing, but for the publicist and combatant the lesson is in the relation of the act and the word to its time. Only when that act of weighing has been performed will the outer public judge Orage in full bulk.

In the Wounds[1]

(MEMORIAM A. R. ORAGE)

Neither the great public, nor the very small public that can afford to pay 7s. 6d. at a shot for its magazines will understand the significance of Orage's death, or be able to answer the question: 'Who was Orage?' until they understand the ideas to which he devoted the last fifteen years of his life:

A. In themselves.

B. In relation to the living economic ideas of this decade *and* the known and undeniable facts of history, the more significant among which are usually concealed from the public, almost never taught by hired professors of either history or economics and often ignored by the very people to whom the poor ape of a public entrusts its most vital affairs, i.e. M.P.'s, members of 'brain trusts', presidents of republics, directors of great financial houses and their most advertised and projecting trained seals.

C. In relation to the gross ignorance in which my generation and yours and our fathers' generation have been reared and in which the generation that followed mine was very largely killed off.

A couple of years ago I had the unpleasant experience of hearing Leon Blum drool for forty-five minutes to the Paris Press Club. Before I could ask him whether his ignorance and his party's ignorance of modern economics was real or pretended, Bill Bird had asked him a technical question, and by the time he had finished evading that question (twenty-two minutes) Sparrow Robertson and the other pressmen present would certainly have assassinated any private guest who had given Leon an excuse for further verbal manifestation. Blum is no more disgustingly ignorant than 80 per cent of French, American, and even British ministers, members, senators and their managers.

Proudhon will be found somewhere in the foundations of perhaps all contemporary economic thought that has life in it. Plenty of people know in vague way that Orage 'started as a guild socialist' and perhaps that Mussolini did likewise, but clear ideas of what guild socialism was when either O. or M. started, are uncommon. Both men found it advisable to move on. I see *three living* varieties of economic thought.

The idea of the corporate state has already entered the domain of action on the grand scale. Gesellism has been tried locally and succeeded.

[1] *The Criterion*, April 1935.

Douglasism went to the polls for the first time in the autumn of 1934, in Australia. And it is with Douglasism that Orage was concerned. 'Social Credit' and 'New Democracy' give weekly and fortnightly counsel to the converted and nearly-converted and to people who know a little about it. I will try to write the next few pages for those who know nothing.

Sometime in 1918 or thereabouts an ex-engineer, ex-head of Westinghouse's Indian branch, then managing an airplane factory noticed that his factory *was creating prices faster* than it emitted the power to buy.

Say that in a month the factory produced £20,000 'worth' of airplanes, but distributed only £17,000 as purchasing power, in wages, dividends, etc. Douglas saw that if his factory was doing so, all other successful factories *must* be doing so in greater or less degree. If factories don't, they go 'bust'.

Dexter Kimball's figures as to the percentage of business failure, the history of American railways, the long muddled and much graphed and charted 'problem of the cycle of crisis' are all eloquent footnotes to which any serious person can refer. Anyone whose mind is capable of receiving impressions from exterior objects, and of correlating the mental stimulae so received, should be able to follow the process of the Major's thought after he made this observation–i.e. a concrete observation of the *fact* in his own factory.

Orage recently made a pregnant remark on thermo-dynamics, the 'second law of thermodynamics' whereby you cannot unscramble eggs.

To the devotee of algebra, six eggs scrambled may equal six eggs unscrambled. There exist also several printed volumes on purely mathematical fallacies.

The Major's *first* observation is on a par with the observation of the falling apple or of the kettle lid lifted by steam: a *point* of departure.

People have asserted that they 'haven't seen it'. The factories where it does not occur, gradually disappear if it continues not occurring for a longer period than they can stand its non-occurrence. No one, so far as I know, has attempted to *disprove* this part of Douglasism either to Douglas, to Orage or to the present writer *by* the simple presentation of the accounts of a firm.

President Roosevelt got as far as saying 'if half a nation can't buy what the other half produces' but he refuses, or has up to date refused, to look at the impasse presented when 'the whole of a nation cannot buy what the *whole* nation produces'.

He is the shiftiest great politician (as distinct from mere cheats and scoundrels) that I can, for the moment think of. The moral cowardice of failing to look at this problem is not quite commensurable by the political expedience or 'political craft' implied. Hence the murmur that he is sold up the river to Governor Lehman's friends (true or false, as may be).

Douglas's perception was that *under* the present accounting system the public's purchasing power can *never* catch up with prices, and that the actual money available can never *buy* all the goods available.

Anybody can or should be able to see the millions of people, ten millions in Britain, twenty millions in America now unable to buy half of what they *want* or even a decent percentage of what they need.

This *objective* fact apparently does *not* penetrate the minds of statesmen and bankers. It merely skims over the greasy pate and causes a transient uneasiness.

Orage's last words over the radio, emerging for Rapallo from the crackle of Alpine thunder were: 'in the gap between Price-values and Income is enough gunpowder to blow up every democratic parliament'.

Admuit. That was a fine sentence to die on.

Mussolini is erecting an assembly *more representative* than the old model parliament, he is working against the 'gap' by a human Italian system, which he has himself stated was not 'an article for export', all of which needn't prevent the intelligent foreigner from learning the truth about Italy, or perhaps acquiring a little of Italy's cultural heritage. Europe has twice before done so, with advantage.

Douglasism proposes to start bridging the gap from a different position. Anyone who *thinks* out the results of the accounting system now raging will see that the deficiency of purchasing power is *not static*, but that the gulf is constantly widening.

The idiocy of mere spasmodic dumping of purchasing power, ought to be visible. Douglas proposes an irrigation system.

The main complaint is: where will the state *get* the money to pay dividends? Why isn't it merely 'persistent, never-ending inflation'?

For Douglasism (itself part of a thought-heritage) proposes to distribute purchasing power to the public via national dividends. And this strikes some people as absurd, or at least as impossible.

These same people often receive dividends from their 'investments in industrial or national bonds'. They often read in newspapers that 'government subsidies have been granted' or that 'doles', etc., are being provided or that 'relief' is provided. *But* the spectacle of nations *pouring* out purchasing power by the million through specific grants, emergency measures and as 'charity' causes no mental cohesion, or no mental activity based on the convergence and interactions of thoughts.

People know that most money is *paper*, or they don't know it, and are unable so to consider it. The Macmillan Commission *admits* that banks create money. Bank-defenders admit that nine-tenths of all money is 'bank money'. The idea that most purchasing power exists either as engraved paper or as entries in account-books is too diaphanous to take root in the public comprehension.

Money is a 'representation of something else', it is or *ought to be* the representation of something solid.

It *ought* to be the representation of something *solid and deliverable* or else of available service (like a ride on the railway or tramcar). Under the present oppression it is often the representation of a mere airy probability (called by its exploiters 'sound banking' or 'sound finance' or 'orthodox economics').

Apart from the deliberate cheats and fools, men of goodwill and partial enlightenment often do honestly wonder *whence* the state *could* draw its power to pay continual dividends (i.e. distribute pieces of engraved paper with a certain regularity) without going bankrupt.

To explain this one is tempted to reach backward into the chasm of history. Once usury was *condemned* by the Church's high wisdom, to the same hell with Sodom, as 'contrary to natural increase'.

But the Church sanctioned the 'increment of association'.[1]

It was a black day for Europe when this distinction was lost. It was also a dull day for England when Insularity raged so that Gourmont's writings on the Dissociation of Ideas failed to receive proper attention, simply as *method* in thinking.

When small merchants could not fill each one his own ship, they banded together, and shared in marine adventure, both peril and profit. When savages hunted, they now and again hunted in bands. A group of men acting together can, in some circumstance achieve more than the *sum* of the possible attainments of the same hundred men acting each on his own.

The difference between these *sums*, is the 'increment of association'.

That increment is essential in the comprehension of the Douglas plan, for which A. R. Orage gave his life.

Five thousand Basutos cannot sling a Baldwin locomotive forty feet into the air, and put it down gently on the other side of a factory.

When men associate not only with other live men, but with the aggregate of all acquired skills and inventions, the increment of *association with* all these skills and inventions adds another dimension to the 'increment of association' an increment so enormous that popular imagination is still incapable of understanding it, and many people are still scared, as of a bogey man.

---

[1] Definitions. *Increment of association:* Advantage men get from working together instead of each on his own, e.g., crew that can work a ship whereas the men separately couldn't sail ships each on his own.

Cultural heritage: Increment of association with all past inventiveness, thus, crops from improved seed; American wheat after Carleton's researches; a few men hoisting a locomotive with machinery. *Social Credit: An Impact*, 1935. Ed.

This new increment is the 'cultural heritage' of Douglas's economics.

Mere *work* is no longer the root of power. That is to say it is *not* the work of the living men actually employed, or concerned in doing a given job, that contributes most to its performance.

Three men doing the work of 3,000, or doing work that 10,000 could not have done, have, let us admit, a particular *part* in the attainment of the results, and should receive special honour or recompense for it. But the ratio between the work done and the worker is *not* what it was in the Dark Ages, or even in 1850.

The *'più alta giustizia sociale'* demanded by Mussolini in the Milan Piazza will certainly take count of the proportion between 'heritage' and immediate physical labour, or living men's skill, implicated in the performance of future production.

In a gross way communism *denies* utterly the proportion in this proposition.

Socialism and various left-over schemes refuse to admit a proportion.

It should be apparent that in this great association there is an enormous source of riches. 'Science has solved the problem of production', etc.

Ever since economics emerged from its primitive stage, in handbooks for bankers, the men who have thought about it have assured us that money must be an 'equivalent'; the medium of exchange must be a true picture of the material represented.

Marx failed to realise sufficiently the root difference between property and capital; property a possession; capital a claim on other men's work, often savagely enforceable. In like manner volumes have been wasted in idle discussion because of failure to take adequate count of the difference between permanent, or long durable, and perishable and quickly perishable goods.

A fixed money can easily represent permanent goods. Two means, and I believe two only have been devised for a monetary and credit system that will simultaneously and steadily represent a conglomerate of durable and perishable goods, one is the Douglasite system of compensated price, the other the Gesellite Schwundgeld, though not in the crude state some Gesellites imagine.

Stampscript can only represent the conglomerate (durable and perishable goods) if issued *in a certain ratio* to fixed money.

Issued in proper ratio it could do a good deal of what Douglas aims at. *But* the ascertaining of that proper ratio would be just as complicated as the computation necessary to decide on Douglas's 'just price'.

No system of economics can dispense utterly with all detail and all computation. Communists and many communisant distributists and cunctative socialists seem to think that by getting rid of tickets altogether you tend to simplify life.

Gesellism lies outside a discussion of Orage's aims. He opposed it. For the moment I shall simply assert that any Gesellism which refuses to take count of a ratio, a proportion between the quantity of fixed money, and that of money requiring a monthly stamp (1 per cent) to keep it valid at par, is not serious.

(Again I assert that three great men studying reality from three different angles, but without personal vanity, whatever their initial oppositions, are bound to converge in measure as they attain complete understanding. My present job is to state Orage's position, referring to other concepts only in so far as they help me define his position.)

The fundamental material reality underlying the Douglas solution of poverty, slums, industrial tyranny, is that the cost of production is consumption.

That is to say a nation during a year is out of pocket, or out of possession of those things it consumes, destroys, sends abroad.

Whether it produce goods (raw and fabricated), buildings, etc. to the value of one billion or ten billion, the material cost of those things is what it exports and consumes, and that destruction includes the wear and tear on the workmen, it includes the depreciation of the national health during the period.

I think it was Albert Londres who remarked on the drivelling mania of the ghouls who govern French Africa: 'you would think when trying to produce, they would consider the necessity "faire du nègre".'

Those of us who in moments of violent meditation are ready to treat financial tyrants as Russians once treated Bojars arrive at this frenzy in considering how the preachers of what they call 'economy' meaning the curtailing of consumption, are prodigal of the life and health of great masses of white populations, Caiaphas and company do not like to think of these things.

The economy which would build up the health of ten million Englishmen, and twenty-five million Americans is not yet come into practice. Only in the Corporate State, and only in Italy has any drive been made toward this objective.

This saving could come by taking heed of other expenditure and of the cost of non-human materials.

Apart from the work that goes into it, the *cost* to England, or Holland or any other country, during a year, of all it makes, of all that grows in its fields *is* the 'consumption' (including export).

Toulousains do not eat the veal they ship to Paris. Platitude! Obvious! But absolutely invisible and incomprehensible to a banker. You don't believe me? All right *ask* a banker. Ask *any* banker.

When a costing system, that is a system for estimating what anything costs, and therefore what people should pay for it in proportion, takes count of this fundamental basis, that system will be heading toward the 'più alta giustizia sociale', it will be heading towards economic justice and you will either have Douglas's 'just price' or you will have something with another name that will be found to be rather like it.

So far no one has had the glittering and transcendent imagination to think out what the difference will be, but then very few first rate or even second rate minds have occupied themselves with the problem.

I have said specifically, and Mussolini knows implicitly, that you can have an enormous margin of economic injustice in a jolly fine social system. By which I mean neither you nor I care a hang whether the steak we have for dinner 'is worth' 2s. 3d., 2s. 9d., or 3s. 8d. (three an' eight pence) so long as it is a prime steak and so long as we can afford to get *enough*. and do get, *de facto*, enough.

Douglas aims high, and wants economic justice. It may be an engineer's blueprint of a state unattainable. Radio and flying were once 'unattainable'.

At any rate Orage writing 'for God' insisted on, or at any rate emphasised justice, though we won't see it in action this summer.

Douglas having invented a mechanism felt, I think, that there was no use *preaching* the locomotive, and that it could be of comparatively little use to people too incurious to investigate its function or too stupid to understand its utility. There is a good deal to be said for this attitude.

On the other hand there is a good deal to be said for stopping, without needless delay, the wholesale murder of great masses of our population. Orage was so built as to feel indignation at the spectacle of skilled biologists labouring to find a remedy for pellagra that would be cheaper than food.

ORAGE

I had no interest in Orage's mysticism and am unqualified to define it. I was thankful he had it simply because it kept him in action. He prized the moral indignation of his contributors. I don't know that it helped the clarity of our writing. But, on the other hand, the lack of it in our contemporaries has not always produced better results, nor on the whole a clearer outlook.

Mere abuleia, or the sheer cowardice that causes a man to shun a decision inside his own mind as to the right or wrong, the rightness or wrongness, the sanity or unsoundness of a given idea or congeries of ideas does not of itself lead to lucidity of perception or precision of judgment however much it may help a ninth rate or even a third rate wordster in the avoidance of immediate trouble.

Orage had the concept: rectitudo. On that rock was his edifice. If the reader knows a better rock let him take it with my benedictions and compliments.

Orage's *rectitudo* demanded justice, justice in the division of the 'eredità culturale', the cultural heritage; of the increment of association.

It demanded that the price charged the plain man and consumer should have a just ratio to the real cost of his food and clothing, and that adequate monetary-tickets should exist.

He did not care particularly who issued the tickets, though Social Credit, as formulated, favours their control by the 'representatives of the people'.

Only within the last few months has a new kind of 'representation of the people' been offered in competition to the very seedy and out at heels Mother of Parliaments or the assembled employees of the Standard Oil and other great American companies gathered in Washington.

This mechanism is a matter of politics. I doubt if Orage had any political talents whatsoever. He was a moralist, and thence an economist.

He loathed above all other animal categories the dog in the manger. Only the descendant of this canine species can hold this against him.

Those of us who saw the Major's point in the first weeks of his first declarations find it rather difficult to unsee it, or to put ourselves in the role of non-perceivers. I don't know how you are to put us in your places. I mean how, for example, are you going to convince the bee that a bee-line isn't the shortest or most convenient to travel.

For three or four years Orage repeated, now soft, now loud, now irate, now ironic: 'consumption is the cost of production. You cannot *cure* unemployment. Unemployment is *not* a disease. We could get all the food and goods needed if the banks would get out of our way, if the banks wouldn't sabotage our exchange and consumption.' And so forth.

Then he took ten years' vacation. The trams of the Lord move slowly. The screw propeller for ships was invented as soon as the paddlewheel.

Three years ago Orage thought the light might have penetrated Albion's occiput. I suppose our old gang was then in at least three corners of the spherical planet.

Any government worth a damn could pay dividends instead of levying taxes. I don't know who *said* it first. It was apparent from Douglas's early propositions.

From early times people have been accustomed to a proportion between public and private ownership. The ratio has varied, from the theoretical total ownership of a sovereign to the theoretical total ownership by '*them*', i.e. the theoretical abolition of all private property.

'Mais, ça appartient à eux', said an orthodox Bolshevik official when

417

I asked him what really was the difference between the Italian present regime and his own.

As I have said above, and will have to repeat a thousand four hundred times in the next semester: property and capital differ. They are not *one* and the same.

You can upholster any and I believe every economic idea (except stamp script) with historic background and precedent. You can ring the changes on town land and crown land, on common and freehold.

You can *not* obliterate the difference between the righteous and the unrighteous, or between the man who will learn (in the old sense of will), the man who *has* the intention of coming to truth, and the man who will not learn.

Every honest man in my time who has started thinking about the nature of money has seen a need to reform the present system of control of it. What is money? how does it get there? who makes it? These questions asked week by week. How do men buy; and how can they?

Who makes the medium of exchange? Who controls them? What guides them? How did they come into power?

Did Rothschild make money or take money, by his swift ride or his agent's swift ride after Waterloo?

Who deserves well, and who ill of the state? of the people?

These questions Orage asked over and over in every new form he could think of.

The gross ignorance of men high in power is demonstrated to me week by week, the tergivisations, the twistings of men in authority are thrown into relief every week on the desk where I am writing. Friendships are broken, and old esteems go by the board when one finds an old friend deficient, deficient in simple honesty, in an accustomed old frankness.

'How can any man trust politicians', writes the friend of thirty politicians. 'You are a Fascist and to hell with all Fascists'. 'Heartfelt thanks'.

'I have never been able to agree with Douglas's scheme, though I accept many of his premises; but your views interest me immensely'.

'Value of your name is appreciated—so can't you manage to do some other kind of work—anything except economics?' Arthur Kitson remarked: the first three professors who started to use my books in their classrooms were removed from their jobs with great promptness.

'I assure you that your views are appreciated and that all of the problems you touched upon are having the thoughtful attention of the administration'. (20 March 1934) 'I assure you he (Roosevelt) does understand that the whole people must be able to buy what the whole people produces'.

Maybe, but by 19 November F.D.R. hasn't, so far as I know, admitted it publicly. Many people seem to think he's been 'sold up the river'.

From the day Roosevelt entered the White House, Orage was perhaps his fairest and most open critic. If his hopes and his rages varied as mine have, his expression was calmer and he seemed less given to excess in either direction.

As to this question of the public's being able to buy its own produce, an answer (for the 94th time one would think it *was* the answer, an answer, the answer, the ultimate answer to the persistent (but from every new head of the hydra) question: *Why* isn't it (Douglas economics) just persistent never-ending inflation?

That answer I quoted in print in 1933. 'Would you call it inflation to issue tickets for every seat in a theatre, regardless of the fact that the theatre has until now been always two-thirds empty *simply* because no such number of tickets was printed?'

Even in Jefferson's time people were saying you 'have to have more money in circulation when you have a greatly increased quantity of goods', meaning that for a higher standard of living it will be convenient to have both faster and more ample exchange of products, and to be adequate the number of tickets, or the accounting, must keep up with this increase of available consumable or usable goods.

Lack of historic knowledge keeps people from comparing life in an industrialised country with life in Doughty's desert Arabia or with life in very dark ages, say about 700 or 800 A.D. when they tell us European production had dwindled, in fact Europe was producing hardly anything save human beings, and there was an oriental market for eunuchs.

Historic detail sometimes starts a man thinking. Orage wrote *into* a public that had been blindfolded by generations of books produced under the heel of the profit system, fouled by the mentality of decades oppressed by university and educational systems warped by the profit system, by a bureaucracy of education, the bureaucrat being a man who avoids 'dangerous' knowledge, who can almost indefinitely refrain from taking, officially, cognisance of anything whatsodamnever that is likely to disturb his immediate comfort or expose him to the least inconvenience or ridicule.

Exempio gratia: Van Buren's memoirs were written in 1861 and published in 1920.

There were, and are, arrears of learning for the public to make up, and against this siltage Orage battled until his last heart gripe. It was the sea of stupidities, not a clean sea, it was the bog, the mud storm and quicksand of obfuscation, the ignorance, the non-correlation, the irritation of the jostled, the gross silence of hired concealers and the utter triviality of 'men great in the public eye', or notorious authors whose royalties rolled in from the continent, or the U.S.A. or the provinces.

'Has he *got* an opinion? Is the x . . . z . . . y . . . q . . . p . . . (or whatever the phrase might be) capable of an opinion?'

We knew that kind of comment in the office. Orage sat in Cursitor Street with a Diogenes lantern of a new pattern; it showed up many curious profiles. Pickthall came in with facts. The young Turks knew somebody was lunching with the high, the *high*, oh very, and so forth. Whatever one lost in those days in nickle plush and Ritz dinners, one gain in the zest for knowledge.

'Very few people', says Edgar Wallace, 'are respected by anyone.'

One of the best tributes in the memorial number of the *New English Weekly* was from a man who, so far as I know, was scarcely acquainted with Orage, and whose authority or importance Orage at any rate professed in private to find wholly beyond his comprehension. I can telescope both that tribute and Wallace's epigram from experience. You could call Orage a damn fool *and* respect him. I don't mean you could do first one and then the other I mean you could do both at once. Usually you knew that the folly was superficial that it meant an insistence on something of greater importance than the fancy style or minor merit of a given case up for discussion, that it amounted to no more than his singleness of intention, and his urge to get along toward his goal.

His 'pickin' daisies' covered most of the artistic activities in his epoch. We who were ten years or more years younger cheered for the superior daisies. Several seemed rather good.

He printed my 'Seafarer' in the old *New Age*, I think he may have printed the first draft of the *Nekuia* (unless it was Granville), he printed my 38th canto, and the 41st went through the press in his last issue. He didn't want it 'dressed up'. For twenty-three years I don't think that either of us ever took the other seriously as a critic of letters, and now thinking of it in retrospect, I wonder how far the difference of view was a mere matter of the twelve years difference in our ages.

I remember his contented discouragement on one occasion, 'Oh well I suppose it just is that I can't make you into a journalist.'

To this day I haven't the faintest idea who *read* that paper. The only man I ever met who had seen my stuff in *The New Age* was an admiral. I was seated in a battleship, one spot where the empire still conserves order and ceremony; where you still get a Bath oliver; where red wine is still called claret, at least by the steward. I accused the admiral (unjustly) of having looked me up in *Who's Who*.

He on the other hand assured me that 'these men are personally honest' meaning several, as I recall it, cabinet ministers, or at least men in high place.

The office was equally in the dark as to my interest, at least I remember one grin of greeting: 'We were just wondering what *you* read in the paper, or how much you look at.'

To weigh Orage at full value the reader is asked carefully to consider the meaning of the next sentences:

Orage wrote in the British Empire. Even I am old enough to remember a time when the Empire was very efficient. I think it was efficient probably because it could make use of a great number of half-wits (bureaucracy) admirably controlled by a very much smaller number of johnnies who were manifestly *all there*.

While the admiral could assure me that his friends were personally honest, i.e. in private dealings, another member of the ruling caste could equally assure me that his cousin so-and-so who was *very* high, had been very much surprised to find so-and-so lunching with so-and-so and addressing him by his front name.

All of which tempts me to a number of less relevant speculations, many possibly pregnant, but all centrifugal, all likely to lead us away from the main theme: Orage's ideal, Orage's concept of justice. You can't get twenty-three years of a man's life into one funeral notice.

The aim concretely was to equate the nation's purchasing power to available goods. And by nation we here must include the aggregate of individuals purchasing goods for their individual needs, as well as mass purchases made for the needs of the public as public.

(Would you, said Lord Tankerville, say you couldn't build roads because you hadn't any kilometres?)

To that end Orage meant, as a Douglasite, that any and every man's earnings were to be augmented by a share of the 'increment of association' (with the nation, and with accumulated means of production).

He meant that the price charged should have just relation to the material cost of the object.

The rest is matter of detailed computation regarding specific cases. It regards particular cases. The state *has* credit. Distribution is mainly effected by means of little pieces of paper, or at least the ultimate distribution to individuals of their daily and weekly supplies is effected mainly by little pieces of paper. The French for fifteen years after 1919 used little brass discs labelled 'Chambres de Commerce de France, Bon pour 2 francs', or '1 franc'. This fact had no more effect on the thought of English economists than had Mallarmé on Rudyard Kipling. Professor Gubbet went there and never knew what he was using. Dealing with England's Gubbets Orage finally wore himself out.

If I have inadvertently left any obscurities in this article, I apologise. I also refer the reader who finds the statement lacking in detail, to a brief shilling pamphlet by Major Douglas *The New and Old Economics* (Scots Free Press, 1 India Buildings, Victoria Street, Edinburgh).

D'Artagnan Twenty Years After[1]

Perhaps there were only two musketeers, that is, three of us in all who had a two barrelled art and the gift of verbal invective. But having had the text bound for preservation and turning back to inspect it, I am moved to demand a reprint at least of some passages. The text is still gristly. Mr. Laughlin brilliantly advocates Gertie Stein as cathartic, the best apology yet. And there may be something to his plea. A single idea expressed in and as a method is easier for half-wits to ingurgitate than a seething mass of ideas bursting through any method and demanding each one its individual capture.

Naturally New Zealand disliked it. Naturally Manchester took six months to discover the satiric propulsion of the Quarto BLAST, 1914.

I turn back to *Exile*, 1927 and find that very little, as indicating metabolism of writing, has occurred in the interim. I turn back to the *Little Review*, 1917/19 and find very little news intervening between that date and the present on the literary frontier. 1923 winter of the same periodical showed a fair list of surrealists with all the subsequent features of that little coterie.

PARIS: clap trap heaven of amative German professor

wrote Wyndham Lewis in 1914 or it may have been 1913 if one allows for delays in printing and the distance between London and Harlesden (where was Mr. Leveridge's print shop).

'WE must kill John Bull,' wrote Mr. Lewis. 'BLAST HUMOUR quack english drug for stupidity and sleepiness, arch enemy of the real, conventionalising like gunshot.' 'Impossibility for Englishman to be grave and keep his end up.' 'Chaos of Enoch Ardens.'

It wasn't the finished thing. It wasn't the finished article. Cocteau in the *Mystère Laic* years later gave us the silk-fine web of indirect criticism. Nothing is new and all good is renewal.

Aristotle spoke the true word about metaphor, the apt use whereof is the true hall-mark of genius.

The hokku is the Jap's test. If *le style c'est l'homme*, the writer's blood test is his swift contraposition of objects.

Most hokkus are bilateral.

> The foot-steps of the cat upon
> The snow:
> Plum blossoms.

[1] *The Criterion*, July 1937.

May seem to the careless peruser to be only bilateral, two visual images; but they are so placed as to contain wide space and a stretch of colour between them. The third element is there, its dimension from the fruit to the shadow in the foot-prints. No moral but a mood caught in its pincers.

> The waves rise
> And the waves fall but you

(this is a hero's monument in Nippon)

> are like the moonlight: always there.[1]

Another dimension. From dead thesis, metaphor is distinct. Any thesis is dead in itself. Life comes in metaphor and metaphor starts TOWARD ideogram.

The live writer in France is Cocteau. The live writer in England has been for over a quarter of a century Wyndham Lewis vorticist.

The ideogrammic method did not wait for Fenollosa's treatise to become current in book form. We didn't wait to know of Fenollosa's existence. Nevertheless 1912–14 London fought its way into the sodden light of that epoch.

1908 saw a stirring. By 1912 it was established, at least in Ormond St., that the cardboard Shaw and the suety Wells were NOT the voice. That Arnold Bennet was inadequate, that British impressionism was too soft.

England was so smug in those days (as in 1937) that *Blast* was regarded as violent. So dynamic is ANY equation that attains any sort of justness whatsoever.

BLAST is a legend. I could fill pages with citations from it and go undetected.

'Chaucer was very much cousin of Villon as an artist. Shakespeare and Montaigne formed one literature.' 'Humour is a phenomenon caused by sudden pouring of culture into Barbary.'

That is Mr. Lewis in *Blast*. So also is: 'Chaos invading concept.' 'Any great Northern Art will partake of this insidious and volcanic chaos. No great English art need be ashamed to share some glory with France, tomorrow it may be with Germany where the Elizabethans did before it. But it will never be French any more than Shakespeare was, the most catholic and subtle Englishman.'

The whole public and even those of us who then knew him best, have been so befuddled with the concept of Lewis as EXPLOSIVE that scarcely anyone has had the sense or the patience to look calmly at his

---

[1] Quoted in Canto XCIII. Ed.

perfectly equanimous suave and equipoised observations of letters. The difference between a gun and a tree is a difference of tempo. The tree explodes every spring.

Any full man, any man who approaches the Renaissance totalitarianism, who refuses to run in the most paying groove repeating himself once a week or once monthly to meet a 'demand' is bound to suffer occultation, to remain three-fourths in shadow because men of little comprehension can not reconcile themselves to, or digest the concept of, intelligence shining in divers places from a centre.

The public (his public) so expects Mr. Lewis to break out philosophically, or in relation to politics and social institutions that no one asks whether his donation to the critique of letters is or isn't in substance equal to Mr. Eliot's.

'The Latins are at present in their discovery of sport ... gush over machines ... the most romantic and sentimental "moderns" to be found. It is only the second-rate people in France or Italy who are thorough revolutionaries.'

'The nearest thing in England to the great traditional French artist, is a great revolutionary English one.'

I repeat: the silky quality of *Le Mystère Laic* is not here. But this was written in 1914. No two writers having any real value completely overlap one another.

When Lewis writes for the eye, he is visible. General formulations in the writing of Lewis or of any man do not and can never attain the vividness of *The Enemy of the Stars*. Why should I open to that play at a time when Mr. Eliot has just been exhorting England over the air to be poetic in dramedy I don't know. *La forza del destino*. Here WAS poetic drama.

Here before the B.B.C. murmured at every fire-side WAS and IS (mehercule) the RADIO DRAMA. Written, printed 1914, impossible of presentation by any medium save the human voice carried through the black air: a DRAMA.

A drama for Radio because no material theatre and no conceivably effective precentor with a megaphone standing in the pit bellowing the stage directions could move the theatre goer as could the proper changes of voice by a great speaker 'on the air'.

The play has waited a technique for its presentation. Cocteau has evolved the technique. First with his own voice and megaphone off stage in *Les Mariés* and in *Antigone*, then with the Columbia discs; much to the distress of the studio director. Cocteau in his fumoir with his discs and his radio, with his oracle that speaks pure cipher, unsurpassable trouvaille; cleaving-stroke of the spirit, moving as no human voice.

Cinq, douze

Cocteau has evolved the technique for Argol. In detail. But *The Enemy of the Stars* had been written before that.

'Immense collapse of chronic philosophy. He bulges all over. Human bull rushes into the circus. He is not even a "star".'

This is pre-war. It is very distinctly pre-Gertie. 'Red of stained copper predominant colour. Overturned cases and other impedimenta have been covered, throughout arena, with old sail canvas.'

One, or at least the present, writer is mildly bored with the tosh emitted during more than a decade by Mr. Joyce's epigons; blather about the revolution of the word. The renovation of the word may stem out of Stendhal. Flaubert was certainly grandfather to any verbal renovation of our time, but the phase specifically touted by Mr. Joyce's Parisians and international penumbra was already in full vigour in Mr. Lewis' writings in BLAST 1914. At a time when Mr. Joyce was still the strict classicist of 'Chamber Music', 'Dubliners' and the Portrait of the Artist as a *beau jeune homme*. The difference being that Lewis' renovation of the word was a vigorous renovation and not a diarrhoetic imitation of Mr. Joyce's leisurely flow and murmurous permuting. Lewis' renovation was conceptual. Joyce's merely, in the main, sonorous, an attraction of the half-awake consciousness to and by similar sounds.

Naturally the abundance of conceptual bustle in Lewis is infinitely less digestible, thence less attractive to writers of mediocre envergure. It is radically inimitable in that it can only come from a think-organism in action, a mind actually initiating concepts, or at least very busily chucking them from one side of a head to another.

'Sudden indignation at Argol acting, he who had no right to act.'

BLAST was regarded as a manifesto, as an action, which it was, but an excessive preoccupation with that particular part of its function has obscured the more durable elements, the level criticism, for example, of the note: Futurism, Magic and Life.

The public was manifestly not ready for the kind of criticism that Lewis then offered 'them'. Mr. Laughlin in his *New Directions* speaks eloquently of the subjects under his eye, but some of them should stand in a wider artographic survey, that is, in relation to what Lewis had printed before Mr. Laughlin started assessing our universe. As, for example, the note on Relativism and Picasso, the attack on the deadness inherent in *natures mortes* by definition (an essay on the then 'latest' Picasso work, namely what he had done 1912–14).

The next note begins:

'A civilised savage in a desert city, surrounded by very simple objects. . . .

'Sculpture of the single sententious or sentimental figure. . . .'

425

The durable malady or limitation of the criticism in *Blast* is not that it is broken and jabby, but that there still hangs about it a 'morning-after'. Lewis had escaped from the polite paragraph but the old inertia of momentum still led him to finish his sentences, often when the complete revelation of idea had been made in a single phrase.

The 'world' in those days was so accustomed to having its sun (intellectual sun) rise in Paris that no one even today remembers that Lewis' remark on Ingres and the recent cult of ugliness preceded Cocteau's clean cut identification of D'Annunzio and Marinetti. So unmoving was the air in the French parlour and dining room that Aragon's generation doesn't yet know that at given date the French were missing a train already gone from the Ormond St. and Kensington junction.

'When an ugly or uncomely person appeared on the horizon of their daily promenade Ingres' careful wife would raise her shawl protectingly, and he would be spared a sight that would have offended him.

'Today the Artist's attention would be drawn, on the contrary, to anything particularly hideous or banal, as a thing not to be missed. Stupidity is . . . etc.'

'A man could make just as fine an art in discords, and with nothing but 'ugly' trivial and terrible materials, as any classic artist did with only 'beautiful' and pleasant means.

'*But it would have to be a very tragic and pure creative instinct.*'

Readers of Lewis are so often startled, or read him so often with the expectation of being startled that they don't wait for the end of his thought.

'The Kaiser had made war on cubism before he made it on England.' 'All the fun in Shaw's plays . . . is based on sport and blood.' The second issue (1915) contains these bits of information and 'A super-Krupp or War's End'.

'And it seems to me that as far as art is concerned, things will be exactly the same after the war as before it.' That sentence illustrates Mr. Lewis' balance and sanity, 1915. A totally different mental equipment from that rampant in the Wells-Shaw-Bennett-Sidney-Webb *bouillabaisse* of half-masted blather which preceded my decade and Lewis' decade.

Just as Gaudier got a great deal of what he intended to say into *The Embracers,* so without anyone's much suspecting it Lewis got a great deal more of a world-map of his own intentions into those two volumes of *Blast,* than anyone has taken the trouble to notice.

These were the intentions of an already consummate combiner of forms, of a man who has mastered the relation of volumes in an art which has actually only two dimensions as its field of expression. As to his colour sense. Compare Lewis 1912 with Max Ernst or Matisse, to take two maxima of the century.

As achieved work in writing you have Tarr, you have the early short stories, and you have the *Apes of God* or at any rate you will have it when its contemporaneity has worn off and a few readers can regard it as an objective manifestation, that is as a work in which figures are 'created', exposed, set forth.

This is the Britain of Fielding, Smollett, Hogarth and Rowlandson, I mean as they were in their strong interiors.

To this catalogue of Lewis' writings, I still wish we might add the unwritten rest of the Crowd Master, which it is now too late for Lewis or for anyone else to conclude.

Of my own contributions to *Blast* the note on Binyon's *Flight of the Dragon* ought to have preceded that on his translation of Dante in my last volume of essays, where it would have been had I not overlooked it.

If this present note can be regarded as spoken to toddlers gathered at one's knee, I should reiterate the sentence on a great deal of Paris being chronologically later than the London of 1914, the best of Paris followed fairly quickly (meaning Picabia then in New York and Dada then suckling in Geneva). The afternoons at Picabia's with Cocteau and Marcel Duchamp were thoroughly *à la page* in 1920–21, but the rest of Paris was not, and so far as I can make out from incipient London 1936–37 there is ten years of time lag still in your city. News is, I suppose, news after a decade if the news reader is overpoweringly earth-bound, spatial, etc., but the velocity is rather that of a fog than of etheric vibration.

The natural antithesis now as it was two decades ago is between Joyce and Lewis. The critic can get a number of useful measurements by it. In Lewis' favour today one is almost driven to the summary that 'at any rate' Lewis has never for five minutes been willing just to sit back and be a celebrity. Herein Mr. Joyce celticly approaches his equally celebrated Irish confrere and predecessor.

LA RICHEZZA È LO SCAMBIO

One theme in the foregoing paragraphs needs exegesis. I am nowhere pleading for mere novelty or mere news value in art. 'We' London 1911–14 were subsequent to a great deal of Paris. For example Fernand Leger in 1902 was doing the kind of drawing which Gaudier did in 1911. I can not believe that any great number of people in England, the U.S.A. or even in Paris know this. I know it only by accident, having lived a few doors from Leger and having by sheer chance turned over a soiled bit of paper amid a heap of his sketches, saying at once: 'My God, Fernand I didn't know you could do that!'

To which the rich slow voice: *Oh voui, mais je pouvais pas PEINDRE.*

That is the measure of Leger's asceticism; of the sobriety of his purpose. The Leger known to the great public, carpet designs, mechanical forms, put aside his facility. Nobody knows him as draughtsman (you could compare Plate XXVII in my 'Gaudier-Brzeska'); all that quick appeal was put aside for the *autre chose*, the thing people didn't know, and that Leger has built up in thirty-five years, impressive perhaps, or at least justly assessable, only when you see Leger's work *en bloc*.

Opulence comes of exchange. There were any number of continental precursings. It was definitely our job, London 1908 to '14 in the workings of one intellectual blood circuit to eliminate our ignorance of ten years' continental plastic and forty years' continental writing.

But Paris post-war had a torpid liver, its digestion was weak and even Voisin's has vanished. We knew we were subsequent, Aragon's generation did not.

The wave that had Picasso as foam rose at least into 1922. And the intellect inside it was Picabia whose mental activities cannot be ignored in any serious chronicle of the decade 1914–24.

You can trace a very vital critical action [*sic*]: Wyndham Lewis, Picabia, Cocteau. Disjunct, not the conscious process of a conspiracy but lively minds meeting a common need *of the period*.

'He discovers the moon once a week' remarked Francis Picabia of Mons. Z.

Picabia is the only man I have ever met who has a genius for handling abstract concepts with the ease and surety a chartered accountant would have with a bill (ordinary) of lading. Bert Russell strikes me as a half wit. The philosophers *de carrière*, the men who write ABOUT what they call thought, etc. and philosophy, are all heavy, incompetent dunderheads, insensitive to one or other part of the spectrum.

If you don't examine 'J. C. Rastaquouère' between 'BLAST' and *Le Mystère Laic* you lose the chronological sequence in those *états du cerveau états de l'âme* wherethrough and whereby 'literature renews itself'.[1]

The definition of *rasta* being: *étranger dont les moyens d'existence sont inconnus*.[2]

'J'ai envie de fabriquer une voiture automobile "artistique" en bois de rose, mélange de pillules Pink. Les pneumatiques seraient en acier et les billes en caoutchouc, comme FUTURISME ce ne serait pas mal.'

Francis, enfant terrible as draughtsman, ten lines to summarise a year's work by Picasso. Francis the only man who was really indignant at the *Mariés de la Tour Eifel* because it was not a new creation from scratch. *Cet homme, il abîme tout. C'est La Tour Eifel de Delauny.*

To my mind this was very unjust, in that it did not credit the energy

---

[1] 'La litterature se renouvelle par les états du cerveau–états d'âme–plus que par la forme ou le sujet, quelque- fois par les grands sentiments qu'on a à sa portée.' Gabrielle Buffet, Intro- duction to Picabia's *J.C.R.*

[2] Quoted Canto CV. Ed.

and real work required to get a given effect from a painter's canvas onto the stage and into action. But it was nevertheless prophetic of what the delightful entertainment *became* the instant Cocteau took his hands off it and the performers were free to break down all Jean's precisions of movement. I mean the stylisation of their gestures, whereof they were limited to one each in the original presentation.

Picabia greeted Marinetti post-war with: 'I dreamt that it was my great-grandfather who discovered America, but not being an Italian he said nothing about it to anyone.'

When we were selecting stuff to be reproduced in a special Picabia number of the ʟ/ʀ. I picked a dozen canvases, then another dozen and said: 'but at any rate not that one'.

'No!' he replied, 'Not that one, *C'est de Picasso*.' As it was, a gift.

Picabia was the dynamic under Dada.

It is you might say 'footless' to present surrealism without its mental *état civile* – merely because 66 pages of Picabia were locked in a cellar by a terrified publisher, and are, thence, little known outside the very active group which had immediate access to them in 1919 and '20.

'Europe exhausted by the conquest of Alsace Lorraine.' *Pauvres êtres tombés par centaine pour la gloire d'un ventriloque.*

> Il y a beaucoup moins
> de choses sur terre
> que ne nous le fait croire
> notre philosophie

Even if Picabia's sole virtue were corrosive, which I don't for a moment grant, Europe in 1919–22 needed ammonia, it needed an *eau de Javel* triple strong, and a man who could cut the barnacles off Picasso, Cocteau, Marinetti, pitilessly but with consummate good humour was an asset to Europe.

I have written more than once that Gaudier Brzeska was the most complete case of Genius I have ever encountered. Put it creative genius, fully equipped, but Gaudier wasn't a danger to everyone in the room. You could have slept or dreamt for twenty minutes while Gaudier was hammering the butt end of a chisel, but you had not the excitement of mental peril which accompanied Francis Picabia. There was never a rubber button on the end of his foil. It wasn't a foil, it was a razor sharp at the point and had thereby the vastly greater pedagogical value.

The intention of this article, in case it may still have escaped any reader, is to assert by implication that the intellectual world of our time, or my time, has contained a reasonable number of large and vivid mental animals, enough to prevent a moderate man's feeling he lives in an absolute desert, and secondly to assert quite openly the trouble there was, the midwifery required, to get *out* of the nineteen hundred and eights (London) or the *fin du siècle dixneuvième* Paris and leave a place free for Prufrock. I mean for a new decade to get started without cerements, without verbal ligatures still binding it to the world of my adolescence, of Lewis's adolescence.[1]

[1] If you take it I am being 'helpful' or providing *documents pour servir*, say that I suggest the following works as subject of essay (with their dates) to the, I hope, much younger critic who will analyse Mr. James Laughlin's *New Directions*.

BLAST 1914; BLAST 1915; Picabia's *J. C. Rastaquouère*; Cocteau's *Mystère Laic*, American translation of which is included in J. L.'s anthology.

Ford Madox (Hueffer) Ford; Obit[1]

There passed from us this June a very gallant combatant for those things of the mind and of letters which have been in our time too little prized. There passed a man who took in his time more punishment of one sort and another than I have seen meted to anyone else. For the ten years before I got to England there would seem to have been no one but Ford who held that French clarity and simplicity in the writing of English verse and prose were of immense importance as in contrast to the use of a stilted traditional dialect, a 'language of verse' unused in the actual talk of the people, even of 'the best people', for the expression of reality and emotion.

In 1908 London was full of 'gargoyles', of poets, that is, with high reputation, most of whose work has gone since into the discard. At that time, and in the few years preceding, there appeared without notice various fasciculae which one can still, surprisingly, read, and they were not designed for mouthing, for the 'rolling out' of 'ohs'. They weren't what people were looking for as the prolongation of Victoria's glory. They weren't, that is, 'intense' in the then sense of the word.

The justification or programme of such writing was finally (about 1913) set down in one of the best essays (preface) that Ford ever wrote.

It advocated the prose value of verse-writing, and it, along with his verse, had more in it for my generation than all the groping (most worthily) after 'quantity' (i.e., quantitative metric) of the late Laureate Robert Bridges or the useful, but monotonous, in their day unduly neglected, as more recently unduly touted, metrical labours of G. Manley Hopkins.

I have put it down as personal debt to my forerunners that I have had five, and only five, useful criticisms of my writing in my lifetime, one from Yeats, one from Bridges, one from Thomas Hardy, a recent one from a Roman Archbishop and one from Ford, and that last the most vital, or at any rate on par with Hardy's.

That Ford was almost an *halluciné* few of his intimates can doubt. He felt until it paralysed his efficient action, he saw quite distinctly the Venus immortal crossing the tram tracks. He inveighed against Yeats' lack of emotion as, for him, proved by Yeats' so great competence in making literary use of emotion.

And he felt the errors of contemporary style to the point of rolling

---

[1] *The Nineteenth Century and After*, August 1939.

(physically, and if you look at it as mere superficial snob, ridiculously) on the floor of his temporary quarters in Giessen when my third volume displayed me trapped, fly-papered, gummed and strapped down in a jejune provincial effort to learn, *mehercule*, the stilted language that then passed for 'good English' in the arthritic milieu that held control of the respected British critical circles, Newbolt, the backwash of Lionel Johnson, Fred Manning, the Quarterlies and the rest of 'em.

And that roll saved me at least two years, perhaps more. It sent me back to my own proper effort, namely, toward using the living tongue (with younger men after me), though none of us has found a more natural language than Ford did.

This is a dimension of poetry. It is, *magari*, an Homeric dimension, for of Homer there are at least two dimensions apart from the surge and thunder. Apart from narrative sense and the main construction, there is this to be said of Homer, that never can you read half a page without finding melodic invention, still fresh, and that you can hear the actual voices, as of the old men speaking in the course of the phrases.

It is for this latter quality that Ford's poetry is of high importance, both in itself and for its effect on all the best subsequent work of his time. Let no young snob forget this.

I propose to bury him in the order of merits as I think he himself understood them, first for an actual example in the writing of poetry; secondly, for those same merits more fully shown in his prose, and thirdly, for the critical acumen which was implicit in his finding these merits.

As to his prose, you can apply to it a good deal that he wrote in praise of Hudson (rightly) and of Conrad, I think with a bias toward generosity that in parts defeats its critical applicability. It lay so natural on the page that one didn't notice it. I read an historical novel at sea in 1906 without noting the name of the author. A scene at Henry VIIIth's court stayed depicted in my memory and I found years later that Ford had written it.

I wanted for private purposes to make a note on a point raised in *Ancient Lights*; I thought it would go on the back of an envelope, and found to my young surprise that I couldn't make the note in fewer words than those on Ford's actual page. That set me thinking, *mehercule*. I did not in those days care about prose. If 'prose' meant anything to me, it meant Tacitus (as seen by Mackail), a damned dangerous model for a young man in those days or these days in England, though I don't regret it; one never knows enough about anything. Start with Tacitus and be cured by Flaubert *viâ* Ford, or start with Ford or Maupassant and be girt up by Tacitus, after fifty it is *kif kif*, all one. But a man is a pig not to be grateful to both sides.

Until the arrival of such 'uncomfortables' as Wyndham Lewis, the distressful D. H. Lawrence, D. Goldring, G. Cannan, etc., I think Ford had no one to play with. The elder generation loathed him, or at any rate such cross-section of it as I encountered. He disturbed 'em, he took Dagon by the beard, publicly. And he founded the greatest Little Review or pre-Little Review of our time. From 1908 to 1910 he gathered into one fasciculus the work of Hardy, H. James, Hudson, Conrad, C. Graham, Anatole France, the great old-stagers, the most competent of that wholly unpleasant decade, Bennett, Wells, and, I think, even Galsworthy.

And he got all the first-rate and high second-raters of my own decade, W. Lewis, D. H. Lawrence (made by Ford, dug out of a board school in Croydon), Cannan, Walpole, etc. (Eliot was not yet on the scene).

The inner story of that review and the treatment of Ford by its obtainers is a blot on London's history that time will not remove, though, of course, it will become invisible in the perspective of years.

As critic he was perhaps wrecked by his wholly unpolitic generosity. In fact, if he merits an epithet above all others, it would be 'The Unpolitic'. Despite all his own interests, despite all the hard-boiled and half-baked vanities of all the various lots of us, he kept on discovering merit with monotonous regularity.

His own best prose was probably lost, as isolated chapters in unachieved and too-quickly-issued novels. He persisted in discovering capacities in similar crannies. In one weekly after another he found and indicated the capacities of Mary, Jenny, Willard, Jemimah, Horatio, etc., despite the fact that they all of 'em loathed each other, and could by no stretch of imagination be erected into a compact troop of Fordites supporting each other and moving on the citadels of publication.

And that career I saw him drag through three countries. He took up the fight for free letters in Paris, he took it up again in New York, where I saw him a fortnight before his death, still talking of meritorious novels, still pitching the tale of unknown men who had written the *histoire morale contemporaine* truthfully and without trumpets, told this or that phase of America as seen from the farm or the boiler-works, as he had before wanted young England to see young England from London, from Sussex.

And of all the durable pages he wrote (for despite the fluff, despite the apparently aimless meander of many of 'em, he did write durable pages) there is nothing that more registers the fact of our day than the two portraits in the, alas, never-finished *Women and Men* (Three Mountains Press, 1923), Meary Walker and 'T'.

For T.S.E.[1]

His was the true Dantescan voice–not honoured enough, and deserving more than I ever gave him.

I had hoped to see him in Venice this year for the Dante commemoration at the Giorgio Cini Foundation–instead: Westminster Abbey. But, later, on his own hearth, a flame tended, a presence felt.

Recollections? let some thesis writer have the satisfaction of 'discovering' whether it was in 1920 or '21 that I went from Excideuil to meet a rucksacked Eliot. Days of walking–conversation? literary? *le papier Fayard* was then the burning topic. Who is there now for me to share a joke with?

Am I to write 'about' the poet Thomas Stearns Eliot? or my friend 'the Possum'? Let him rest in peace. I can only repeat, but with the urgency of 50 years ago: READ HIM.

[1] *The Sewanee Review*, Winter 1966.

434

Index

INDEX

INDEX

INDEX

INDEX